RN
EGE
RY

$10.00

The railroad from Boston to Albany, opened to traffic in 1841, was the first major trunk line completed in America, and it established important precedents for nineteenth-century railroading. Contrary to past assumptions, the road was built less as a result of Boston's urge to compete with the Port of New York than because of the desire of Boston and Springfield business leaders to open the interior of Massachusetts to industrial development.

The situation of Massachusetts in the 1820's was unique. Unlike New York and Pennsylvania with their newfledged economies and their large western hinterlands in the first flush of development, Massachusetts had an old economy with its agriculture undermined by the westward movement and its profitable trade within the British Empire destroyed by the Revolution. Its need was to industrialize.

Mr. Salsbury describes the response of Massachusetts to the completion of New York State's Erie Canal in 1825 and then analyzes the complex political and economic forces within Massachusetts that prevented the construction of a purely state-owned railroad to link Boston with Albany. By 1831 a textile boom provided the incentive and the resources necessary for the construction of a railroad from Boston to Worcester as a private venture. The success of the Boston & Worcester, along with the increased confidence of the public, then induced the state to lend financial support

various aspects of Ameri
industrial history. He te
University of Delaware.

*Center for the Study
of Liberty in America*

Jacket design by Frank Williams

CASTE

LIBRARY

The State, the Investor, and the Railroad

A PUBLICATION OF

THE CENTER FOR THE STUDY OF

THE HISTORY OF LIBERTY IN AMERICA

HARVARD UNIVERSITY

The State, the Investor, and the Railroad

THE BOSTON & ALBANY, 1825-1867

by Stephen Salsbury

HARVARD UNIVERSITY PRESS
CAMBRIDGE, MASSACHUSETTS   1967

HE
2791
.B714
S3

© COPYRIGHT 1967 BY THE
PRESIDENT AND FELLOWS OF HARVARD COLLEGE
ALL RIGHTS RESERVED
DISTRIBUTED IN GREAT BRITAIN BY OXFORD UNIVERSITY PRESS, LONDON
LIBRARY OF CONGRESS CATALOG CARD NUMBER 67-20881
PRINTED IN THE UNITED STATES OF AMERICA

THE WORK OF THE CENTER FOR THE STUDY OF THE HISTORY OF LIBERTY
IN AMERICA HAS BEEN SUPPORTED BY GRANTS FROM
THE CARNEGIE CORPORATION OF NEW YORK

TO ROMA CONNOR SALSBURY
AND RALPH THOMAS SALSBURY

Foreword

FOR MORE THAN A CENTURY, railroads were regarded as an obvious blessing to the American economy. A society always sensitive to the need for transportation accepted the assurances of promoters automatically and optimistically, and historians looking back upon the process readily associated the expansion of the nation with the development of the railroad network. It hardly seemed necessary to ask why the roads were built or to investigate the reasons for the institutional form they took.

In recent decades, however, the railroads have fallen upon hard times, of which the abandonment of marginal lines and the pleas for public assistance are the symptoms. Significantly, it is in these same decades that their historical role has been opened to reexamination. Recent econometric studies have called into question the obviousness of the railroads' advantages over other contemporary forms of transportation and have raised doubts about the profitability of these ventures even to their promoters.

Yet the railroads were built if not for abstract calculations of gains and losses then for other reasons; whether they should have been constructed or not, they had an important effect upon American political and economic institutions. They appeared at a moment when the distinction between public and private enterprise was still vague, and they required large amounts of capital and exceptional entrepreneurial and managerial skills. That the railroads emerged as private rather than as governmental ventures and retained that character was a significant feature of American development that demands explanation.

To understand the railroads' evolution, it is necessary to go beyond the conventional general accounts and to examine in specific detail the interplay of forces that affected policy. There have been useful analyses of state development, but these need to be supplemented by more information about the individual roads. Professor Salsbury's enlightening work subjects to a rigorous analysis the road that established the leading precedents for nineteenth-century development.

Oscar Handlin

Author's Preface

OLD AGE is an affliction that in time descends upon all economies. When a region or nation becomes densely populated and when the pursuits upon which it depends for sustenance become either uncompetitive or outmoded by technological change, it has grown old. Some economies, like people, age rapidly, while others remain young even after the passage of many years. Although much of the United States is too new to have encountered old age, some parts of it have lived with the problem for at least 175 years.

Between 1776 and 1830 the American economy passed through two important, interrelated changes. The Revolution destroyed the bonds linking the thirteen colonies to the British Empire and thereby disordered most of the trading patterns that had evolved over 150 years. The defeat of the British and their Indian allies opened the way for the exploitation of the West. America ceased to be a narrow rim hugging the Atlantic and became an inward-looking continental power. Opportunity thereafter favored those of the thirteen original colonies which could most readily attract the western trade.

The fate of the four great Eastern seaboard cities—Boston, New York, Philadelphia, and Baltimore—seemed to hang in the balance. New York responded to this challenge with the Erie Canal, which opened in 1825, and Pennsylvania quickly followed with a decision to build its own canal from the Susquehanna River to Pittsburgh, completed in 1834. In 1827 Baltimore, after a brief flirtation with canals, launched the Baltimore & Ohio Railroad, which however did not reach the West until the 1850s. Massachusetts lagged; it did not start any project until 1831, when it chartered the Boston & Worcester Railroad, which became the first link in a line to Albany that was finally opened in 1841.

Massachusetts' position was unique. Both New York and Pennsylvania had young economies; indeed the western parts of those states were in the first flush of development. Baltimore had still another problem. Most of its route west passed through other states, so that Maryland could not follow the lead of Pennsylvania and New York in building a state-owned transportation link to the West.

Massachusetts, though it controlled most of its own route, faced the most serious challenge of all: that of an old economy. The Revolution and the westward movement had undermined its twin pillars of strength, commerce within the British Empire and agriculture. The decision to build a Boston to Albany railroad was as much influenced by the problems of "old age" as it was by the pressures generated by the lure of new opportunities in the West.

This book owes a substantial debt to Oscar and Mary Handlin's *Commonwealth, A Study of the Role of Government in the American Economy: Massachusetts, 1774–1861*. The Bay State emerged from the Revolution with a vigorous, interdependent economy. In the words of Oscar and Mary Handlin "in the trading and fishing towns, commerce, the prosperity of which benefited the artisan and shipowner, seaman, and shopkeeper, supplied a nucleus of common concern. And many farmers too were aware . . . that they lived in a hinterland, the business of which was to supply the coastal towns with food and with products for export."[1] Massachusetts, too, had a strong tradition of cultural, religious, and ethnic unity. Almost all its people were Protestant with Calvinist roots. The politically incompatible elements had fled as loyalists during the Revolution; those who remained regarded the "Revolution . . . [as] a risk all had assumed together; all would share the success or failure, the danger or satisfaction."[2] The newly independent state also inherited a tradition that placed little emphasis upon differentiating which responsibilities in the economy were governmental and which were private. Indeed, from the earliest colonial times, as Bernard Bailyn in his *New England Merchants in the Seventeenth Century* demonstrated, provincial Massachusetts governments had supported or regulated such widespread ventures as fur trading and iron making. The essential homogeneity of the state—ethnic, cultural, political, and economic—made cooperation between public and private agencies natural and easy. This should have provided a receptive ground for state railroad building.

The nineteenth century, however, brought an end to the old unity. The economy split into opposing factions. After the Revolution commerce first lagged, then boomed, bringing vast capital accumulations into the hands of a few, and then, toward the end of the Napoleonic Wars, again became depressed. The control of money and credit appeared to gravitate from the old mercantile houses to entirely new institutions called banks. Agriculture declined, as did many of the cities and towns dependent upon trade. Large-scale industrial production begun after the War of 1812 was by the third decade of the century a vital part of the state's economy. By 1825 the fracture of Massachusetts' economic "Commonwealth" had been nearly completed. There were deep social and cultural changes as well. Disparities between rich and poor increased, and by the 1840s a permanent laboring class existed. Finally, in the same decade, large-scale immigration, beginning with the refugees from Ireland's potato famine, shattered Massachusetts' religious and ethnic unity.

The division of the state into opposed groups did not rule out government action in any sphere but made it difficult for the state to act in any venture that favored only one section or one interest. By the Civil War the government's main concern focused upon mediating among the various groups.

This book attempts to place the railroad in the general framework of the political and economic changes within the Commonwealth. It outlines the division of Massachusetts into opposing economic interests and emphasizes the dislocations that resulted from age. First a canal then a railroad to Albany became identified with Boston's commercial survival, but economic conflict within the state blocked the Commonwealth's assumption of such a project. The rising manufacturers took up the idea and supplied the energy to launch it. Finally, the two railroads that linked Boston with Albany developed from adjuncts to other economic interests into forces distinct from those which had created them. The book attempts to demonstrate how each railroad became a different kind of institution with its own tradition and individuality. The men who controlled the two roads tended to shape their actions in response to the actual problems they faced, not in conformity with any preconceived notions or patterns.

At this point I should like to express my general indebtedness to Oscar Handlin, who supervised an initial study of the Boston to Albany railroad as a doctoral dissertation and whose constant encouragement, many helpful suggestions, and most of all inspirational example have made this work possible. For financial aid I acknowledge the help of the Center for the Study of the History of Liberty in America, which generously provided the money to retype the entire manuscript and prepare it for publication. I also should like to thank Robert Lovett, Curator of Manuscripts and Archives at the Baker Library of the Harvard Business School, and his assistant Eleanor Bishop, both of whom went beyond the call of duty to make the Boston & Worcester and the Western manuscripts available. I am also grateful to Robert Spalding of the United Fruit Company, Ralph Goodwin of East Texas State University and Paul Taylor of Sweet Briar College for their helpful criticisms of the manuscript in its formative stages. I am also indebted to Loring F. Wilcox, Chairman of the Research Committee of the Railway and Locomotive Historical Society for his help in selecting illustrations from the society's archives.

Stephen Salsbury

NEWARK, DELAWARE
DECEMBER 1966

Contents

Illustrations

The Boston & Worcester Railroad's *Meteor,* built in England by Robert Stephenson & Co. in 1834. Courtesy, The Railway and Locomotive Historical Society.

facing page 10

View north up Lincoln Street, Boston in the 1840s. Boston & Worcester freight house at right, and the Beach Street Station, left. From a stock certificate of the Boston & Worcester. Courtesy, Manuscripts Division, Baker Library, Harvard Business School.

facing page 10

George Bliss. Courtesy the Railway and Locomotive Historical Society.

facing page 11

Western Railroad: Crossing over the Hudson & Berkshire Railroad in the mid-1840s. Reproduced from *Bradbury & Guild's Rail-Road Charts, Boston to Albany,* 1847.

facing page 42

Western Railroad: Fourth Stone Bridge in the Berkshire Hills in the mid-1840s. Reproduced from *Bradbury & Guild's Rail-Road Charts, Boston to Albany,* 1847.

facing page 42

Western Railroad: An original stone arch bridge near Chester, 128.21 miles west of Worcester as it appeared about 1914. Courtesy, The Railway and Locomotive Historical Society.

facing page 43

The Western Railroad's *Superior,* built in the corporation's Springfield shops in 1859. Courtesy, The Railway and Locomotive Historical Society.

facing page 170

The Western Railroad's *Arizona,* built in the corporation's shops in 1866. Courtesy, The Railway and Locomotive Historical Society.

facing page 170

The Boston & Worcester's *Express,* a 28 ton coal-burning passenger locomotive built in the corporation's own shops. Courtesy, The Railway and Locomotive Historical Society.

facing page 171

Chester W. Chapin. Reproduced from Moses King, *King's Handbook of Springfield,* 1884.

facing page 202

Boston & Albany Railroad: Train crossing the Hudson River from Greenbush to Albany. From and engraving on a Boston & Albany stock certificate. Courtesy, Manuscripts Division, Baker Library, Harvard Business School.

facing page 203

The Boston & Worcester and Western promoted through freight business from Boston to the West, even as the bulky grain and flour traffic from the Erie Canal to Massachusetts Bay languished. Courtesy Manuscripts Division, Baker Library, Harvard Business School.

facing page 234

The Boston & Worcester's *Union,* a coal-burning passenger locomotive built by William Mason & Co., 1865. Courtesy, The Railway and Locomotive Historical Society.

facing page 235

Tables

(Five tables which serve as appendixes. See Table of Contents.)

Maps

Charts

The State, the Investor,
and the Railroad

CHAPTER I

The Economic Revolution in Massachusetts, 1830

1. WESTWARD EXPANSION AND ITS EFFECT

IN 1830 BOSTON CELEBRATED the Massachusetts Bay Colony's two hundredth anniversary. In two centuries the struggling settlements on the Atlantic's edge had grown into a flourishing and powerful state with over 600,000 citizens. The Commonwealth had led the way to revolution and independence and had entered the new Federal Union with a buoyant optimism.

But the next four decades had changed the air of optimism into one of near desperation. The country as a whole had expanded. Hundreds of thousands of home seekers had moved through the Appalachian mountain passes into the Mississippi Valley. In rapid order Kentucky, Tennessee, Ohio, Louisiana, Indiana, Mississippi, Illinois, Alabama, and Missouri took their places beside the eastern thirteen states. Compared with the growth of the nation, Massachusetts seemed to stagnate. From the first census in 1790 to that of 1820, the population of the whole United States had increased 150 per cent. Massachusetts, however, grew by only 30 per cent, and the state's westernmost county, Berkshire, lost population.[1] The census of 1830 showed that Massachusetts had fallen from second in population in 1790 to eighth place, being outdistanced by the frontier states of Ohio, Kentucky, and Tennessee and by her Atlantic coast rivals, New York and Pennsylvania.[2]

Bostonians did not have to look far to find the key to New York's success. Situated at the mouth of one of the continent's great rivers, New York City lay at the eastern end of the only natural trough that pierced the rugged mountain barrier separating the entire Atlantic seaboard from the vast Mississippi Valley and Great Lakes regions. This trough followed the Hudson River north to the vicinity of Albany and then turned westward along the bed of the Mohawk River to Rome, where it continued to Buffalo, using a depression that served as an ancient river outlet for the Great Lakes during the ice ages. In this manner Lake Erie and the sea were linked by the famed "water level route."[3]

With the Indians and the English gone, New Yorkers moved quickly to take advantage of this superb gateway to the West. Under Governor De Witt Clinton's leadership, the New York Legislature approved state construction of the Erie Canal, a project that would allow uninterrupted water navigation between Manhattan and Lake Erie. In the fall of 1825, all New York celebrated the marriage of the Great Lakes with the sea.

This great internal improvement sparked an unparalleled boom in the Empire State. Between 1810 and 1830 her population almost doubled from about 1 million to nearly 2 million. The Erie Canal opened New York's interior agricultural lands, making the Genesee Valley a major national granary. Commerce pouring eastward along the canal made New York City the undisputed commercial center of the United States.

New York's success stirred the admiration and envy of her seaboard rivals, which unlike the Empire State, all looked westward to a high mountain backbone stretching from Georgia to Maine. Each wanted to tap the commerce of the interior but could not do so without vast expenditures. By 1830 several had taken decisive steps to create large-scale internal improvements. South Carolina, spurred on by Charleston, was constructing a railway to the west. Maryland was building the Chesapeake and Ohio Canal and the Baltimore & Ohio Railroad. Pennsylvania, however, had the most ambitious scheme, a 15 million dollar, 322-mile state-built canal and railway which would pierce the Allegheny Mountains with tunnels and inclines.[4] Despite this activity Massachusetts lagged, unable to make any decision about internal improvements.

The Bay State's paralysis was not because it failed to recognize the importance of transportation. In fact, Nathan Hale, the editor of the Boston *Daily Advertiser*, in 1829 emphasized that "without some improvement in the means of communication, the population of the interior parts of the state has nearly reached its maximum."[5]

Although a small state, barely 200 miles long and with an average width of little more than 60 miles, Massachusetts was divided by complex interests. The state contained four distinct geographic regions. The eastern third, a deeply indented coastal plain with a shore line of over 700 miles, included the counties of Essex, Middlesex, Suffolk, Norfolk, Bristol, Plymouth, Barnstable, and the island counties of Dukes and Nantucket. Back from the coast was Worcester County, dominated by a range of low hills that separated the eastern seaboard from the Connecticut Valley. Next was the Connecticut Valley itself, cutting a 30-mile swath from north to south in the western half of the state, and which comprised the counties of Franklin, Hampshire, and Hampden; and finally in the west was a mountain wilderness, the county of Berkshire. Despite their great diversity, the four regions shared a common need: improved transportation.

2. EASTERN MASSACHUSETTS—THE FALL OF OCEAN COMMERCE AND THE RISE OF INDUSTRY

The ocean dominated the way of life in eastern Massachusetts, and along the many fine bays and deep-water harbors could be found nineteen of the twenty-two cities and towns in the state with a population of over 4,000.[6] Favored initially by abundant natural resources for shipbuilding and by the protecting influence of British colonial regulations, ocean-borne commerce became the very soul of the region's economy. Even when cut adrift from the bonds of empire, commerce seemed to thrive. Newburyport, in the extreme north of Essex County at the mouth of the Merrimack River, built a canal westward to Hampton and captured the interior lumber trade. At the same time her merchants continued to exploit the West Indies market. Thus Newburyport's population doubled between 1776 and 1810, and its shipping tonnage increased from 12,000 tons in 1790 to 30,000 tons in 1806.[7]

To the south in Essex County was Salem, in 1790 the sixth largest city in the United States, with a population of nearly 8,000.[8] A vibrant, growing seaport before the Revolution, Salem reached its peak between 1790 and 1810. Her captains sailed to the East Indies, Calcutta, and China and brought home

3

oriental treasures. Her population grew to over 12,600 by 1810, and imposing mansions lined her residential streets.[9]

Still further south was Boston, the commercial metropolis of New England. Its population of 18,000 in 1790 made it the third largest city in the United States, and its commerce revived spectacularly after the Revolution.[10] Boston prospered because it became a great world marketplace. It gathered the products of India, China, the East and West Indies, and rural New England in its warehouses and then shipped them out again not only to American markets via a thriving coastal trade but to European customers as well.

Massachusetts accumulated a huge capital, invested in ships and port facilities, together with a constantly increasing surplus that needed continual reemployment in new trading ventures. A typical merchant like John P. Cushing had as late as 1832 more than $360,000 invested in ten different trading voyages and an additional $200,000 tied up in Boston commercial property.[11]

The Commonwealth's maritime prosperity received its first staggering blow from the Napoleonic wars. Strife abroad at first seemed to benefit American commerce since neutral New England ships were free to supply both England and France. Yankee merchants also fell heir to a portion of the British West Indies trade since the English merchant marine was occupied elsewhere. During this era Massachusetts had 310,000 tons of shipping engaged in foreign commerce—37 per cent of the total for the United States and almost double that of the next most important ship-owning state, New York. In the single year of 1807 this fleet brought its owners $15,500,000 in freight money alone, or more than the entire capital value of the fleet! In addition merchants received even greater gains from buying cargoes cheap and selling them at inflated prices in Europe.[12]

But the war also had its perils. England, determined to thwart American trade with France, proclaimed a blockade of the continent. France retaliated by declaring British ports under blockade. Caught between the maneuvers of the struggling giants American shipping became the victim of high seas searches and seizures. Angered by this violation of neutral

4

rights Congress passed, over the protests of the New England merchants, the embargo, nonimportation, and nonintercourse acts, which vainly tried to force British and French recognition of American rights. Then came the War of 1812. Nearly eight years of embargo, nonintercourse, and war fell heavily on Massachusetts. The worst hit were the smaller ports, especially Plymouth, Salem, and Newburyport, which never regained their former glory.[13] Unused ships and wharves rotted, and the capital normally engaged in foreign trade went unemployed.

Peace did not restore Massachusetts' maritime prosperity. Europe carried its own trade, and England closed much of her empire to American ships. Even more important, the Bay State began to feel the effects of expansion westward. When most of America's population, industry, and agriculture lay within a few miles of ocean transportation, any town with a good harbor, resourceful seamen, and capital to invest had a chance to become a major seaport. Boston, Newburyport, Salem, Marblehead, and Beverly developed into thriving centers of trade without any significant back country. Expansion into western New York and the Ohio Valley changed this.

By the second decade of the nineteenth century a large proportion of the nation's agricultural wealth traveled hundreds of miles through the interior to reach a seaport. When the Erie Canal opened in the 1820s thousands of tons of lumber, staves, beef, pork, flour, flax seed, peas, beans, and whiskey flowed into New York City.[14] These were exactly the articles New England had been sending to the West Indies. In return New York sent westward huge quantities of merchandise. In addition to the trade that had to pass through New York, the unrivaled commercial facilities built up there—banking connections, wholesale firms that specialized in supplying consumer goods for the western market, grain exchanges, wharves, the greatest number of ships entering and departing from any Atlantic port, and the best transportation connections to the interior—attracted business that had formerly gone to Massachusetts. Hartford, Springfield, New London, and even Providence merchants began to find a trip to New York more rewarding than one to Boston.

Eastern Massachusetts operated under a particular handicap.

5

The Berkshire Mountains thwarted communication with the West, and the coast lacked easy access even to the interior parts of the state. No navigable river or waterway except the Merrimack penetrated more than a few miles inland. Boston was fortunate enough to be linked by canal to the Merrimack and thus had access to a considerable hinterland in Middlesex County and New Hampshire. No other port in the state had this advantage.

Thus "the first few years of world peace were the severest test that maritime Massachusetts had ever met."[15] Newburyport, with its West Indies commerce diverted to New York and its interior lumber and provision trade drawn to Boston by the Middlesex Canal, declined in population from 7,634 in 1810 to 6,375 in 1830. Other once thriving Essex County ports met similar fates.[16] Even mighty Salem was unable to hold her lucrative trade with the Orient, and her population remained almost stable. New Bedford, Gloucester, and Provincetown prospered only because they exploited the great Atlantic whale, mackerel, and cod fisheries.[17]

Boston, however, continued to grow; its population nearly doubled between 1810 and 1830. It captured much trade from the smaller Massachusetts ports, and the rising textile industry required a large tonnage to ship in cotton and to export finished goods. But in 1830 even Boston seemed to be declining. While New York City's total foreign commerce increased from over 490,000 tons in 1826 to nearly 550,000 tons in 1830, Boston's tonnage actually dropped from 233,000 tons in 1826 to 206,000 tons in 1830.[18] In 1830 Massachusetts imported less in terms of dollars than at any other time since the records for imports and exports began to be separated in 1821.[19]

In December 1828 an anonymous writer in the Boston *Courier* expressed the desperation that was driving the merchants to seek new investment for their capital. New England, he argued, lacked a back country and was no longer competitive with New York. As a result, Newburyport was as "silent as if a perpetual Sabbath reigned in her streets . . . ," and Salem, once the center of a thriving India trade, looked "back with melancholy regret . . . in the . . . conviction that manufactures alone can resuscitate her."[20]

As foreign trade declined, the capital formerly engaged in shipping sought employment elsewhere. Fortunately for Eastern Massachusetts the ebb of commerce coincided with the rise of textile manufacturing. Although Samuel Slater introduced advanced English technology and the use of water power to run American cotton mills as early as 1789, the industry started slowly. The Bay State's merchant princes, with their wealth earning fabulous sums in the China, European, and East Indies trade, spurned investment in textiles. It was possible to triple capital in a single successful voyage to the Far East. In contrast, manufacturing offered risks nearly comparable to shipping but rewarded adventurers with a mere 6 to 7 per cent annual return.

During its first two decades, therefore, smallness characterized the American cotton industry. The early plants grew up mainly in southeastern Massachusetts and Rhode Island, especially at Fall River and Providence. As late as 1831, the average capitalization of the over one hundred mills in Rhode Island was less than $40,000.[21]

After 1810, however, the picture changed. The blow struck at New England commerce by embargo, nonintercourse, and the War of 1812 made a few commercial magnates receptive to industry. The very factors which ruined the importing business and dried up opportunities in shipping created favorable conditions for manufacturing. Thus Francis C. Lowell, a well-to-do Boston merchant, convinced a few of his mercantile friends to put their idle capital to work in a large-scale cotton industry.[22] In 1813, Lowell started the Boston Manufacturing Company, located on the Charles River at Waltham. This corporation began with a capital of $300,000. Associated with Lowell in this venture were ten men who furnished about 95 per cent of the capital. These included Patrick Tracy Jackson, who in partnership with Joseph and Henry Lee had made a fortune importing cotton goods into Boston from Calcutta; Nathan Appleton, who had grown rich shipping pot and pearl ashes to Liverpool and importing British goods to sell in his Boston store; and finally Israel Thorndike, and his son Israel Thorndike, Jr., who made their fortune in shipping at Beverly.[23]

The Boston Manufacturing Company succeeded far beyond

its promoters' most sanguine hopes. In 1817 it declared a dividend of 17 per cent on the capital stock, and for the next ten years dividends fluctuated between 12 and 27½ per cent.[24] Excited by these profits, the proprietors decided upon expansion. Having exhausted the potentials of the Charles, they turned to the largest and most powerful river in eastern Massachusetts, the Merrimack. At Pawtucket Falls, between Chelmsford and Dracut, they took control of an old canal, converting it into a sluice to supply water to turn cotton spindles. On this site in 1822 rose the Merrimack Company, the first of four corporations that by 1828 had a total capital of $2,000,000.[25] These ventures prospered, sometimes paying more than 20 per cent per annum on the money invested.[26]

The cotton revolution produced widespread changes in the life of eastern Massachusetts. Around the factories on the Merrimack, Lowell sprang into a full-fledged city—in 1830, the eighth largest in the Commonwealth, and in 1840 the fourteenth largest in the United States.[27] The success of the textile factories reoriented the thinking of many wealthy merchants, who rushed to control the state's water privileges. One by one the commercial men shifted their investments from shipping to manufacturing. William Sturgis, who in partnership with John Bryant had formed a house specializing in the trade of the Pacific Northwest and had accumulated a fortune of over $1,000,000, invested heavily in the Lowell developments.[28] Nathan Appleton's cousin, William Appleton, who had grown wealthy as an importer of British dry goods and in the Canton trade, invested over $110,000 on the Merrimack.[29] Even Harrison Gray Otis, who had championed shipping interests in Congress, succumbed and purchased for $100,000 the control of the Taunton Manufacturing Company, which produced cotton, woolen, and iron goods.[30]

But shipping had gone through periodic depressions and had always revived to become more lucrative and important than ever. Many merchants expecting just such a pattern kept their money employed in commerce. John P. Cushing, for example, had a total wealth of more than $810,000, and as late as 1832 not a penny of it was invested in industry.[31] Others like Bryant and Sturgis, although heavily committed to the development of manufactures, also kept substantial sums tied up in the China and Calcutta trade. To all, even those who felt that Boston and Massachusetts were finished as a great commercial emporium, the decay of ocean commerce was a sad thing. Harrison Gray Otis in his inaugural speech as Mayor of Boston in 1829 lamented that great fortunes were no longer accumulated in shipping, but he thanked the "Giver of all Good" that factories made possible a modest prosperity.[32]

The triumph of the protectionist Nathan Appleton over Henry Lee, a free trader and East India merchant, for the Suffolk County congressional seat in the election of 1830 indicated that a majority of Boston voters favored industrial development at the expense of shipping. Despite this, for the next forty years there would continue to be a declining but still powerful and vocal minority that would devote its full energy to bringing about a day when ships would again crowd the quays of Boston, Salem, Beverly, and Newburyport and pour forth upon their docks cargoes from India, China, Europe, and the West Indies as in the days before Jefferson's hated embargo.

3. AGRICULTURE, INDUSTRY, AND TRANSPORTATION IN WORCESTER COUNTY

Directly to the west of coastal Massachusetts, the state's second great economic region, Worcester County, was also undergoing revolutionary changes. Its streams abounded in medium-sized water privileges, which created a vast potential power for light industry. The biggest blight upon the county was its lack of transportation. Most of it lay over 40 miles from the nearest navigable water: the Connecticut River on the west, Massachusetts Bay on the east, and Narragansett Bay to the south. By 1830, however, it ranked as the most populous county in the state with more than 84,000 citizens living in its fifty-four towns. Despite its population, the county had no cities, the largest town being its thriving shire seat, Worcester, with 4,173 inhabitants, the nineteenth town of the Commonwealth.[33]

Before 1800, agriculture dominated Worcester County. Its farmers, hampered by a long expensive haul over the wretched roads connecting them with their markets either at Boston or in the Connecticut Valley, produced only those things that could withstand a high transportation cost. The farmers' most salable product was livestock, especially hogs and cattle. These they walked to market or slaughtered and then packed the salted beef and pork into barrels for shipment to Boston or Springfield for export in the West Indies provision trade.[34] In addition, there was a ready market for cheese and poultry. But high transportation costs prevented the export of apples, the major orchard crop, although cider brandy was sent to the seaboard.[35] The other important activity was the manufacture of pot and pearl ash from the hardwood forests that covered the county. The ash, like salt beef and pork, was placed in barrels and carted to the coast for export, mainly to England.[36]

This agrarian economy created no large cities or great wealth. Only in Worcester and in two or three other towns were the merchants able to accumulate even a small amount of capital. Most of the county's inhabitants, however, were neither rich nor poor, but possessed "that middle state of prosperity which . . . so often has been termed golden."[37] With middle-class prosperity went education for a great many of the county's citizens. A farmer like Isaac Davis of Northborough sent his son John to Yale. After graduation young Davis studied law and in 1815 gained admission to the bar. Ambition drove him to the county's largest town, Worcester, which could offer him full employment for his legal talents.[38] Thus began the career of a man who became a United States Senator and the Governor of Massachusetts. Another future governor, Levi Lincoln, also started as a Worcester lawyer.

A third great family arose when Stephen Salisbury opened in 1767 a Worcester branch of the Boston commercial house of Samuel and Stephen Salisbury. The business prospered and earned its proprietor a modest fortune, which his son, the second Stephen Salisbury, inherited in the 1820s.[39] The Salisbury establishment, although the largest in the county, was typical. Farmers brought to the store their salt pork, beef, poultry, pot and pearl ash, and cider brandy and exchanged them for credit to buy the English and West India goods that Salisbury imported through Boston.

Figure 1

The Boston & Worcester Railroad's *Meteor*, built in England by Robert Stephenson & Co. in 1834.

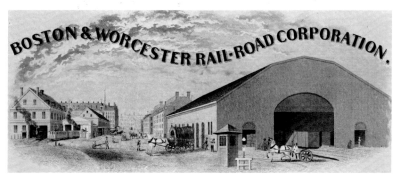

Figure 2

View north up Lincoln Street, Boston in the 1840s. Boston & Worcester freight house at right, and the Beach Street Station, left. From a stock certificate of the Boston & Worcester.

Figure 3

George Bliss, who became president of the Western Railroad in 1842, is discussed in Chapter XI, "The Embattled Mr. Bliss."

The nineteenth century's opening years dealt a crippling blow to Worcester County's agrarian economy. Everything it grew, the rich virgin land in upstate New York and the new western states produced cheaper and better and without the handicap of 40 to 50 miles of land cartage. In consequence the county's growth slowed, and some of the region's prosperous towns began to decline. In the decade after 1800 the county showed a population gain of less than 4,000, while Essex County on the coast increased by 10,000.[40] Many of the younger generation were leaving.

To combat rural decay, county leaders formed the Worcester Agricultural Society, which emphasized scientific farming. Speakers before it urged the use of fertilizers such as fish heads and bones and plaster of Paris to curb soil exhaustion and increase yields.[41] But high freight rates prevented any except the richest farmers from importing these soil restorers. Plaster of Paris sold for $3 to $4 a ton in Boston and faced transportation charges of about $8 per ton to most Worcester County communities.[42]

The society also encouraged agricultural specialization. Speaking before it in 1825, George Tufts argued that Worcester County must abandon uneconomic crops like grain and concentrate on production for the new industrial and urban markets. He recommended dairy farming and wool growing.[43] The agricultural reformers spoke strongly for better transportation. Warmly praising turnpike construction, Oliver Fiske urged in 1823 that private capital furnish the money for a canal between Worcester and Providence. Only the introduction of an artificial waterway could secure the county's growth, Fiske concluded.[44]

Indeed cheaper transportation was vital to the region's future agricultural prosperity. The lack of it prevented pork, beef, hay, potatoes, cider, apples, truck vegetables, dairy products, and poultry from reaching the expanding industrial cities around Boston and Lowell at prices that were competitive with similar produce brought by water from Maine and New York. Of the 120,000 cords of firewood consumed yearly in Boston, Cambridge, and Charlestown 100,000 cords arrived in vessels from Maine, but not a stick came from timber-rich Worcester

County.[45] No matter how much the region improved its husbandry, planted the right crops, or restored the soil, all was in vain unless a market could be found. And the more the region specialized in the production of a few cash crops, the more necessary a market became. It is doubtful that Worcester County could have adopted scientific farming, had it not been for the beginning of industrialization in the area.

Worcester men watched the founding of the textile industry at Providence and Fall River and almost immediately initiated ventures of their own. In 1790, Cornelius Stowell, a Worcester clothier, began a small factory to manufacture print calicoes, carpets, dye and dress woolen goods.[46] From this start the industry grew, until in 1837 there were in Worcester County sixty-six woolen mills, which had a total capital value of more than $1,800,000 and which employed almost 2,500 people. These factories consumed over 3,740,000 pounds of wool, more than a third of the total for all of Massachusetts.[47]

Soon manufacturers demanded more fleece than could be produced locally. By 1837, the Worcester County mills consumed more than fifty times the wool raised in the county and more than four times the entire production of Massachusetts, thus creating an important need for better transportation connecting the area with the nation's major wool-growing regions, Vermont and upstate New York.[48]

Local merchants also sparked the cotton industry in the county. Typical was George T. Rice, a Worcester hardware dealer who in 1830 built a modest cotton factory on Mill Brook.[49] By 1837 Worcester County had a total of seventy-four such factories and had, of all Massachusetts counties, the second largest capital investment in its mills and consumed the second greatest amount in raw cotton, all of which had to be transported inland from either Providence or Boston.[50]

Expansion in textiles created a third great development, the start of an important metalworking complex. The demand for carding and spinning machines and looms caused Ichabod Washburn and William H. Howard to start a textile machine factory at Worcester in 1820. This was the beginning of a long career during which Washburn turned Worcester into a major steel and iron center. In 1835, the town's leading merchant,

Stephen Salisbury, II, financed Washburn in a new wire manufactory, demonstrating once again the close association between
local mechanics and merchants in the county's industrial
development.[51]

The demand for iron stimulated the growth of foundries. In
1825 William A. Wheeler, who had begun his career as an
ironmaster in 1812, started an ironworks with the financial aid
of George T. Rice, H. W. Miller, and A. D. Foster. In 1826
this became the Worcester and Brookfield Iron Foundry with
furnaces in both towns.[52]

Concurrently with the rise in iron production came a boom
in the fabrication of all kinds of consumer goods which laid
a solid foundation for the emergence of a complex and diver-
sified industrial economy in the county. By 1837 the area manufactured for the national market large quantities of scythes,
axes, plows, firearms, wire, and wire sieves.[53] The county had
also assumed second place in Massachusetts in the making of
boots and shoes, producing in 1837 more than 2,350,000 pairs.[54]

Worcester County's industrialization was quite different from
that of eastern Massachusetts. There were no great capitalists
such as the Appletons and the Lawrences, and the county's
water power, while lending itself to medium and small factories, was not big enough to attract the large cotton mills of
the Merrimack Valley.[55] The force behind industrialization
came from the county's own merchants, mechanics, and
farmers who poured their entire resources and energy into
manufacturing when agriculture was waning.

The growth of scientific farming and the rise of industry
intensified Worcester County's need for better transportation.
Farmers, merchants, and millowners all demanded improvement, but few had the money to pay for better roads or canals.
The towns, which traditionally had built and maintained the
roads, were reluctant to vote funds. The agriculturalist, fight-
ing for his very life against the challenge of western produce,
could not be expected to pay large assessments for new roads.
The other alternative, payment of the road tax in labor, was
unpopular and hence impractical.[56] Thus highway construction
fell almost by default into the hands of private individuals
whom the state chartered as turnpike corporations with author-

ity to build roads along specified routes and to collect tolls for their use. In this manner Boston and Worcester were connected in 1809. Although a help, these roads left the region's main transportation problem unsolved. Turnpike corporations generally proved a bad investment. Even if they did build a highway, they seldom had the financial strength to maintain it. Turnpikes, once built, tended to deteriorate rapidly. But even at best they were greatly inferior to canals, and Worcester County agriculture and industry needed something that would match water transportation to compete with other inland regions like upstate New York.

Canals were more expensive than highways. Geography dictated against easy construction of any artificial waterway between Worcester and the Massachusetts coast; so all attention became focused on the best available route to the sea, the Blackstone River Valley between the town of Worcester and Rhode Island's Narragansett Bay. It was not until the 1820s that effective action was taken toward realizing this dream. The cost of such a project was over $750,000, and Worcester County had what little capital it possessed too heavily committed to industrial expansion to initiate an improvement of this magnitude. The main impetus, therefore, came not from Worcester but from Providence, which hoped to capture from Boston the trade of central Massachusetts.[57]

Worcester officials gave their enthusiastic support to the Blackstone Canal. But over $500,000 of the $750,000 that the waterway cost came from Rhode Island. The canal's completion in October 1828 gave Worcester County its first decent outlet to the sea. Soon thousands of tons of coal, iron, cotton, wool, corn, salt, flour, molasses, oil, gypsum, and leather floated up the waterway to supply the county's industrial and agricultural requirements. But even this great internal improvement failed to serve the county's needs adequately. It touched but a small portion of the region, and during four or five winter months ice thwarted all commerce upon it. Financially it was a failure. In its first two full years of operation the canal collected tolls of just over $20,000 or less than 1 per cent per annum on the more than three quarters of a million dollars invested in it.[58]

Thus Worcester County began the year 1830 in a state of economic upheaval and uncertainty. Its farmers faced financial ruin unless they could restore their soil and raise specialized crops for the expanding urban market. The storekeepers and mechanics had staked their meager capital and full energy on the building of factories. Both the new industrialists and the agriculturalists welcomed the Blackstone Canal even though it destroyed traditional ties with Boston and threatened to make the whole area an economic appendage of another state. To Worcesterites the canal was their first effective artery of communication with the outside world, and of even greater importance, it had been constructed without draining away their precious capital. To Worcester, transportation had to meet two main tests: first, it had to equal waterways in efficiency; second, it had to impose no financial burden upon the county. If it met these two qualifications, they supported it no matter what route or form it took.

4. INDUSTRY AND TRANSPORTATION IN THE CONNECTICUT VALLEY

Directly to the west of Worcester County lay the broad and fertile Connecticut River Valley. Its three counties—Franklin, Hampshire, and Hampden—comprised a total area just slightly larger than Worcester County. Through these three counties the Connecticut River flowed from north to south, forming a great natural highway that afforded easy access to the ocean southward through the state of Connecticut. Nature endowed this valley with water-power resources rivaling those of the Merrimack River. Especially significant were the Chicopee, Ware, and Millers Rivers, which, although they originated in the Worcester highlands, achieved their full force only in their lower reaches. On the western side of the valley, too, were major power sites on the Westfield and Deerfield Rivers, which rose in the Berkshire Mountains and flowed east to join the Connecticut.

The Connecticut Valley attracted settlers early. Starting in 1635, immigrants gradually took up the rich bottom land, and two important inland trading centers arose: Springfield and

Northampton. By 1830 Springfield had become the seventh largest town in Massachusetts, with a population of nearly 7,000, while Northampton had about half that number.[59]

From the 1630s until the beginning of the nineteenth century, a prosperous agrarian economy flourished in the Connecticut Valley. The farmers of the three river counties were not handicapped by lack of transportation and grew a large variety of products for export. Aside from livestock, pot and pearl ash, the region produced considerable wheat, oats, barley, and Indian corn.[60]

The valley's economic power centered in the merchants, who with the ministers, lawyers, and doctors controlled the political and social life of the area. From its founding, Springfield was the valley's most important town. Just a few miles up the Connecticut River from the state line, the town enjoyed an excellent natural position for its role as the commercial center of western Massachusetts.

Springfield's most important citizens were the Dwights. This dynasty gained its power through a general store started by Josiah Dwight in the 1750s. Like the Salisbury establishment in Worcester, the Dwight store gathered the farm produce and exported it in the West Indies trade. Under a son of Josiah Dwight, Jonathan, the firm became the largest concern in western Massachusetts.[61] But the same factors that undermined Worcester County's agriculture were at work in the Connecticut Valley and threatened Jonathan Dwight's commercial empire.

Three of his sons, Jonathan, Jr., Edmund, and Henry, were educated at Yale, where a relative, Timothy Dwight, presided. Jonathan, Sr., apparently recognized the rural decline, for about 1810 he began to shift his assets into new ventures. In 1814 he became a founder and the initial president of Springfield's first bank. Associated with him as a director was his son Jonathan, Jr.[62]

Meanwhile Edmund went east to Dedham, where he studied law under Fisher Ames. Here young Edmund met Boston's most influential merchants and politicians, for Fisher Ames was the high priest of New England Federalism, and around his dinner table gathered the Lowells, Cabots, Lawrences, Appletons, Lymans, and Quincys, as well as Harrison Gray Otis, Ignatius Sargent, and others who later became the backbone of the rising cotton industry.[63] Thus began a relationship that ripened into a firm alliance between Springfield's elite and that of Boston. In 1809 Edmund married the daughter of Samuel Eliot, a successful Boston merchant.[64] After completing the law apprenticeship, Edmund retired to Springfield and took an active part in the family business.

Around the Dwights grew a strong clique recruited largely from the old local aristocracy, which, although it held a high social position, was unable in the region's agricultural economy to achieve substantial wealth. What possessions it did accumulate were usually limited to real property and stores not easily converted into cash. The economic gulf separating Springfield's leaders from the rest was narrow indeed. No one in the valley could rest secure in his position or think of retirement as did many Boston and Salem merchants in the period between 1810 and 1820.

Of central importance in the Dwight group were two young lawyers, George Bliss, Jr., and John Howard. Young Bliss's father graduated from Yale during the American Revolution and became Springfield's leading lawyer. George, Jr., following family tradition, attended Yale and then studied law in his father's office. Although he was admitted to the bar in 1815 and earned a reputation as a shrewd and resourceful lawyer, he seemed to regard his practice as a steppingstone to real estate speculation and other more lucrative activities. John Howard started as an attorney with an office on the second floor of the Dwight store, but in 1823 he took a $1,000 a year position as cashier of the Springfield Bank, a job he retained until he was made the bank's president in 1836.[65]

The Springfield clique eagerly sought new economic opportunities that were not dependent upon the region's decaying agriculture. The big change came when Edmund Dwight moved to Boston in 1822 and became the business partner of James K. Mills, a relationship that lasted until Dwight's death in 1849.[66] Here Dwight came into daily contact with his old friends, the men who were harnessing the Merrimack's water power. Dwight, who grew up on the Chicopee's banks, immediately saw it as an ideal site for large factories, and so he set to work to form a union between the rising Springfield men and the Boston capitalists which he hoped would found an industrial empire in the Connecticut Valley.

In 1822 Jonathan Dwight, Jr., purchased the "land and water power on the south side of the Chicopee River at Chicopee Falls . . . for himself and his brother Edmund."[67] In 1823 the Massachusetts Legislature chartered the Boston and Springfield Manufacturing Company with a capital stock of $500,000, which immediately bought the Chicopee land from the Dwights. The initial investors in the new cotton enterprise included Jonathan and Edmund Dwight and George Bliss of Springfield and Israel Thorndike, Harrison Gray Otis, Samuel Eliot, and James K. Mills of Boston. By 1825 the mill's first units started production, and in 1828 the corporation took a new name, the Chicopee Manufacturing Company.[68]

The building of industrial Springfield proceeded in a manner almost identical with that occurring simultaneously in the Merrimack Valley. Patterning their operation after the Locks and Canals Company at Lowell, in 1831 the Springfield industrialists formed the Springfield Canal Company, which bought from the Chicopee Manufacturing Company the canals along the river and all excess land. The new organization acted as a real estate developer; it built additional factories and supplied water power to run them.[69] Between 1831 and 1841 the Canal Company constructed three large cotton and woolen mills on its holdings. In 1832 it built the Cabot Manufacturing Company with an authorized capital of $1,000,000.[70] Its incorporators included Jonathan Dwight and George Bliss of Springfield and Boston's Harrison Gray Otis, Israel Thorndike, and Samuel Eliot. In 1836 William Appleton, Augustus Thorndike, and Henry Cabot of Boston started the Perkins Mills, with a capital stock of $500,000. In 1841 the Dwight Manufacturing Company, the last of the large factories on the lower Chicopee, was established; its major investors included Edmund Dwight, William Sturgis, and Thomas H. Perkins.[71]

Thus while most of the Connecticut Valley was undergoing an agricultural slump, Springfield and the Chicopee Valley were in the midst of an active industrial boom, which spread

18

only slowly to Hampshire and Franklin Counties. With the growth of textile mills came the need for better transportation. Despite the close association between Springfield and Boston capitalists, the Worcester highlands blocked overland communication between the two towns. A freight traffic survey taken in 1828 showed that nearly all commerce went south down the Connecticut to Hartford.[72]

In 1830 a new link with the south opened, a canal that started in Westfield, Massachusetts, and terminated in New Haven, Connecticut. This 2 million dollar enterprise, sponsored by New Haven merchants, was incorporated as the Farmington Canal Company in Massachusetts. In 1834 this waterway reached Northampton, and it seemed to Boston observers to open to New York, through its satellite New Haven, the trade of the entire Connecticut Valley.[73]

Without a new route between Springfield and Boston, it seemed only logical that New York, and not the Massachusetts capital, would gain from the industrialization on the Chicopee. Certainly New York City, which already had a large trade with the southern states, could supply raw cotton for the mills; and its position as the chief importer and exporter for the West by way of the Erie Canal made it an ideal place to procure wool. And as a market for finished goods New York had no peer. Thus the very boats that brought raw materials and other goods from New York up the Connecticut would take back finished textiles to the emporium on the Hudson. On the contrary water communication between Springfield and Boston by way of the Connecticut was impractical. Not only was it almost twice as far to the Massachusetts city, but Boston, lacking any direct link with the West, was decidedly inferior to New York as a distribution point. To some it seemed inevitable that many capitalists would transfer their offices from Boston to New York and combine investment, purchasing, and marketing at one central location.[74]

Two important factors bolstered Boston's position. The Springfield development was secondary to and controlled by the same men who were responsible for the even larger textile ventures on the Merrimack. As long as eastern Massachusetts and southern New Hampshire held a commanding lead in cloth manufacture, Boston would keep its position as a major cotton and wool importer and as a market for finished cloth. Furthermore, water transportation, although the best available in 1830, was not well suited to Connecticut Valley manufacturing. Canal and riverboats were slow, insurance was high, and for four or five months out of every year ice stopped navigation.[75] Even more vexing, unlike the Lowell mills, which stood along the Merrimack with its connection to the Middlesex Canal, none of the Chicopee factories had direct access to water transportation. Boats could not ascend the Chicopee, and all freight had to be carried in wagons from the Connecticut. For the Dwight developments at Cabotville and Chicopee Falls this meant an irritating haul of from 2 to 6 miles.

The 1820s marked a turning point for the Connecticut Valley's transportation system. This period saw the culmination of improvements that cleared the Connecticut River for steamboat navigation from southern Vermont to the sea and saw the opening of a canal that by 1834 offered an uninterrupted artificial water highway from Northampton to New Haven. These events weakened the commercial bonds between the valley and Boston and drew the entire region into New York City's trading orbit. At the same time industrialization created a powerful and growing demand for internal improvements that were not subject to the caprice of geography and weather and that could link the vast power resources of central Massachusetts with the outside world.

5. BERKSHIRE COUNTY: THE STRUGGLE FOR TRANSPORTATION

West of the Connecticut Valley lay Berkshire County, the smallest of Massachusetts' economic regions. A continuation of the Vermont Green Mountains commanded the entire eastern half of the county, towering from 1,600 to 2,000 feet above the Connecticut River, effectively isolating the more habitable portions of the region from the rest of Massachusetts. The western slopes of these Berkshire Hills were drained by two major river systems, both of which rose in the central part of the county. The Housatonic, a rushing stream often broken by rapids and waterfalls, carved its way southward through the towns of Pittsfield, Lenox, Stockbridge, Great Barrington, and Sheffield. Then it flowed into the state of Connecticut and finally emptied into Long Island Sound. The Hoosic, equally rapid and powerful, rushed northward through the towns of Cheshire and Adams and then through a corner of Vermont and into New York State, where it joined the Hudson above Troy. Along the banks of these two rivers lay the best land and the largest towns in the county.[76]

Berkshire County was populated later than any other part of the Commonwealth. Not until after 1744 did a substantial number of settlers find their way across the granite ridges into the county's more fertile western portions.[77] Until the start of the nineteenth century Berkshire relied upon farming. Like the Connecticut Valley, it raised livestock and a considerable amount of wheat and rye, which its farmers carted as much as 30 miles to the market towns of Hudson, Albany, and Troy on the Hudson River. The agricultural boom was short-lived; by the 1820s the county did not even raise enough grain for its own needs and had to import it from Albany. Soil exhaustion and then the opening of the rich upstate New York lands by the Erie Canal spread a blight upon the region. By 1810 Berkshire's population reached a peak of 35,787 and then started to decline.[78]

Only the beginnings of industry checked this trend. "Berkshire seems destined to become a great manufacturing district," wrote the Reverend Chester Dewey in 1829. "The facilities for the application of water power in Adams, Pittsfield, Dalton, Lee, Otis, Stockbridge, and Great Barrington are very great."[79] Indeed by 1830 the county again started to grow, and several of its villages had high hopes for the future. By that time six towns had a population of more than 1,800, the largest being Pittsfield, which had just over 3,500 inhabitants, followed by Adams, Great Barrington, Sheffield, Williamstown, and Lee, in that order.[80] All were widely separated, Adams and Williamstown in the northwest corner of the county, Pittsfield and Lee in the center, and Great Barrington and Sheffield in the southwest. All these towns were rivals since none was large enough to see itself secure as the region's most important trading or industrial center.

Lack of capital, numerous small mill sites unable to attract factories on the scale of those on the Chicopee, and inadequate transportation slowed the area's growth. Consequently early industry was limited to small mills financed by local entrepreneurs. Abundant marble and granite quarries and iron deposits attracted the capitalists' attention as much as the mill sites around which grew paper mills and woolen and cotton factories.

Typical of the county's development was the town of Lee, which in 1827 was a thriving village of almost 1,800. It contained six paper mills, two woolen factories, two iron furnaces, a forge, a gunpowder mill, three furniture shops, nine saw mills, and eight retail stores. Lee's nearest outside market was nearly 40 miles away at Hudson, and in 1826 more than 2,200 tons of raw materials and finished goods were teamed between the two towns. Lee was about 150 miles from New York City, and it cost $7 a ton to ship goods there, of which $5.50 went for the 40 miles between Lee and Hudson while the remaining 110 miles of river transport cost but $1.50.[81] Although Lee was actually closer to Boston than to New York City, there was no commerce at all with Boston, and the Berkshire town even found it difficult to send representatives to the General Court.

Pittsfield too was an embryonic manufacturing center. Among the town's leading industrialists were Lemuel and Josiah Pomeroy, who in 1827 owned and operated a woolen and cotton factory in which more than $130,000 had been invested.[82]

Transportation was the most serious obstacle slowing Berkshire manufacturing development. In 1828 the county's shippers paid over $108,000 or an average of $5.88 per ton to move less than 19,000 tons between Berkshire towns and the Hudson or Connecticut Rivers.[83] Local industrialists used every means at their command to create better connections with the outside world. The county's mountains made canals impractical, so the first three decades of the nineteenth century saw the emphasis on turnpike construction. In 1797 the General Court chartered the Third Massachusetts Turnpike Corporation, which constructed a road from Pittsfield through Dalton,

Hinsdale, and Worthington to the Connecticut River at Northampton. Rugged hills and canyons forced a large capital outlay, but the project never paid a dividend since repair costs devoured all toll receipts.[84]

Dissatisfied with the third pike and undaunted by its failure, the Pittsfield industrialists obtained a charter for the Pontoosac Turnpike from Pittsfield through the pass of the Westfield River to Springfield.[85] Lemuel Pomeroy headed the new company, and he viewed the pike not as a means for private profit but as a public service designed to facilitate Berkshire County's trade. Hence he tried to lure Berkshire, Hampshire, and Hampden counties into joint construction of a free public road along the proposed route. Only when these efforts failed did the private corporation build the highway. In 1830 the Pontoosac Turnpike was completed for the full 50 miles between Springfield and Pittsfield, but the road must have been a flimsy affair since the whole capital stock invested in it amounted to but $10,000.[86] Even with this improvement, freight transportation to New York City by way of Springfield was difficult. All goods had to be teamed 50 miles to the Connecticut River, where they were loaded onto a river steamer bound for Hartford. There another transfer was necessary since the large ocean-going steamboats used on the Hartford-New York run could not proceed up the Connecticut beyond Hartford.[87] If the shipper used the new Farmington Canal between Westfield and New Haven, which opened simultaneously with the Pontoosac Pike, two changes also had to be made—the first at Westfield to the canal and the second from the canal boat to a steamer at New Haven. This route did, however, reduce the land cartage from 50 to 35 miles.

The irksome changes and poor connections on the Connecticut Valley route channeled most Berkshire traffic to the Hudson River, which had cheap, frequent, and direct steamship service to New York City. Thus, although transportation was gradually improving, Berkshire County still felt itself isolated in 1830. Its merchant-industrialists eagerly sought some type of internal improvement that would give their enterprises the same access to markets enjoyed by the Chicopee and Lowell developments and which would put an end to the 30- to 40-mile horse-drawn transportation which stood between them and the rest of the world.

6. COMMERCIAL RELATIONS BETWEEN ALBANY, TROY, AND MASSACHUSETTS

Between the Massachusetts state line and the Hudson or North River lay a hilly section of New York State slightly more than 20 miles wide. This area's main importance in 1830 lay in the fact that it was an obstacle between Berkshire County and its natural outlet. But along the Hudson itself were two booming cities, Albany and Troy. They were born to be rivals. Both were located at the eastern end of the Erie Canal, and both hoped to parlay this advantage into commercial greatness. Albany, New York's capital and second largest city, occupied a high hill on the west side of the Hudson River 140 miles upstream from New York City. Stimulated by the Erie Canal in the decade between 1820 and 1830, Albany doubled in population from 12,000 to 24,000 and became the eighth largest city in the nation. During the same decade Troy, located just six miles upstream from Albany but on the opposite bank, grew even faster. Troy's population spurted from just over 5,000 to more than 11,000.[88] The two cities each built terminals to handle the thousands of canal boats that arrived each season. The Trojans were especially anxious to funnel the western trade through their town. They realized that much traffic would be interchanged between canal boats and steamers, and they hoped that the transfer point would emerge into a commercial emporium that would rival New York City. "Let this place be made the *head of steam navigation on the Hudson . . . ,*" urged the Troy *Post* on May 13, 1823.[89] Significantly, when the Erie Canal opened on October 8, 1823 the first boat to carry merchandise west was the *Trojan Trader*.[90]

Troy's success was watched carefully in the south. A suspicious Trojan declared that "Albany viewed 'this growing prosperity of their neighbors with an evil eye,' and considered it as 'an encroachment upon their native rights.' "[91] Albany did not intend to be left out, for in 1823 with the cooperation of the city fathers and the town's leading merchants a special commission created by the New York State Legislature set about to build a giant shipping terminal for Albany. The result was a great basin with docks and wharves that accommodated 1,000 canal boats and fifty larger vessels.[92]

If in 1830 Albany and Troy looked West, it had not always been that way. About 1800 the Hudson Valley towns saw their main opportunities eastward, in Massachusetts and Vermont. Besides Troy and Albany, the town of Hudson, 29 miles downstream from New York's capital, had equal hopes for greatness. Anxious to attract business, Hudson's merchants sought a turnpike charter in 1799. The resultant Columbia Turnpike ran east to West Stockbridge, Massachusetts, and captured the trade of Lee, Great Barrington, and Pittsfield.[93]

Simultaneously Albany moved to link itself with Massachusetts by building two turnpikes. The first ran southeast from Greenbush opposite Albany to connect with a road to Pittsfield at the Massachusetts state line. The second ran northeast from Greenbush to tap the trade of northern Berkshire County, especially that of Adams and Williamstown.[94]

Troy attracted considerable Berkshire business by way of the turnpikes constructed under Albany's leadership. And though its first efforts went to build a toll road west toward Schenectady, Troy never lost sight of the eastern trade. In 1827 the Trojans started planning for a pike northeast to Bennington, Vermont. This $100,000 project became a reality in 1831 and soon took its place as an important source of the city's commerce.[95]

Although the Erie Canal diverted attention from Massachusetts and Vermont, Albany and Troy still demanded improved transportation eastward. Both cities saw that an overland artery east to the Massachusetts coast would enhance their position as interchange points and help lure the commercial emporium away from New York City to the upper Hudson basin. At the very least, better communication with Massachusetts would build the two cities' hinterland and bring additional business supplying the growing industrial centers of Berkshire County. But there was always the possibility that a new mode of transportation, perhaps the novel and untried railroad, could replace the Hudson as an outlet to the sea. Sharp in the minds of the

Troy and Albany men was the winter ice, which choked all shipping three to four months each year. A railroad would solve this problem, and if it happened to divert the summer trade to Boston, so much the better.

But even if not one bushel of grain destined for the markets of Europe or the West Indies could be weaned away from New York City, there was still a thriving trade between eastern Massachusetts and the Erie Canal to be accommodated. The withering of agriculture and the growth of manufacturing in Massachusetts had turned every area of the state into a region which imported breadstuffs and raw materials and which in turn scattered to the world markets the products of its factories. The logic of the situation was obvious to all. The West—upstate New York, Ohio, Michigan, Indiana, and Illinois—produced grain, meat, wool, and hides. Massachusetts consumed these products and in return sent westward shoes, iron machinery, shirts, wool garments, cotton cloth, and a hundred and one additional items. This natural trade was destined to grow, but already in 1830 it amounted to more than 30,000 tons annually between Boston and Albany alone.[96] Of this amount not less than 5,000 tons represented manufactured goods going west. In addition the fisheries of Gloucester, Marblehead, and Cape Cod sent to Albany nearly 25,000 quintals of codfish plus a like number of barrels of mackerel.[97] Eastward went "75,000 barrels of flour together with large quantities of timothy seed, peas, [and] wool."[98] Worcester, too, imported large amounts from the West.[99]

In 1830 this commerce could move between Massachusetts and Albany in just three ways. The first, the land route between Boston and Albany (via Worcester, Springfield, and Pittsfield), was suitable only for passengers and mail. A correspondent for the Boston *Courier* recommended the Boston and Albany stage only for those who wanted to see the country "or whose health requires exercise." The roads were "extremely rough and hilly; the horses and coaches . . . not of the highest order; and the rate of travel tediously slow."[100] Any substantial trade by land was impossible.

All other methods of reaching Albany depended upon water. The fastest of these, the steamboat, was usually taken by passengers and was used for the shipment of high-value merchandise. Every morning at five o'clock stages left Boston for both Providence and Newport. Here they connected with steamers for New York City which reached there late the same day. At New York the traveler stayed overnight and then embarked the next morning on one of the steamers plying the Hudson between Manhattan and Albany. The Boston *Courier* advised the steamboat *North America,* which left the city at seven in the morning and arrived at Albany before night. The paper praised the roads from Boston south to Newport and Providence as straight and good, and the stages as smooth and fast. The total fare for the trip was $10—$2 for the stage, $6 for the boat from Providence to New York, and $2 from New York to Albany.[101] Passengers or freight from Worcester County had an even easier time since the Blackstone Canal linked Worcester with Providence. From Springfield passengers could travel the entire distance to Albany by steamboat, changing boats at Hartford and New York. This trip consumed two days and the fare was about the same as that between Boston and Albany.

Although steamboats carried nearly all passenger traffic between Massachusetts and Albany, most freight went by schooner. In 1830 two major companies, the Boston, Albany and Troy Packets and the Boston and Albany Despatch Line, offered weekly service between the Massachusetts capital and the Erie Canal. These two companies alone had a fleet of nine ships. In addition, at least sixteen independent vessels competed for the Boston to Albany commerce.[102]

Sloops and schooners served eastern Massachusetts well. They were ideal for the bulky grain trade from the Erie's terminal to Boston and Providence. The cost of shipping by boat was small. The customary rate for flour was $4.50 per ton including insurance, but sharp competition often lowered the charge to $2.50 a ton. By comparison teamsters demanded $10 a ton just to haul goods the 45 miles between Boston and Providence.[103] Certainly cities with direct water transportation, especially Boston, Worcester, and even Springfield had such easy access to the national grain basket that there was little, if any, economic justification for a new route to Albany. But the Industrial Revolution created new transportation demands not easily met by sloop navigation. Power sites, not proximity to canals or navigable rivers, determined the location of the manufacturing town. The growth of places like Lee, Pittsfield, Chicopee, Palmer, Framingham, and Ludlow underscored the need for improved land transportation.

The very nature of industrial traffic was different. Grain moved seasonally. It was harvested in the summer and moved to the coast from July to November. The same was true of wool. Sheep were shorn in the summer and wool moved to market well before winter. Thus when ice blocked navigation there was little agricultural produce to be shipped. Industry ran throughout the year. Factories produced both winter and summer, and although they might stockpile raw materials during the ice-free months, the demands of the market, not the growing season, regulated output. The businessman had to meet heavy competition. He often had to ship west during the winter so that his goods could arrive in time for the spring trade. A fickle market could cause a sudden spurt in demand that required more wool or cotton in the dead of winter. And for the first time speed in delivery became important. If goods sent west for the spring trade did not arrive in time, the western storekeeper would have to sell them at a loss or keep them in stock for a full year to realize a profit. Factories that could promise fast and sure delivery had a great competitive advantage.

Measured against these requirements, sloop navigation was unsatisfactory. Its major advantage, cheap movement of bulky goods, was counterbalanced by the ability of manufactured articles to afford relatively high freight rates. A ton of flour was worth perhaps $35 at most, but a ton of shoes twenty times that amount. The shoe manufacturer wanted speed and reliability, but the Boston and Albany shipping route was "closed for three months in the year [at] all times dilatory, and . . . subject to accidental delays, the duration of which, cannot in any instance be computed beforehand."[104] The normal time consumed by water transport from Boston, Worcester, and Springfield to Albany was two weeks. This, of course, was in addition to the time, expense, and inconvenience of the road haulage necessary to reach navigable water from most Massachusetts factories.

Massachusetts in 1830 had all the trouble of a mature economy undergoing a drastic metamorphosis. Booming industrial towns stood beside decaying seaports. Places like Newburyport and Beverly, lacking power resources, lived on in the hope of a commercial revival. Their reaction was retrenchment, and their capitalists either retired from trade to wait for better days or moved to Boston and invested in manufactures. The great merchant capitalists were split: some still spurned industry; others shifted some investments into textiles but continued heavily committed to shipping; still others went over completely to manufacturing.

Throughout Massachusetts soil exhaustion and the competition of western land stalked agriculture. Since well over half the state's population lived on the land, the plight of the farmer dominated thinking in a majority of the state's villages and towns. Farmers welcomed the intrusion of manufacturing into Worcester County, the Connecticut Valley, and the Berkshire region, for it meant new markets and a chance for survival. But all actively opposed expenditures by their town governments or the state which might bring new taxes. The country store owners who formerly relied on the agricultural trade were forced to join the Boston capitalists in the movement toward industrialization or to start new factories on their own. In either case, industry completely absorbed most inland capital.

The transportation picture was confused. Geography had split Massachusetts into four separate economic units which, for the purposes of communication, might as well have been separate states. There was no adequate way to move goods from east to west across the Commonwealth. It cost about four times as much to move a ton of freight the 40 miles from Boston to Worcester as it did to send it the 200 miles between Boston and Albany.

In some ways transportation had improved. Canals and the removal of river obstructions had opened up large areas of Worcester County and the Connecticut Valley. But as helpful as these improvements were, they were inadequate to meet the state's growing needs, and for Boston the Blackstone and Farmington Canals meant commercial disaster, for both tended to draw business away to its commercial rivals, Providence, New Haven, and New York. For much of Massachusetts, especially the hilly sections of Berkshire and Worcester Counties and parts of the Connecticut Valley, canals were impractical. Finally the growth of industry demanded a better kind of transportation than could be furnished by water—one that was faster, more reliable, and one that could continue to operate in the winter as well as the summer.

Almost every part of Massachusetts stood to benefit from improved transportation. The industrialist needed better access to his factory, a surer means for receiving his heavy raw materials, and a more rapid way to send his finished goods to market. Boston needed an artery to the West to hold its position as the commercial metropolis of the Northeast. And the farmer's dream of scientific agriculture and growing specialized crops hinged upon his power to send his produce quickly and cheaply to the new industrial centers.

Yet despite this universal need, the year 1830 saw Massachusetts in a heated controversy over internal improvements. The argument raged over a radically new form of land transportation, the railroad, which had already been adopted by Maryland and South Carolina in their efforts to link themselves with the West. To some in Massachusetts the issue seemed clear. Either the Bay State would build a railroad to the Erie Canal at Albany, or the Commonwealth would become an economic backwater.

The Issue of State Aid

THE RECENT REINTERPRETATION of the relationship of government to economic activity in nineteenth-century America has taken two forms. First, there has been an attempt to show that from the Revolution to 1830 public policy, especially at the state level, favored government economic planning in the form of the widespread promotion of internal improvements designed to stimulate general economic development. Second, there has been an effort to measure quantitatively governmental contributions to internal improvements with the goal of proving that they were decisive in providing social overhead capital.

The second proposition became the subject of heated controversy. Carter Goodrich and his students emphasized the quantity of capital provided by government. Harvey Segal, for example, found that 73 per cent of 188 million dollars invested in canals prior to the Civil War came from government.[1] With respect to both railroads and canals Goodrich argued that "Recent studies . . . have shown that the volume of government investment was greater than had been believed, both in absolute figures and in relation to the total canal and railroad investment, to the total national investment, and to the total budgets of governmental authorities."[2]

Goodrich and his followers have not gone unchallenged. Douglass North in 1966 asserted that "all too often present ideological attitudes of scholars toward government intervention have influenced their perspective toward the past." He called for "an unbiased, systematic examination of the extent to which the activity of government at all levels did or did not actually promote economic growth," an analysis he believed had not yet been undertaken.[3] Elsewhere North maintained that this would involve more than a mere totaling of dollars invested. "If the government indeed played a significant role and accelerated economic development, it is necessary not only that quantitatively its contribution would have been important, but alternatively the resources without government intervention would have been used far less efficiently." That this was the case was not at all clear. Government investment in canals in the 1830s, for instance, came in a period of full employment of resources; as a result, the foreign capital attracted by government led to a reallocation of resources from one type of economic activity to another. "The net contribution at best was the differential productivity between, on the one hand, the kinds of economic activity that would have existed without government support and, on the other, the government investment in canals." In the light of the widespread failure of the canal system, it was not "self-evident that this was a net positive contribution."[4]

The factors involved in building a railroad from Boston to Albany throw significant light on the problems of measuring the "stimulating effect" of government money by statistics alone. On the surface the figures seem to provide a dramatic demonstration of the primacy of government support. The railroad, when finally finished in 1842, represented a total capital investment of $9,000,000. Of this, $3,000,000, or one-third, was private in the form of stock subscriptions. The remaining $6,000,000, or two-thirds, came as a result of government action. Yet to the question "Did government initiate the Boston to Albany railroad?" the answer must be a clear no. The chapters that follow demonstrate why the state did nothing despite an elaborate effort to force it to initiate internal improvements. The legislature considered canals and railroads too novel, too untried, and financially too risky to merit aid. As long as internal improvements appeared to be certain financial failures, no matter how generally beneficial to the rest of the economy, the state was too timid to take the initiative. Only after the Boston and Worcester and its two sister systems the Boston & Lowell and Boston & Providence, private corporations financed entirely by private capital, conclusively demonstrated that railroads were both practical and profitable, did Massachusetts finally agree to aid an Albany railroad.

The state's support of the Western Railroad was essential since the road was constructed during a period of national financial crisis when private capital was not abundant. And the almost immediate profitability of the Western would seem to qualify the railroad, even under the standards of Douglass North's strict formula, as a wise investment. But this might substantiate his argument that with the return of prosperity and the conclusive demonstration in Massachusetts that railroads were profitable, private capital would have soon built the line anyway. Certainly the Western Railroad's ability to pay all the interest upon its large debt and a 6 per cent dividend within three years after the system had been finished indicates that the route was not a "developmental" project in H. Jerome Cranmer's sense—that is, a road built to open up a region in advance of actual transportation requirements—but was rather a line able to exploit an already considerable traffic potential.[5] The state may have advanced the Western's construction by as much as five years. But in Massachusetts private risk capital initiated the railroad, which only then attracted government support. This experience stands in marked contrast with post World War II America, where government in such fields as atomic energy and space exploration has broken the new ground only to have private capital in the form of investments in power stations and communications satellites follow.

The development of the Boston & Albany must be understood in the light of early nineteenth-century American conceptions of the proper role of the state in the economy. Louis Hartz and Milton Heath have argued that the governments they studied followed well thought through programs in which the state undertook the responsibility for economic planning.[6] Hartz, anxious to slay "the myth of laissez faire" described Pennsylvania's ambitious internal improvement projects and concluded that the state adapted the mercantilist ideas of the British Empire to the post-independence era. "Government assumed the job of shaping decisively the contours of economic life."[7] Heath saw an even more specific state role in the South in general and in Georgia in particular. "There were two theories concerning state support of railroad construction in the South," he wrote.

33

One was that the state should assist all projects in some more or less uniform fashion, a policy exemplified most fully in Virginia and Tennessee. The other theory was the one developed in Georgia, that the state should confine its efforts to a single large project that was designed to confer a general benefit upon the entire state and to stimulate efforts widely in private and local construction of complementary and auxiliary railroad lines; and, furthermore, that the state should embark a sufficiently large sum—preferably the entire cost—to assure reasonably prompt completion of the work."[8]

Laissez faire is a myth, at least as far as the building of canals and railroads is concerned. But the states did not follow well thought through plans for the guidance and stimulation of economic development. Assistance to a few key projects and widely scattered speeches of local politicians to influence votes on a specific measure are not evidence of a theory of government aid.

The Massachusetts story is a perfect example. The Commonwealth had no dearth of leaders who proposed schemes for state-owned canals and railroads, and the appropriate propaganda supplied a theoretical basis for such plans. Yet the history of internal improvements in the Commonwealth disproves the existence of a generally held theory of the state's role in such works. Nor is there evidence of mercantilist carryover from pre-Revolutionary days. Indeed the first major internal improvements, the Middlesex Canal and the turnpikes, were private. Only when these failed did the promoters of inland transportation turn to the state. It is significant that Nathan Hale, who led the fight for a Boston to Albany line and who at an early date supported a state-built railroad network, constantly shifted his position as circumstances changed. In a six-year period he supported a purely state-owned system, a mixed enterprise, a wholly private corporation, and then a mixed enterprise again. Hale was typical of most Massachusetts advocates of internal improvements. The Bay State men responded not to theories but pragmatically to each problem, taking the side of private, mixed, or public enterprise as the specific situation warranted.

The most recent attempt to analyze the beginnings of the

Boston to Albany railroad, Julius Rubin's *Canal or Railroad? Imitation and Innovation in the Response to the Erie Canal in Philadelphia, Baltimore and Boston,* examines the internal improvements that extended westward from these three seaport cities in the decade after the Erie Canal opened.[9] He asks why Pennsylvania responded immediately to New York's challenge with a state canal, Baltimore soon after with a private railroad that later received some government aid, and Boston much later with a railroad. He denies "that extremely small disparities in situation, information and timing could have produced such large differences in response."[10] The explanation for the difference in behavior, he holds, lies in the attitudes of the leading men of each city. These attitudes among other things reflected the traditions of the three cities. Boston was conservative, and Nathan Hale "cautious," Baltimore "daring" and "innovative," and Philadelphia "panic" stricken and "imitative."[11]

The chapters that follow lend no support whatever to Rubin's conclusions. Massachusetts' decision not to build a canal and to construct a railroad made sense in both economic and political terms and definitely did result from the state's particular situation. The Boston press between 1826 and 1830 revealed that the city was deeply concerned about its declining position as a port and was frenetically eager for some link to the Erie Canal. More zealous advocates of such a program than Nathan Hale and his paper, the Boston *Daily Advertiser,* would be difficult to find. Why then did not Boston build a canal in 1826, when an engineering study revealed that one could be constructed at a great cost? The answer lies in economic and political reality. Politically the canal was dead from the start because it was regarded as a money-losing proposition and because Boston exercised small influence in the Commonwealth. The farmers who controlled the state legislature saw little merit in a canal that would bring in cheap western farm products to ruin their markets, and moreover they would authorize no project that might add to a tax burden they already considered too heavy. Private capital also refused to build a canal. While it was true that merchant shipping in Massachusetts and Boston was declining, textile manufacturing was beginning to offer a large-scale and highly profitable alternative form of investment.

Boston was not dying and its capitalists knew it. Yet in 1826 the industrial base was not sizable enough or dispersed enough to demand a railroad to the West.

Not until large-scale cotton mills for the Chicopee and Connecticut Valleys were either planned or under construction did Boston industrial leaders become interested in a transportation artery westward across the state to Worcester, Springfield, and Albany. The Boston to Albany railroad was not primarily a response to the Erie Canal (although the rhetoric left over from the initial reaction lingered on, as did shipping interests) but the result of a concerted drive by manufacturing groups who wanted transportation to inland factory sites.[12] This new industrial base did not become strong enough to take action until after 1830, when the success of England's Liverpool and Manchester Railway proved railroads practical beyond any doubt. Timing was of vital importance. Had the rural dominated Massachusetts General Court supported Boston's initial cry for a westward internal improvement in 1826, as the Pennsylvania Legislature supported Philadelphia's demands that same year, the Bay State would have selected a canal over a railroad.

Furthermore Rubin's implication that Pennsylvania's decision to build a canal was unwise is based largely on hindsight. Considering the crudeness of railroads in 1826 and the extremely slow pace at which transportation innovations historically had evolved, the Pennsylvania decision makers could not have anticipated that railroads would mature in ten years to a point where they would render a canal obsolete. Rubin's argument that railroads offered a practical alternative to canals as early as 1825 ignores the widespread view, even in England, that horses were equal to or better than steam engines. The Stockton and Darlington steam locomotives did not convince many people at the time that a transportation revolution was at hand. Had the railroad failed to develop, the Pennsylvania Canal, despite the fact that it probably could not have challenged the Erie, would have assumed a major role in the development of that part of the Keystone State through which it ran, and the project would have gone down in history as a brilliant achievement.

36

Rubin's distinction between canals as "imitative" and railroads as "innovative" seems meaningless. Neither form of transportation originated in America. Both came from England. New York State and Pennsylvania both borrowed the English experience and technology, which at the time seemed best to meet their requirements. And in Massachusetts, the Boston & Worcester Railroad and its counterparts the Lowell and Providence lines, were near copies of the Liverpool and Manchester.

But Rubin's main error is in his analytical technique. He bases his explanation of the decision-making process in the three cities upon an analysis of the arguments posed for the various projects and makes no attempt to determine the power structure in each region. In Massachusetts he lumps together the legislature, business, and shipping interests and the supporters of internal improvements. It would be more fruitful to analyze not the arguments in behalf of internal improvements but the character of the groups for and against the projects and their relation to the economies of their regions. This study of Massachusetts indicates that an explanation of Pennsylvania's action will emerge from an examination of the Philadelphia and back-country economy joined to a study of arguments and an analysis of the members of the legislature who voted for the canal. In Baltimore, where, like Massachusetts, private initiative took the lead, a detailed study of the business leaders is in order. Baltimore took action in 1827. This rapid decision might be explained if it could be determined that unlike Boston's capitalists, who had attractive alternative investments to shipping in textile manufacturing, Baltimore's prosperity remained largely tied to trade, and hence the city and its business leaders, threatened by the Erie Canal, took immediate steps to protect the only major source of prosperity. While such areas are beyond the scope of this study, the analysis of Massachusetts makes it very clear that the Commonwealth acted in response to its particular situation; without a detailed examination of the politics and economies of Pennsylvania and Maryland, it is dangerous to postulate that their problems were similar.

Because of the scarcity of inland transport, no one in the 1820s in Massachusetts opposed internal improvements, but disputes about routes and financing dashed the hopes of every railroad proposal until 1830. The route problem reflected diversity of interests. A railroad or canal constructed from Boston west to Albany or Troy met almost automatic hostility from other Massachusetts seaports, especially Newburyport, Ipswich, Salem, and the island counties of Dukes (Martha's Vineyard) and Nantucket. These places, undergoing a deep commercial depression, felt that what little shipping they still enjoyed would be siphoned to Boston if that city became the terminal of a line of communication to the Mississippi Valley.

Public financing of such a project, which might lead to higher taxes, was more than the coastal ports could bear. In the interior, too, routing was a problem. A single line the length of the state could not please everybody. The improvement could run through the southern part of the state, through the center, or along the northern border. Any project built along the northern or southern routes would leave a substantial portion of the Commonwealth as much as 30 to 60 miles from it. And for most people 30 miles was as bad as 100. Even the central route left many places 20 to 30 miles to one side, and this compromise had the additional disadvantage of bypassing such important towns as Worcester, Fitchburg, Springfield, and Pittsfield—all of which demanded that the improvement run through their community as the price of support.

Even more vexing was financing, which could be effected privately through the charter of a corporation, publicly by the creation of a state agency, or by a mixture which would involve state and possibly municipal purchase of stock in a semiprivate corporation. But any plan would have to enjoy the support of the state government.

Massachusetts politics in the 1820s was as much in a state of flux as its economy. From 1812 until 1822 the state's voters elected Federalist administrations with clocklike regularity. By 1823, however, the Federalist Party was on its death bed. The very pillars of its support—merchant shipping and entrenched property rights—were crumbling, for the economic revolution sweeping the state challenged all old interest groups and forced even the most conservative to reevaluate their positions. In 1823 the Federalist Harrison Gray Otis received a sound trouncing in the election for governor at the hands of the seventy-year-old Dr. William Eustis, a Bostonian, Republican, and veteran of the Revolution.[13]

In 1825 all Federalist opposition melted, and the Republican nominee, Levi Lincoln, received over 35,000 ballots as against a combined vote of less than 3,000 for his opponents.[14] Lincoln, a Worcester lawyer receptive to the state's growing industrial needs, was returned to office for eight consecutive yearly terms until 1834, when he was succeeded by another Worcester lawyer, John Davis. The period of Lincoln's administration was one of realignment and political chaos; issues rather than party dominated.

One center of controversy exploded over corporations and vested rights. In 1828 the General Court chartered a company to build a free Boston and Charlestown bridge less than 400 yards from an established toll span. Immediately a bitter fight rocked the state. Men of property felt that the legislature had struck a mortal blow against all corporations, charging the state with violation of contract and virtual confiscation of private property.[15] After prolonged legal action, the United States Supreme Court in 1837 ruled against the toll bridge, maintaining that the grants of a state legislature gave no implied rights but only those privileges explicitly conferred by the words of a charter.[16]

In the long run railroads benefited from the Supreme Court's decision. If the Charles River Bridge proprietors had been upheld, the established turnpike and canal corporations could have blocked the new railroad lines that threatened them. But in the short run the controversy had a devastating effect on plans for the private financing of internal improvements. When the legislature authorized construction of the free bridge, it diminished the value of every corporate charter. If a profitable internal improvement could be undercut by a parallel line chartered at the legislature's whim, there was little incentive for venturing money in such an enterprise.[17] Thus capitalists came to insist upon charters which specified exclusive rights to traffic for a certain period of time. Such demands only made it harder to obtain legislative approval for a charter that would satisfy both the investors and the public.

Another great issue concerned reform of the General Court. The Massachusetts Senate was elected on the basis of the proportion of state taxes each county paid, an arrangement that favored Boston.[18] The lower house was no more satisfactory. In theory over 1,000 representatives were entitled to seats. In practice, however, the annual membership varied enormously. The legislature met twice each year, for a short session in June and for a long winter sitting. In much of the state it was hard to find people willing to spend one-fourth of their time in Boston. Most towns, therefore, sent representatives only when an issue that affected them was under consideration. This explains why Boston elected but seven members in 1827 and sixty in 1830. Between 1825 and 1830 the membership varied from a low of 177 in 1825 to a high of 496 in 1829.[19]

These arrangements came under heavy criticism in the 1820s. But proposals for a change always raised the question of which section of the state should control the General Court. As it was, the small towns could veto any measure by flooding Boston with representatives. The question was important because it influenced the nature and the amount of taxation.

Massachusetts, with substantial sections of its trading and farming regions in decline, was allergic to taxes.[20] Each group within the state suspected that it would suffer from an increase. Boston feared that, if the declining rural and other seacoast towns had too much power, they would attempt to raise all revenue in the city by bank taxes and other levies upon commerce. On the other side, the farming areas and the ports felt that if Boston and the new industrial towns had the upper hand, they would reduce commercial and industrial taxes and place most of the charges upon land and agricultural wealth. Furthermore, Boston and several other towns, which were pushing hard for an artery to the West, might involve the state in a large program of internal improvements, and the bill would fall upon depressed towns that would not share in the benefits.[21] Disagreement over reapportionment prevented any constitutional reform until 1831.

Massachusetts hotly debated an even more vexing question: whether or not the state should build a railroad to link its capital with Albany on the Hudson. The issue was not new.

The Commonwealth had been the first American state to build a major canal. In 1793 the Middlesex Canal had been chartered to bring the trade of all Middlesex County and most of New Hampshire to Boston. Significantly this improvement was undertaken by private capital, but the state fixed the toll. In 1794 the directors of the new corporation created 1,000 shares of stock, of which 800 were taken and on which assessments between 1794 and 1806 amounted to a total of $610 for each share.[22]

The history of the Middlesex Canal cast a cloud over all proposals for Massachusetts internal improvements between 1810 and 1831. All told, the canal's stockholders invested a total of $592,000, or more than the entire authorized capital of the Boston Manufacturing Company at Waltham. Although the canal was completed in 1804, not until fifteen years later did its directors declare the first dividend, which amounted to a mere $15 a share, or slightly more than 2 per cent upon the capital invested. Instead of improving as population and industry moved into Lowell, the canal dividends actually fell to $9 a share in 1827, $8 a share in 1830, and nothing in 1831. The project was "a financial failure from the end of the first year of business to the day, fifty years later, when the last boat traversed its nearly abandoned works."[23]

Horse-drawn wagons waged an active and often successful campaign to capture the traffic between Boston, Middlesex County, and New Hampshire. The canal forced teamsters to lower their rates, but shippers often preferred to pay higher land charges rather than patronize the boats. In 1827 the Lowell factory owners used the canal to ship heavy raw materials from Boston to their plants; however, they sent nearly all their finished goods back by wagon, partly to force down canal rates, but also because wagons were faster, provided door-to-door transportation, and were free of winter ice. The millowners would be the main force behind the railroad, which eventually destroyed the canal.[24]

The private turnpike corporations, which attempted to meet the demands for better transportation between 1800 and 1810, also proved disastrous for investors. The $420,000 Newburyport Turnpike, which linked Newburyport and Boston, a "remarkable instance of enterprise and miscalculation," lay almost unused since the people continued to travel on the old road.[25] Even when pikes were heavily traveled, they still proved a financial horror. The Boston and Worcester Turnpike, chartered in 1805 and opened for traffic in 1809, was the wonder of its day. It knifed across the countryside in an almost straight line, shortening the distance from 45 to less than 38 miles. The corporation financed itself by issuing 600 shares with a par value of $250 each. The completed road cost just under $150,000, but unfortunately the stockholders were not able to sit back and watch the money roll in. Although a few dividends were paid, the company seldom earned enough to keep the road in repair. In 1817 the corporation's bridge over Long Pond burned, and the directors had to assess each share a total of $66.50 to rebuild it.[26] Since none of the early corporations enjoyed limited liability, stock ownership always carried with it the possibility of large payments to meet any debts contracted by the company. But if the stockholders were not protected against exploitation, the people of the Commonwealth were. The General Court carefully fixed the location of toll gates and specified the exact amount to be charged.[27]

Financial disaster cooled the ardor for private construction; there was a great lessening of turnpike and canal building between 1810 and 1825. Capitalists refused to invest in what they considered hopeless enterprises. The decade of the 1820s therefore saw a massive attempt to get the state government to undertake what private individuals would not.

Few events received greater attention in Boston than the construction of the Erie Canal. Since this project coincided with Massachusetts' commercial decline, local observers were quick to advocate a similar program to cure the Bay State's ills. In 1825, Massachusetts' Governor Eustis urged the General Court to authorize commissioners to survey and determine the feasibility of a canal from Boston to the Hudson River. The legislature responded favorably; three commissioners were appointed and Colonel Loammi Baldwin was named engineer.[28] Speaking before the legislature on January 4, 1826, newly elected Governor Levi Lincoln anticipated the report of the commissioners. The proposed canal was practicable, he argued,

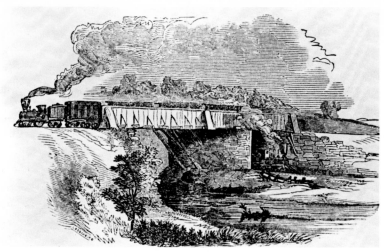

Figure 4

Western Railroad: Crossing over the Hudson & Berkshire Railroad
in the mid-1840s.

Figure 5

Western Railroad: Fourth Stone Bridge in the Berkshire Hills in
the mid-1840s.

Figure 6

Western Railroad: An original stone arch bridge near Chester, 128.21 miles west of Worcester, as it appeared about 1914.

Figure 7

Western Railroad: An original stone arch bridge near Middlefield, 128.88 miles west of Worcester. Concrete bridge to the rear built in 1913.

and "the interests of the Commonwealth require its execution." There was no hazard in the venture, and no enterprise could be "more beneficial to the agricultural, manufacturing, and commercial interests of the State, than the opening of a water communication from the capital through the populous, productive, and flourishing western counties of the Commonwealth."[29] Lincoln further recommended that the legislature enlarge the powers of the commissioners by making them a permanent board of internal improvement.[30]

Instead, when the legislators saw the report, they abolished the commission, thereby killing the prospects of a canal.[31] Loammi Baldwin had indeed found two "practicable" routes from Boston to the Connecticut River, but he recommended a northern canal running to Fitchburg and then down the Millers River to Greenfield. West of the Connecticut Baldwin preferred a route that ascended the Deerfield River to the foot of Hoosac Mountain, to be pierced with a 4-mile tunnel, thus bringing the canal to the Hoosic River, which it would follow the rest of the way to the Hudson near Troy. Baldwin advocated that they bore under Hoosac Mountain since it could be navigated without locks in but one hour and twenty minutes, while the only feasible alternative route bypassed Hoosac Mountain through Vermont and involved 18 miles of canal with 228 locks, which would take two days to traverse.[32]

The magnitude of Baldwin's proposal can be measured against the Erie Canal, which had a total rise and fall of less than 670 feet, requiring but 77 locks in its 353 miles.[33] In contrast Baldwin estimated that the 100-mile portion of the canal between Boston and the Connecticut River alone would require almost 400 locks to overcome a total rise and fall of more than 1,950 feet. Even more staggering was the cost, an estimated $6,000,000 including $940,000 for the tunnel under Hoosac Mountain. The section between Greenfield and Boston was estimated at $3,000,000, or more than the entire authorized capital of the four textile mills that Boston industrialists were erecting or planning to build on the Merrimack at Lowell.[34]

These estimates were not received kindly by a legislature that hesitated to raise enough money to pay a $50,000 state deficit. Nor, considering the dismal financial record of previous internal improvements in the state, could private investors be expected to furnish such an enormous sum. In addition, the estimates did not go unchallenged. David Henshaw wrote acidly in the Boston *Courier* of February 28, 1826, that, using the data of the report itself, a minimum of fifty-two years would be required to finish the Hoosac Mountain tunnel.[35]

This was a poor year to propose major internal improvements in Massachusetts. Merchants were then beginning to abandon shipping in favor of industry, and few businessmen had enough confidence in the commercial future of Boston to invest the millions necessary to connect their city with the Great West. Moreover, the factory still had to prove itself. Prospects looked favorable, but involved a daring gamble. Most of Lowell was yet to be built, and industrial Springfield was still a vision in the minds of the Dwights.

Furthermore, the canal did not meet industry's requirements. The Baldwin route avoided Worcester, Springfield, and Pittsfield, the three most active interior factory centers. In any case, waterways diverted large amounts of water that industry might need in a drought. Worcester County and Rhode Island manufacturers in 1823 had therefore opposed the Blackstone Canal, which threatened to rob them of power for their 20,000 spindles. Later, during severe droughts riots broke out when angry millowners dumped huge quantities of stone into the locks in order to hold the river water to run their factories.[36]

The legislature's rejection of Baldwin's canal focused attention upon the new and untried railroad. It was only slowly that this new form of transportation emerged as the clear answer to Massachusetts' needs, for although primitive railways had long moved coal in English and Welsh mines, they had only recently become full-blown rivals of canals and turnpikes. In November 1825 the Boston *Daily Advertiser* reported a startling development in England, the opening of the Stockton and Darlington Railroad. Although it was built to haul "coals, lime, bricks, and lead from the mines to the sea," this was no ordinary colliery line. It connected the towns of Stockton and Darlington, 12 miles apart, and with its branches had a total length of more than 32 miles. From the start the Stockton and Darlington employed awesome steam locomotives, each drawing "besides a tender containing fuel and water, 24 wagons made entirely of iron, and weighing 23 cwt. each, and when loaded containing 53 cwt. of coals each. . . . The engines, thus loaded, [moved] at the rate of about 4 miles per hour, carrying each a weight of about 95 tons."[37]

Massachusetts was not far behind in adapting rails for the movement of heavy freight. Early in 1826, at the instigation of an engineer, Gridley Bryant, and a merchant, Thomas Handasyd Perkins, the General Court chartered the Quincy Granite Railroad to haul the stone being mined for the Bunker Hill Monument three miles from the quarry near Quincy to tidewater. This project was completed on October 7, 1826. The first Massachusetts railroad rested on a foundation formed "by digging a trench 2 feet wide, and about the same depth, which was filled with stone compactly laid without mortar." The ties, placed 8 feet apart, were huge blocks of granite 7½ feet long and weighed nearly a ton each.[38]

Perkins, in the Boston *Advertiser,* described the rails as made of pine timber set "six feet apart from outside to outside." Each rail was "12 inches deep, by 6 inches wide—upon top of the pine rail [was] a strip of oak, 3 inches wide by 2 inches thick, and upon the oak [were] plates of iron ⅜ of an inch thick by 2½ inches wide. The wooden rail [was] secured from changing its position by an iron stay which [was] fastened between the oak and pine by nails, the other end of the stay entering a hole drilled three inches into the [granite tie]."[39] Perkins planned to substitute all granite rails as the initial wooden ones rotted. But in many places he felt that iron rails, like those used in Great Britain, were preferable to stone, and he became an early advocate of tariff removal on English rails since American iron cost $150 a ton compared with $62 for the British product delivered in Boston. Each car on the Quincy railroad hauled 4 to 5 tons, and a single horse normally pulled two cars at a rate of 3 miles an hour.[40]

It took vast imagination to see that the rickety, horse-drawn Quincy railway would in less than ten years revolutionize inland transportation and would eventually bring even the mighty Erie Canal to its knees. But Perkins' interest in railroads probably stemmed from necessity rather than vision, for he was at

this very time transferring his wealth from commerce to industry, and he was on the verge of making large investments in
the factories on the Chicopee River at Springfield. It is not
surprising, therefore, that in January 1826 he and several other
Bostonians petitioned the legislature to finance surveys for a
railroad from Boston to the Hudson.[41]

Although a committee reported a measure authorizing the
"Governor to appoint three Commissioners and an Engineer" to
investigate a railroad, the house refused to act. The time was
not ripe. Even a man favorable to internal improvements like
Governor Lincoln still looked upon railroads with a jaundiced
eye. Lincoln, who had actively supported the Blackstone Canal,
questioned the value of railroads in a speech at the opening of
the June 1826 session of the legislature. "The more extended
and beneficial influence of Canals in the general improvement
of the country" seemed to him decisive. A railroad was "a mere
passage way for travel and transportation" and canals were
superior "for the accommodation of the infinite variety [of
freight] in weight and bulk."[42]

Although the railroad had suffered an initial defeat, after
1826 a growing number of Massachusetts' leading citizens
began to rally about it as the answer to the transportation
requirements of the state's farmers, merchants, and industrialists. The most important and influential of the converts was
Nathan Hale, editor of the Boston *Daily Advertiser*. Hale was
born in 1784, the son of a Congregational minister in Hampshire
County, Massachusetts.[43] He bore the name of his father's
brother, the revolutionary patriot who had but one life to give
for his country. Young Nathan graduated from Williams College in 1804 and then studied law. Although he eventually was
admitted to the bar, his mind ran more to science, and between
1805 and 1810 he taught mathematics at Phillips Academy in
Exeter, New Hampshire. In 1811 Hale came to Boston, where
he started a law practice, but he soon drifted into newspaper
work. In 1814 he purchased the *Daily Advertiser* and became
its editor. For nearly forty years its columns reflected his
strong-willed personality.

In many respects Hale was an idealist. His long association
with railroads yielded him but little personal profit. He bought

railroad stock only when he thought his purchases would encourage others to do so, and as soon as railroads became established he held no stock in them at all.[44] His salary as a railroad executive always remained modest. After he fought a successful battle for internal improvements, he turned his major attention to bringing into Boston an abundant supply of pure water from the hills of Middlesex County. Few were as devoted to civic welfare as Nathan Hale.

In his entire career as lawyer, newspaper editor, water commissioner, and railroad president, he was closely associated with the elite of Boston society. He felt most comfortable in the company of the Adamses, Otises, and Quincys, the merchant aristocracy that ruled the Massachusetts capital. "While there was a Federal Party, the *Advertiser* was a Federalist journal; when and while there was a Whig Party, the *Advertiser* was a Whig journal; and during the years that marked the decadence of one and the rise of the other of these parties, the 'era of good feeling' . . . the *Advertiser* was found approving all that was good and opposing all that was wrong or unjust in the administration of public affairs by any party."[45] What was good and just did not always clearly reveal itself. More often than not, however, right turned out to be the policies that pleased the merchant aristocracy. But the 1820s were trying times for the men of commerce. At the beginning of this decade Hale strongly opposed the tariff, though by 1830 he had second thoughts on free trade. His indecision resulted in bitter attacks by Joseph T. Buckingham, editor of the rival Boston *Courier*.[46]

Hale's views on the relative importance of industry and commerce explained why he emphasized so strongly the railroad's role in increasing trade between Boston and the "extensive and fruitful region which lies west and north of Albany." The railroad was a method of snatching from New York the vast commerce of the West, especially during the winter months when the Hudson was "entirely obstructed by ice." A railroad from Boston to Albany "would afford a channel . . . equal in point of regularity and safety to steamboat navigation and equal in rapidity to the common navigation of the river; though far inferior to the latter in cheapness." Therefore a large part of the vast trade from Albany to New York which is invariably interrupted early or later, every winter by the frost, would "eventually find its way by the railroad to Boston."[47]

The *Advertiser* argued that Boston could not afford delay, and Hale twisted the 1830 census returns to prove a decline in the city's population.[48] Unless a means of internal communication was developed with Albany, Boston would wither away. The vision of "restoring" Boston at New York's expense loomed large in the thoughts of New Englanders between 1831 and 1841, when the railroad to Albany was built. To this dream Hale committed himself body and soul, and from the *Advertiser* poured a perfect flood of railroad propaganda.

Not everybody in Boston approved. The *Courier's* editor, Joseph Buckingham, referred to him as a self-proclaimed "unrivalled scholar in the mathematical sciences, and the very SIR ISAAC NEWTON OF RAILROADS AND CANALS!"[49] Such criticism hardly phased Hale, who continued his campaign unabated. Hale was not above slanting the news to favor his cause. The *Advertiser* reported with zest the anticipated trials of Peter Cooper's now famous steam locomotive, the *Tom Thumb*, on the Baltimore & Ohio Railroad. But when Cooper's engine, much to the delight of railroad skeptics, lost a race with a horse on August 25, 1830, Hale's paper made no mention of it. Instead the *Advertiser* lamented that the *Tom Thumb* was slower than expected but reported that the trials had "fully proved the efficacy of this mode of propelling the cars, whether for passengers or freight."[50]

Caught up with Hale in the fight for a western railroad were other men of vision who dreamed of private gain rather than of civic betterment. Not the least among them was Boston's David Henshaw, a gouty, outspoken bachelor and an admirer of Napoleon Bonaparte who evoked strong responses from nearly all who met him. His friends toasted him as "A Hercules in intellect, and a Democrat in principle . . . worthy and capable of any station within the gift of the executive," who had "presided with equity" when he was President Jackson's collector at the port of Boston.[51] To his enemies he was a "shrewd, selfish, strong-minded (but . . . corrupt hearted) man," who as soon as he received the sword of authority as collector of customs "wielded it with a sternness and contempt of official

48

life, worthy of Nadir Shah, or any other sanguinary despot."[52] Henshaw himself minced no words. He spoke out for his causes with force and determination. An ardent follower of Jackson, Henshaw lustily cheered "this modern Hercules" who had prostrated with a single blow the Second Bank of the United States, that "monied monster, with its hydra-heads, which designed to crush and strangle our liberties in its venomous folds."[53]

Henshaw was born in Worcester County at the town of Leicester in 1791, the fifth son of a small farmer. Young David received a common education at Leicester Academy, but when he was sixteen, his father apprenticed him to the House of Dix and Brinley, Boston wholesale druggists. In 1814 David became a full partner. The drug enterprise was just a stepping-stone to wider fields. Using his profits, he entered banking, and by the middle of the 1820s he was a director of three new institutions: the Commonwealth, Franklin, and Market banks. Here he met the hostility of the entrenched mercantile class and of the Bank of the United States, which regarded him and his banks as speculative upstarts. Although he for a while owned enough stock in an older conservative bank to make him a director, the icy attitude of the other directors, who suspected that Henshaw's interest was to borrow and not to lend, soon forced him to withdraw.[54]

Next he moved into real estate, in which he became heavily involved with the Warren Association, which aimed to fill up some tidal flats in South Boston, thus creating new valuable lands just across the water from the crowded Boston peninsula. Significantly, the Commonwealth Bank loaned the Warren Association between $180,000 and $250,000 to enable it to proceed with its land development.[55] Henshaw's connection with South Boston real estate speculation brought him face to face with another entrenched interest. The land promoters in their zeal to make their property more accessible to Boston in 1824 applied to the legislature for permission to build a free bridge from Wheeler's Point to South Boston. Since this would compete with an established toll bridge, the application met open hostility from the proprietors. Henshaw's argument that the legislature could charter new corporations and that the new interests should pay only for the property actually taken and should not be liable for diversion of travel from established works carried the day, and in 1826 Governor Lincoln signed a bill authorizing Henshaw's bridge. Thus ended an early version of the famous Charles River Bridge controversy.[56]

Politically Henshaw had a full and eventful career. In the gubernatorial election of 1823 he worked hard to defeat Federalist Harrison Gray Otis.[57] Like many politicians Henshaw floundered about with no definite political home during the final part of the Era of Good Feeling. Although he had favored William H. Crawford and opposed John Quincy Adams in the national arena, he supported an Adams ally, Levi Lincoln, on the local stage. In 1826 Henshaw was elected as a Republican to the lower house of the Massachusetts General Court. But Lincoln's opposition to the Warren Free Bridge soon separated the two men and in the end Henshaw found himself snubbed by the conservative Republicans and running for the state senate on an anti-Lincoln ticket put up by "citizens friendly to a Free Bridge over the Charles River."[58]

Henshaw was virtually forced into the arms of Andrew Jackson. Determined to make the most of his new alliance, Henshaw organized a hard core of supporters who worked unceasingly for Jackson's election. Although they failed to carry Massachusetts in 1828, Henshaw had become the state's leading Democrat, and Jackson rewarded him with the collectorship of the port of Boston, one of the Federal government's most important and lucrative positions.

Henshaw used his new power to attack his old enemy, the Bank of the United States. When he saw that Jackson distrusted it, Henshaw petitioned Congress to allow himself and others, including several conservative Boston merchants, to establish a new bank to replace Nicholas Biddle's institution.[59] Although Congress failed to act on this proposal and rechartered the old bank, Henshaw had the last word. Jackson's veto of the bank bill stood, and Henshaw was credited with influencing Jackson to strike a final blow at Biddle's bank by the withdrawal of Federal funds in 1833. The Boston politician profited enormously from this move since Federal money was then deposited in "pet" state banks, among them his own Common-wealth Bank.

Henshaw's long career had its bleak spots. In 1838, the failure of the Commonwealth Bank revealed that it had engaged in many unsound and speculative practices, including unwise loans to the Warren Association.[60] While Henshaw was not involved in anything illegal, and the collapse did not ruin him financially, the affair marred his public career. At about the same time he split with Martin Van Buren, Jackson's successor, and fell from power in the Massachusetts Democracy. In 1843 Henshaw had one last fling at major public office when President Tyler appointed him Secretary of the Navy. Although Henshaw's many enemies prevented his confirmation by the Senate, he served in the position for several months with force and dignity.[61]

Henshaw's life is the record of a man who knew what he wanted and how to get it. Ambition consumed him; his goals were wealth, power, and influence. His first success came in the drug industry, a business regarded by many of the day with contempt. In Boston he found himself outside the ruling mercantile group, which controlled the banks and commercial life of the city. Henshaw thought big; his ego prevented him from gradually easing his way into established circles, and he boldly created his own banks, newspapers, and corporations, which ran afoul of established institutions. Henshaw never opposed wealth, but fought the vested powers that hindered his various enterprises. His career was a long fight for economic opportunity. But he strongly supported the idea that "business corporations, excluding banks and all large corporations for trading in money, when judiciously granted and suitable regulated, seem to [be] generally beneficial and the natural offspring of our social condition."[62]

The proposal for a railroad from Boston to Albany, therefore, counted David Henshaw as one of its earliest and strongest backers. That it was new and speculative did not deter him, for he fully believed, along with an anonymous writer in the Boston *Courier* "that the first stroke upon a rail road would add a third part to the value [of Boston's real estate]."[63]

Standing with Hale and Henshaw as an early railroad sup-
porter was another resident of eastern Massachusetts, William
Jackson. Born in 1783, he came from an old New England
family from which he inherited a 54-acre homestead in
Newton.[64] Jackson spent his early life in Boston, where he
managed his own candle and soap manufactory until he retired
in 1820. Like Henshaw, Jackson was not a member of Boston's
ruling aristocracy. But unlike the Democratic politician, Jackson's dreams were less of national prominence; he preferred to
be a big man in a small town, and his interests did not clash
directly with vested property rights. Instead he tried to capitalize on his importance in Newton, seizing opportunities created
there by the general growth of the Massachusetts economy.

Jackson's main involvements were in local banking and real
estate development. He was the founder of Newton's first
savings bank and was its first president, a position he held
from 1831 to 1835 and again from 1848 until 1855. He was also
the initial president of Newton's first commercial bank, which
opened for business in 1848. In the 1840s he became the first
big developer of Newton suburban land. He laid out several
subdivisions including Walnut Park, Waban Place, and Auburn-
dale. He was the first man to sell real estate in Newton by
the foot.[65]

Politically Jackson was a maverick, being drawn into many
of the reform movements. He was a strong temperance man,
and he belonged successively to the Anti-Masonic, Whig,
Liberty, and Free Soil parties. He served several times in the
lower house of the Massachusetts General Court, including
the years 1830 and 1831, when the railroad question was under
consideration. By 1833 he represented Newton in Congress,
where he served two terms as an Anti-Mason. Later he was
a perennially unsuccessful candidate of the Liberty Party for
governor, lieutenant governor, and member of Congress.

Jackson saw improved transportation as a key to the Commonwealth's growth. He argued that railroads would produce
benefits similar to those brought by the Erie Canal, which
"although [it] cost more than eight millions . . . already netts
7 or 8 per cent per annum." But return on capital invested was
only a small part of the profits. "The increased value of the

two strips of land on each side of the canal, three miles wide, is in all probability equal to the whole cost of the canal," he asserted. Furthermore, "the advance on the real estate in New-York City, fairly attributable to the canal, cannot be less than twenty and perhaps thirty millions of dollars."[66] Jackson, Newton's great real estate developer, was keenly aware of the close relationship between internal improvements and land values. That knowledge did not fail him during his many years of association with Massachusetts railroads.

"In no part of the state has a warmer zeal been manifested for the establishment of a western rail road, than in the county of Berkshire," wrote Nathan Hale in 1827.[67] This was almost entirely due to the influence of a single man, Theodore Sedgwick, Jr., of Stockbridge, who caught railroad fever in 1826. Sedgwick's father had been prominent in Massachusetts politics throughout most of his lifetime, being from 1789 until his death in 1813, "either a representative or senator in Congress or a judge of the [Massachusetts] Supreme Court."[68] Young Sedgwick also entered politics; during the period when the railroad question was under discussion, he represented his native Stockbridge in the lower house of the General Court. He was also a business associate and friend of the Pittsfield industrialist, Lemuel Pomeroy.[69] Sedgwick became the spokesman for the frustrated Berkshire men who were desperately trying to forge a satisfactory link with the outside world. His first article appeared in 1826 in the Pittsfield *Sun*. From then on railroad propaganda poured from his pen. Berkshire County, he wrote, has an "unlimited supply" of water power, but without transportation it is worth "not a cent." A railroad, he asserted, would "break down the barriers between the cities and the country," and investment capital would flow "into it like water."[70]

Henshaw, Jackson, and Sedgwick looked to England's 30-mile Stockton and Darlington and to the puny 3-mile Quincy Granite Railroad on the coast of Massachusetts and saw a means of land transportation superior to any yet devised. From the first they shaped the public's conception of railroads and then stayed on to build and run them. The railroad clique's immediate task, however, was to sell the idea. Looking back to his role in the campaign, Theodore Sedgwick said he had to teach "first, the effects of internal improvements generally; secondly the peculiar benefits arising from facilitating communication with the market, and the superiority of the railroad to every other method of accomplishing this object; thirdly the mechanical effects of railways, and their applications; and, lastly, their peculiar local advantages."[71]

Hale's *Daily Advertiser* kept its readers abreast with every railroad development both in Europe and America. Hale missed nothing favorable to his cause. He printed long descriptions of the Stockton and Darlington Railroad. He covered in detail Maryland's great effort to link itself with the West, the Baltimore & Ohio Railroad. Hale maintained that railroads not only worked but made profits as well. "The directors of the Baltimore and Ohio Rail-road . . . have declared a dividend of two and a half per cent," he reported on January 10, 1831. This profit, he emphasized, was paid out of the earnings received for operating just 13 miles of single track.[72]

But no enterprise received more attention than England's Liverpool and Manchester Railway. This project, the most ambitious of its day, was the world's first modern railroad. Unlike the Quincy Granite or the Stockton and Darlington, which were both built primarily to haul specific commodities, the Liverpool and Manchester was a true common carrier. It arose from the needs of industrial Britain and connected England's second greatest port, Liverpool, with the bustling factory city of Manchester, which was slightly more than 30 miles inland.[73]

The Liverpool and Manchester Railway was a private corporation chartered in 1826. It opened in 1830 and from the first, it competed with, not supplemented, the established canals and turnpikes. It served Manchester's textile mills by rapidly moving raw cotton from Liverpool inland and, in return, carrying finished manufactured products from the factories to the sea. Although much of this industrial traffic had been won away from horses and wagons, which had plied well-maintained turnpikes, the railroad also cut deeply into canal business, successfully moving heavy items such as iron and coal. In addition the railroad hauled passengers, driving from the turnpikes every competing stagecoach. In short the new railroad hauled everything presented to it, from the smallest package of cotton shirtings to the bulkiest loads of coal and iron.[74]

In its construction, the proprietors of the Liverpool and Manchester built with a bold and lavish hand. Their railroad stretched across the countryside in an almost straight and level line, piercing hills with deep cuts or tunnels, and crossing rivers, and depressions on high bridges or huge fills. In motive power too, the Liverpool and Manchester led the way, for it was on this line in October 1829 that the famous Rainhill trials proved beyond doubt the efficiency of the steam locomotive.

Nathan Hale watched the Liverpool and Manchester with rapt attention and, starting in 1829, he printed dozens of articles describing every detail of the English railroad. On November 23, 1829, Hale asserted that the British experiments proved "that locomotive engines . . . will travel thirty miles an hour, and with such an equal and steady motion that passengers while travelling at that rate can read and write."[75] Hale printed pictures and exact details on the performance of Robert Stephenson's *Rocket* and the other locomotives tested at Rainhill.[76] When the trials were finished, Hale concluded that a new transportation era had been born. Rails and locomotives, he claimed, are better adapted to traveling with speed, safety and economy than canals, and best of all, "these advantages . . . may be secured on any line of communication where the income . . . is sufficient to defray one half the expenses of a canal, it being very certain that a railroad can be built and maintained at less than half the expense of a canal."[77]

No account was too lavish or dramatic for Hale. On December 9, 1829, he quoted the speculation of a writer in the Liverpool *Times*, "But if a speed of thirty miles an hour has already been attained [by locomotives], what good reason is there that we should not in the process of time accomplish sixty miles per hour? Nay why should we stop there?"[78] Certainly Hale saw no cause for pessimism. In January 1830 he reported that the stockholders of England's most profitable canal, the Sankey, were about to drain it and lay a railroad on the old

bed. Next he said that the stock of the Liverpool and Manchester had advanced from a par of £100 to £171 a share.[79]

Even in 1830, after the Liverpool and Manchester opened
for regular traffic, Hale continued his barrage. In April 1831
he recorded a feat which proved that the full powers of locomotive engines had been "as yet very little understood." Stephenson's latest locomotive, the *Sampson*, had hauled a train of
thirty freight cars with a gross weight of more than 151 tons
the 33 miles between Liverpool and Manchester in two hours
and twenty-one minutes, consuming less than 20 shillings'
worth of fuel.[80] The Liverpool and Manchester "proved conclusively" that railroads could and would answer the transportation needs of Massachusetts.

Hale left nothing to the imagination. Long articles elucidated
the advantages that each interest group in the state could
expect from a railroad to Albany. This great work would enable
the Connecticut Valley farmers, who were "almost excluded"
from the Boston market to send East their hay, apples, cider,
and potatoes. A new opportunity would open, he argued, for
Worcester County firewood. In 1827 wood sold for $6 to $8
a cord in Boston, and because of its bulk it could not be teamed
more than 15 to 20 miles. A railroad, Hale asserted, would
allow farmers who sold wood for $2 a cord in Worcester to
send it to the Massachusetts capital at a handsome profit.[81]

Industry had even more to gain. In 1828 Springfield would
consume 600,000 pounds of cotton, all of which had to be
shipped up the Connecticut River. Rail transportation would
facilitate the movement of this cotton, and it was even more
vital for the factory developments that were at the time being
built at Ware and Palmer. Without a railroad, the Ware Manufacturing Company had to team its freight 65 miles from
Boston at a cost of at least $10 a ton.[82]

But Hale addressed his most passionate and effective appeals
to Boston's mercantile interests. The Massachusetts capital,
argued a writer in the *Advertiser*, had grown strong through
the trade of an extensive back country, which had included
"Rhode Island, Connecticut, New Hampshire, Vermont, and
the western part of New York" as well as Massachusetts. But
the steamboats on the Hudson, the improved navigation on

the Connecticut, and the Blackstone Canal, had by 1829 reduced Boston's hinterland "to limits, within a usual circle,
which may be descried from the cupola of the State House."[83]
A forceful editorial in October 1828 chided Boston. Providence,
it argued, had constructed the Blackstone Canal "notwith-
standing the discouragement and dissuasion of those nice cal-
culators who have steadily predicted that the whole capital
invested in it would be lost." And Boston was losing the race.
"Lumber and lime . . . and other heavy articles which had
heretofore been carried in large quantities [from Boston] to
the county of Worcester have already been shipped . . . directly
[from] Providence." And Worcester traders "have also made
arrangements to procure their goods from New York."[84] A few
weeks later the *Advertiser* lamented that "last year [1827]
molasses was carried by land at a great expense to the New
Worcester Distillery; but who can ever expect to see another
hogshead transported by land, without a railway? Our trade
with the interior, and the coasting trade dependent on it are
gone, without this indispensable improvement."[85]

The propaganda hit its mark, and by 1829 the original band
of railroad enthusiasts had been joined by a strong and powerful group. One of the first to change his mind was Governor
Levi Lincoln, who urged every session of the legislature from
1827 through 1830 to support a railroad between Boston and
Albany. His speeches sounded as if Hale himself had written
them. "The astonishing results of the recent scientific experiments in Europe, in the application of Steam to produce moving power, by which time, and distance, and weight are alike
overcome, to a degree almost incredible" inspired a "confidence
in this manner of conveyance, which neither the incredulity
of the timid, nor the obstinacy of the prejudiced [could] longer
resist."[86]

Among the most important and active railroad converts were
the rising industrialists. The list of advocates in central Berkshire County reads like a stockholders' roster of Pittsfield
industrial concerns. Of the eighteen official Pittsfield delegates
to a railroad convention held in January 1828, at least five held
stock in the Pittsfield Cotton and Woolen Factory; they included
Joseph Merrick, David Campbell, Jr., Thomas A. Gold, Samuel

Colt, and Lemuel Pomeroy. In 1831, when it seemed as though Massachusetts would not act to secure a railway between Boston and Albany, Lemuel Pomeroy presided at a meeting that demanded that Berkshire County go it alone and build a railroad from Pittsfield to Albany in cooperation with New York State.[87]

In Springfield, too, the industrialists became ardent railroad supporters. Both Jonathan and Edmund Dwight lent their names freely to railroad petitions; and George Bliss worked in the legislature to ensure that any line to the West would pass through Springfield.[88] The Boston investors in the Chicopee Valley textile mills joined their Springfield brethren. Harrison Gray Otis was particularly active; he signed petitions urging legislative action, wrote articles for the *Daily Advertiser,* and as Boston's mayor from 1829 to 1831 he took the opportunity to urge a western railroad in his inaugural speeches.[89]

In Boston support came from every group. Industrialists like Samuel and William Lawrence, Francis Jackson, and Nathan Appleton united with free traders and merchants like Andrew Allen, William Foster, Joseph Coolidge, and Robert Shaw in the belief that a railroad would serve both commercial and industrial interests with equal facility. So well did Hale do his selling that when in a Boston town meeting on February 11, 1829, railroad advocates put the question "shall the city government be authorized to purchase stock in a railroad?" the assembled citizenry answered with an overwhelming 3,055 yeas to 59 nays.[90]

To whip up a frenzy for railroads was one thing; to build them was quite another, and between 1827 and 1831 a bitter debate raged on the question of whether they should be constructed by the state or by private corporations. Few people of the day had doctrinaire views. Most citizens supported or opposed a state-owned railroad according to how they thought it would affect their own pocketbooks. Significantly, nearly all railroad enthusiasts, especially the wealthy industrialists and merchants, felt that the Commonwealth, not private enterprise, should undertake the project.

The most telling argument against internal improvements was not their impracticability but their cost. Although Hale maintained that a railroad cost only one-third to one-half as much to construct as a canal, even he estimated in 1827 that a single-track railway could not be laid down for less than $12,000 a mile.[91] At that rate more than $2,400,000 would have been needed for a line from Boston to Albany. No matter how hard Hale tried, he could not dispel the idea that internal improvements would be unprofitable. Private capital, already reeling from the decline of shipping, shied from investing so large a sum in such a questionable enterprise. William Jackson in 1829, arguing for a state-built railroad, admitted that there was a general conviction that the project would not pay the interest upon its cost. But "if at this moment," Jackson observed, "the Erie canal tolls paid but 2 per cent instead of 6 to 8 upon its cost, is there an individual who now hears me who would not say, that the act which sanctioned its construction was not one of the wisest and most profitable, too, that was ever passed by any Legislature of New York?"[92]

Jackson emphasized that the public nature of a railroad made it worthy of state support. He raised the specter of monopoly: "When the Legislature of New York gave the Fulton company, the exclusive steam navigation of its waters they knew not what they did."[93] Jackson felt that private construction of a Boston to Albany railroad might be just as great an error. "It is perfectly obvious," he argued, "that the greater ease, greater speed, and greater certainty of this mode of conveyance would secure an almost entire monopoly of this business . . ." Jackson concluded that the stage fare between Boston and Albany was $8, but that passengers could be moved profitably by rail at a charge of $3. "In the hands of a private corporation," he asked, "what is there to prevent the fare from being kept at $8?"[94]

Similarly the *Essex Gazette* commented that a western railroad was "in truth . . . a state measure . . . in which the interests of the whole Commonwealth are to a greater or lesser extent involved." The *Gazette* observed that after the Charles River Bridge fiasco no private persons would support a railroad or any similar public work without an iron-clad monopoly for a specific period of time and a free hand to fix rates. A railroad, it continued, was no more "visionary" than Fulton's steamboat, and the Massachusetts representatives and senators ought to realize that fact so that if they voted to "throw this boon into the hands of a private corporation, they may at least know what they are giving away."[95]

The strongest argument for public construction came from western Massachusetts' Theodore Sedgwick. Isolated Berkshire County with its small population and even smaller assessed valuation had much to gain from a railroad and little to fear from higher taxes if the enterprise should turn out to be a burden upon the state's ratepayers. Asserted Sedgwick, "the mode of constructing the road; its direction; its connection with other communications; the regulation of the travel; of the tolls whether high or low; whether upon tonnage and passengers, or upon either alone, are all public concerns, and this [should not] be left to the decision of owners living at Salem, Boston, Worcester, Springfield, &c."[96] Sedgwick saw that Berkshire's interests were not Boston's. Pittsfield wanted low rates for its goods, which went relatively short distances to Albany or Boston. The day might come when a private management, controlled by the merchants of Boston, would institute ruinously low rates on grain from the West and, in order to make a profit for the stockholders, would make up the loss by raising local freight and passenger rates as high as the traffic would bear. This kind of discrimination against certain customers in favor of others would be less likely under public than private ownership, Sedgwick reasoned.

But most of the pressure for a state railroad resulted from the sentiment so clearly expressed by Nathan Hale: simply that railways "cannot be effected without the aid of the government."[97] Hence all effort focused upon the General Court. Despite the initial failure of railroad efforts in the winter 1826 legislative session, agitation did not die. At the next meeting in June 1826, the lower house of the General Court, urged on by Boston's Dr. Abner Phelps and Worcester's Emory Washburn, formed a select committee to investigate a railroad to the West, and the legislators ordered it to report back to the lower house at the winter session in 1827. The Phelps committee, although it had no funds and made no actual surveys, sent questionnaires about the state seeking information on likely routes and the amount of traffic a railroad could expect to haul. In January 1827 the Phelps committee made a report extolling the virtues of rail transportation and asking for the appointment of three commissioners and an engineer, who would make a professional survey of the Boston to Albany line. The committee recommended an appropriation of $5,000 to pay for this. But the legislature balked at so large a sum, and although on February 22, 1827, it created a board of internal improvements consisting of three commissioners, nothing was done by them because of a lack of funds.[98]

In the legislature that convened in June 1827 the railroad question met with more success. The propaganda campaign waged by Hale, Phelps, and Sedgwick was beginning to win over men of influence. Upon the urging of Josiah Quincy, then Mayor of Boston, the General Court authorized the appointment of two commissioners and an engineer to survey the Boston to Albany route, and even more important, it appropriated $10,000 to finance the project.[99]

The two commissioners, Nahum Mitchell of Boston and Samuel M. McKay of Pittsfield, and the engineer, James F. Baldwin, made their report to the General Court in January 1828. They considered two possible routes: a northern line from Boston through Cambridge, Belchertown, Northampton, Adams, and Williamstown to Troy and a southern line from Boston through Framingham, Worcester, Springfield, Pittsfield, and West Stockbridge to Albany.

Baldwin made accurate surveys only on the southern route, concentrating his efforts on the portions from Boston west to Newton and across the Berkshire Hills from Springfield to Albany. Since steam had still to prove itself, Baldwin made all his estimates for horses. Even so, he presented a convincing case, and Governor Lincoln in presenting the report to the legislature commented that "the results to which the Commission have already arrived, may be considered as fully establishing the practicability, within the reasonable application of means, of the construction of the road."[100] Lincoln's speech reflected the thoughts of many Bay Staters, who for the first time, were beginning to realize the full possibilities of a railroad to Albany.

CHAPTER III

The Rejection of State Initiative

JANUARY 1828 marked the turning point in the campaign for a Boston to Albany railroad. Up to this time there had been no serious possibility of state action, but Baldwin's favorable report, the worsening of Boston's commercial position, the growth of industry along the Chicopee, and the constant barrage of railroad propaganda were beginning to create a solid demand for action. In response the General Court in March 1828 established a new board of internal improvement consisting of nine of the Commonwealth's most distinguished men. They were Governor Levi Lincoln, Nathan Hale, Stephen White, David Henshaw, Thomas W. Ward, Royal Makepeace, George Bond, William Foster, and Edward H. Robbins, Jr.[1] At the same time the New York Legislature, acting under the pressure of Albany and Troy interests, made provisions to cooperate with Massachusetts in the survey of that portion of the Boston to Albany route within the Empire State.[2] Nathan Hale assumed the leadership of the new board, which immediately hired two engineers, James Baldwin to continue his survey of the Boston to Albany route and James Hayward to examine a line between Boston and Providence.

The railroad efforts did not go unchallenged. A new legislature met the following June, and in the house of representatives a vocal minority, largely from Essex County and from inland country towns, which feared that additional surveys might lead to more taxes, opposed Hale's request for $8,000 to finance the board's operations. The prorailroad forces carried the day by a vote of 141 to 72 because the towns that would benefit from the proposed Albany and Providence railways took care to send enlarged delegations to the lower house. Boston, for example, increased its representation from nine to forty-one, while Essex County allowed its numbers to decline from forty-five to forty-two.[3] Thus Hale received a free hand to submit a plan to the legislature for railways from Boston both to Providence and to Albany.

The board made its report on January 16, 1829. Governor Lincoln, in an address to the General Court, had already urged its favorable consideration. "The examinations and surveys," he said, "will appear to have resulted in an entire assurance of the practicability of the great improvements which have been contemplated, and in presenting the strongest inducements to the Government and People, to encourage them to their immediate undertaking."[4]

The report, a thick 197-page document, printed by the press of the *Daily Advertiser*, contained a comprehensive description of the proposed work, extensive maps, and detailed estimates of costs and probable traffic. The commission's work was done more than nine months before the successful Rainhill trials on the Liverpool and Manchester Railway, and its proposal called for little more than a magnified Quincy Granite Railroad. It recommended a double track line following a southern route from Boston through Framingham, Worcester, Springfield, Pittsfield, West Stockbridge, and then through New York State to Albany. The southern line, the report maintained, was superior to both a northern or a central route because in the south the Worcester ridge could be crossed at an elevation of 918 feet, and the Berkshires at 1,440 feet, whereas the northern route, which was the next most attractive, crossed the Worcester summit at an elevation of more than 1,000 feet and the Berkshires at 1,886 feet.[5]

For power the report contemplated horses. Coal, the fuel for steam locomotives, was too expensive in Massachusetts, while oats and other food for horses was both cheap and abundant. "The facts show," the report asserted, "that the cost of transportation on a rail road in this country, by horse power, will be less than in England, by either horse or steam power."[6]

On the question of locomotives hung the whole problem of how the railroad would be operated. There were two choices. It could be treated as though it were a canal or turnpike furnishing only the track and relying on private individuals to supply the horses and wagons. The railroad would do nothing but maintain the track, and all the work of soliciting and moving the passengers and freight would be handled by a great number of other individuals or companies, which would compete among themselves for business, charging a comprehensive rate and in turn paying a toll for the use of the facilities.

The second choice involved railroad ownership of all moving equipment, as well as the road itself. Of course steam implied a single ownership since locomotives were too expensive and too complicated for private individuals to own and operate. Besides it would have been unthinkable to have on a single railroad a large number of steam engines which were not under the close supervision, both in running and in maintenance, of one management.

The board of directors left the whole question of operation decidedly ambiguous. Most of the cost estimates were solely for the construction of the roadbed and track and did not include money for either animals or wagons or their maintenance. Further, all the revenue statistics were in terms of tolls, which would be charged per ton of goods or per passenger for movement over the railroad. The report clearly indicated that there would be further charges to cover the cost of vehicles and power. At the same time the other parts of the report strongly hinted that the railroad itself might operate all passenger service.[7] Obviously, the board of directors was side-stepping a dangerous issue. If the railroad was to be treated as a "super-turnpike," many or most of the stagecoach operators and teamsters hauling passengers and goods between Boston and inland points would have had opportunities to transfer their efforts to the railroad. But if the railway owned all the equipment, the independent operators would be frozen out. The evidence clearly indicates that Hale, at least, felt that the railroad should have complete control both of track and vehicles, but that he preferred not to raise this potentially explosive issue unless forced to do so.[8] The issue did not arise because the average person in Massachusetts, including most of the legislators, did not understand the full implications of a railroad.

Engineer Baldwin predicted that the roadbed and finished superstructure would cost about $16,000 per mile.[9] At this rate it would have taken at least $3,200,000 to construct the entire line between Boston and Albany. The directors maintained that the whole amount could be borrowed and that the railroad would earn enough to pay the interest upon that sum and to finance repairs as well. Their calculations assumed that the money could be had at annual interest rates of between 4½ and 6 per cent. This meant that the project would have to receive each year a minimum of between $144,000 and $192,000 just to pay the interest. The directors apparently felt that a negligible $8,000 a year would suffice for upkeep, for they asserted that a yearly income of $200,000 would be more than adequate "to cover the interest [at 6 per cent] together with the cost of repairs and superintendence."[10]

The entire traffic estimate was an attempt to show that the railroad could earn the necessary $200,000 a year and thus pay its own way. But also written unmistakably into the document was the realization that there were two, almost conflicting types of traffic between Boston and Albany. The through business moved the entire distance between the Hudson and Massachusetts Bay, and local shipments traveled only part of the length of the line. It was the through traffic—commerce that moved from the Great West through Albany carrying wheat, flour, lumber, and salt beef from the interior to the coast—which many Boston merchants saw as the key to the commercial revival of the Massachusetts capital. But to take this business away from New York City, any railroad would have to go into direct competition with water transportation on the Hudson River. Significantly, although the report talked grandly of increasing Boston's prosperity "from an easier intercourse with the interior,"[11] it without fanfare wrote off the possibility that a railroad could do more than capture the existing trade between Boston and Albany. The report pointed out that sloop navigation moved flour between the Hudson and eastern Massachusetts at a charge of between $2.50 and $3 a ton and that the railroad could do it no cheaper than from $2.59 to $2.97 a ton. Because of speed and convenience, "either rate," continued the directors, "would probably be low enough to secure to the railroad the carriage of all the flour between Albany and Boston."[12] Unstated, but clearly implied, was that the directors had not even seriously considered that the railroad could move flour from Albany to Boston as cheaply as

$1.50 per ton, the customary charge on the Hudson between Albany and New York City. Thus the directors passed over the question of Boston's competition with New York City. Even more important were the figures for the over-all freight traffic. Of the approximately 102,000 tons that the railroad could expect to haul each year, they estimated that less than one-third, or about 29,000 tons, would be through business between Boston and the Hudson. The remaining two-thirds, or more than 70,000 tons, would be local traffic. In terms of projected revenue, the through traffic was even less important since the directors estimated that it would produce less than $29,000 of the total projected freight revenue of $143,000.[13]

Clearly the directors saw that the railroad would depend for its success primarily on local, not through, business. Of course some local traffic would help commercial Boston. In fact a Boston to Worcester line was absolutely vital if the Massachusetts capital had any hope of retaining the commerce of Worcester County, which was beginning to slip away to Providence down the Blackstone Canal. But this effort was purely defensive, that is, it protected a trade that Boston had traditionally enjoyed; it did not build a new trading area. If Boston were to cut into New York City's business, it would need much lower rates on the railroad than the directors proposed.

But could rates be lowered to divert the business of the Great West from New York to Boston? An examination of the directors' estimates shows that they proposed to charge the through traffic at a much lower rate than the local business. Thus the Boston and Albany freight would pay a toll of but ½ cent per ton per mile, while all local traffic would pay a toll of 2 cents per ton-mile. The directors justified the rate differential on the grounds that a higher toll on through traffic would prevent the railroad from competing with the sloops that plied between Boston and Albany via the Hudson and Long Island Sound. Since the tolls represented only the payment for the use of the rails and did not include a charge for the vehicles, power, and manpower that would move the goods, the directors reasoned that the total cost to move a ton between Boston and Albany would amount to $1 for tolls plus an additional $1.57 to $1.97 for vehicles, power, and manpower. Thus to compete for the New York City traffic, which moved down the Hudson at $1.50 per ton, the railroad would have to drop the $1 toll altogether.[14]

These estimates pointed up sharply, if inadvertently, the potential conflict between local and through traffic. In fixing the rates of toll, the directors kept in mind that the railroad would be burdened with a fixed yearly charge of at least $200,000 for interest and upkeep, which always had to be paid whether the railroad moved one ton or a million. In setting the Boston and Albany through tolls at one-fourth of the local charges, they were following sound business practices, for if the through tolls were higher, the railroad would have been unable to compete with the sloops and thus would have lost $29,000 a year in tolls that could have gone toward meeting the fixed charge of $200,000. In other words, not carrying the Albany to Boston through traffic at reduced rates would have had the effect of raising local tolls still further since then the entire burden of the $200,000 fixed charge would have had to be raised from local business alone.

But the directors could not justify forcing rates down low enough to capture the traffic of the West, which was flowing toward New York City. This could only have been done if no tolls on through traffic were charged. Thus, if the railroad competed for the Albany to New York City business, the through traffic would have made no contribution toward paying the fixed charge. This would have forced local shippers to subsidize through traffic, for it would have placed the entire burden of the fixed charges upon the local traffic.

In setting the tolls, the directors assessed against both through and local traffic the amount of the fixed charges they felt each could afford to pay. By this action, they asserted that the railroad could capture the entire existing trade between Boston and Albany, but they ruled against an attempt to divert the western trade from New York to Boston. Being men of political wisdom, the directors did not emphasize this. Only when the railroad was finally completed to Albany did the conflict between the merchants, who hoped to make Boston the commercial metropolis of the East, and the local shippers burst into full swing. Throughout the nineteenth century each management of the Boston and Albany route would face the same problem. In short, each management would have to decide whether to favor commercial Boston or local factories, farms, and businesses. Much of Massachusetts' future was in the hands of the managers who shaped the rate policies of the Boston to Albany railroad.

The directors concluded that the traffic in 1829 alone would be sufficient to enable the railroad to operate in the black, but they bolstered their argument by claiming that the railroad would be significant in the encouragement of economic growth throughout much of the state. It would, they maintained, spur industrial expansion in Worcester County, along the Chicopee River, and in the Berkshires, and it would help the farmer.[15] Further, it would have a beneficial effect on real esate. "It will perhaps not be rash," the directors continued, ". . . to suppose that the building of the railroad would produce an immediate rise, in the aggregate value of lands, and real estate, in the Commonwealth, more than equal to its whole cost."[16]

All this was preparatory to the final recommendation of the directors, that the state assume the entire burden of constructing the Boston to Albany railroad. "It is the opinion of the Directors," they concluded,

> that works of such magnitude, and on which public accommodation so essentially depends, should be under the control of the government of the state. To enlist in such works the enterprise of individuals or corporations, it will be necessary to make a grant of privileges, which it will be difficult to define with sufficient limitations, to secure all the interests of the public, while at the same time they are made broad enough to induce a sufficient investment of capital for the enterprise. They therefore recommend that the construction of these works shall be undertaken [by the state] that an authority be given for raising such sums of money as may be necessary for the works, by the sale of stocks bearing an interest of 4 1/2 per cent per annum, and reimbursible in not less than fifteen or twenty years, for the payment of which the faith of the state shall be pledged, and for meeting the annual interest of which sufficient taxes shall be provided.[17]

68

In other words, the directors asked that the state borrow no less than $3,000,000[18] and commit itself to possible interest payments of $144,000 annually plus the eventual retirement of debt, after a period of fifteen to twenty years. Of course Hale and the other directors were certain that the state would never be called upon to meet the interest payments or to retire the debt; on the contrary, they argued that the work would return a handsome profit to the Commonwealth in the years to come.

But the General Court was unwilling to act immediately. The lower house sent the report to a committee headed by Theodore Sedgwick which on February 23, 1829, reported back with a ringing endorsement of state aid to railroad construction; but it also proposed that the question be postponed until the new legislature, which would meet the following June. The recommendation was accepted, and thus the railroad became the central issue in the April–May 1829 state elections.[19]

Few proposals aroused greater sentiment in Massachusetts than a state railroad. In Boston, Hale made a successful bid for reelection to the state senate. While Hale stood as a National Republican, his railroad coconspirator, David Henshaw, ran unsuccessfully for the state senate on the opposition Jackson ticket, dramatic evidence that Boston's railroad enthusiasm was not confined to one party or class.

But the main struggle centered in the elections to the lower house of the General Court. On May 1, 1829, Hale demanded that Boston send its full legal representation to the lower house. "We have observed," he wrote, "that in several parts of the state, towns have been urged to send their full number of representatives, for the special purpose of opposing . . . the railroads recommended by the last legislature. . . . This makes it important," he continued, "that Boston and other towns which think favourably of the projected improvements should have in the legislature their fair proportion of the representatives." In response to this plea Boston increased its numbers in the lower house from forty-one to fifty-six.[20]

But in depressed Newburyport, a place that could conceive of no results from a railroad except, possibly, as an addition to the tax bill, the town met and elected its full quota of representatives. Not satisfied with this, the town meeting instructed their legislators to oppose the railroad measure at all costs. "Were there no men in Newburyport with whom the citizens could trust their interests without special instructions?" asked Hale bitterly. Across the Commonwealth each town weighed similar questions, and when the campaign was over, 496 men had been elected to the lower house, compared with 345 in the previous session and 197 in 1825. This represented the greatest number since the separation of Maine from Massachusetts in 1820.[21]

During the election, railroad opponents formed a solid wall of hostility. Opposition came from several sources. Most coastal regions outside the Boston area had no use for the railroad. Places like Newburyport, Salem, Plymouth, Cape Cod, and Nantucket feared additional taxes for a project they felt could never benefit them. The farmers of Middlesex and Norfolk Counties, who sold their produce in Boston, joined the coastal opponents. They saw that a railroad would make it possible to ship into the metropolis potatoes, hay, cider, apples, eggs, butter, and vegetables from interior Massachusetts. Naturally the idea of being taxed to open the Boston market to their competitors did not appeal to rural Middlesex and Norfolk Counties.[22] Central and western Massachusetts were badly split. With but few exceptions, only those towns that were to be served directly by the new railroad favored it. Those off the line opposed it, reasoning that an improvement 20 miles away was as good as none at all. Since most of these villages were undergoing severe agricultural depression, they were not in the mood to pay for something that did not benefit them.

Arguments against the railroad were surprisingly responsible and logical. Even Joseph T. Buckingham, the editor of the Boston *Courier*, who had written in 1827 that a railroad from Boston to Albany would be a "project which every one knows, who knows the simplest rule in arithmetic, to be impracticable . . . and which if practicable, every person of common-sense knows would be as useless as a railroad from Boston to the moon,"[23] had been won over to the idea that railroads might be of benefit. He now opposed the Boston to Albany project because he felt it went to the wrong place, for he had become

70

a leading advocate of a line from Boston to Vermont and Lake Champlain.[24]

Some papers did ridicule the claim that a railroad would be efficient. A correspondent for the *Essex Register* made an elaborate set of calculations proving that a railroad could not carry freight between Boston and Albany at less than $20 a ton! The writer concluded that it was very "plain . . . that not a barrel of flour, beef, pork, or anything else, will ever be diverted from the natural channel of the North River, and the established market of New York, to come over the rail road to Boston."[25] Hale answered this with comparative ease, but he seemed almost powerless to counteract an issue raised in a series of articles published in April 1829 in Northampton's *Hampshire Gazette*. This paper saw the railroad as a threat, for it would hurt the farmers of the Connecticut Valley by allowing "the farmers of New York and Ohio, who cultivate a soil much more productive than ours . . . to supply our markets cheaper than we can, not only Boston . . . but the smaller markets at Westfield, Springfield, Chicopee Factory and other manufacturing villages near the road, and thereby in some degree exclude our products." Next the *Gazette* attacked the cost estimates presented by the Directors of Internal Improvement. Engineers, the paper maintained, were fallible, and to make matters worse, they normally erred on the side of too low an estimate. The *Gazette* feared that Baldwin, Hale, and the prorailroad group had fabricated low construction estimates in order to lure the state into the project. "In our opinion," said the *Gazette*, "it will be unsafe for the public to rely with confidence on the estimates of this or any other Engineers. We are convinced that the Western Rail Road, will cost over four and a half millions of dollars, or from 40 to 50 per cent more than the [Hale-Baldwin] estimate, and we are willing to give our reasons." Then followed a formidable and lengthy list of estimates compared with the actual costs of such projects as the Erie Canal, the Hudson and Delaware Canal, and others, which all indicated that original costs projected by the engineers had been far too small. Then the paper reminded its readers that English railways cost $22,000 a mile, as compared to the Hale-Baldwin estimate of $16,000.[26]

The *Gazette* argued that until the cost of the western railroad had been determined, no satisfactory answer could be given to such an inquiry as "Will the tolls pay the interest and repairs? If not," speculated the paper, "how heavy a tax must be levied annually upon the people to make up the deficiency? will it be 5,000 or 100,000, or $150,000?" The editor warned that it was doubtful that, if the railroad cost only the $3,250,000 estimated by the engineer, its income "will be sufficient to defray the annual charges of interest, repairs, and superintendence." But, concluded the writer, "should it cost *four millions and a half*, and the more we examine the subject, the stronger is our belief that it will exceed that sum, a burdensome tax must be paid annually by the people, many of whom will derive no advantage from the road."[27] The weight of logic was heavy on the side of the *Gazette*. Had not every internal improvement in Massachusetts, whether canal or turnpike, failed to pay adequate dividends upon its stock? And it seemed doubly unfair to farmers to ask them to pay for a railroad that could only help their competitors.

When the legislature met in June the prorailroad forces were none too certain. Governor Lincoln made an especially strong appeal on the railway's behalf. He asserted that it was vital to Boston's commercial prosperity and stated that upon the growth of Massachusetts' capital city hinged the future of the entire Commonwealth.[28] Unfortunately, the legislature had before it the unpopular issue of direct taxation. After much debate the General Court enacted a tax of $75,000 "to be assessed in proportion to the property owned by each person on the first of May" 1829.[29] This was the first direct levy since the year 1824, and it was an ill omen for the railroad legislation, whose supporters found that the senate was evenly balanced "not varying more than a vote or two either way, and that if a vote [were] taken the decision might [be] with the presiding officer." The house was even more doubtful. Neither side seemed anxious for a test, so the General Court, with the consent of both sides, put the railroad question over until the session of January 1830.[30]

In the six-month interval after the legislature's adjournment, prorailroad forces sampled opinion across the state and concluded that the lower house of the General Court would never vote for a state-owned railroad. The cost specter raised by the *Hampshire Gazette* had crystallized solid opposition to any program by which the state would carry the entire burden. Meanwhile the spectacular Rainhill steam trials made Hale and his followers even more confident that a railroad could succeed. Therefore they decided to submit a revised plan to the General Court when it reconvened in January. Theodore Sedgwick sounded the new note in an article for the *Berkshire Journal*. He called for a "union between the state and individuals."[31] The new proposal was that the state charter a corporation with a capital stock of $3,300,000 of which the Commonwealth would take but $1,100,000, and private individuals the rest. The state would not be obligated unless the public actually took its full share. This plan limited state interest payments to 4 or 5 per cent of $1,100,000, or to about $50,000 a year. Thus if the railroad did not pay, which Hale assured the people would not be the case, the Commonwealth would not face an overwhelming tax burden.[32]

Therefore, in January 1830 the legislature debated not a full-blown state work but the question of whether the Commonwealth should aid private individuals who would assume the major financial responsibility of throwing a railroad across the Berkshires from Boston to the Hudson. The debate centered in the lower house; it was heated and acrimonious, and it lasted almost two full weeks. The leading railroad spokesmen were Theodore Sedgwick, William Jackson, and Royal Makepeace, who served with Hale as one of the directors of internal improvements. Sedgwick made the usual references to the decline of Boston's commerce and the necessity for providing transportation to the Berkshire, Worcester, and Springfield industrial areas. "It is the duty of the state," he said, "to do something for giving employment to the people, at a time when private investment of capital has been so disastrous."[33]

Allied with Boston's commercial and industrial interests was an important segment of the state's fishing industry. Speaking for them, Marblehead's Representative Green said the fishermen asked only for a railroad. "A few years ago," commented Green, "they brought to market 800,000 quintals of codfish in a year, now they bring but 150,000. But with a railroad," he maintained, there would be "1,000 men employed in the fishery from the town of Marblehead . . . and fresh codfish might be swimming in the ocean one day, and found 200 miles distant in the country on the next day, and it was not unlikely that they might be able to deliver fresh cod in Ohio."[34]

Speaking against the Boston to Albany railroad was Representative Brooks of Bernardston, a little village north of Greenfield on the Vermont line. "Much time," he said, "has been expended . . . to prove what everybody who had attended to the subject was long ago convinced of—that rail roads are a superior method of internal communication to any other that has been hitherto invented." But he argued that it was an "idle dream" to think that a line through Springfield to Albany would help the people of Hampshire and Franklin Counties, for to use it would necessitate hauling goods in "common wagons . . . ten, twenty, or thirty miles." He ended by vowing that "he should stand as firm as possible against the delirious project of a rail road to Albany, but should do all in his power in favour of a road to Vermont."[35]

To this Representative Perkins of Becket, in Berkshire County, replied that although he favored a Boston to Albany route, he would vote for any line rather than "put the whole improvement at hazard." Since the Albany line ran but six miles from his door, he favored it, but he added that he had a poor opinion of a legislator who said, "if the railroad don't *go to my house*, it shall not *go at all*."[36]

Lurking in the background was the fear that the $1,100,000 proposed state subscription represented just an opening wedge, and that the railroad to Albany would cost far more than the estimated $3,200,000. It was well known, argued Representative Baylies of Taunton, that "railroads in England cost $25,000 per mile, and [that] the Liverpool and Manchester would cost $100,000 a mile." Baylies reasoned that since labor and iron were cheaper in England than America, the true cost of a Boston to Albany line might be $20,000,000. "It was idle," he concluded, "to say that the State ventured only $1,100,000. If individuals did not pay their assessments the State would have to back up the whole expense."[37] For most legislators this

Figure 8

Western Railroad: Through the Berkshires, deep rock cutting 129
miles west of Worcester in the mid-1840s.

Figure 9

Western Railroad: Third Stone Bridge in the Berkshire Hills, as it appeared in the mid-1840s.

thought was frightening indeed; they had just used every means at their command to avoid laying a direct tax of $75,000, and the prospect of starting a project that might result in yearly expenditures of more than $800,000 was unthinkable.

On January 30, 1830, the house smothered the railroad bill by a vote of 283 to 162. Almost solid delegations from Boston and the towns of Worcester, Springfield, and Pittsfield supported the act, and they were joined by a scattering of representatives from the rest of Massachusetts, but it was not enough to overcome the combined opposition of almost the entire seacoast outside Boston and the part of the interior that felt it would not be served by the railroad.[38]

This vote, lamented Hale, is the result of "jealousy, arising from the manner in which the legislature is constituted, which leads members to act exclusively on the principle of serving their own towns."[39] The Northampton *Courier* put it even more bluntly: "Let the route of the contemplated rail road be laid through every village of the Commonwealth, and by the threshold of every representative's door, and we question whether they would, individually, stop to inquire into the expediency of involving the state."[40]

Certainly few, if any, of the opponents voted against the measure because they had scruples against government aid or operation of internal improvements. As if to emphasize this, just two days after the defeat of Hale's dream, Representative Cogswell of Ipswich, a vociferous opponent of state support for an Albany railroad, introduced a bill into the house which advocated a double-track system from Boston to Ipswich to be built entirely at the Commonwealth's expense.[41]

The legislature's smashing defeat of the western railroad scheme did not end the public aid dreams of its promoters, for they still hoped that Boston would lend its credit to the project. Municipal support of railways was not novel, for in 1827 Baltimore had subscribed to $500,000 of Baltimore & Ohio Railroad stock.[42] There was general sentiment for similar action in Boston; indeed its citizens in February 1829 had voted overwhelmingly for municipal purchase of railway stock, but the matter had been allowed to drop pending the General Court's treatment of Hale's plea for a state railroad.[43]

Now that the legislature had rejected Hale's proposal, railroad supporters once again turned to Boston. If Hale's propaganda campaign had done nothing else, it had whipped the city into a frenzy, for he had managed to convince nearly everyone that it was declining, and he had linked a railroad inseparably with its commercial revival. But not all Bostonians shared this view. A small minority, mainly composed of property owners, seemed satisfied with the city's growth and looked upon community support of internal improvements as a measure that would raise their taxes. They prepared to resist any effort to involve the municipality in a railroad scheme. This small but determined group found a friend in Joseph T. Buckingham, who had long disputed Hale's claim that Boston was on its deathbed.

Through his paper, the *Courier*, Buckingham waded into the fight. "Is Boston in a state of decline?" he asked. "The popular reply to the question is, Yes: and the man who should seriously ask it [at a town meeting in Faneuil Hall] would probably be laughed at for an ignoramus, or hissed and hooted down as a fool. If," continued Buckingham, "he should gravely attempt to maintain the negative, he might run the hazard of being clad in a straight jacket and carted off to the insane hospital."[44]

In this spirit Boston met to decide whether it should support a western railroad. The city fought the issue out in a series of town meetings that took place on July 12, August 2, and August 9, 1830, at Faneuil Hall. The actual question under debate was whether the town meeting should request the city council to ask the legislature to pass a law authorizing Boston's subscription to not more than $1,000,000 of stock in a railroad to the Hudson.[45] The railroad's cause was popular; most citizens favored immediate action and were in no mood to tolerate delay. Men of the stature of George Blake, former United States district attorney and the owner of considerable Boston property, argued that a railroad was certain to succeed and that it would enhance real estate values. Therefore Blake felt that the people ought to adopt municipal aid prior to the next meeting of the General Court in January 1831.[46]

Not all property owners agreed. A spokesman for the minority was Alexander Townsend, who owned the Marlboro Hotel and a sizable amount of other Boston property.[47] At the meeting on July 12 Townsend, amid a chorus of boos and jeers, branded city railroad aid as unfair since it put the entire financial burden in case of failure upon the owners of real property. But, Townsend added, he would be glad to subscribe to a few shares of stock in a private corporation. At the meeting on August 2, when Townsend attempted to move indefinite postponement of the entire question, the assembly went mad. Exasperated, Townsend remarked that "if they hissed they would only make a hiatus in his remarks but he would stand there until the flesh rotted from his bones, or they hissed themselves out of breath, before he would give way to anything but a motion to adjourn, or a call to order from the chair." Mayor Harrison Gray Otis tried to restore order but succeeded only partially.[48]

At the next meeting on August 9 the citizens voted 1,966 to 532 to request the city council to ask the General Court to grant Boston authority to subscribe to stock in a railroad.[49] The victory of the prorailroad forces, however, was Pyrrhic since the opponents of municipal aid made it clear, both at the town meeting and in the newspapers, that they felt that the Massachusetts constitution made it illegal for cities to subscribe to any public work outside their own boundaries. The antirailroad forces left no doubt that they would challenge in the courts any law authorizing the city to purchase railroad stock.

This threat proved effective. Railroad supporters realized that to link internal improvements with a measure of doubtful constitutionality might result in lengthy litigation and delay.[50] Hale, in an editorial in the Boston *Advertiser*, opposed municipal aid: "To urge [the railroad] forward in a manner not generally acceptable, will be running the hazard of exciting a permanent opposition on the part of [many] who may ultimately lend a voluntary co-operation."[51] Thus ended the attempt to secure municipal aid for the railway to Albany.

The failure of government to act forced the question of internal improvements back on the shoulders of private capital. Fortunately, the success of the Liverpool and Manchester and the dividend paid by the Baltimore & Ohio from the receipts of the first year of its operation inspired growing confidence

77

just as New England manufacturing interests began to fully appreciate the value of rails over turnpikes and canals. The close association between railroads and industry was shown by the fact that Massachusetts' first effective railroad charter was granted in June 1830 to a group of Lowell industrialists.[52] This group, headed by Patrick Tracy Jackson, received permission to construct a railroad virtually on the banks of the Middlesex Canal between Boston and Lowell. Despite the rising enthusiasm of the private interests, construction of any railroad in 1830 was uncertain. Initial Boston & Lowell stock offerings went unsubscribed, and the building of the Boston & Albany still seemed as far away as ever. Mayor Harrison Gray Otis, writing for the Boston *Advertiser* in May 1830, summarized the problem. For an object of such magnitude as a railroad to the Hudson "millions will be requisite" and "it would be delusive to expect" capitalists to invest so great an amount "until it can be demonstrated to a moral certainty that it would produce regular and sure dividends."[53]

What was needed, added Otis, was convincing proof that railroads would work. This could only be accomplished by a bold experiment financed by interested private persons who were willing to risk a small sum to prove that a railroad would serve industry and commerce and pay dividends as well. Although such a demonstration might be accomplished on the proposed Boston and Lowell, Otis emphasized that there was urgent need to make a start on a western railroad. Therefore he recommended that the state charter a private corporation with a capital of $400,000 the stock of which would be sold in shares of $100 each. This company would build a single-track railroad for a distance of about 40 miles inland, probably to Worcester.[54]

It did not take railroad supporters long to rally around Otis's idea. Hale on January 20, 1831, advocated the construction with state aid, if possible, or entirely at private expense if necessary, of a road from Boston to Worcester. The steam locomotive, he remarked, made a single track as effective as a double-track system operated by horses. Using steam, the whole project could be accomplished at a cost of no more than $600,000.[55]

In a last desperate bid for state aid, Harrison Gray Otis and others petitioned the General Court in March 1831 for incorporation to construct a railroad from Boston to Worcester. Otis's bill required the Commonwealth to subscribe one-third of the stock, or $200,000. William Jackson argued that it had now been demonstrated in the United States and in England that a single-track railroad could be built for $8,000 or $9,000 a mile. This meant that $600,000 would be adequate for a 40-mile line to Worcester. He further maintained that revenue from passengers alone would pay the interest on the capital.[56]

But the legislature would have none of it. Representative Brooks of Bernardston spoke for the majority when he observed "that converts multiplied with astonishing rapidity from the Boston delegation, when the project was to have the state enlisted, but they came in very slow when the city was to be enlisted. The people at a distance," he continued, "could not see the propriety of taxing them[selves] to carry such a project into effect." A Boston and Worcester railroad, maintained Brooks bluntly, would operate almost for the sole benefit of Boston, and he said "to the people of Boston if they wanted a rail road they ought to make it."[57]

When the June 1831 session of the legislature met, western railroad supporters did not even propose state aid, for they knew it was futile. Although Hale had not abandoned the idea that state participation in a Boston to Albany railroad was both necessary and desirable, he realized that until railroads demonstrated that they were not potential tax burdens, no state aid law would pass the General Court. The editor of the *Daily Advertiser* also believed that a Boston to Worcester railroad could operate at a profit. Fortunately, several wealthy industrialists agreed with him. Therefore Hale put himself at the head of a group who petitioned the legislature for a charter to construct a railway to Worcester. Thus on June 23, 1831, the General Court created the Boston & Worcester Railroad, a corporation that was to build as an experiment the first leg of what Hale hoped would become Boston's artery to the Great West.

CHAPTER IV

The Boston & Worcester Charter: A Triumph of Private Interest

THE BOSTON & WORCESTER CHARTER was a strange and misleading document because it was the culmination of a long series of unsuccessful efforts to initiate Massachusetts railroad development. Earlier the legislature had insisted on a mass of restrictions giving the state control of rate making and protecting the people from transportation monopolies. Investors rejected these concepts just as the General Court refused public aid. The legislature reached an impasse in 1831. The antimonopolists and regulators on the one hand and the supporters of public aid on the other still hoped to win. But it was obvious to all that without some compromise there would be no railroad. The result was a charter that contained a large measure of sham. It appeared to regulate rates but did not, and it seemed to throw open the tracks to all, while it wrote into fine print a provision giving the management a monopoly of all vehicles. The wording of the charter saved face for the regulators and antimonopolists, but the substance gave to the private investors nearly everything they desired.

The Boston & Worcester's charter defined the railroad's relation to the Commonwealth. This was one of the three original Massachusetts charters as well as one of the first in the United States, and it had a profound effect on the development of railroads and on their position in society.

Until 1831 most of the great internal improvements had been government projects—the Erie Canal in New York State, the Pennsylvania System, and the Ohio Canals. Even private corporations started in the late 1820s like the Baltimore & Ohio Railroad and the South Carolina Railroad and Canal Company had substantial government backing.[1] But the first three Massachusetts railroads, the Boston & Lowell, the Boston & Providence, and the Boston & Worcester, were wholly private and received no state or municipal aid. The initial patterns they set endured; even the later policy of state railroad promotion did not significantly alter the private direction and operation of railroads in the Commonwealth.

The outcome was the result of the fact that in 1831 the vast majority of Massachusetts citizens desperately wanted railroads yet considered all internal improvements unprofitable investments. Since they feared state taxes, they were willing to let private individuals build the railways. The major issue, therefore, became not whether the Commonwealth ought to grant private charters but rather how much and what kind of power the state should give corporations which would undertake the construction.

The railroad agitation reached its zenith when monopolies were under vigorous attack in Massachusetts and in the nation. The Warren Free Bridge controversy and Jackson's war against the Second Bank of the United States forced investors to demand safeguards in any charter proposing that private money engage in an enterprise with a public character. As the railroad fever spread, the majority of citizens became progressively more tolerant of these demands. The result was a charter that paid lip service to public rights but actually put tremendous power into the hands of the investors. A western railroad controlled the future of most of the state, influenced industry in almost every county, held the key to the revival of agriculture, and could make or break Boston's bid to become the East's commercial emporium. Rate and service decisions could encourage or discourage Boston's competition with New York as a market for grain or the emergence of on-the-line industry. Significantly, the charter gave the directors an almost free hand to run their railroad as they saw fit.

The Boston & Worcester charter created a corporation with 10,000 shares of capital stock.[2] Unlike the Middlesex Canal or the Worcester Turnpike, the Boston & Worcester Railroad enjoyed limited liability. If the railroad failed, the stockholder lost only his original investment. The charter fixed the par value of each share at $100 in a deliberate attempt to involve many small and middling investors. This contrasted sharply with previous Massachusetts practice, for each Middlesex Canal share represented a $740 investment, and the par value of the shares in the great Lowell and Springfield textile mills was $1,000. The industrialists who promoted the Boston & Lowell continued this tradition and set the value of shares in that railroad at $500 each.[3] But all railroads chartered in Massachusetts after 1831 followed the Boston & Worcester's lead. That road attracted a large group of stockholders that included wealthy merchants and great captains of industry together with small-time businessmen, shopkeepers, and lawyers who had money to risk or who felt that it was in their interest to encourage railroad development.

The charter gave all power to a board of directors of "not less than five members" to be elected annually by a vote of the stockholders. Each share had one vote, except that no one proprietor could cast more than one-tenth of all votes no matter how many shares he owned.

Because the promoters estimated that the construction of the Boston & Worcester would take from two to three years, it was understood that the whole $100 due on each share would not be needed immediately. Nathan Hale made it clear that the entire $1,000,000 capital would be called for only as the work progressed. Thus the initial subscribers paid for their stock in several assessments of between $10 and $20 each over a period of two years. This again made the stock attractive to smaller investors who could obligate themselves for shares without immediately putting up much cash.

Apart from specifying that the corporation would have a president, treasurer, and clerk, the charter left the company's entire administrative and operational structure to the discretion of the board. The directors' power was limited only by their having to receive an annual vote of confidence. They controlled both the vehicles that moved over the line and the rates, issues on which hung the development of the modern railroad. The control of all vehicles running over the road made it possible for the directors to adopt any new technological innovations. The rate-making power was necessary to attract investors.

Like the report of the board of directors of internal improvements in 1829, the 1831 charter was ambiguous as to whether a railroad was a superturnpike or a new kind of transportation in which all vehicles were to be owned and operated by one management like the Liverpool and Manchester Railway. The pressures toward the first course were great. The Boston *Advertiser* during April and May 1831 reported the intense bitterness of the English stagecoaches, teamsters, and freight forwarders put out of business by the Liverpool and Manchester when it decided upon exclusive railroad ownership of all engines and carriages upon its line.[4] To independent stage operators and freight haulers the railroad was a threat unless they could transfer their operations to it.

Therefore, it was not surprising that section five of the Boston & Worcester charter specified that the road could be used "by any persons" who complied with basic rules to be formulated by the directors. This undoubtedly satisfied most citizens that the way was clear for the railroad's general use in the same manner that a turnpike was open to the wagons and coaches of all upon payment of a toll. The charter's state-purchase clause further reflected the superturnpike concept, for it maintained that "after such purchase, the limitation [that a central authority could fix rules binding upon vehicles using the road] provided in the fifth section of this act shall cease and be of no effect." Clearly state purchase would open the railway to all without restriction.[5]

But section five ensured that under private management the "transportation of persons and property, the construction of the wheels, the form of the cars and carriages, the weight of the loads and of all other matters and things in relation to the use of said road shall be in conformity to such rules, regulations and provisions as the Directors shall from time to time direct." Section three gave the directors power "to purchase and hold . . . engines, cars, and other necessary things in the name of the corporation." Thus the charter contained key provisions that enabled the private management to monopolize all vehicles. Section three approved of railroad ownership of rolling stock and the steam locomotive. Safety and effective maintenance demanded that all locomotives be controlled by one management, and section five gave the directors power to rule off the road any equipment not suitable for a steam railroad. Clearly, unless the state purchased the line, which was highly unlikely, considering the Commonwealth's past rejections of state financed internal improvements, the railroad's management could monopolize its system.

But the charter's ambiguities invited challenges. The first came in 1838 when the Seekonk Branch Railroad claimed the right to run locomotives over the Boston & Worcester and gave the latter's charter as authority. The Worcester's directors acted quickly; they prohibited any train not drawn by the corporation's motive power. They resolved, however, to "provide locomotive[s] with skillful enginemen . . . for the moving of cars and carriages [of other railroads] at all reasonable times and at such rates as may be fixed by the board of directors." Furthermore, they specified that "no car . . . shall be loaded or unloaded on the railroad between the two terminations thereof, except by direction of the Superintendent or some agent of the corporation."[6] Thereby the Worcester agreed to haul the cars of "foreign" systems behind its engines, but reserved the right to exclude any equipment not meeting certain standards. The Seekonk did not pursue its claims further.

Later, however, in 1844 and 1845 the Western Railroad demanded that it be allowed to enter upon and use the Worcester's tracks. The B&W again refused, and the Western carried its case to the legislature, which responded by confirming the Worcester's position. "No locomotive engine or other motive power," stated the resultant law, "shall be allowed to run upon any Rail-Road constructed by authority of this Commonwealth, except such as belong to, and are controlled by the Corporation owning and managing such road unless by the consent of such Corporation." But the General Court did require that every railroad "at reasonable times, and for a reasonable compensation . . . draw over their road the passengers, merchandize, and cars of any other Rail-Road Corporation."[7] The latter phrases made mandatory a policy that the Worcester had followed from the very first, the interchange of cars with connecting systems. However, the Western's sole purpose in trying to run trains upon the Worcester's tracks was to force the latter to haul the former's freight and passengers at lower rates. This attempt failed completely, for the legislators confirmed the Worcester's monopoly of motive power and their specification of "reasonable compensation" for hauling the Western's cars left the rate question as much a matter of argument as before.

In reality sections three and five of the Charter were a clever ruse. Nathan Hale and other Boston & Worcester supporters knew that an open provision giving the railroad company a monopoly of vehicles upon its line would incite opposition. Hence they wrote into the charter phrases that seemed to throw the tracks open to all upon payment of a toll, as was customary on turnpikes. But at the same time, by giving the directors power to own and operate steam engines and to fix exact specifications for all rolling stock, they ensured that the railroad could effectively monopolize its own road. Hale clearly understood that a railroad required single ownership of both the tracks and the equipment. Writing for the *Advertiser* in July 1830, he explained, "there is just this difference between the proprietors of a canal and those of a rail road. The former are like the owners of a turnpike, to whom it is wholly immaterial who, or what moves thereon, so [long as] there be moving enough to yield a revenue. The latter are like the turnpike too; but they must be owners also, of all the stage coaches, wagons, carts, and carriages, and horses, and must employ all who drive; and all persons who are necessary through the whole extent to load and unload every vehicle."[8] That most contemporaries did not understand this concept undoubtedly facilitated the charter's passage through the legislature.

Hale also envisioned the steam locomotive. Significantly, when the Worcester's board of directors made its first report in 1832, it endorsed the recommendation of their engineer, that steam locomotives be used in preference to either stationary engines or horsepower.[9]

Even more important to investors was the power to control rates. Previous charters for internal improvements had usually fixed the tolls. This was true of both the Middlesex Canal and the Worcester Turnpike.[10] Private railroad promoters, however, demanded a free hand to set rates and a guarantee against the construction of competing railroads. They were determined to avoid another Charles River Bridge fiasco.

But in 1830 most legislators still desired to fix rates and opposed giving any railroad a monopoly of traffic. Thus, although the General Court rejected state aid for either an Albany or Providence railroad, it granted charters to several private corporations which, if acted upon, would have resulted in a rail network radiating from Boston to Providence, Berkshire County, and Vermont.[11] But the legislature struck from each of these charters provisions endowing the proposed corporations with exclusive rights to build a railroad along their routes.[12] Furthermore, the charter of the Franklin Railroad to Vermont set maximum tolls of 3 cents per mile on a ton of freight and 2 cents a mile for each passenger.[13] The abortive Boston, Providence, and Taunton charter was more flexible. It gave initial freedom to set rates, but if after four years of operation profits exceeded 10 per cent per annum, the legislature could reduce rates so that the shareholders would receive no more than 10 per cent.[14]

The charters created in the winter of 1830 produced no construction. Thus, facing a growing popular sentiment for railroads, the legislature capitulated to the investor's demands. The General Court gave the Boston & Worcester a thirty-year monopoly of traffic decreeing that "no other Rail Road other than the one hereby granted shall within thirty years from the passing of this act be authorized to be made leading from Roxbury, Brookline, Cambridge, or Charlestown to any place within five miles of [Worcester]." The surrender on rate making was even more complete, although here it was cloaked by words which at a casual glance seemed to give the legislature authority to reduce dividends of more than 10 per cent on the total capital invested. In the charter's terminology:

> a toll . . . hereby is granted and established for the sole benefit of said corporation upon all passengers and property of all descriptions, which may be conveyed or transported upon said road, at such rates per mile as may be agreed upon and established from time to time by the directors of said corporation. . . . Provided, however, that if at the expiration of ten years from and after the completion of said road the nett income or receipts from tolls and other profits, taking the ten years aforesaid as the basis of calculation shall have amounted to more than ten percent per annum upon the cost of the road, the legislature may take measures to alter

and reduce the rate of tolls and other profits in such manner as to take off the overplus for the next ten years calculating the amount of transportation upon the road to be the same as the ten preceding years.

The Boston & Worcester directors did not take the "limitation" on their powers very seriously, for their first report emphasized that they would be free to establish rates that would produce dividends in excess of 10 per cent.

By the charter, the Directors are authorized to establish such rates of toll . . . as they think fit. . . . These rates . . . however, will be at the expiration of ten years from the completion of the road, subject to the revision of the Legislature, and if at that time it shall appear, that the income . . . has amounted to more than ten per cent per annum, it will be in their power to order a reduction of these tolls for the next ten years, to such rates as on the business to the ten years then expired, would have given only an annual income of ten per cent. On such a graduation of tolls for the second ten years, the corporation will have the benefit of any increased business, from the increase of the population or other causes in the progress of the ten years, for swelling the income of the second ten years above ten per cent, so that if the average of the first ten years should be equal to ten per cent income, the average of the second ten would, probably, be equal to twelve or fifteen per cent.[15]

In effect, the charter exempted the Boston & Worcester from any rate regulation for its first ten years. And even after ten years had elapsed, the charter limited the legislature's power to fix rates to but once every decade. There were only two additional restrictions to the directors' rate-making authority. The legislature retained the option to set tariffs on goods transported over the Boston & Worcester from connecting railroads, and finally the charter gave the Commonwealth the right to purchase the railroad from its stockholders after an initial period of twenty years. But investor interests were carefully protected since the state was to pay the full par value of the stock plus 10 per cent interest per annum from the time the capital was paid in. The Commonwealth could, however, deduct from this amount all dividends paid out by the railroad prior to state purchase.

On all other questions of rate fixing, the charter was silent. There were no requirements for uniform charges on all classes of goods, and nothing prevented special concessions to through as opposed to local traffic. On these matters the directors had complete freedom.

The charter's rate-making concessions were widely recognized. Nathan Hale argued that they made the Boston & Worcester a good investment. "The charter," he asserted, "is more liberal in its restriction on the dividends than that of the Liverpool and Manchester road. It gives to the directors the authority to establish tolls at their discretion with the only restriction that at the end of ten years the Legislature shall be authorized to reduce them, from that time forward, in case they produce a net income of more than ten per cent. . . ."[16]

But all were not reconciled. Hale, himself, in the days when he had fought for a state-owned railroad, had argued that "to enlist in such works the enterprise of individuals or corporations, it will be necessary to make a grant of privileges, which it will be difficult to define with sufficient limitations, to secure all the interests of the public, while at the same time they are made broad enough to induce a sufficient investment of capital for the enterprise."[17] In September 1832 a self-styled "Friend of Internal Improvements" warned of the price the Commonwealth had paid for allowing a private corporation to build the Boston & Worcester. The railroad management, he said, would surely fix their rates so as to drive competing stages and wagons from the road; and this, of course, would lower transportation costs; but what, he asked, was there to ensure that the public would get the full benefits and savings made possible by rail transportation? "It may be taken for granted that so long as the rail road will have nothing to fear from competition the proprietors will fix their rates of freight so high as to secure a handsome profit, after paying all expenses." The legislative restriction of dividends was largely an illusion, he maintained, for the only provision on this point was that after ten years, if the annual dividend had exceeded 10 per cent, the legislature could reduce the current tolls to such rates as on the average

88

of the previous ten years, would produce a 10 per cent dividend, and the tolls so fixed would become the rates for the next ten years, after which the legislature could make another reduction on the same principle. "This does not restrict [the railroad] from making a profit of 20 per cent, if they can, or any other rate for the first ten years and if at the expiration of the period the rates of tolls should be reduced, this very reduction, as well as the probable increase of population in the country, will serve again to increase the amount of profits for the second ten years much above ten per cent."[18]

This "Friend of Internal Improvements" foresaw that the state had created a powerful vested interest astride one of the Commonwealth's most important and densely populated routes of travel. The Worcester road, secure in its monopoly of a profitable local business, would, he predicted, lose interest in extending the railroad west to less lucrative fields and might in the end block Boston's bid to attract the trade of the Erie Canal. On the other hand, he felt that a state railroad would plow the profits back into new lines making possible the building of a unified route to the Hudson.

On all operational matters the charter said nothing. No provisions directed the quantity or kind of service or required special safety measures. No mention was made of abandonment of track. All these matters and the many others that today are closely supervised by the Interstate Commerce Commission and the various state regulatory bodies were left to the directors' discretion.

The legislature, however, insisted that the railroad should keep no secrets. To this end the directors were to report annually to the General Court the company's receipts, expenditures, and operations. As if this were not enough, the charter added that the corporation's books "shall at all times be open to the inspection of any Committee of the Legislature." Stiff penalties would result from failure to so comply.

The charter strictly limited management in its use of the power of eminent domain, for it was here that the railroad clashed with vested property rights. The corporation needed the authority to lay out the line according to sound engineering practice. And the directors had complete freedom in selecting both the route and the location of the terminals. But the charter ensured full protection and compensation for any property owner whose land might be seized or damaged. Before any real estate could be taken, the company had to make an accurate survey. The property owner then had to be given an adequate description of the land required. In most cases the law envisioned that the railway and the landowner would reach a voluntary agreement on the price to be paid. If this could not be done, then the county commissioners were to serve as arbitrators. If the county commissioners' decision still did not satisfy, then either party could bring the case before a court where a jury would decide.[19] This process minimized unfair land seizures and protected the railroad from the tactics of land speculators.

Besides ordinary private property, the railroad crossed over two special kinds. These were private internal improvements such as the Blackstone Canal or the Worcester Turnpike and public highways and roads owned by the towns along the route. In such cases the railroad had the power to raise or lower any road or canal so that the tracks could pass over or under the other artery. In no instance, however, could the railroad block or obstruct the old roads or canals. The charter provided that towns or parties dissatisfied with relocations could take their cases to the county commissioners. If the railroad refused to make the alterations directed by the commissioners, the injured party could then make the changes on its own and charge the railway. This provision established a relationship between railroads and highways that has remained unchanged. It made the railroad responsible for the upkeep of any bridges or underpasses. Future legislation would clarify even further the railroad's duties in regard to grade crossings and maintenance of bridges and underpasses, but from the very first the railroad was meant to take full financial responsibility for the cost of highway crossings. While comparatively unimportant at the time, such expenses became a significant drain on railroad revenues in the latter part of the nineteenth century and have remained so ever since.

The Boston & Worcester's charter served as a model for that granted to the Western Railroad in March 1833. The Western completed the line to the Hudson by laying track from Worcester to Albany.[20] Both charters were an almost blank check given to private companies in return for construction of internal improvements that most contemporaries thought would be financial liabilities. Both charters conferred a thirty-year monopoly of traffic and gave almost a complete freedom from any type of governmental control either in the area of rates or of services offered.[21] Freed from government restraint, the directors had unlimited power to experiment, and during the more than thirty years that the charters of the Boston & Worcester and the Western remained in effect, the main patterns of American railroading emerged. Interchanging of cars between systems, through ticketing of passengers and freight over many roads, mass movement of commuters, effective handling of mail and express, emphasis on safety for both crews and passengers, express and local passenger service, and nearly all the other features we associate with modern railroads had their start during this period. But most significantly from the first both the Boston & Worcester and the Western became true common carriers. The monopoly of motive power and cars by the companies and the absence of any effective alternative method of transportation made it necessary for the new railroads to move every conceivable kind of freight and passenger traffic. Thus grew the tradition that railroads would carry anything from a bag of feathers to a letter or a slab of marble. And even more important, this service was offered on a regular basis that could be depended upon in the winter as in the summer, and the trains ran whether no passengers or a thousand presented themselves at the station. In this sense railroads were different from all the transport systems that preceded or followed them, for no other single transportation method has ever attempted to perform such a wide variety of services. Canals, inland shipping, highways, pipelines, and airways—all cater to highly specialized transportation markets. From the beginning, however, the Boston & Worcester and the Western not only met the highly specialized requirements but general needs as well.

Although the Worcester and Western roads were free from direct governmental regulation, their managements were not immune from public pressure. Massachusetts was an old and highly developed state with many powerful and varied interest groups. In many respects the story of these two railroads is the history of how these powerful groups exerted pressures to force the railway managements to serve particular interests. At first the various factions battled to control the boards of directors. It is important to note, however, that groups which failed to dominate management did not attempt to institute direct state regulation but rather tried to create competing lines. Thus in the middle of the nineteenth century when certain groups became dissatisfied with the rate structure of the Boston & Worcester and Western roads, the dissident forces turned not to the legislature for laws prescribing state rate regulation, but asked the Commonwealth instead for direct aid in schemes to build a competing line.

The general effect of the charters, therefore, was to emphasize the role of private initiative in transportation development. Thus the state no longer served as the mainspring of internal improvements as had been the case in New York, Pennsylvania, and Ohio. When Massachusetts rejected Hale's plan for state railroads, the Commonwealth moved into a passive position. Later, when the Bay State did become active in the support of railroad building, it acted not as the developing force but as an adjunct to private corporations.

CHAPTER V

The Construction of the Boston & Worcester

THE BAY STATE's new industrial ventures seemed to bear fruit all at once. "This year has been one of unprecedented prosperity in the Country, and particularly so to enterprising Merchants and Manufacturers," wrote the Lowell industrialist William Appleton in 1831.[1] The boom grew in intensity and magnitude until it was pricked by the financial panic of 1837.

During these prosperous years the Boston & Worcester got its start. The company received its charter on June 23, 1831, and in May 1832 the stockholders authorized the directors to locate the railroad and begin construction. Workmen turned the first shovelful of earth on August 14, 1832. More than a year and a half later on April 16, 1834, a diminutive steam engine jerkily pulled a string of passenger cars the 8 miles from Boston to Newton, thus inaugurating Massachusetts' first regularly scheduled passenger train. Originally this service consisted of three daily-except-Sunday round trips to Newton, but by November 1834 the trains ran more than 33 miles to Westborough, three-quarters of the way to Worcester. On July 4, 1835, the first train ran the 44 miles from Boston to Worcester, and the following week full freight and passenger service was established.

By 1838 the Boston & Worcester had proved itself, both as a means of transportation and as a profit-making enterprise. The success of the road and of its two sister lines, the Providence and the Lowell, produced startling reversals in public and governmental attitudes. Throughout the state railroad schemes sprang up; and when financial panic undermined the support of private capital, the General Court stood ready to shore up the boom.

The first few years set the patterns that dominated the railroad's history for more than three decades. Of major importance was the emphasis on passenger and local traffic, for it was the hauling of people, not freight, that made success possible. From the first the Worcester was a local railroad, catering to local needs.

Nathan Hale, the first president, guided the Boston & Worcester through its early years. Serving with him on the board of directors from 1831 to 1839 were men who represented Boston's varied interests including banking, real estate, wholesale and retail merchandising, investing, and manufacturing.[2] Some like David Henshaw and William Jackson had played an important role in the fight to secure state aid; others like Eliphalet Williams, William Sturgis, George Morey, and Daniel Denny had remained in the background during the initial struggle.[3] Eliphalet Williams was a leading Boston politician who had been president of the city's common council and had waged an active campaign for the protectionist Nathan Appleton when the latter ran for Congress in 1830. But Williams' main importance lay in his position as the cashier of Boston's powerful City Bank.[4]

William Sturgis represented the old-line shipping aristocracy and the new industrialists. Through his continued activity in the firm of Bryant and Sturgis, he kept an interest in the Calcutta and China trade, but he also recognized the ebb of commerce and as a hedge invested heavily in the new cotton mills at Lowell and Springfield. Sturgis carried conservatism over into railroading. The railway, like any other business, was a safe and profitable place to put money. He opposed wild speculation, for a well-run road should serve the public and simultaneously produce dependable dividends as did the textile mills.[5]

George Morey, a lawyer, had built up a modest fortune mainly as a trustee cautiously investing other people's money. In addition to being a director, he served the railroad as clerk and treasurer.[6] Daniel Denny, like David Henshaw, came to Boston from Leicester, Massachusetts. In Boston Denny entered the domestic dry goods business and accumulated more than $200,000 before retiring to enjoy the fruits of his labor.[7]

The Boston men's most serious problem was financing the

railway's construction. Despite Nathan Hale's spirited attempts to prove that railroads were profitable, most men of wealth remained skeptical. But these same citizens also recognized that something was necessary to rescue Boston from the decline of the 1820s. They approached the railroad not as a money-making scheme but as a patriotic duty that would indirectly aid their factories and businesses and protect their land values.

The Boston & Worcester depended entirely upon the sale of 10,000 shares of stock at $100 a share.[8] To encourage a widespread interest, the promoters made it easy to take shares. When the subscription books opened in Boston and in Worcester, a prospective stockholder paid only an initial assessment of $1 for each share with the assurance that the $10,000 so raised would be spent only if all the shares had been subscribed and that it would pay for a detailed survey of the route and the line's potential earning power. No one would be finally committed until after the survey, when the stockholders would meet to decide whether or not to proceed. The directors made it known that subsequent assessments would be levied at the rate of $20 to $30 each year as the construction progressed.[9]

Even these terms, which offered the stock on the installment plan, did not attract a rush of investors. The general prosperity Massachusetts enjoyed in the 1830s discouraged the purchase of railroad stock. The mere fact that "well managed Manufacturing establishments of Wool & Cotton . . . earned twenty per Cent on [their] whole capital [in 1831]" deterred investment in a venture that had, according to the general consensus, little chance ever to return more than a bare 2 or 3 per cent per annum.[10]

In the town of Worcester, which stood to gain heavily from the railroad, only eighteen persons subscribed. Significantly 50 of the 250 shares there were taken by the merchant and industrialist Stephen Salisbury; another factory owner, George F. Rice, subscribed for 25.[11] In general the Worcester entrepreneurs were busy using their limited capital to build iron, woolen, cotton, and leather factories, and they had little money to divert to internal improvements. Almost the entire financial burden fell upon Boston.

In all, including the Worcester shareholders, 238 individuals and firms subscribed for an average commitment of about 40 shares. The list reads like a mercantile, political and industrial directory of Boston's great families. Three of the Appletons, Samuel, William, and Nathan, took a total of 313 shares. Edmund Dwight and his partner, James K. Mills, between them signed up for 150 shares. Harrison Gray Otis took 163, William Jackson 50, Whitwell, Bond & Company 164, David Henshaw 100, Thomas H. Perkins 50, and Joseph Coolidge 164. Even Daniel Webster took 163 shares.[12]

Although this illustrious group met on the first of May 1832 and voted to go ahead with the Boston & Worcester, many proprietors had great reservations. Toward the end of 1832, when rumors circulated that the corporation was in a "very unpromising state, and that the directors were mad in attempting to go on with it," the shareholders rushed to sign a petition calling for a special meeting to consider abandoning the work. Nathan Hale and his board, however, made an able defense of the railroad's progress and thereby managed to win a unanimous vote of confidence from the stockholders.[13]

Nevertheless, if the railroad had depended upon the original subscribers to follow through on their pledges and pay the assessments, it would have failed. In June 1835, when the first train ran to Worcester, only 41 of the original 238 stockholders still held shares in the corporation, and these held less than 17 per cent of the total. Indeed most of the initial stockholders hurried to get out as soon as they paid their first assessment. Harrison Gray Otis dumped his entire 163 shares early in 1832. Asserting that railroads were a poor investment, William Appleton boasted of selling his 100 shares in 1832 at a good profit. The other Appletons did the same. Patrick Tracy Jackson was not so fortunate, for he took a $600 loss when he sold his 100 shares in November 1832.[14]

Luckily, others stood ready to support the stock. Among the new investors were certain Massachusetts banks to which businessmen preferred to shift the risk. By 1835 several Boston banks controlled almost 20 per cent of the Worcester stock. The City Bank, whose cashier Eliphalet Williams was a director of the railroad, held nearly 1,000 shares. And David Henshaw, supported by the Commonwealth Bank, owned almost 500 shares. A year later in 1836 the Market Bank held more than 1,200 shares.[15]

Even more significant was the migration of much stock to New York. By 1835 Manhattan controlled about 45 per cent of the Worcester Corporation, and on a single day, August 28, 1835, the New York exchange saw over 771 shares of Boston & Worcester stock traded.[16] The Bostonians recognized the importance of this market, and in 1833 they elected George Shipman, a New York stockbroker, to the railroad's board of directors. In 1836 New York was represented on the Worcester board by R. H. Winslow. Concomitantly the railroad opened special books in New York to facilitate the transfer of shares and the payment of dividends in that city.[17]

The construction period demonstrated the Massachusetts investors' basic conservatism. Never again was so high a proportion of Boston & Worcester stock held outside the Commonwealth. The Boston men wanted the railroad, and they supplied the initial momentum, but they were only too happy to let others take the financial risk during the experimental years. Only after the Worcester road became a blue-chip investment did Bostonians again buy shares, and by 1840, when there was no longer a need to woo New York money, the director from the Empire State was quickly dropped and replaced by a Massachusetts man.[18]

The most important problem aside from financing was the selection of the route. Beyond the obvious requirements of building a line that was short and level and reasonably inexpensive, it was necessary to pick the route that would generate the most business. The directors aimed for a line to serve as a "main trunk," capturing the traffic between New York City and Boston, between Boston and Albany, and, if possible, the commerce moving from Boston northwest to Greenfield and Vermont along the Millers River Valley. The charter allowed the directors complete freedom to locate the right of way, and they gave careful consideration to both a northern and a southern route. The northern line from Boston through Waltham, Sudbury, Marlborough, Berlin, and West Boylston provided easy access to the Millers River and tapped the trade of the upper Connecticut Valley and Vermont. But the directors finally selected a southern line running from Boston west through "Brighton, Newton, Needham, Natick, the southern part of Framingham, the north part of Hopkinton, the south part of Southborough, Westborough, Grafton, and the eastern part of Worcester," a route that could dominate all traffic between Boston and New York City by way of Connecticut and make the Boston & Worcester the first leg of a Boston to Albany line.[19] In the planning stages at least, the directors envisioned their line as the trunk of a great network radiating from Worcester south to Norwich and west to Springfield and Albany, thus tapping both the southern and western trade. Nathan Hale saw clearly that a Norwich route could compete effectively with the Boston and Providence for the trade of New York City. Hale also felt that an all-rail route to New York could be built through Worcester, Springfield, Hartford and south to Manhattan Island.[20] It was no accident, therefore, that although the Boston & Worcester became a locally oriented railroad, it was also always a vital link in a great intersectional transportation network connecting Boston with New York City and the Great West.

To fix the right of way's exact location, the board hired a professional enginer, Colonel John M. Fessenden, a graduate of the United States Military Academy. Colonel Fessenden started his career in internal improvements working for the Chesapeake and Ohio Canal, but he soon moved on to the Baltimore & Ohio Railroad.[21] Fessenden was determined not to repeat the mistakes that had badly hurt that road, on which sharp curves and steep grades prevented the use of English steam engines. Fessenden recommended that the Boston & Worcester have no grades that rose more than 30 feet in a mile or curvatures with a radius of less than 1,000 feet.[22]

He therefore laid the route along river valleys wherever possible. From Boston the line ran along the Charles to a point near Newton Lower Falls, where it crossed the river into Needham.[23] From there it ran through nearly level land passing Long Pond in Natick to Framingham, where it began to follow the Concord River to Westborough. The worst grades lay in the last 10 miles. Between Westborough and Grafton was Cutler's Summit, 380 feet above the terminal in Boston. The most formidable grade lay between Grafton and Worcester; it led to a pass 490 feet above sea level, occurring just before the railroad descended into the town of Worcester, which itself was 455 feet higher than Boston. In the days before the bulldozer and dynamite, when all cuts and fills had to be made by men wielding picks and shovels and using horses and wagons, finding an economically feasible route required many surveys and much imagination.

The art of locomotive building was so primitive in 1831 that Fessenden made all estimates on the assumption that the engines would weigh but 4½ tons. Even with easy grades and curves, he calculated that such a locomotive could only haul a maximum of 36 tons at an average speed of 6 miles per hour. To achieve an average speed of 20 miles an hour, the load would have to be reduced to 10 tons.[24]

Originally the directors had thought that landowners would be happy to have the railroad run through their property since it was common knowledge that internal improvements increased the value of adjacent real estate. Acting on this theory, the directors estimated that a mere $21,000 would suffice for all land costs and fencing. But the first attempts to make purchases produced a rude jolt. "In that portion of the road which passes through Brighton and Newton the lands . . . are held at a high rate, and the proprietors in general are unwilling to make any abatement on the account of any advantage to result to them from construction of the road," lamented the directors in 1833.[25] Even those who owned vast acreages remote from Boston refused to give their land to the railroad. Before negotiations were through, the Boston & Worcester paid more than $365,000 for rights of way and other necessary property.[26]

The railroad normally selected the route deemed best by Colonel Fessenden and negotiated with the property owners or resorted to eminent domain. But alternative routes could be used to avoid local opposition and condemnation procedures. Most men in 1831 greatly underestimated the influence that railroads would have upon community development. The survey through Framingham discovered two good routes. The best line, from the engineering standpoint and from that of serving the town, lay along the Worcester Turnpike through

Framingham Centre. But the Wheeler Brothers, who owned stock in the turnpike and who maintained the leading store in the Centre, violently opposed the railroad. They advocated that it be built along the alternative survey a mile and a half to the south. They reasoned that a railway running alongside the turnpike would dry up their own traffic, destroying the value of the turnpike stock and reducing the business at their store. Bowing to the local pressure the railroad chose the southern route. The events of ten years dramatically demonstrated the Wheelers' error. Banishing the railroad to South Framingham did not save the turnpike. Instead the new railway station became a magnet that drew business away from the Centre. A new town, still the heart of Framingham, rose where the trains stopped. Belatedly the Wheelers reversed their opposition and attempted to revive the Centre with a branch from the main road.[27] But in general along most of the Worcester line a passive attitude permitted engineering considerations to determine its specific location.

Such was not the case, however, at the two terminals. Although it was only partially realized in 1831, the site of the depot and freight facilities in Boston was to have far-reaching effects upon the city's future rivalry with New York for the Great Western trade. Successful competition for the flour and grain export business demanded a terminal adjacent to the warehouse and deep-water wharf facilities used by the ships engaged in overseas commerce.

Instead the Worcester road's weak financial position and Boston's topographic configuration dictated the location of the eastern terminal. In 1831 any approach to Boston involved an enormous expense and great engineering problems. The city proper occupied a small peninsula connected to the mainland only by a narrow tongue of land running south along the present Washington Street to Roxbury. A railroad approaching Boston from the west had two basic choices. Starting in Brighton, it could cross the Charles River into Cambridge, running past what is now Central Square to the vicinity of the present Longfellow Bridge. Here it would cross the Charles again and terminate near the present North Station. This route had the drawback of two costly river bridges and many street crossings in Cambridge. The final terminal would have been shared with the Boston and Lowell Railroad, which was then building to the city from the north.

The alternative route skirted the Charles River's southern banks and required a mile and a half of bridges and embankments to cross the Boston Water Power Company's full and receiving basins, which occupied most of what is now Back Bay. This put the railroad terminal not far from what is today South Station.[28]

The Worcester's directors delayed their decision by starting construction at Brighton, 3 miles from Boston proper. Aware that the initial 2 miles might cost more than $100,000, or over one-tenth of the railroad's entire capital, the directors cast about for a way to lessen this expense. The result was marriage between the Boston & Worcester and a land speculation scheme in Boston's South Cove, which at the start of 1833 was a 75-acre mud flat lying at the southern edge of the city due east of Washington Street and south of Kneeland Street.

With the knowledge that the railroad created an opportunity for profitable real estate development, a group of Boston capitalists applied to the legislature for a charter that would permit them to buy and fill in the mud flats. The General Court responded by chartering the South Cove Corporation in February 1833. Edward H. Robbins, a "born speculator" who "after many ups and downs" came out rich became the corporation's president; Josiah Quincy, Jr., its treasurer; and Ellis Gray Loring its clerk.[29] In order to lure the Boston & Worcester into the cove, the new corporation offered to sell to the railroad slightly more than 2 acres, which would have at least a 150-foot frontage on navigable water for a price not to exceed $35,000. In addition the Cove Company offered a bonus of $75,000 and a guarantee to pay all land damages incurred by the railroad in crossing the neck of land between the Water Power Company's empty basin and the South Cove property.[30]

Delighted, the Boston & Worcester accepted. Superficially the deal promised everything. It supplied almost free land on Boston's southern edge, and it gave the railroad direct access to a pier site on navigable water. But the advantages proved illusory. Although the Boston & Worcester built a wharf, the

101

deep-water ships used in ocean commerce were unable to enter the cove. In their haste to solve financial problems, the railroad's directors failed to notice that even in the early 1830s all vessels of large draft were either going to the northern part of the Boston peninsula or to piers across the river in Charlestown. The directors soon realized their mistake. At a meeting in June 1834 they complained that the South Cove Corporation was filling in too much land and was not planning for deep-water channels. But the real estate company would not reverse its policy.[31] The public, however, did not notice the absence of overseas shipping facilities until after the completion of the railroad to Albany. Then bulk grain shipments through the port of Boston faced a 2- or 3-mile horse cartage between the railroad terminal and deep-water piers. This situation was not satisfactorily remedied until after the Boston & Worcester merged with the Western Railroad to form the Boston & Albany in 1867.

The news that the Boston & Worcester Railroad was to build across the Back Bay sent the Water Power stocks tumbling to one-half of their former value.[32] Alarmed shareholders feared that the railroad would fill in so much of the basins that a large part of the water storage capacity would be destroyed. The Water Power directors felt that by blocking the railroad, they could restore the value of their stock, and they refused to negotiate for a right of way across their basins. The Boston and Worcester thereupon invoked the procedure of eminent domain, laid out a right of way 5 rods wide across the full and receiving basins, and immediately started to construct bridges and fills. The Water Power Company's reaction was swift; they commenced a chancery suit in Massachusetts' Supreme Judicial Court for an injunction to halt all work, arguing that their charter gave them the exclusive right to use the Back Bay marshlands and that a later grant could not permit another corporation to use the same flats. This suit challenged the entire concept of eminent domain and a favorable ruling would have hampered internal improvements throughout the Commonwealth. The court refused to issue the injunction, and the work on the railroad continued uninterrupted. But the question of compensation for damages remained, and this issue hung fire for many years before a satisfactory settlement was worked out.[33]

At Worcester the problems were less complicated. Again the directors' main desire was to provide an inexpensive terminal able to accommodate all other railroads that might be constructed into the town. From the first the Boston & Worcester planned to share a joint station with the Norwich & Worcester Railroad and the proposed Western Railroad to Albany.[34] Therefore the Boston and Worcester directors purchased nearly 100 acres about a mile south and east of the village. But the local businessmen knew more about the effect of railroads upon land values than those of Framingham, and they insisted that the tracks run right to their Main Street. When the railroad complained of the cost, several businessmen donated land in the center of town.[35] But the Boston & Worcester also developed the area on the outskirts of town into a freight terminal and engine yards.

From the beginning, the engineer and the directors agreed that the railroad should be constructed in the most solid and permanent manner possible. The line was just a shade over 44½ miles long. For purposes of construction the road was divided into forty-eight planes "of which eighteen measuring about fourteen miles [were] level." The other thirty had different rates of inclination, the least of which rose 4 feet to the mile, and the steepest 30. To maintain an easy gradient, the railroad was forced to dig two long 40-foot-deep cuts through solid black rock at Cutler's Summit in Grafton and at the system's high point just before entering Worcester. Otherwise it required only minor cutting and filling.[36]

The line had two major bridges. The first, a 1½ mile-long viaduct over the full and receiving basins of the Boston Water Power Company, had 1,700 feet of wooden trestlework and a solid earth embankment held in place by masonry walls. To ensure free passage of water from one side of the basins to the other, the embankment was broken by several graceful stone arches, whose piers rested on piles driven below the water level. The railroad tried hard not to reduce the water-storage capacity of the power company, and to compensate for filling in part of the full basin, the contractors enlarged the pond by removing over 9,000 cubic yards of earth from adjacent marshland.[37]

The second major bridge crossed the Charles River at the Newton-Weston town line; it had a 120-foot wooden span resting "on abutments of substantial stone masonry rising 30 feet from the surface of the water."[38] Throughout the rest of the line the railway employed masonry bridges to cross the numerous small rivers and streams. Typical were two graceful arch bridges constructed of granite with hammered joints that spanned the Concord River.

The railroad also went over or under 33 public highways and roads. For these crossings Colonel Fessenden designed wooden bridges resting on granite abutments. The line also crossed 32 public roads at grade, all of which places became potential points of collision between trains and horses, wagons, and pedestrians.

Although the directors ordered the roadbed graded to a width of 24 feet, or wide enough for a double track, to save money, only a single track with turnouts for passing every 6 miles was constructed at first.[39] Since this was very much a pioneer railroad, uncertainty marked Colonel Fessenden's initial report on the superstructure. He made estimates for two different types of iron rail, which he recommended be laid upon stone blocks.[40] By the time construction started, however, Fessenden decided upon rolled iron edge rails weighing 40 pounds to the yard. These he specified should rest on cast iron chairs weighing 15 pounds apiece. The chairs, spaced 3 feet apart, were fastened to transversed cedar ties. Experience on the Baltimore & Ohio had shown that stone was not a proper foundation, for it lacked elasticity, and the constant pounding of the trains not only gave a rough, jolting ride but loosened the rails and wore them badly.[41] Wood proved an ideal substitute.

As the crews laid the track, they dug a continuous trench 2 to 3 feet deep under each rail. Into these ditches they rammed stone rubble as tightly as possible to serve as a foundation upon which to lay the ties.[42] This method was unsatisfactory since the center part of the tie still rested on plain earth. The freezing and unfreezing of the ground during the first winter (1834–

1835) twisted the ties out of place along much of the roadbed. The railroad then adopted the technique of laying a gravel foundation almost a foot deep the entire width of the road, and embedding the ties completely in the crushed rock.[43] By 1836, with the exception of the cast iron chairs, the roadbed had assumed the basic form that it maintains to this day.

The organization of construction followed traditional patterns. There was in 1831 no single contractor in Massachusetts capable of building a work the size of the Boston & Worcester. The largest previous projects had been the cotton factories on the Merrimack, and the Middlesex and Blackstone Canals. Neither of the two internal improvements had been built by a single contractor. The Worcester directors followed the precedent of the turnpike and canal builders before them; they divided the road into a great many small segments and hired separate contractors to take charge of each section.

This system had one great advantage. It relieved the railroad of having to deal with all the problems of the organization and the supervision of construction. During the building period the directors put all real authority in the hands of two men: the engineer, John Fessenden, and the agent, William Jackson.[44] The engineer and his assistants surveyed the line and marked out the exact locations of the grades, fills, and bridges. He divided the road into more than 50 sections; some were single masonry bridges, others were a mile or more of road to be graded. The agent first dickered with the landowners for title to the right of way and then, after competitive bidding, awarded construction contracts to the low bidders. Contracts for the grading and masonry on the first division, extending 13 miles from Boston to Needham (Wellesley) were let in mid-1832, and the full 21 sections of that division were finished, ready for the laying of the superstructure by December 1833. Additional contracts were executed for laying the track, and this was finished to Needham by July 3, 1834. Similar procedures were followed for the other divisions, and iron rails reached Worcester by the first of July 1835.

The large number of small contractors produced excellent results. Colonel Fessenden made careful cost estimates for each section. In every case a contractor bid below the estimate.

The builders all managed to fulfill their obligations except where the railroad cut through solid black rock at Cutler's Summit and at the junction of the fifty-first and fifty-second sections at Worcester Summit. Here excavation proved extremely difficult, and the railroad had to pay sizable sums above the original bids to finish the work.[45] This system produced no great companies and made no man rich. Instead, it divided work among about 75 different contractors, none of whom received as much as $80,000.

The building of the Boston & Worcester and its sister railroads created a vast new market for all kinds of materials. Some, like the stone for retaining walls and bridges or wood for ties and trestles, were procured locally. But the railroad demanded large quantities of new items, many of which in the early 1830s were not available in Massachusetts or even in the United States. The most important were iron rails and rolling stock, including steam engines and cars.

In the 1830s England led the world in railroad technology. Its mills and factories had catered to the Stockton and Darlington and Liverpool and Manchester railways. By 1832 British industry stood ready to meet the flood of orders that began to pour in from railroads in America and England. Nathan Hale, Colonel Fessenden, and William Jackson had followed the growth of the Liverpool and Manchester, and they naturally turned to an English supplier for needed rails and equipment.

Actually they had little choice. The surge in demand had reduced the cost of rails in England from £12 a ton in 1827 to £9 in 1831, and simultaneously the quality had improved. In 1832 the price fell still further. These reductions made it possible to land English iron on Boston docks at $64 a ton, including all shipping charges, insurance, and a tariff of 25 per cent. By comparison American iron was both inferior in quality and in short supply and could not be delivered in Boston at less than $120 a ton. These facts alone produced a strong incentive to import even small quantities of iron. But rails were needed in large amounts. Fessenden estimated that it would take more than 3,600 tons of iron just to lay the single track between Boston and Worcester. Even at English prices

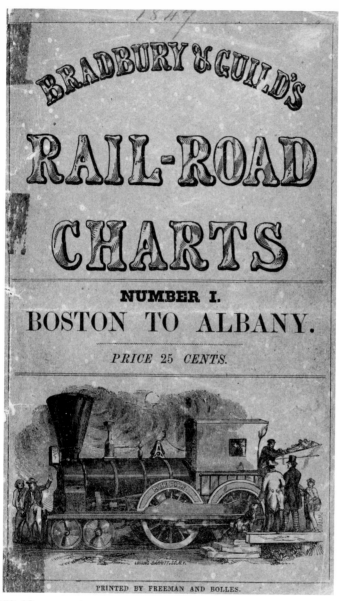

Figure 10

The Boston & Worcester locomotive *Mercury* on the cover of an 1847 tourist guide.

Figure 11

Western Railroad: Interior of the Springfield engine house as it appeared in the mid-1840s.

this would cost more than $230,000.[46] No management could have considered the purchase of American iron in 1833. Instead the Boston & Worcester together with several other railroads formed a lobby in Washington to press for the elimination of the tariff, a move that had the backing of most of Massachusetts' leading industrialists including Nathan Appleton and Thomas H. Perkins. Congress in July 1832 passed a law to refund the tariff when railroad directors certified that the iron had been laid down permanently on their system.[47]

England's industrial superiority did not weigh so heavily in the field of locomotives. It took neither great quantities of raw materials nor elaborate factories to build steam engines that weighed only about 6 to 9 tons. They could be fabricated in a dozen or more foundries along the Atlantic seaboard. The Baltimore & Ohio's predicament had stimulated widespread interest in American locomotive construction, and by 1832 several manufacturers in the United States sought locomotive orders.

In mid-1833, when the Boston & Worcester directors decided to purchase four locomotives, they had an open mind. Since there was no significant difference in price between English and American engines—both cost between $4,500 and $6,000—the decision rested on speed in delivery and performance.[48] Physically the Boston & Worcester had been built in conformity with the design of the Liverpool and Manchester. The Worcester road had the same gauge and grades and curves, which made it possible to employ the type of locomotives constructed for the Liverpool line by Robert Stephenson at his works at Newcastle-on-Tyne.[49]

But the purchase of English motive power had serious drawbacks. Facilities for repair and adjustment could be found only in a shop capable of building motive power. This made American, and preferably Boston, machine shops essential. Therefore, while the directors placed all their orders for iron in England, employing the House of Baring as agents, they divided their initial purchases of locomotives equally between American and British manufacturers. They bought two engines from Robert Stephenson and one each from Colonel Long in Philadelphia and from the Mill Dam Foundry in Boston.[50] The British engines were the world's best; the American were frankly a gamble.

Colonel Stephen H. Long, a West Point graduate, made his first mark in western exploration. The peak in the Rockies that still bears his name stands as a monument to his exploits in Colorado. In the early 1830s Long became associated with Philadelphia's William Norris, who was destined to become one of America's best known locomotive builders. In June 1833 Colonel Long approached the Boston & Worcester with an offer to build a 6-ton anthracite coal-burning locomotive at a cost of $4,500. After some discussion the directors agreed. A few months later when the Colonel suffered financial reverses, the Boston and Worcester advanced him $3,000 to complete his engine, which he finally delivered in January 1834.[51]

The Mill Dam Foundry's locomotive resulted from the initiative of the Boston & Worcester directors. The engine was a 9-ton version of a smaller Stephenson machine, which the Boston & Lowell loaned to the foundry to serve as a model.[52]

When the Boston & Worcester started service in April 1834, the two 6-ton Stephenson locomotives, the *Meteor* and the *Comet*, and the Mill Dam Engine, appropriately called the *Yankee*, all ran well; but the Long machine proved a failure. The railroad's impending completion caused the directors late in 1834 to order four more Stephenson locomotives from the Barings, which all went into service by August 1835. But the romance with English motive power was fast drawing to a close. Passenger traffic proved unexpectedly heavy, and by August 1835 the Boston & Worcester needed more engines.[53] A rash of breakdowns and the inability of the Stephenson locomotives to haul heavy passenger trains up grades at "normal" speeds caused J. F. Curtis, the road's newly appointed superintendent, to recommend the purchase of motive power from new sources. Immediately orders went out for one engine each from Bury's Locomotive Works in Liverpool, England, M. W. Baldwin in Philadelphia, Pennsylvania, and the machine shops of the Locks and Canals Corporation in Lowell, Massachusetts. The Bury engine, christened the *Lion*, went into operation in January 1836; it was the last English engine ever ordered by the Boston & Worcester.[54]

In three short years the difficulties of purchasing locomotives from across the sea and the desire to have motive power designed specifically for the Worcester's requirements created a need for locally built engines. Orders from the Middle States proved only a stopgap until New England builders could fill that need. The emergence of the Boston & Worcester provided a powerful stimulus for the growth of heavy industry in the Bay State.

To provide passenger and freight cars, the directors turned to firms that constructed stagecoaches in New York City, Hoboken, and Baltimore. But simultaneously the railroad placed orders with Kimball and Davenport in Boston and Osgood Bradley in Worcester. Between 1835 and 1842 the Boston and Worcester bought locally hundreds of additional cars. This, too, created a new heavy industry in Massachusetts.[55]

Building and equipping the Boston & Worcester shattered Colonel Fessenden's original cost estimates. To raise the needed money, the stockholders on May 4, 1835, voted to enlarge the stock by an additional 2,500 shares. This was but the first of several increases, which by 1838 raised the corporation's total capital to $1,700,000. In 1832 Colonel Fessenden predicted that the whole railroad including the cost of land, roadbed, track, engines, and cars could be finished for no more than $900,000 or approximately $20,500 a mile. The road actually cost nearly double that estimate or more than $1,600,000, which was equal to about $38,000 a mile.[56] Fessenden knew his business, and some of his estimates were remarkably accurate. His calculations for the cost of grading and masonry, for example, proved nearly correct. Some additional costs were for the viaduct over the Water Power Company's basins in Boston and for retaining walls and extra drainage found necessary after the line went into operation.

The items that forced the railroad nearly to double its original capital were land, equipment, and terminal, shop, and station facilities. Both the directors and the engineer miscalculated land costs, but the underestimates in the case of equipment and buildings stemmed from Nathan Hale's deliberate attempt to minimize the full costs. If a prospectus had placed the cost at $1,600,000 or more, there would have been few takers for the stock. The engineer, therefore, made only token allowances for engines and cars and did not make any provision at all for depots, shops, or terminal facilities.[57] The imperfect realization on the part of the general public and of most investors as to the nature of railroads allowed these estimates to pass unquestioned. But by 1838 nearly $300,000 had been spent for cars, stations, and buildings. In reality capital costs had just begun. An ever-expanding business soon required a double track, enlarged terminals and shops, more rolling stock, and branch lines. In 1860 the Boston & Worcester had a total stock of 45,000 shares, representing a paid-in capital of $4,500,000.[58]

The Boston & Worcester's appearance upon the Massachusetts scene was dramatic and exciting. In March 1834 the railroad put into operation the first steam locomotive ever to run in the Bay State, and a crowd gathered at Boston's Tremont Street terminal just to watch it run. "It was the first time we ever saw one [a locomotive] in motion," wrote a correspondent in the Boston *Evening Transcript*, "and we candidly confess that we cannot describe the singular sensation we experienced, except by comparing it to that which one feels when anticipation is fulfilled and hope realized. We noted it as marking the accomplishment of one of the mighty projects of the age, and the mind, casting its eye backwards upon the past, as it was borne irresistibly onward, lost itself in contemplation of the probable future."[59] "I saw today for the first time a Rail Way Car," wrote Christopher Columbus Baldwin, the distinguished librarian of Worcester's American Antiquarian Society in his diary on August 1, 1834. "What an object of wonder! How marvellous it is in every particular! It appears like a thing of life. The cars came out from Boston with about an hundred passengers and performed the journey, which is about thirteen miles in about forty-three minutes. I cannot describe the strange sensations produced on seeing the train of cars come up. And when I started for Boston it seemed like a dream."[60]

The first train into Worcester on July 4, 1835, brought out the largest crowd in the town's history. People lined the tracks for a mile on either side just to catch a glimpse of the engine as it flashed by.[61] The State Lunatic Hospital released the less violent of its inmates to witness the great event, one of whom remarked upon seeing the locomotive, "Well it beats the very devil. I never before saw a critter go so fast with such short legs."[62]

On Saturday, July 5, 1,500 curious people descended on the railroad to make the round trip between Boston and Worcester. To accommodate this throng, the company ran two eleven-car trains, each hauled by a pair of locomotives. The trains each made two round trips over the system without accident or delay.[63]

For most the first ride on the Boston & Worcester was an unforgettable experience. The traveler of 1835 leaving Boston made his way "to the train of cars" which stood "under their long sheds with the locomotive engine puffing impatiently." The engineer's men were "busy oiling the wheels and storing the fuel," while "the captain of the cars" arranged the passengers and secured the baggage. Seated either "with twenty or thirty others in . . . a coach, with a broad aisle . . . and stuffed seats" or in a compartment, the traveler felt the cars pull away and in a few minutes was "rolling on with immense force and velocity" over roads and bridges, marshes and water, "now shooting across the plain, now riding along a high embankment over a ravine, now winding through a fruitful and luxuriant valley." For the first fifteen minutes he was likely to "feel a little pale," running "along at the rate of twenty miles an hour, within six inches of the brink of an embankment twenty feet high." These feelings, however, soon subsided and left the passenger "the pleasure of actually flying" without danger.[64]

CHAPTER VI

Running the Boston & Worcester, 1834–1842

THE BOSTON & WORCESTER'S DIRECTORS had to strike out boldly on their own to solve the problems of labor force organization, schedules, rates, and fares. No previous railway had been in operation long enough to provide a satisfactory precedent. The directors wished to prove, once and for all, that railroads were a profitable investment. Nathan Hale understood that "the success of the three railroads leading from this city [Boston]" would "inspire . . . confidence in enterprises of the same kind in other places," and he felt that the Boston & Worcester was the key to Massachusetts railroad development.[1] Dividends would attract private capital and might also persuade the Commonwealth to lend its credit for a line to Albany. Therefore the controlling principle that guided the Worcester management during the years between 1834 and 1840 was that of earning a profit upon the road's capital investment.

Although Hale and the other board members made the broad policy decisions, they took little active part in the road's routine management, and they received only nominal compensation for their services.[2] As the system neared completion, the importance of the engineer, Colonel Fessenden, diminished, and the main responsibilities devolved on two officials, the agent, William Jackson, and the superintendent, James F. Curtis.

William Jackson, who received the corporation's top salary of $3,500 a year, continued to direct all new construction and in addition took charge of maintaining the track, buildings, and terminals. To run the trains, the railway created a new carrying department and placed it under Superintendent Curtis, who was paid $3,000 a year.[3] The directors set the ground rules for hiring, one of which specified that "no person be employed to take charge of the engines or of the cars or to act in any other service of this corporation who shall not wholly abstain from the use of ardent spirits."[4] But they left recruitment to the superintendent and agent, requiring only that all persons hired must be approved by the board of directors. In most cases this was a formality.[5]

The superintendent initially hired two kinds of employees: those who ran the trains and those who managed the depots, yards, and shops. The depot masters at the two terminals, Worcester and Boston, had the full responsibility for keeping the engines and cars in repair and ready for use. The Boston depot master also supervised the repair and machine shops established in the South Cove adjacent to the passenger and freight stations at Beach and Lincoln Streets. Each terminal also had a freight master who received all merchandise, weighed it, issued receipts for it, and collected the money due on it. Elsewhere along the line resident agents at seven different stations handled the freight. All the nonoperating employees with the exception of the laborers working in the shops or in the track gangs received annual salaries ranging from $400 to $1,000.[6]

In contrast the operating men normally received a daily wage ranging from $1 to $2. The train crews consisted of an engineer, fireman, conductor, sometimes called the carsman, and one or more brakemen. Although the engineer had complete responsibility for the care of his locomotive, on passenger runs he was under the command of the conductor, who gave the orders as to when and where to stop and start. The conductor also collected fares from passengers who were unable to or chose not to buy tickets from the station agents. Freight trains ran without a conductor and were under the direction of their engineers, who stopped at every station to take on or to discharge merchandise.[7]

Circumstances forced the Boston and Worcester to concentrate initially on passengers. Freight demanded station agents, facilities for storage, crews to load and unload goods, and a large variety of cars. But passenger traffic could begin with a single locomotive and a few coaches. Depots and station agents were not essential since fares could be collected on the train.

Therefore, on April 16, 1834, as soon as the workmen finished the 8 miles of line between Boston and Newton, the directors inaugurated passenger service. The whole operation used but a single locomotive, the Stephenson-built *Meteor*; and the schedules consisted of three round trips daily "leaving Boston at 6 and 10 A.M. and 3:30 P.M., and returning at 7 and 11:15 A.M. and 4:45 P.M."[8] The trip from Boston to Newton was made in twenty-eight minutes at an average speed of 18 miles per hour. The directors asserted that "the engine may be made to travel at a much more rapid rate with apparent safety, but this speed has been thought sufficient for the usual rate of travelling."[9]

On November 15, 1834, the railroad extended service to Westborough Center about 35 miles from Boston. The new schedule called for two round trips daily leaving Boston at 7 A.M. and 3:15 P.M., and Westborough at 8 A.M and 2:45 P.M. The railroad used two trains. In the morning the train outbound from Boston to Westborough met the inbound cars at Hopkinton. In the afternoon the trains met at Needham. Stages to or from Worcester connected with all trains, and there was a coordinated rail and stage service between Boston, Hartford, Springfield, Northampton, and Uxbridge.[10] A booking office in Boston sold combined rail-stage tickets to any one of these points. November 1834 also saw the beginning of freight service, but at first the railroad carried almost a negligible tonnage.

The real test came when the line was opened to Worcester on July 4, 1835. After that date passenger traffic doubled as the cars carried 16,000 people each month. And freight assumed importance with an average of about 1,000 tons hauled monthly.[11] The surge of business required three daily passenger trains in each direction as well as a single trip each way by a freight train. The passenger cars steamed over the 45 miles between Boston and Worcester in two hours and forty-five minutes, and the freights took twice that long.[12]

The first few years of operation were a superintendent's nightmare. The Boston & Worcester ran on its single-track line without any signals at all. Superintendent Curtis, aware that collision lurked around every corner, adopted a scheduling system that aimed for rigid control of all train movements. Because his road was relatively short, the superintendent could have the daily passenger trains leave Boston and Worcester at identical times, for example at 6 A.M., 12 noon, and 4 P.M.[13] Thus the inbound and outbound cars could meet at Framingham, the halfway point, and each train could reach its destination well before the next one was scheduled to start.

Curtis timed freights out of Worcester and Boston directly behind the morning passengers, and carefully prescribed where they would meet other traffic. All this worked beautifully provided that there were no breakdowns or extra movements, for the whole arrangement depended entirely upon each train being at the right place at the appointed time.

But sooner or later every engineer faced the perplexing problem of what to do when a train he was supposed to meet was overdue. The rules required him, after forty-five minutes, to detach his engine from its cars and run it ahead to aid the late train.[14] This risked running head-on into a locomotive speeding to make up lost time. Miraculously, however, no scheduled train ever collided with another during the early years. The railroad's wrecks all involved an unscheduled repair train, which emerged as the system's Jonah.

The first incident occurred in October 1837 when a Boston-bound passenger running at full speed plowed into several cars of the standing gravel train near Westborough. Although the passenger engine leaped the tracks and careened into a field, no one was seriously injured, but all were badly frightened.[15] Less than a year later in October 1838 a regular freight rammed the gravel train again. This wreck killed the freight's engineer, Hiram Bridges, who left behind him a widow and several children.[16]

These two accidents exposed a serious problem. In 1838 two connecting railroads were under construction at Worcester: the Western leading to Albany and the Norwich & Worcester running south to Connecticut. Both these lines would funnel a large quantity of new traffic onto the Worcester road, requiring an increase in scheduled trains. To make matters worse, the directors planned to make a bid for the Boston–New York City business by connecting with the steamboats at Norwich.

A daily train that could not have a precise schedule would then appear on the line since storms, winds, and fog often played havoc with the steamship timetables.[17]

In the case of the first wreck the directors took swift action. They met on October 31, 1837, and dismissed the gravel train's overseer for keeping his engine and cars on the main line when he knew the regular train was due. They further recommended that the gravel train be banished from the road altogether.[18] Of course this was not possible, and within a few weeks the repair train emerged again under a master who the superintendent hoped would be more careful.

But increasing traffic demanded more effective action. Urged on by Superintendent Curtis, the directors on February 6, 1839, ordered double tracking of 7 miles of main line between Natick and Hopkinton.[19]

Closely connected with the task of keeping trains on time were the operational hazards of the first winter. Critics maintained that the New England climate would halt trains. Hale termed such assertions rubbish; the winter of 1834–1835 gave the railroad a chance to prove itself. The first troubles came in December, when near-zero temperatures stalled the steam engines by freezing the water before it could be fed into the locomotive boilers. The railroad solved this by heating the water in the storage tanks. But snow was the real enemy, and heavy falls caused much delay and blocked the line completely for three days.[20]

Late trains produced bitter comments from some passengers. The editor of the Northampton *Courier* was stuck on a westbound train that took six hours to make the normal two-hour run between Boston and Westborough. The editor flayed the Worcester management as "deceptive and incompetent" and charged that when the engine on his train got stuck in a snow drift, the engineer had to run to the nearest farm house to get horses to help free the locomotive. Hale answered his critics with an editorial in the *Daily Advertiser*. "We believe," he said, "that the experiment of running Locomotive Engines in such a climate as ours, with the thermometer below zero, has never before been attempted, and it was expected that difficulties would occur, which experience only could overcome. Pipes freezing, wheels slipping on the rails when covered with ice, are impediments which have never been known in England, and which it is acknowledged have on two or three occasions this winter caused detention on the road. To remedy these evils no pains of expense have been spared. Means have been provided to warm the water in the tender, and snow scrapers have been invented, which it is believed will effectually clear the rails as the engine passes, and prevent all such accidents in the future."[21]

To fight snow, the railroad hired special crews with horses at Newton, Needham, Framingham, and Westborough to plow the track after each storm. If the first winter disillusioned some of the passengers, it hit the company's finances even harder, for during the months of December, January, February, and March the railroad sustained a net operating loss of nearly $3,000.[22] During the second winter (1835–1836) the road fared better. It earned an operating profit of almost $900 for the same four months, but storms still plagued the trains. Despite all precautions 2 feet of wet, slushy snow followed by intense cold tied up traffic for more than a week.

By the third winter, however, experience began to win. Superintendent Curtis made all station agents responsible for keeping open a section of track and ordered them to get out during snow storms and clear the road with a team of two horses and four men. In addition special engines ran over the line with snowplows and kept the trains running through the winter of 1836–1837. The improved organization and increasing business enabled the road to make a substantial profit during this period.[23]

Many operating hazards were daily, rather than seasonal. More than thirty grade crossings made the steam engine an intimate part of every town along the line. Fearful citizens predicted that locomotives, horses, and pedestrians would not mix. Hale argued that railways were safe and that if people exercised "normal" care they had nothing to fear.

But the trains had hardly started to run when a spectacular crossing accident confirmed the forebodings of those who saw the iron horse as a fire-breathing monster. In late August 1834 at Newton Crossing, Isaac Hurd, out for a spin with a young lady, drove his carriage in front of an oncoming passenger train. The locomotive killed the horse, reduced the chaise to kindling wood, and left the two badly frightened young people sprawled in a ditch. On September 1, 1834, Hurd stood with his lawyer before the Worcester directors demanding compensation. Alarmed, the board took immediate action to prevent the recurrence of such an accident. The directors prescribed that large white signs be erected on every public highway where it crossed the railway, bearing the warning "LOOK OUT FOR THE ENGINE AND CARS." They also ordered the superintendent to put bells on all locomotives which the firemen would ring vigorously upon approaching crossings.[24]

The following week the directors decided to erect gates attended by a watchman at three busy crossings in Boston, Brighton, and Newton. "With the care which has now been taken on this railroad," commented Hale, "We conceive there is no room to apprehend accidents from this source. If travelers on the highways suffer themselves to be run over, it will be from their own carelessness."[25]

Public feeling ran high on the subject, however, and the legislature left nothing to chance. On April 8, 1835, it passed a law requiring all railroads to put up signs at grade crossings bearing the inscription in "capital letter of at least six or nine inches: RAIL ROAD CROSSING—LOOK OUT FOR THE ENGINE WHILE THE BELL RINGS." And to ensure that the bell would ring, the General Court decreed that all engines be equipped with a bell weighing at minimum 35 pounds, and the legislators decreed that it be rung "at a distance of at least eighty rods from the place of crossing." Finally the legislature empowered the selectmen of any town to force a reluctant railway to install crossing gates and employ watchmen.[26]

The legislative action regulating crossings pointed up the initial relationship between railroad corporations and the Commonwealth. The state lawmakers refused during the early years to prescribe safety measures that interfered with train movements or other matters that affected only those who used the railroad. The General Court also rejected bills attempting to require the companies to provide alternative transportation when snow blocked the tracks. But the legislature acted quickly

118

when the railroad challenged established interests. This was true whether it threatened landowners or the users of roads and highways. The effect was to give the corporation a free hand where railroad patrons only were concerned. The directors scheduled trains as they pleased, raised or lowered fares at will, and in large measure fixed maintenance and safety procedures with no outside interference.[27] Only when the corporation conflicted with innocent bystanders did the legislature act to protect vested rights. Towns had a right to the safe use of their roads, and landowners had a right to expect just compensation for damages caused by railroad construction.

The first years of operation produced some radical changes in the opinions of the railroad proponents. The early promoters argued that Boston must push a railroad westward to keep the trade of Worcester County, regain the business of the Connecticut Valley, and tap the commerce of the Erie Canal. They mentioned passenger traffic as an afterthought.[28] The Boston & Worcester directors' first report predicted that most of the revenues would come from hauling goods. They asserted that the railway would capture the freight normally moved between Boston and Worcester and would stimulate a "great increase in the transportation of some articles, such as wood, ship timber, hay, potatoes, charcoal, mineral coal, lumber, stone, and plaster."[29]

Actual experience confounded these predictions. "The supposed number of travellers on the route of the Boston and Worcester Railroad, according to the estimate of the directors before its construction, was 54,000 per annum, or 174 daily. The average number of travellers thus far . . . has exceeded 400 daily. It is probable that the number of passengers the first year . . . will be equal to three times the estimated number," chortled Nathan Hale in August 1835.[30] Passenger loads from July 1835 through December ranged from 12,000 to 16,000 in the summer months but dropped to half that number in the winter. The first full year of operation, 1836, confirmed that the early passenger surge was no passing fancy. Considerably more than 100,000 people rode the trains that year, and every month of 1836 showed an increase over the corresponding month of 1835.[31]

The board realized that the "transportation of persons is much more productive of profit than that of merchandise," and they aggressively encouraged passenger traffic.[32] With the exception of banning all rail movements on Sunday, the new company attempted to tailor their timetable to business demands. When during the winter of 1835–1836 the number of riders fell to about half that of the summer months, the directors voted to cut the daily round trips between Worcester and Boston from three to two. But when travel increased the following spring, they restored the third train.[33]

Not content with monopolizing the passenger business generated by the towns directly on the tracks, the railroad attempted to lure riders from afar. The Worcester management cooperated with stagecoach operators, who from the first were treated as allies rather than rivals. The railroad established stage connections with trains at various points by offering a cash bonus to the stage for each passenger delivered to the cars. In April 1837 the first such arrangement went into effect when a stage from Waltham met all trains at the West Newton station. Later in 1838 the railroad established through stage-train fares between Boston and Keene, New Hampshire; Brattleboro, Vermont; Norwich, Connecticut; and Albany, New York.[34] Passenger traffic boomed, and with the exception of the panic year of 1838 receipts from this source rose annually.

If the passenger business surprised, the freight traffic disappointed. Whereas the directors estimated the movement of more than 30,000 tons annually, in 1836 the trains carried just over 17,000 tons.[35] In addition the directors found that handling merchandise required large capital expenditures. Although passengers could be accommodated without benefit of stations or great terminals, freight needed costly facilities and agents at every station. In Boston alone the outlay for terminals, wharfs, and warehouses was enormous. The impending completion of the Western Railroad to Albany and of the Norwich & Worcester to the Thames River in Connecticut caused the directors in 1838 to embark on a vast expansion program to serve freight. They purchased land in Boston's South Cove at a cost of more than a quarter of a million dollars and built on it a $160,000 warehouse.[36] This giant building covered nearly

1¼ acres, and it was entered by four separate tracks. Inside crews could load inbound freight directly "from the cars [onto] a platform level with the floor of the cars; and the outward freight [was] loaded from a similar platform upon the other side." The building had scales, which weighed freight "with or without the cars, and . . . apparatus for transferring cars from one track to another."[37] The railroad also built storehouses for bulk items such as grain and cotton and constructed a wharf on the channel that lay at one edge of the South Cove.

Besides buildings and yards, freight required large quantities of rolling stock. During the year 1837 the company had four times as many freight as passenger cars, but revenue from hauling goods amounted to only $80,000 as compared with the $120,000 produced by the passenger department.[38] Freight trains also increased track maintenance since heavy merchandise cars wore the rails at a greater rate than the lighter passenger coaches. As the years went by, freight expenses continued to exceed those for passengers. In 1844, for example, the Boston & Worcester's passenger revenues amounted to more than $240,000, and the cost of doing this business was about $115,000. By contrast the road expended $118,000 to bring in freight revenues of only $176,000.[39]

Throughout the Boston & Worcester's thirty-five-year life the passenger income continued to top that from merchandise, and the freight costs remained higher than those of hauling people. The directors came to regard passenger traffic as the road's mainstay. The Worcester management soon found local freight quite lucrative, too. But the goods from other roads, especially the Western, which at times tried to ship large quantities of flour and grain from Albany to the seacoast at low rates, produced little if any profit. Instead this traffic required large capital outlays in cars and engines as well as in terminal facilities.

The poor showing made by freight during the Boston & Worcester's early years resulted from the directors' misunderstanding. Initially, they did not recognize that large capital improvements were vital to attract freight and that industry and agriculture needed several years to adjust to the new service. In time, however, freight business like passenger traffic soared well above the original estimates. During the year 1841, for example, more than 40,000 tons moved over the Worcester line, compared to the estimate of 30,000 by the directors in 1832.[40]

In their 1832 calculations the directors erred when they assumed that nearly all freight moving between Boston and points within 15 miles of the tracks would use the trains. The directors' conclusions resulted from a survey of traffic on seven major roads leading from Worcester and Middlesex County points to Boston. They estimated that these channels carried about 30,000 tons, of which at least a third was moved by individual farmers taking butter, cheese, pork, wool, and other produce to market. Superficial logic indicated that the rails would carry this traffic since the directors proposed rates of $2.50 a ton, or about one-third of the charges exacted by commercial haulers between Boston and Worcester.[41]

An analysis of the freight business of 1836 indicates that the railroad did divert traffic from the professional teamsters. In that year the trains moved nearly 15,000 tons westward from Boston along the line toward Worcester. This consisted largely of merchandise bound for stores and raw materials for use in factories, especially wool, cotton, coal, and iron. But from Worcester toward Boston the cars carried less than 3,000 tons or just one-fifth of the westbound freight. Most of this consisted of lumber, furniture, and factory products. At first little agricultural produce moved to market by rail.[42]

The reason was clear. Farmers traditionally hauled heavy loads to market. They had their own teams and wagons and the time to make the trip. In fact those who were several miles from the railroad found it nearly as much trouble to cart their produce to a station as to take it directly into Boston. It took a while for farmers to grasp the new frontiers created by rail transportation and time for the railroad to exploit new freight sources. Dairymen were the first to seize the new opportunities. The iron horse made it possible to ship milk into Boston from any point along the Worcester tracks, and in 1837 the company put special cars on passenger trains to take fresh milk into Boston each morning and return the empty containers in the evening. In 1838 the business generated by dairy produce, eggs, and other farm products grew to such proportions that the railroad put on a special freight train to handle it.[43] Simultaneously the Worcester encouraged livestock shipments by setting low carload rates for cattle, sheep, hogs, and calves to the Brighton Cattle Market near Boston.[44]

Industrial traffic, too, grew slowly. At first the railroad accepted freight only at stations. This forced many factories located directly on the tracks to receive and ship goods from a point several miles distant. At the request of several industrialists the directors on May 11, 1835, authorized side tracks to any property adjoining the road, provided the owner guaranteed to ship at least 250 tons a year.[45] Here again volume developed slowly, but starting in 1838 the directors were flooded with requests for spur tracks.

Proper rate making was vital to traffic generation. But no management in the 1830s had experience in this field. Elementary cost factors such as the wear and tear on rails, ties, bridges, cars, and locomotives were not capable of accurate estimates. Not until the 1840s could operating costs be fixed with any degree of confidence.

But to Hale and his board there was only one real consideration, and that was a rate structure that would produce at least a 6 per cent annual dividend. During the period of partial operation from April 1834 until July 1835, the directors set fares at about 25 per cent below the stage rates. The results were heartening; in the first year the trains carried about 100,000 people and earned nearly $36,000. Encouraged, the directors fixed the Boston to Worcester fare at $1.50 or 50 cents below what the stages charged. The board also designated one car on each train a second-class coach, on which fares were reduced 25 per cent. This car, the directors specified, was primarily for the laboring class. The social stigma attached to the second-class coaches, soon called "Irish cars," must have been considerable because although they were run all through the Boston & Worcester's history, they never carried more than 20 per cent of the total passengers, and in most years less than 10 per cent.[46]

The summer passenger flood in 1835 boosted revenue well above the directors' most optimistic predictions. During one two-week period in July and August, passenger receipts topped $7,000, which equaled one-fifth of the railroad's income for its entire first year of operation.[47] The rosy glow faded when winter brought sharply increased operating expenses and a decline in passengers. This together with the disappointing freight revenue caused the directors to consider raising the passenger fares. Hale felt that the company had no alternative because although the trains earned a handsome operating profit, they did not make enough money to pay the 6 per cent dividend that Hale maintained was vital to ensure future railroad growth in Massachusetts. Strongly opposed to raising fares were Daniel Denny and David Henshaw, who argued that in the long run low fares would serve the public better and would earn a greater profit for the railroad as well. The summer passenger rise in 1836 staved off an immediate fare increase, but during the following fall the seasonal passenger slump together with the continued slowness of the freight business again raised the specter of fare boosts. This time Hale, firmly backed by Eliphalet Williams, who as cashier of the City Bank represented one of the road's largest stockholders, proposed that the fare between Boston and Worcester be raised to $2 with corresponding increases to stations along the line. On November 17, 1836, the directors voted five to three in favor of the increase, thus restoring fares traditionally charged by the old Boston and Worcester stages. In theory the increase was to last only during the period from December through March, the months of lean traffic and high operating expenses.[48]

It is difficult to assess the fare boost's effect on travel since it is impossible to separate the people who were discouraged from using the trains because of the high fares from those who were deterred by the panic that broke in 1837 and lasted into 1838. The directors were pleased with the results, however, for they made the new tariff structure permanent, keeping it until April 24, 1839, when they reduced the fares to the original levels of July 1835.[49] Despite a slight drop in passenger volume in 1837, the receipts increased. Although in 1838 passenger revenue dropped about 8 per cent, by 1839 the railroad felt secure financially, and the directors attempted to increase riding and income by a fare cut. The results surpassed the most sanguine estimates, and by 1840 passenger revenue soared more than 50 per cent above the 1838 level.[50]

During the first few years the Worcester board took a cautious attitude toward passenger-fare experiments, for they were unwilling to risk disturbing their major source of income until the railroad was solidly established. In the period from 1835 through mid-1839 the directors refused to make any special rate concessions aside from second-class coaches. They also opposed reductions for customers who rode the trains daily. The issue arose when George Denny applied for a yearly ticket that would entitle him to unlimited rides for the price of $400. Speaking for the board, which rejected this application, a directors' committee composed of David Henshaw, William Jackson, and Eliphalet Williams maintained that if Denny's plea were granted, it would force the railroad to make similar concessions to all regular customers, thus lowering the line's passenger income.[51] By 1839, the road had gained a firm foundation, and the 6 per cent annual dividend seemed secure. Therefore, the board became receptive to experimentation and established local commuter service and reduced rates for regular users.[52]

During its first years the railroad was able to maintain the old stage fares because it offered a radical improvement in service. Trains turned a trip that had formerly consumed most of the day into a short two and three-quarter hours' journey. The speed and ease the cars afforded were clearly apparent to all, and the railroad carried not only those who had used the stages, but it attracted many who had driven their own carriages.

But speed and comfort, so vital to the passenger business, were not so important for freight, for which cost and ease of handling were paramount. Fixing freight rates proved complex and baffling. The period of partial operation from April 1834 until July 1835 demonstrated that even rates substantially less than those charged by teamsters produced a freight volume far below the original estimates.

Fortunately the large and profitable passenger traffic gave the directors latitude to experiment. A freight rate of $2.50 a ton from Boston to Westborough fixed in 1834 proved disappointing even though it was only a third of teamster charges.[53] Still experimenting, the railroad set the initial rates per ton from Boston to Worcester at $3.50. This was competitive with boats between Worcester and Providence on the Blackstone Canal, and it was $5 a ton less than horse and wagon cartage.[54] However, the directors soon found that a straight tonnage charge on all goods was not practical. Even though the railroad was too short to have a conflict between local and long distance or "through" freight, it still had to recognize that some commodities had such low intrinsic values that they could not afford a high tariff. Furthermore there was an imbalance of traffic; the trains carried five tons toward Worcester for every ton they moved toward Boston, and many cars rattled empty as they returned eastward along the line.

The whole question of rate revision came to a head in 1837. Indecision and uncertainty plagued the board; for two weeks they lowered the rates on coal, lumber, lime, and plaster. Then after much discussion they authorized a completely new rate schedule, which went into effect in November.[55] Although the new tariff retained the basic levy of $3.50 per ton on general merchandise between Boston and Worcester, it set special rates to encourage shipments of specific items. Coal, plaster, pig iron, and sand, sent in quantities of not less than 50 tons went at $3 per ton. Simultaneously the charge was raised for extra bulky, valuable, or dangerous items like feathers, domestic wool, and oil of vitriol.

To stimulate the flow of traffic toward Boston, the directors lowered the general merchandise rate (Worcester to Boston) to $3 per ton and fixed the charge for lumber at $2 per ton. The board also set a scale to way stations between Boston and Worcester. Charges ranged from a maximum on general merchandise of $3 per ton at Grafton to $2 at Framingham.[56] However, the railroad in effect made the Framingham tariff a minimum rate. Therefore it cost $2 whether a shipper sent goods 8 miles between Boston and Newton or 22 miles between Boston and Framingham. The only exception was for items the cars would not otherwise carry; thus the trains took coal between Boston and Newton for 84 cents a ton in quantities of 50 tons or more.

The tariff schedule of 1837 contained two principles that guided the Boston & Worcester management throughout its history. The first of these was that freight rates ought to reflect the value of the product carried. This axiom, which became standard on every railroad in the country, was forced on the Worcester management by hard experience. Coal, for example, was in 1837 just beginning to rival wood as a fuel for heating and for use in blacksmith shops and forges. The value of a ton of Pennsylvania coal delivered in Boston was about $7.50.[57] The freight rate on coal, whether $3 or $3.50 per ton represented a huge part of its cost delivered in Worcester. Since coal was locked in sharp competition with wood, the price at the Worcester depot might determine whether it could compete or not. Hence the railroad found itself in a position where setting a rate of $3.50 per ton might drive coal from the market and thus eliminate hauling it as a source of revenue. The problem facing the Boston & Worcester management was to determine whether the railroad could afford to take coal at a rate that would allow it to sell in Worcester and still produce a "profit" for the corporation—a tricky operation. The railroad would find it "profitable" to haul coal as long as that commodity paid the direct cost of its transportation (labor for loading and unloading, the cost of providing cars, locomotives, fuel, et cetera) plus a modest amount that could be applied to the general operating and fixed costs of the system (maintenance of track, locomotives, terminals, management, capital, et cetera).

If the railroad hauled all freight at the rate charged for coal, it would lose money. But the corporation made up for this on items like wool, for which the transportation costs were only a small part of the article's value. A charge of $4 per ton on wool was hardly noticed since that product sold in 1837 for between 30 and 50 cents per pound or from $600 to $1,000 per ton.[58]

The Worcester management could justify moving coal at a low rate as long as the charge paid the whole direct cost of its transportation and made a contribution, even a slight one, to the general operating and fixed costs of the line. A rate for coal that paid operating and fixed costs as well as a dividend to the stockholders might drive coal from both its market and

127

the trains; high rates on low-value commodities, therefore, tended to remove the contribution they might otherwise make to fixed and operating costs, thus leaving the entire burden of these charges to fall upon other goods. In brief, not hauling coal might have resulted in still higher charges for wool, cotton, and high-value manufactured items.

The problem in rate making came in the determination of the exact transportation expenses. This involved separating the passenger from the freight expenses, and the fixed from the operating costs. In this process there was much confusion and room for error, especially in the first twenty years, when the expenses for such basic items as renewal or repair of rails, bridges, locomotives and cars was not known for certain or became submerged in capital expansion programs.

For the first ten years all attempts to determine the precise operating costs were rough approximations. It was impossible to find the break-even point for hauling any item and thus difficult to "justify" any rate. The directors, therefore, set rates on the principle of "what the traffic would bear" rather than on a detailed knowledge of what was "right" for both the railroad and the product. Pragmatic freight rates worked well as long as bulky, low-value articles made up a small proportion of the freight. But pragmatism backfired when, after the opening of the Western Railroad to Albany, a flood of flour and grain poured on to the Boston & Worcester, all of which needed the lowest possible rate in order to make Boston competitive with New York as a port city.

Thus after 1841 the Worcester management found itself in a trap of its own making. They had built into their rate structure the principle of charging only what the traffic could afford. They had done this with the idea that they would carry no item at a loss—that is, below the out-of-pocket operational costs. Unfortunately the Worcester board was unable to pinpoint the exact costs of operation. It was, therefore, vulnerable in the fight over rates against the combined interests of the Western Railroad and Boston's grain and flour exporters. This debate lasted for twenty-seven years, or until the Worcester road was merged with the Western to form the Boston and Albany Railroad.

The second major principle contained in the freight tariff of 1837 was that of a high minimum charge. The flat rate of $2 per ton on all general merchandise made those who shipped a ton 8 miles to Newton pay almost two-thirds of the cost of shipping the same ton to Worcester. The directors clearly understood that distance alone was not an adequate guide. Many costs such as loading and unloading, providing terminals, cars, and station agents were the same whether goods moved 1 mile or 40 miles. It was therefore easy to justify the high minimum rates. This question became vitally important because after the completion of the Western Railroad to Albany, the Worcester line thought of itself as a giant 40-mile terminal in its dealings with the Western. The concept of high terminal costs became almost a fixation with the Worcester directors, who argued that the road's huge investment in stations, yards, warehouses, and other facilities in Boston ought to be an important consideration when joint rates were set for the two corporations. This, too, became a matter of bitter dispute between the Worcester and the Western when they attempted to divide joint receipts.

The Worcester management faced constant demands from big shippers who wanted special concessions. The board could meet these requests by lowering the charges across the board on the shipment of certain items in quantity, as they had done with coal; but it was also possible to make special contracts with individual customers. The railroad made the first such arrangement in April 1837 with Robert Earle of Worcester, giving him a nine-month contract to ship lime, flour, and plaster from Boston to Worcester at reduced charges. The directors, instead of renewing Earle's privileges, made the concessions granted to him part of the general tariff in 1839.[59] The railroad, however, did not abandon individual agreements and continued in the 1840s to make them in both passenger and freight service.[60] At no time did the directors attempt to rig competition, but general public mistrust and fear of abuses caused the General Court in 1850 to outlaw all special rate agreements and to require that freight tariffs be printed and publicly displayed and that any concession apply on equal terms to all shippers.[61] From that date on, the railroad placated pressure groups by building into the regular tariff charges that favored certain items.

On the whole the Boston & Worcester's early rate and fare policies were sound. By keeping passenger fares at high levels the directors ensured the inflow of money to pay dividends, and this in turn secured the additional funds for expansion. Between 1835 and 1842 the railroad more than doubled its capital from $1,000,000 to $2,300,000. This money—raised by the sale of new stock, which always sold at prices in excess of its $100 per share par value—went toward the construction of terminal facilities, the purchase of new equipment, and the double-tracking of the entire distance between Boston and Worcester, which was finished in 1843. In addition the railroad always enjoyed a superior credit rating, which was useful in the negotiation of short-term loans at low interest rates.[62]

In the matter of freight tariffs, the directors, while at all times cautious, set rates that were competitive with the water competition on the Blackstone Canal and that cut the cost of land transportation at least in half. The freight policy avoided rash experimentation that might have plunged the road into financial chaos or that might have resulted in unpopular rate increases in the future. Instead the Worcester management laid the basis for a slow but steady growth of local traffic. This allowed industrialists and farmers to build new factories or to raise new products dependent upon the railroad with the certain knowledge that rates would remain stable or would gradually be lowered. By 1839 the road found itself in a position to make significant reductions in both passenger and freight charges.

If President Hale led his system toward a conservative rate-making policy, he took bold action to initiate dividends. The first train had not yet steamed between Boston and Worcester when the board of directors formed a committee to investigate the company's revenue with a view toward paying a dividend.[63] This committee, under Hale's chairmanship, made its report on June 26, 1835. Although it found that the railroad had not received more than $60,000 in passenger and freight revenues and had incurred expenses of nearly $40,000, it recommended a 2 per cent dividend amounting to $25,000. Thus the committee proposed that the railroad pay in dividends $5,000 more than the trains had actually earned. Hale obscured this by a bit of financial sleight of hand; he added to the freight revenue a sum of $6,250, which he maintained was due to the railroad for hauling its own goods, some "3,000 tons of iron and 500 tons of sleepers and other materials to Needham, Hopkinton, and Westboro," moved during construction.[64] In effect the committee proposed to pay out as a dividend the money the stockholders had paid in as capital.

A close examination of this report indicates that the railroad's ability to pay a return upon its stock in July 1835 depended solely on an optimistic view of the corporation's future revenue. This point is emphasized by the fact that Hale's committee underestimated the road's expenses (car and locomotive maintenance and track repair) by charging most of the funds for these items to the construction account. Thus to declare a dividend in July 1835 was to gamble on a sharp revenue increase, which fortunately did occur. Hale's rosy view of the company's future earnings was not shared by the entire board, for two directors, George Bond and David Henshaw, voted against the majority.[65]

Six months later there was no doubt about the road's ability to pay a return on its capital. The only question was how much. This time a committee composed of Eliphalet Williams, George Bond, and George W. Pratt determined that the trains had earned a net profit of slightly more than $51,000. They recommended, and it was unanimously agreed, to pay out $50,000 of this as a 4 per cent dividend.[66] Even here the committee underestimated the road's expenses for upkeep, although they allowed twice as much for this purpose as the Hale committee had six months previously. In August 1836 President Hale and Eliphalet Williams made a strong bid to force through a further 2½ per cent dividend and thus realize their goal of a 6 per cent per annum return upon the stock. To add power to this drive, R. H. Winslow made a special trip to Boston from New York and put in one of his rare appearances at a board meeting. But the other directors pleaded caution and defeated the dividend by a vote of six to three.[67]

The passing of the second dividend in 1836 and the increase

in passenger fares that fall put the Worcester road in a strong position to weather the panic of 1837. Encouraged by a substantial increase of gross revenue during 1837, the railroad declared two dividends totaling 8 per cent. Although this proved too high a rate to maintain, the road never thereafter paid less than a 6 per cent return. The constantly increasing passenger and freight traffic allowed the company to maintain its 6 per cent rate and even pay as high as 10 per cent some years on a capital that grew to $4,500,000.

The Boston & Worcester's operation from 1834 to 1840 demonstrated that railroads were practical beyond the most sanguine claims made for them during the promotional era of the 1820s. The success of the Worcester and of its two sister roads, the Lowell and the Providence, created a railroad mania that swept through Massachusetts with the speed of lightning. Not only had Hale and his colleagues proved that the iron horse could carry people and freight at the unheard of speeds of 20 and 30 miles an hour, but they demonstrated that investors could reap a substantial profit from such an enterprise. In less than a decade Hale's grand experiment managed to break through the prejudice and reluctance that had blocked private finance and state support of a railroad to Albany. By 1840 private and state resources found themselves working side by side to lay bands of iron to connect the capital of Massachusetts with the capital of New York.

CHAPTER VII

Financing the Western Railroad

IN MARCH 1833 the Massachusetts General Court granted the Boston & Worcester's directors a charter, which vested in them control of a new railroad company that had the right to build a line westward from Worcester to Springfield and thence to the New York boundary in Berkshire County. This charter resulted from Nathan Hale's belief that the Boston & Worcester was only the beginning of a great trunk route to Albany, and it made certain that any such enterprise would funnel into the Boston & Worcester.

The legislature molded the new body, termed the Western Railroad Corporation, after the initial Bay State railway laws. The Western Corporation received a thirty-year monopoly of the traffic between Worcester and Hampden County and the freedom to charge tolls, which could be regulated by the state only after ten years, and then only if they produced a net income of more than 10 per cent per annum on the railroad's capital. The Western had until December 1, 1838, to locate its line, and the owners of the Worcester railroad were to have first preference in the purchase of the stock. Thus by all logic the Boston to Albany railroad should have come under the control of a single management with a single purpose. Such, however, was not to be the case.

During the Worcester line's construction, the Western's charter lay dormant, awaiting the outcome of Hale's grand experiment. But the beginning of train service on the Worcester in 1834 sparked renewed interest in the Western. In that year, a railroad fever swept through America, and projects multiplied by the dozens in each state. In New England all important towns had one or more railroad schemes afoot. High on the list of projects was a line linking New York City with Boston. Hartford in particular envisioned itself as a way station on a direct route between Boston and Manhattan. In 1835

Hartford's General Johnson proposed that his city build directly to Worcester to intercept the B&W and at the same time forge a line southward toward New York City.[1] For a short while the effort to bind the Empire State's metropolis with Massachusetts' capital eclipsed the dream of a line from Boston to Albany.

The Western Railroad also had its strong advocates in Albany, Pittsfield, Springfield, and Boston. Berkshire County, tired of its isolation, was determined to secure better communication with its markets. Industrial Pittsfield, which had vainly supported a state railroad from Boston to the Hudson, quickly lent its backing, but its main effort soon focused on building between the New York State line and Albany or Hudson. The two New York cities responded favorably to this idea since both were anxious to expand their trade with western Massachusetts. Bowing to this pressure in May 1834, the New York Legislature chartered the Castleton and West Stockbridge.[2] This road had the united support of Albany's merchants and Pittsfield's factory owners, whose products still went via costly turnpikes to markets along the Hudson River. These promoters planned to make their road the New York connection for the Western Railroad, if such were ever constructed, but they were ready to act alone if necessary.

The chief Massachusetts advocate of the Albany road was the Pittsfield textile manufacturer Lemuel Pomeroy, who whipped up enthusiasm at meetings both in Berkshire County and in New York State and led the list of stockholders in the new company.[3] Writing in July 1835, he lamented that nothing had been done to activate the Western, but he was "determined to have a railroad from this place [Pittsfield] to the state line [and on to the Hudson], and that *forthwith*."[4] Four months later Albany's Hermanus Bleeker, speaking in Boston's Faneuil Hall, expressed the same sentiment when he declared, "whether Boston decide[s] to make the Road from Worcester to West Stockbridge or not, the Road from Albany to West Stockbridge will be built."[5]

No single Bay State community had more hopes for the Western Railroad than Springfield, for in 1835 that Connecticut River town stood on the threshold of a great boom. The first

134

of its giant textile mills was just swinging into full production, and the local men in conjunction with Boston capitalists were planning additional factories. Springfield's leaders felt that their town could become the unchallenged commercial emporium of western Massachusetts if only they could make it the Connecticut Valley's transportation hub.

George Bliss, who was deeply involved in Springfield's banking, real estate, and industrial development, led the railroad forces there. Bliss saw his native town locked in a battle with Hartford for the supremacy of the Connecticut Valley. The move for a "direct line" between New York City and Boston seemed to him part of a clever plot to make Hartford the trading center of central Connecticut and western Massachusetts. Bliss noted that Hartford proposed not only a railroad from Worcester to Hartford and on to Manhattan, but also a line from Hartford to Albany. This plan threatened the Western Railroad with competition along its entire length. It would be difficult enough to raise capital without this menace; but with it the Western was through.[6]

Bliss therefore pushed for a railroad between Hartford and Springfield, and for the activation of the Western charter so that both the Boston–Albany and the Boston–New York traffic would pass through his native town. In January 1835 the Springfield *Gazette* summed up local sentiment: "We have but little apprehension that the citizens of Boston . . . will be disposed to avoid this town by extending [the Boston & Worcester] directly to Hartford, merely to facilitate commerce between Boston and New York, when by coming directly to this town, the same object may be nearly as well attained, and at the same time the trade of this section of the state which now principally goes to the city of New York be secured to our own metropolis."[7] The large Boston investment in local industry increased the town's confidence in the Western's early construction.

A mass meeting on February 16, 1835, called for a convention to be held in Worcester on March 5 to consider the building of a railroad between that place and Springfield.[8] Nearly one hundred delegates from towns along the proposed line attended, and they enthusiastically supported moves to activate the Western charter. The only exception was the Worcester delegation, which believed that the extension of the railroad from Boston past its terminus in Worcester would be injurious to its business interests.[9] Out of this meeting came a committee headed by Bliss, which raised $7,000, mainly from Springfield merchants, for an accurate survey of the line between Worcester and the Connecticut River.[10]

A delighted Hale made the Boston & Worcester's engineer, Colonel Fessenden, available to the committee for the survey. Fessenden's report, reprinted in the Hampden *Whig* of July 30, 1835, estimated that the Springfield to Worcester railroad would cost $1,200,000 and that it would earn a net income of more than 16 per cent per annum.[11] This document received wide circulation and served in lieu of a prospectus for the Western's stock solicitations.

Meanwhile the backers of the New York–Boston direct line called a railroad convention at Worcester on July 2, 1835. This move, together with an act passed by the Connecticut Legislature in May 1835 that chartered the Worcester and Hartford Company "to construct a Railroad from the termination of the Hartford and New Haven Railroad, in Hartford, to the northern boundary of the State, in the most direct and feasible route towards Worcester . . . ," frightened the Western's proponents.[12] They turned the Worcester convention into a general railroad assembly attended by representatives from over one-fifth of all the towns in Massachusetts and Connecticut. Speakers advocated three main roads: the Worcester–Springfield line presented by George Bliss, the Worcester–Norwich line proposed by John Rockwell and the Worcester–Hartford "direct line" urged by General Johnson.[13] Although the gathering took no action, popular enthusiasm together with pressure applied by Springfield convinced the directors of the Boston & Worcester to open the books for stock subscription in the Western on August 3, 1835.

This act brought the Western proponents face to face with the problem of finance, the nemesis that had stalked the Boston to Albany line for over a decade. Compared with the Western, the Worcester was a puny effort indeed—only one-third the length and free of the construction problems involved in rising over 1,800 feet above the Connecticut Valley. Engineers maintained that a road with an easy grade could be built across the Berkshire Hills, but this would require deep cuts, high bridges, and long tunnels, which would raise construction costs well above those on the B&W.

The 44-mile Worcester road had been capitalized at a million dollars, but in 1835 experience indicated that its real cost would run to $1,500,000 or more. Even the Western's most ardent supporters found it impossible to maintain that their road could be built for less than 3 million dollars, or three times the Worcester's initial capitalization. To make matters worse, the country through which the Western passed was sparsely populated. Springfield had but 8,000 people, and Pittsfield not more than 3,600. Passenger traffic, which had been the backbone of the Worcester's revenue, would flow less readily on the Western, and even the promise of a greater amount of freight could not be taken with too much optimism after the Worcester's experience.

The Western's charter called for a total capital of 2 million dollars. The Worcester's directors, in consultation with the Springfield men, decided not to seek an increase; it might be impossible to raise a larger sum, and the 2 million dollars would be enough to get trains running from Worcester to Springfield and from Pittsfield or Lee to the state line, where they would connect with the Albany & West Stockbridge. The success of these segments would make it easy to get additional capital, or if not, state aid would complete the route.

Nathan Hale realized that Pittsfield and Albany had but little capital and that even Springfield could raise no more than $200,000, but he had high hopes that Boston and New York City would buy most of the shares. He had good reason for his confidence; by 1835 New Yorkers held almost 45 per cent of the Worcester Corporation and an equally large segment of the Boston & Providence.[14] Earlier, in fact, Hale refused an offer to sell the Western's entire stock in Manhattan because he feared that "it might throw the whole enterprise into the vortex of the stock gambling operations of Wall Street." In addition the

Boston editor felt that this might deliver the railway, so vital to Massachusetts' commerce, into the hands of its greatest rival.[15]

Reality soon smashed Hale's optimism. An intensive ten-day campaign disposed of only 13,000 of the 20,000 shares. Boston subscribed for 8,500 shares, and Springfield and other Massachusetts towns took 4,500, but "the subscription fell short of the anticipation . . . in the city of New York."[16]

The Western's promoters quickly interpreted this rejection as proof that the Boston to Albany line struck at the heart of New York City's Erie trade. To emphasize this, Hale printed a letter dated in New York on August 13, 1835, which read: "We shall not for our part subscribe a cent which shall tend to divert any part of the business of this city to Boston. The Bostonians are a very clever and enterprising people, but we shall not let them *come Yankee over us*, so far as to make a road to direct our trade to their city with our means."[17] The Hale strategy won the railroad substantial support in New England's metropolis.[18] Amasa Walker, a leading shoe merchant, asserted that a railroad to Albany "would be to Boston what the great Erie Canal was to New York, vast in expense, but magnificent in results. The citizens of Boston . . . alone must do the work. The New Yorkers are too good judges of the case . . . to give their money to an enterprise which they know would be injurious to their city."[19]

The Western found its staunchest advocates among Bostonians interested in manufacturing, wholesaling, and ocean commerce. Edmund Dwight and his partner James K. Mills together with Thomas H. Perkins, William Appleton, Abbot Lawrence, William Sturgis, and Israel Thorndike had financed Springfield's industrial development and had a stake in improving transportation to that city.[20] Almost equally enthusiastic were the heads of Boston's big mercantile houses, such as Amasa Walker and Thomas B. Wales. Walker had come to Boston from North Brookfield, a town halfway between Worcester and Springfield on the proposed Western Railroad. He started his career as a shoe manufacturer but later founded the Boston house of Allen, Harris, and Potter, which became one of the nation's largest wholesale shoe concerns.[21] Writing

BOSTON AND WORCESTER
RAILROAD.

WINTER ARRANGEMENT.

On and after Tuesday next, November 1st, the Accommodation Trains will run daily, except Sundays, as follows :—

Leave Boston at **7 A. M., 1 P. M. and 3 P. M.**
Leave Worcester at half past **6** and **9 A. M., and 4 P. M.**

The first and last trains from Boston, and the second and third from Worcester, will connect with the trains of the Western Railroad.

The first and second trains from Boston, and the second train from Worcester, will connect with the Norwich Railroad.

THE NEW YORK STEAMBOAT TRAIN,
VIA NORWICH,

Will leave Boston at **4 P. M.**

A Mail Train will run on Sunday. From Worcester at half past 6 A. M.; from Boston at **2 P. M.**

☞ All Baggage at the risk of its owner.

WM. PARKER, Superintendent.

Boston, October 25, 1842.

D. CLAPP, JR. Printer....184 Washington St.

Figure 12

The winter advertisement of 1842 finds the Boston & Worcester Railroad emphasizing through travel to New York City and Albany.

Figure 13

The Boston & Worcester's *Fury,* a 22-ton wood-burning passenger locomotive built by Seth Wilmarth, a South Boston locomotive builder in 1849.

Figure 14

The Western Railroad's *Addison Gilmore* as it was upon its construction in 1851 prior to its rebuilding as a 4–4–0. This was the first locomotive to be constructed by the Western Railroad in its own shops.

under the pen name "South Market Street," Walker flooded the *Daily Advertiser and Patriot* with articles which stressed that without a direct western outlet Boston's commission houses would become satellites of New York.[22]

The outstanding spokesman for the old overseas shipping magnates, who still felt that Boston could rival New York as a port, was Josiah Quincy, Jr., whose father had served as Boston's mayor from 1825 to 1829. Josiah, Jr., had been nurtured in New England's tradition of ocean commerce, and Boston wharf property held a high place among his many interests. He took a leading part in the South Cove Corporation, and he dreamt of western grain flowing to European markets through Massachusetts Bay. Quincy became the champion of those who fought for low freight rates on breadstuffs moving from the West to the port of Boston.[23]

The men of eastern Massachusetts who rallied to the Western were in a peculiar position. They wanted the line, but they hesitated to take the financial risk of building what they considered a poor investment. The fact that 1835 was a boom year only seemed to increase the lure of textile plants, for New Englanders found it hard to pass up investments that paid an average dividend of 15 per cent in favor of a railroad projected through the wilds of western Massachusetts.[24] And New York's rejection did not increase the enthusiasm of the conservative Bostonians, who still wanted to minimize the probable loss by diffusing the stock ownership.

The railroad promoters decided to make a thorough canvass of all Boston and nearby towns in a final effort to sell the remaining 7,000 shares. A mass meeting at Faneuil Hall on October 7, 1835, heard Daniel Webster proclaim that Massachusetts was, or at least ought to be, very little "worse off than New York. If New York has a great navigable river," he maintained, "Massachusetts has what New York wants, a vast sea coast. What both wanted was a great line of artificial communication running inward to the West. New York has constructed hers and has other mighty works of the same character in progress; and all that Massachusetts needs, is by a work of very moderate extent not merely to recover the trade of her own territory, but to acquire a fair share, a large and

139

growing share of the commerce of the boundless West."[25] The meeting voted to appoint a committee of six persons for the City of Boston at large, and three additional men in each ward and three men each for South Boston, Charlestown, Lynn, Cambridge, and Roxbury to solicit subscriptions for the Western Railroad.

After the meeting, the canvassers went out with instructions from Edward Everett to miss no one from "capitalist to car-man."[26] It was a long, hard process, and the promoters found it necessary to call another assembly on November 20, but finally on December 5, the last share had been subscribed. Something of the spirit of this effort can be detected from this passage in the diary of Josiah Quincy, Jr., who served as one of the Boston solicitors.

> Nov. 24, 1835. I went over the list of the voters in my ward to find out who had not subscribed in order to call upon every man who is able, to learn whether he is willing to help out with this great undertaking.
>
> November 25, 1835. Went round with Mr. Edmund Dwight to obtain subscriptions for the Western Railroad, and they all with one accord began to make excuses. Some think the city is large enough and do not want to increase it. Some have no faith in legislative grants of charters since the fate of the Charlestown bridge, and very few say they won't subscribe. It is the most unpleasant business I ever engaged in.[27]

When the smoke of promotion cleared, the railroad found itself with more than 2,800 individual stockholders who held an average of between eight and nine shares each. Since more than one hundred persons owned nearly 40 per cent of the stock, the majority held between one and four shares, or no more than $400 worth at par value.

More than 15,000 shares, or 75 per cent of the total, were held in Boston and its suburbs. Springfield subscribed for almost 2,000 shares, or 10 per cent, and Albany for less than 3 per cent. New York City held a mere 180 shares, and the remaining amount, about 10 per cent, or 2,000 shares, was pledged for by subscribers in various towns along the line, mainly in Berkshire County. Worcester's attitude toward the railroad can be gauged by the fact that its citizens held not a single share![28]

The railroad's financial rock was the Boston industrial community, particularly that part of it involved in the Springfield factories. James K. Mills took 200 shares, which made him the railroad's largest single stockholder, but the list of those who subscribed for more than 100 shares also embraced Nathan Appleton, A. & A. Lawrence & Co., William Lawrence, Thomas H. Perkins, and Israel Thorndike of Boston, as well as George Bliss, D. & J. Ames, Jonathan Dwight, and Henry Sterns of Springfield.[29]

On January 5, 1836, the stockholders at their first assembly elected a slate of directors that included George Bliss, Edmund Dwight, Thomas B. Wales, William Lawrence, and Josiah Quincy, Jr.[30] Before adjourning, the shareholders urged the directors to seek state aid. Three days later the board made a Boston merchant, Thomas B. Wales, president; Ellis Gray Loring, clerk; and Josiah Quincy, Jr., treasurer. Two basic problems confronted the new management: the commencement of the work on the line and the raising of capital. Finances were by far the more pressing issue. The directors were aware that it was easy to get people to sign stock pledges but that it would be difficult to make them pay their assessments. Many citizens had taken shares merely to get rid of the canvassers, secure in the knowledge that a subscriber could pay the first $5 assessment and surrender his stock with almost complete immunity.[31] Also hanging over the road was the fear that the project could not be finished even if the entire capital of 2 million dollars were raised. Thus as almost the first order of business the directors decided to press for state aid, which they believed would supply the needed additional funds and encourage the original stockholders to meet their assessments.[32]

The directors knew that any scheme for government support required a turnabout by the legislature. But now the railroad promoters were better prepared than ever before to convince the General Court that the time had come to aid internal improvements. Prosperity surged through the Bay State in the period from 1830 to 1837. Massachusetts was beginning to reconcile itself to the decline of ocean shipping, to the loss of the West India trade, and to the decay of the old agricultural order. The new generation had its eyes on industry. The new trends quieted earlier fears that a depressed Commonwealth could ill afford a project that might fail financially and throw a crushing tax burden upon waning seaports and decadent rural villages.

Furthermore the dramatic construction of the first three Boston railways convinced all but the most confirmed doubting Thomases that these ventures were practicable and profitable. Most Bay Staters were too conservative to want to risk much of their own substance in so novel an enterprise, but these same men were now willing to allow the state to take the chance. The new prosperity and the hope that railroads could eventually pay their own way caused every town to envision state aid for a line to its door. Gone was the feeling that only one grand trunk route could be constructed. Governor Everett's Whig administration was soon advocating state support for a railroad network radiating from Boston to all parts of his Commonwealth.[33]

Against this background the Western launched its campaign for 1 million dollars of state support. To manage the effort, the directors selected two of their number experienced in the ways of the legislature. George Bliss and Justice Willard seriously investigated three main approaches: a direct subscription by the state for 1 million dollars of stock, indirect aid by a government guarantee of railway bonds, or the incorporation of a special bank with a capital of 5 million dollars, which for twenty years would pay its annual tax to the railroad instead of the state.[34]

Although Bliss and Willard preferred outright state purchase of the railroad's stock, they decided that the effort had a better chance on Beacon Hill if government aid were coupled with the bank issue.[35] Bliss's strategy worked better than he dared hope. Jackson's war on Nicholas Biddle and the Bank of the United States produced substantial Massachusetts sentiment for a large central bank that could fill the vacuum that would be created by the destruction of Biddle's institution. Over 1,700 Bostonians had petitioned the legislature for permission to establish a state bank with a capital of 10 million dollars.

142

William Lawrence, one of the Western's directors, who also sat on the General Court's committee on banks seized this opportunity. The bank advocates eagerly welcomed the Western's overtures, and the two groups quickly combined forces by writing into the proposed charter of the "State Bank of Massachusetts" a proviso requiring its directors to buy 1 million dollars of Western Railroad stock.[36]

The union of the bank and the railroad frightened the Democrats, who opposed the formation of a "monster" monied institution. But this time the towns friendly to the Western Railroad had sent representatives to the General Court in large numbers. Even more important, the railroad had won significant support in Franklin and Hampshire Counties, including the editors of the influential Northampton *Courier* and the Greenfield *Mercury*.[37] The railroad's friends worked ceaselessly to create the impression that their project had the overwhelming approval of the whole Commonwealth.

The combined onslaught shattered opposition, especially after a motion to postpone the whole issue to the next General Court failed by a large vote. In a desperate move to defeat the hated monied monster, the Democrats, led by Representative Hubbell of Lanesboro, sponsored a bill that divorced the bank from the railroad. Hubbell's act simply increased the Western's stock by 1 million dollars to be subscribed by the state. In addition the bill specified that three of the railroad's nine directors be appointed by the legislature. The house gave this measure its rousing support, voting for it 243 to 9. The senate, too, approved, except that the upper house amended the act to require that the state pay its assessments only if 75 per cent of the same assessment had also been paid by the private shareholders. This ensured that the individual stockholders could not shirk their payments and throw the entire financial burden upon the Commonwealth. Governor Everett signed the act, and the state became a one-third partner in the Western on April 4, 1836. Meanwhile, separated from the railroad, the state bank was dropped.[38]

Massachusetts did not finance its purchase of railroad stock out of tax revenue, but by state scrip sold in London as each assessment fell due. To pay the interest and eventually to redeem the scrip, all dividends received upon the stock went into a special sinking fund along with one-half of all money raised by the sale of state-owned land in Maine. The result was happy.[39] After 1845 the Western paid regular dividends, which by 1857 were sufficient to redeem the scrip. By 1845 the railroad's shares sold on Boston's stock exchange at par value, and they became a real asset to the Commonwealth, which in 1854 used 3,700 of its shares to endow the Massachusetts school fund.[40]

The Commonwealth's decision to become a partner in the Western produced joy in the railroad camp; for the first time a railway to the Hudson seemed within grasp. In April 1836 the board ordered engineers to fix the road's location between Worcester and Springfield. Simultaneously, the directors set about collecting the initial $10 per share necessary to formally activate the company.[41] This, however, proved no easy task, for although nearly 90 per cent of the shareholders paid with little hesitation, the remainder had either moved away leaving no address or confessed that they had taken stock merely to start the railroad, but that they had no intention of paying any assessment beyond an initial $5. Fortunately the Western had a sum of several thousand dollars contributed by Harrison Gray Otis, David Sears, and a few other rich Bostonians, and the directors used this money to pay the initial $10 on each delinquent share.[42]

Major construction started in January 1837. In April the directors laid the fifth $5 assessment to raise funds for grading the line between Worcester and Brookfield. But almost as they did so, the financial panic of 1837 broke. This storm made the difficult task of collecting assessments an impossible one. Overnight loose capital vanished; the Western's directors estimated that their stockholders sustained losses of 20 million dollars.[43] As more and more shareholders pleaded financial embarrassment, the directors succumbed to the inevitable and postponed payments.[44]

In the midst of the financial panic the engineers delivered another shock. Their new surveys revealed that rails between Worcester and the New York state line could not be laid for less than 4 million dollars or over 1 million dollars more than the highest previous estimate.[45] The railroad seemed doomed. In May, William Appleton and William Sturgis requested the board to stop all work until the corporation's financial status was clarified, and the directors ordered the engineers to stop accepting bids for grading on that part of the line between Brookfield and the Connecticut River.[46]

In desperation the promoters turned again to the state. In a bid to lay the problem before the public, Emory Washburn, then one of Worcester's representatives in the General Court and a future governor of the Commonwealth, bluntly stated that "every effort on the part of the stockholders has been exhausted—every scheme has been tried to its utmost limit, and nothing remains for them but to abandon the enterprise, or for the Legislature to grant prompt, adequate and efficient aid."[47]

Washburn put the problem clearly. Until 1837 both the Worcester and the Western had been financed wholly by the sale of stock in the United States, mainly in Massachusetts and New York. Both companies had overlooked the large reservoirs of foreign capital in Britain and in continental Europe. When pounds had been needed to purchase English iron or locomotives, the Worcester directors had bought British exchange from Boston banks with dollars raised in America.

But in 1837 the Western could no longer ignore foreign capital. The Commonwealth had a negligible debt and one of the largest and wealthiest populations in the nation. In addition it had a reputation for fiscal integrity unmatched by any other state in the Union. The proponents of public aid argued that the monetary crisis made it imperative to leave "the shattered remains of private fortunes, to fill the usual channels of a reviving course of business" and to extend the state's credit as a "shield" over the railroad.[48]

The Western's shareholders put forth definite proposals at a special meeting held in Boston's Old Court House on November 23, 1837. They recommended that the state underwrite $2,400,000 in bonds, an amount equal to 80 per cent of the railroad's capital. In return, the stockholders agreed to give the state a first mortgage on the road, in which they had invested $600,000, which equalled a payment of $20 on each share.[49]

The bid for state aid received wide support throughout the Commonwealth. Financial crisis had not destroyed the hope that eventually a railroad to Albany would earn a profit. Speaking before the legislature, Emory Washburn argued that to abandon the work would be to delay for years if not forever, the prospect of an artery to tap the trade of the Great West. "Six hundred thousand dollars," he emphasized, "have already been expended . . . every dollar of which will be lost. Farms along the line of the road have been cut up and injured by the work already done, and individuals who have generously given up their lands for the public use, will find themselves deceived in the hope that their sacrifices were to enure to the public benefit."[50]

The railroad itself in its "Address to the People" added other arguments, not the least of which was that specie from abroad would ease the financial crisis in Massachusetts by bringing new money into local banks and by allowing construction to proceed, thus giving employment to thousands. "If we arm the . . . banks in Massachusetts with $2,400,000 of exchange on England, it will furnish in the spring an amount more than sufficient to pay our cash balance then due to Europe and to New York, and we can then resume specie payments without any curtailment."[51] But the most telling point of all was that the "State can make the loan, and will neither be obliged to raise the money nor assume the management of the road."[52] The railroad's revenue would more than pay the interest upon the bonds and would retire them without any direct or indirect monetary contribution from the state. The taxpayers of the Commonwealth would not find it necessary to contribute a cent. The General Court referred the proposal to a joint committee headed by Emory Washburn which hammered out a bill that set the pattern for future state aid to Massachusetts railroads. On February 21, 1838, the legislature passed the bill.[53]

This legislation was a model of sound state action in conjunction with responsible private enterprise. It allowed the

146

railroad to use the state's strong credit position. Private loans in 1838 bore interest rates of 8 to 12 per cent. But the state of Massachusetts was able to market its securities at less than 5 per cent. The new law gave maximum protection to the Commonwealth.[54] It scaled down the amount of the loan from $2,400,000 to $2,100,000, which represented 70 per cent of the railroad's capitalization. In addition the legislature insisted that to qualify for the aid, the stockholders must pay in a further $10 per share, thus increasing their stake to $30 a share, or collectively to $600,000 for the private investors as against $300,000 for the state.

The state issued a scrip "in the name and behalf of the Commonwealth . . . expressed in the currency of Great Britain" and payable in London in thirty years which bore interest at 5 per cent per annum. Rigid restrictions prevented misuse. The Commonwealth's treasurer was not to deliver the bonds to the railroad in amounts larger than $300,000, and upon each application for an installment the governor and the council were to ascertain that "two thirds of the proceeds of the scrip previously delivered" were "faithfully expended" for the construction of the road.

The act created a sinking fund into which any premium received from the sale of the bonds was to go along with a sum each year equal to 1 per cent on the amount issued.[55] The treasurer of the Commonwealth and the treasurer of the Western Corporation were made the sinking fund's commissioners responsible for investing the money according to ways strictly defined by law.[56] The state-aid proponents asserted that the premiums from the scrip sales together with the yearly sums paid by the railroad and the interest accrued from investing this money would be more than sufficient to retire the bonds upon maturity. So well was the program conceived that the sinking fund actually did come within a hair of meeting these expectations. In all, the state of Massachusetts issued 4 million dollars of bonds, of which slightly more than one-third were sold above par, raising a sum for the sinking fund of nearly $140,000. The other two thirds, amounting to nearly $2,500,-000, were sold at a discount of approximately $180,000.[57]

During its first few years the Western earned only enough

to meet operating expenses and the interest payments on the outstanding bonds. Therefore the railroad did not pay the required annual 1 per cent to the sinking fund until 1844.[58] From that year on, however, the company made regular contributions as required by law. Despite the slow start, the Western's yearly payments and wise management of the fund produced a sum that totaled nearly $3,660,000 on January 1, 1871, the date on which the 4 million dollars of bonds became due.[59] The Boston & Albany Railroad, which assumed the responsibility for the Western's obligations after 1867, found it a simple matter to refinance the remaining amount in funded bonds due in October 1875. These were retired on time, extinguishing all liabilities that the state of Massachusetts contracted in its support of the Western Railroad.[60] Thus ended the Bay State's first experience in railroad aid, an effort that did not cost the taxpayers a cent.

The legislature, after making certain that the Commonwealth's interests were protected, entrusted the railroad with the details of the scrip's management. Therefore it fell upon the Western's directors to find buyers for the bonds and to meet the interest payments punctually. An early resumption of construction demanded quick negotiation of the bonds. The depressed state of the American economy made it unlikely that they could be sold at home. Nor was it practical to appoint a special agent to market them in Europe. Treasurer Josiah Quincy preferred to deal with an established English banking house that would provide the railroad with "money in advance of sales and thus furnish the means of going on immediately with the work."[61]

The Western's directors on April 30, 1838, signed an agreement with London's Baring Brothers. The Barings promised that, upon receipt of the bonds, the Western could draw in advance £90 sterling for each £100 sterling of scrip. In return the railroad gave the Barings complete freedom to sell the Massachusetts notes at any price. The London house further undertook to pay the interest and principal when they became due. For their services the Barings charged "one per cent for negotiating the . . . certificates, one per cent on the amount of dividends of interest for discounting remittances and

148

paying interest, and one-half per cent on reimbursement of the principal."[62] By terms of the contract the Western's directors forwarded the money to the Barings to meet all payments for interest and principal as they fell due.

The marriage of the Western and the Barings served the railroad well, for in effect the London investment house agreed to deliver $1,890,000 (90 per cent of $2,100,000) to the railroad. The Baring's commission and charges came out of the remaining $210,000. The London bankers, therefore, assumed the risk of selling the bonds at better than 90 per cent with any amount above that figure, less of course the charges agreed upon, going to the railroad. If the bonds sold at less than 90 per cent, the Barings took the loss. This contract was especially valuable since the state issued the scrip only in amounts of $300,000 as the construction progressed. This meant that the negotiation of the bonds would last two to three years, while the market price for the securities of American states might change. Yet the agreement protected the Western against any drop below 90 per cent—a fact that the Barings came to regret.

At first scrip sales went well. During 1838 and 1839 the Barings sold over $1,200,000 of it at an average price of 3¼ per cent above par.[63] In addition the railroad drew the full 90 per cent on the remaining scrip (some $810,000), thus receiving from the Barings a total of about $2,000,000. This money enabled vigorous prosecution of the construction. During 1838 and 1839 the directors concentrated activity on that part of the road lying east of the Connecticut. On October 1, 1839, the 54 miles of track between Worcester and Springfield were finished, and the first train steamed between Boston and the Connecticut Valley.

It soon became evident, however, that building costs between Worcester and the state line would soar at least $1,500,000 above the $3,000,000 the company had at its disposal. Then the corporation faced the problem of whether to raise the additional money by assessments on the stockholders or by an application for another credit grant from the state. The stockholders on December 12, 1838, voted almost unanimously to ask the state to issue $1,500,000 of new scrip on terms similar to those of the previous grant.[64]

A special joint committee of the legislature supported the Western's request. The committee stressed that an "attempt to collect any considerable amount from the private stockholders would be entirely unavailing" and asserted that such a move "if inforced by vigorous process of law . . . would bring severe suffering on worthy citizens."[65] A law of March 23, 1839, authorized the state to issue new scrip to the amount of $1,200,000 if the shareholders paid two more assessments (the seventh and eighth) of $5 each. The new legislation also raised the number of state directors from three to four out of a total of nine. An attempt of Northfield's Samuel C. Allen to have the state purchase complete control of the line was soundly beaten, affirming the General Court's deep aversion to outright state management of internal improvements.[66]

The new loan of the state's credit seemed to solve the Western's financial problems. Baring Brothers offered to negotiate the new scrip on the same terms as the old, except that they reserved the right to limit the amount of money that could be drawn in advance. The railroad signed the new agreement but specified that the Barings could not sell the bonds below 95 per cent of par value.[67]

The Western entered 1840 with confidence. It had completed its line east of the Connecticut and was well started on that part of the road between Springfield and West Stockbridge on the New York State boundary. But the beginning of 1841 found the corporation back before an appalled General Court asking 1 million dollars of new scrip. This time the legislature was unsympathetic. Charges of mismanagement filled the air, but the need for additional funds was genuine.

Construction in the Berkshires had been more expensive than anyone had imagined. The railroad explained: "Whoever considers that we have to break asunder the continuation of the Alleghany Mountains and to cross more chains than one;— that in 13 miles of Mountain Passes, we have 21 bridges, some of which are 70 feet above the stream;—and that nature has interposed an almost insuperable Barrier between us and the Great West,—will deem the cost of the Western Rail-Road, rather below, than above, what might have been expected."[68] The expense of laying the track across the mountains, together with the unexpected costs of finding a firm foundation for the piers of the Connecticut River bridge, which had to be built on a bed of quicksand, had added between $500,000 and $700,000 to the original estimates.[69]

The Western also needed money for a proper connection from the Massachusetts state line to the Hudson River at Albany, some 39 miles away. The engineers had made all their calculations on the assumption that the road would be built only to the state boundary. Another corporation chartered in New York was to raise its own capital and build the line from West Stockbridge to the river. Two cities, Hudson and Albany, had eagerly sought to take advantage of connection with the Western. But only Hudson followed through. That town's merchants saw a railroad as a way to make their center an equal of Albany and Troy. In 1835 they raised a capital of $250,000 to construct the Hudson and Berkshire, which opened for business in October 1841.[70]

But Hudson's road was not satisfactory. Hastily constructed with sharp curves and steep grades, it had rails too light for the locomotives used between Springfield and Worcester. Besides the H&B went to the wrong place. Boston looked to Albany and the Erie Canal, not to a town 40 miles downstream which could never develop into an important point of transshipment for products flowing between the Great West and the Atlantic.

The Western's directors deemed it imperative to build a line directly to Albany. A charter for such a road existed, but little had been done to use it until April 1840, when the city of Albany pledged to loan its credit to the extent of 1 million dollars for the benefit of the Albany & West Stockbridge line.[71] The plan was simple; the city issued 1 million dollars of scrip, part of which it used to purchase the outstanding West Stockbridge stock.[72] The city then agreed to lease the entire road to the Western, which would build and operate the Albany line as an integral part of its own system.

By terms of permanent contracts signed in 1840 and 1841 by the city of Albany, the Albany & West Stockbridge Railroad, and the Western Railroad, the city agreed to turn over 1 million dollars of scrip to the West Stockbridge company. That road in turn agreed to deliver the scrip and all rights under its charter for the life of that instrument, to the Western. That railroad promised to negotiate the Albany bonds, to set aside 10 per cent of the proceeds therefrom ($100,000) as a start for a sinking fund to retire the scrip, to pay all interest upon the bonds, and to make an annual payment of 1 per cent on the 1 million dollars to the sinking fund.[73]

In addition the Western was obligated to use the proceeds from the Albany scrip to build and equip the railway between the Massachusetts boundary and Albany. The Western agreed to procure on its own resources any funds needed beyond the money realized from the sale of the scrip. After construction the Western was to provide all service over the Albany & West Stockbridge. The agreement was invaluable to the Western, for it meant absolute control over its New York connection.

But the contract left the Western with a severe financial headache. The Albany aid effectively raised only $900,000 as against the estimated cost of the whole road, which was slightly more than $1,400,000.[74] Thus, to fulfill its obligation, the Western Railroad had to find an additional $500,000.

The needs of the Western were real enough; the problem was to convince the legislature. To do so, the railroad embarked on a vigorous propaganda campaign. Leading the attack was Peter P. F. Degrand, one of State Street's leading brokers and a founder of the Boston Stock Market. Joining with Degrand were men from all parts of the state, including such familiar faces as Pittsfield's Lemuel Pomeroy and Julius Rockwell; Springfield's Charles Stearns and George Bliss; and Boston's David Henshaw, George H. Kuhn, George Pratt, and James K. Mills.[75]

In a plea to the legislature P. P. F. Degrand wrote flamboyantly that *"a Contract of Transportation, very fortunately made, with the Albany and West Stockbridge Rail-Road Company, and with the City of Albany,* in the true enlightened spirit of mutual interest, HAS PLACED, IN OUR OWN HANDS, THE KEY OF THE WESTERN RAIL-ROAD,—by securing to us the control of the construction and management of the 38 miles of Rail-Road, from the Line of our State to the very mouth of the Erie and Champlain Canals;—thus giving us possession of the long-sought Prize." Surely, he went on, it could not be our purpose "to stop our Rail-Road, at West Stockbridge, in a morass. . . . It was the mouth of the Erie Canal, which we sought . . . it was for this that we did move onward." Just one more million will complete the road, chanted the Western's supporters. This "trifling sum" representing a charge of but $1.36 per citizen was not too much to ask.[76]

Debate in the General Court was long and bitter, but in the end, Massachusetts capitulated. The lawmakers voted on March 12, 1841, to issue $700,000 of new scrip. They made it clear, however, that this would be the last such aid given, and they insisted that to receive the bonds, the stockholders must contribute an additional $20 per share, bring their entire investment to $60 per share, or to a collective total of $1,800,000.[77] The General Court wrote into the bill the usual safeguards and decisively defeated efforts to give the state a majority of the railroad's directors.[78]

Those who thought that the new scrip would end the Western's financial woes soon had a rude shock. In 1841 as bills due equipment suppliers, contractors, and the like accumulated, Treasurer Josiah Quincy, Jr., noted that the sales of Massachusetts bonds grew more difficult. In fact ever since the initial sale of slightly more than $1,200,000 of Massachusetts scrip at above par in 1838 and 1839, the Barings had found the market for Bay State securities poor. Englishmen sensed that some American states like Indiana, Maryland, Michigan, and Pennsylvania had overextended their borrowing and might default or suspend interest payments on their debts. This feeling tarnished Massachusetts bonds, and they could no longer be sold above par. To widen the appeal of Western scrip, the Barings in June 1840 asked permission to make the dividend warrants payable in Paris and Amsterdam as well as in London. Even this action could not stem the tide, and by 1841 the Barings were still unable to dispose of the full $2,100,000 of the original Massachusetts scrip.[79]

The London bankers returned the second issue of $1,200,000 to Massachusetts, where Josiah Quincy, Jr., placed it in the hands of various Boston and New York banks as collateral for loans.[80] But things went from bad to worse. Pennsylvania, with a total state debt of over $33,000,000, began to teeter on the brink of financial disaster. In August 1842 it failed to meet its interest payments and created a crisis in which the Western was unable to sell its remaining Massachusetts scrip at par.

The need for more money was urgent, and the Western faced the prospect of selling the scrip at a large discount or calling for new assessments from the stockholders. In January 1842 the directors still "had not supposed that any further assessments would be necessary to complete the road." But, "the novel and dangerous doctrines advanced by some of the States in regard to the validity [of debts contracted for internal improvements], and the refusal or neglect of others to meet the interest upon their debts . . . operated abroad to discredit and depress the price of all State stocks . . . and prevent sales except at a ruinous sacrifice."[81] The bonds of the United States government offered at 6 per cent also hurt the Massachusetts 5 per cent notes.

In January 1842 the directors had sought the advice of four of their major stockholders. Abbot Lawrence, Nathan Appleton, William Appleton, and William Sturgis unanimously recommended that the treasurer call for the payment of the rest of the money due on the capital stock. This amounted to $40 per share, or some $1,200,000.[82] The directors implemented this recommendation and resumed assessments. By the end of 1842 the full par value ($100) on each share had been assessed and collected.[83]

This still left the problem of selling the scrip. The depressed state of the security market continued, and the Western's management finally decided to dispose of the Massachusetts scrip at a price that would yield 6 per cent, as Federal bonds did. P. P. F. Degrand auctioned away the final $280,000 of these securities in December 1842 at prices ranging from a high of $87 to a low of $84 and ¾.[84] In a final summation Josiah Quincy, Jr., reported that the railroad had received a total of $3,835,000 from the $4,000,000 of Massachusetts scrip. This meant a loss of nearly $165,000. The Albany bonds fared about as well. The railroad realized about $970,000 from them for a loss of about $30,000.[85]

When in 1842 the first train puffed over the completed

Western and Albany & West Stockbridge railroads, a total capital of $8,000,000 had been expended. By contrast, the short Boston & Worcester had cost but $1,700,000, all of which had come from the sale of stock to private individuals at par value. The financing of the Western and Albany roads was a complicated and mixed affair. Just slightly more than one-third of their total capital, or $3,000,000, represented stock, of which $1,000,000 was held by the state of Massachusetts.

The remaining 5 million dollars had been raised by loans guaranteed by the Commonwealth and the city of Albany. This bonded indebtedness had a profound effect on the Western's history, for bonds, unlike stock, forced huge annual fixed interest and sinking-fund payments upon the railroad. Because the Western faced interest charges of 5 and 6 per cent on 5 million dollars as well as a further 1 per cent on the same sum for the sinking funds, it had an annual fixed cost of $310,000, which had to be paid whether the trains ran or not.[86]

Table 1. Sources of capital, 1842:
BOSTON & WORCESTER AND WESTERN RAILROADS

WESTERN RAILROAD			BOSTON & WORCESTER RAILROAD	
Stock		$3,000,000	Stock, private	$2,700,000
Private	$2,000,000			
State	1,000,000			
Bonds		5,000,000		
State	$4,000,000			
Albany	1,000,000			
		$8,000,000		

The railroad management felt the effects when it came to fixing rates. Dividends could be passed; indeed the Western went until February 1845 without declaring a single dollar of return upon its 3 million dollars of stock. But the interest and sinking-fund charges could not be omitted. The failure to meet a single payment on the scrip would have struck a mortal blow at the credit of Albany and Massachusetts.

The city and the state would have had to make up any default from tax revenue or like Pennsylvania be branded fiscal irresponsibles. Any financial reverse would therefore draw the railroad into politics. The legislators had guaranteed the Western's debts in the belief that the Commonwealth would never expend a cent of tax money. Hence the whole weight of the state and its four directors was thrown behind rates and fares that would provide enough money for both operating expenses and interest payments. The importance of fixed charges can hardly be overestimated. For the year 1842 the Western's total operating costs amounted to less than $270,000.[87] This meant that the interest and sinking-fund charges of $310,000 loomed larger than any other factor when it came to setting rates and fares.

The year 1842 marked the end of the honeymoon between the maritime interests of Boston and the industrialists who pushed the railroad to aid factory developments in Worcester County, the Connecticut Valley, and Berkshire County. From that date on, the shipping interests became dedicated to a fight for low through rates designed to lure the bulky agricultural commerce of the Great West from New York City to Boston. The industrialists, however, wanted moderate and reliable rates on the local traffic originating along the line from Boston to Albany.

The opening of Boston's long awaited artery to the West forced its management to make a decision as to whether it should attempt to divert the flow of the Erie Canal to the Bay State. To bid for the western trade meant direct competition with the Hudson River. In the debate that followed, Boston's shipping interests advanced low-rate theories, which many considered risky. For several years low rates hung in the balance. The fact that the railroad's fixed payments were larger than the operating costs placed the company in a poor position to experiment with "risky" tariffs. Success would have been hailed by all, but failure to earn enough to pay the fixed charges would have caused a financial crisis in Albany and on Beacon Hill. This at all times weighed heavily on the decisions made by the Western's management.

CHAPTER VIII

Rails Across the Mountains

THE WESTERN RAILROAD'S LEADER comparable to the Worcester's Nathan Hale was George Bliss. A Springfield lawyer, politician, land speculator, and industrialist, Bliss early joined the fight for a Boston to Albany railway. The stockholders elected him a member of the first board of directors in 1836, and for the next decade he remained either a director or played a major role in the company. From 1836 until 1842 he was general agent, a position similar to but more powerful than the one William Jackson held in the Boston & Worcester organization. In 1842 Bliss became president with the understanding that he would act as a full-time manager, giving to that office an importance that it had not had under Thomas B. Wales, who lent the presidency his prestige rather than his full time and talents. In 1843 Bliss remained a director, but he failed to win reelection to the presidency. By 1844 he resumed the presidency, which he retained until his retirement in 1846.

Throughout this ten-year period Bliss, more than any other man, molded the company and gave it lasting form. He guided the selection of the route, raised a strong voice in the purchase of locomotives and cars, and most important of all shaped the line's sound financial structure. He believed in deferring dividends if necessary, and he opposed risky rate experimentation. His policies were not always popular, but in the end they triumphed, and at his retirement the Western had a fiscal strength and a tradition of freight rates and passenger fares that remained with the system throughout its life.

There was little in common between Hale and Bliss or their careers. Hale had taken up the cause of railroads in a burst of patriotic fervor, never expecting to earn a living from them. He got along well with his fellow directors. Never until 1846 did the Boston & Worcester board seriously challenge Hale's leadership.

By contrast, Bliss had a stormy time. By 1836 the public was no longer ignorant of railroads; most people realized the relationship between route selection and land value. More significantly, the Western was no local line; it was a great regional artery with the dual purpose of opening up the industrial and agricultural heart of Massachusetts and of linking the port of Boston with the West. As soon as the trains began to run, a bitter fight developed for control. Boston's shipping interests demanded rock-bottom rates for passengers and freight coming from Albany. The local industrialists and agricultural interests feared that low through rates would be unprofitable and would cause local traffic to bear ruinously high tariffs. Legislators in the General Court who had placed the Commonwealth's full faith and credit behind 4 million dollars of the railroad's bonds insisted that the Western maintain a strong financial structure, which would ensure prompt payment of the interest charges and the sinking-fund obligations. Even the Worcester road had a vital stake in the Western's policies, for Hale's line, which served as the final leg of the Boston to Albany route, wanted to make a profit on all traffic to and from the Western. Land speculators and equipment suppliers also added to the explosive situation.

Bliss's troubles were also in part the result of his economic background and personality. Despite his association with Springfield's elite, Bliss began the 1830s with his fortune still to be made. His father had given him an education and a place of respect in the community but little ready cash. In 1825 Bliss furthered his social position by marrying Edmund Dwight's sister.[1] Like David Henshaw, Bliss had a driving ambition for both political power and economic wealth. But unlike Henshaw, the Springfield lawyer had no need to fight entrenched interests. Indeed Bliss had only to use his connections to make his mark in the Commonwealth.

Springfield elected Bliss to the General Court in 1827, and for the next three decades he was a familiar figure on Beacon Hill, where he soon assumed legislative leadership in the Whig Party. In 1835 Bliss became president of the senate, and in later years he served as speaker of the house of representatives. During his first terms in the legislature Bliss seized upon the railroad as a perfect vehicle for developing his Chicopee River factory lands. When in 1836 he became formally associated with the Western, Bliss had built himself a widespread reputation as a clever political leader and a shrewd lawyer. But none of his speculative ventures had yet borne fruit. He still earned his livelihood primarily through the practice of law and was still looking for his big economic opportunity.[2]

George Bliss was a natural choice to assume the major responsibilities of building and managing the railroad. He knew western Massachusetts; his name commanded respect and confidence there; and his experience in the General Court was invaluable. Bliss welcomed the opportunity, but only on the condition that he be paid a substantial salary for his efforts. He made it quite clear from the start that he could not afford to take the position as full-time agent for less than $10 a day.[3]

While Bliss acted as counsel for the railroad in the effort to win state aid, the board of directors authorized him $10 a day plus expenses, and later they set his salary as agent at $3,000 a year. Bliss often commented that this was less than he earned as a lawyer and that he had to make a financial sacrifice to take the job.[4] Later Bliss became a strong advocate of raising the salaries of the company executives, especially the president and the treasurer. In fact he voted to increase the president's salary from an annual $2,000 to $3,000 in 1842, the year he assumed that office. To Bliss, demands for high pay seemed not only reasonable but just compensation for a job that was both difficult and exacting. But to the opponents of his policies, Bliss's initial stipend of $10 a day as counsel and his vote as a director to raise the salary of an office he was about to fill became targets of attacks on his integrity.

Bliss's detractors accumulated further fuel by an examination of his real estate dealings while he served as agent. From time to time Bliss bought land along the right of way, and in Springfield he held several lots adjacent to one of the proposed routes through the city.[5] Bliss's enemies found it easy to charge him with manipulating the route selection to favor his speculations and with profiting from his official position. These insinuations caused Bliss no end of grief.

More of Bliss's troubles came from his strong-willed, stubborn, icy personality. Bliss himself gave this account of his early life: "I attended the common district school kept by a female until eight years old [1801], and then was transferred to a school kept by a man. Out of school I wandered about on the streets or engaged in play with every boy I could find. My father when at home was very rigid in his family government and discipline, controlling me more by fear than affection, as was the wont in those days."[6] The early years produced a man whom one of his relatives later described as "cold, learned, dry, just, hard, [and] unloveable."[7] His youth instilled self-reliance, drive, and determination, but it also created a man who was self-righteous and proud. Once Bliss decided upon a course of action, he stuck to it regardless of the consequences. Things often became a "matter of honor" with him, and as he once wrote in a letter to an associate, "I [can] consent to nothing which even by implication, [could] have a stain upon my character, or excite a suspicion of the purity of my motives."[8]

Bliss expected to gain ample monetary rewards for his services and found nothing wrong with asking for and receiving high salaries or using his information to build his private fortune because, in the main, he ran the railroad with a skillful hand and always for what he thought were the best interests of the Commonwealth. He worked tirelessly to secure the shortest and most practicable route between Worcester and Albany. He kept a close watch on contractors and suppliers to make sure that the Western got its full value for all the money spent during construction. His policies toward dividends, rates, and fares, while controversial, were designed to place the railroad on a solid financial footing. Never did Bliss speculate in the company's stock or use his position to raid the railroad's treasury. Most of his troubles came from his uncompromising, self-righteous, and at times tactless personality and from the attacks of those who opposed his basic policies.

After the railroad consolidated its financial position, its big problem was to survey and purchase a right of way from Worcester to the state line at West Stockbridge. The responsibility for the route selection lay with the agent, George Bliss, and with the company's engineers. Disagreement troubled the

Western's board from the first, for the hiring of the engineers produced a sizzling controversy.

The directors appointed a committee to find suitable talent to make surveys across the Worcester Highlands and the Berkshire Mountains. The committee's majority, after a thorough investigation, recommended two West Point men, Major William Gibbs McNeill to act as chief engineer and Captain William Swift to serve as resident engineer. The West Pointers had a solid record of experience with railroads—Swift with systems in Connecticut and in the Middle Atlantic states, and McNeill with the Baltimore & Ohio. But their association with the Army alienated a substantial group who opposed the concentration of the best and most lucrative railroad jobs in the hands of a small clique of military academy graduates.[9]

Popular opposition to the army men focused in Francis Jackson, who besides his position as a Western director, was the South Cove Corporation's agent.[10] Jackson's minority report called for "free competition among our practical and intelligent working men in preference to confining the choice to the graduates of West Point, who . . . are notoriously unfit for the practical purposes of general direction and superintendence of such a work. It cannot be expected," he continued, "that any institution can take boys from the lap of wealth, luxury, and idleness and fit them for all the duties of such an enterprise."[11] Jackson viewed the military men as wasteful and more charmed with the "beauty of a bridge [or] the imposing appearance of a viaduct . . . than the plain and homely attributes of utility and economy."[12] The majority of the Western's board thought otherwise, however, and on March 25, 1836, they hired the two West Pointers, giving McNeill a part-time supervisory contract to run for four years at $10,000 for the entire period. Swift was to devote his full time to the railroad, and for this he received a salary of $4,000 the first year and $5,000 for each succeeding year.[13] In 1837 McNeill brought his associate George W. Whistler, better known as Whistler's father, into the company, thus completing the system's top engineering staff.[14]

The Western Railroad fell naturally into two sections of

approximately equal length: the first east of the Connecticut between Worcester and Springfield and the second west from Springfield to the state line at West Stockbridge. Circumstance dictated that the road east of the Connecticut be constructed first, for the comparatively dense population held the lure of immediately profitable traffic, and the eastern portion was relatively easy to build since it crossed the rolling uplands that separated the Blackstone's watershed from that of the Connecticut. By contrast the near wilderness west of Springfield required lengthy surveys and huge expenses; the Berkshire Mountains were the most formidable barrier faced by any railroad in the world up to that time. Beginning in April 1836, the Western's management turned the full attention of the newly hired engineering team toward finding a precise location for the tracks between Worcester and Springfield.

There were troubles both in selecting the line between the cities and in finding suitable approaches and stations in the two terminals. Between Worcester and Springfield, engineers encountered unexpected obstacles. Previous surveys had disclosed that the Chicopee River Valley was the natural path for most of the distance; but the major difficulty was in discovering a way out of the valley of the Blackstone and across the highlands between Worcester and the Chicopee River. In the 1830s even a small hill was a major challenge. The shortest distance from New Worcester to East Brookfield at the Chicopee's head was a scant 11 miles, but between these two towns stood a high ridge that loomed between 500 and 900 feet above the Worcester station. Early reports gave hope that the railroad could use a pass providing nearly direct access to the Chicopee Valley, but accurate surveys soon indicated that this route could be built only with grades six to seven times as steep as any on the Boston and Worcester and that this route suffered from curves too sharp for steam engines.

These findings required a search for a new pass. A detailed survey of the entire ridge for a distance of 9 miles both to the north and south of Worcester discovered a line that ran from the Blackstone River south around a hill known as Henshaw Ridge through the town of Charlton. This turned the 11 miles between New Worcester and East Brookfield into more than seventeen, but after still further investigation the management had to adopt the Charlton summit location.

This 17-mile portion of the Western had nearly as much rise and fall as the entire 44-mile Boston and Worcester road. Hale's system had its major summit 500 feet above the railroad station in Boston and a mere 34 feet above the Blackstone River at Worcester. By contrast the Western's Charlton summit, just 12 miles from the Blackstone, lay 430 feet above the Worcester station and over 900 feet higher than Boston. Even so, the Charlton pass required extensive rock cutting, which placed the tracks in a gash more than 40 feet below the ground level. Another measure of the difference between the two railroads was the steepness of the grades. On the Worcester the maximum rise was a gentle 30 feet per mile, and only a bit more than one-fourth of the line had grades even that steep. But almost all of the Western's first 17 miles had inclines that exceeded the Worcester's maximum, and for two of the miles the rise was 60 feet per mile, a commentary on both the difficulty of the terrain and on the technological advance in steam locomotives which had occurred during the four years since Colonel Fessenden had designed the Worcester road.[15]

From East Brookfield to the Connecticut the engineers had a fairly easy job, for they had but to follow the Chicopee River through the towns of West Brookfield, Warren, Brimfield, Palmer, Wilbraham, and Ludlow to Springfield some 54 miles from Worcester and a full 99 miles from Boston. Over this section the Western lost nearly all its hard-won elevation, for Springfield lay just over 70 feet above Boston's Back Bay.

If engineering considerations determined the route around Henshaw Ridge and along the Chicopee Valley, the same cannot be said for either the location of the tracks or the stations in Worcester and Springfield. These questions produced fights that opened wounds which did not heal for more than thirty years. The controversy over the Worcester depot was especially significant, for it threw light both on the split that developed between the managements of the Western and the Worcester railroads and on the concepts of railroading in the mid-1830s.

Hale's railroad had approached Worcester from the southeast and had terminated at Hathaway's farm, a mile from the village center. Not satisfied with this location, leading local merchants aided the railroad in the purchase of land on Main Street, just two blocks from the heart of town. Although the B&W directors established the passenger station on Main Street, they erected yards, engine houses, and freight facilities on Hathaway's farm. Hale had made an "express stipulation" with the owners of adjacent land in the town that railroads approaching the B&W's Main Street station would be granted an easement, thus making it possible for lines from both Albany and Norwich to terminate at the same location.[16] He wanted each company to construct separate passenger stations on land abutting the Boston & Worcester's terminal. He felt that there would be no through passenger service but that each system would run its trains into adjoining depots and that passengers would change cars by walking the few feet from one station to the next. Although the Worcester management did not envision through passenger trains, they did plan for a physical connection among the railroads at Hathaway's farm, where the three companies would share a joint freight terminal and would interchange freight cars.[17]

The Worcester Corporation formulated these plans alone since neither the Western nor the Norwich & Worcester was more than a paper corporation at the time. When the Norwich Corporation became active, it immediately purchased an acre abutting the Boston & Worcester's Main Street station and proceeded to follow Hale's plan almost to the letter.[18] Such was not the case with the Western.

The Boston & Worcester had counted on full cooperation from the Western, which it completely controlled.[19] But the terms of finance wrenched the Western from the Worcester railroad almost as soon as the new corporation was organized. And the problems facing the Western's management were of such a nature as to bode ill for a smooth relationship between the two corporations.

In 1836 Hale's system vibrated with life and optimism. Passengers clambered aboard the trains in ever-increasing numbers, and even freight shipments began to show a decisive upsurge. Dividends started to flow, and the Worcester's stock, although still largely controlled by New Yorkers and Boston bankers, began to be considered an attractive investment. Simultaneously the Western reposed in despair. Zealous promoters had forced the company's 2 million dollars of stock into the reluctant hands of Boston and Springfield citizens who had a pessimistic outlook for dividends. And preliminary engineering surveys in the Berkshire Mountains and along Henshaw Ridge bolstered early fears that even with state purchase of an additional million dollars of stock that the Western's capital resources were insufficient to build a railroad from Worcester to West Stockbridge. Against this background a committee composed of George Bliss, Captain Swift, and William Jackson wrestled with the job of finding a depot location in Worcester.

In mid-1836 Captain Swift headed an engineering team that investigated three different approaches to the town: the Hale proposal to run the line into a terminal near the Worcester Corporation's Main Street station with an extension southeast along the B&W tracks to Hathaway's farm, where joint freight facilities and yards would be located; a route leading to a free depot site in north Worcester, which was to be provided by Stephen Salisbury and other prominent local businessmen; and a line suggested by Swift himself, which skirted Worcester Village's southern edge running directly to Hathaway's farm, where it was proposed to build both the freight and passenger terminals.[20] After considerable discussion the committee rejected the Salisbury site because it would draw the Western's tracks more than a mile out of the way. Against Hale's plan Bliss and Swift raised three objections: it lengthened the distance between Boston and Springfield by about a quarter of a mile; it was undesirable in principle to separate the freight from the passenger terminals; and a Main Street passenger station would cost almost twice as much as unified facilities on Hathaway's farm.[21] Bliss felt that the cost differential was particularly important in view of the Western's capital shortage.

The Bliss-Swift recommendation brought a hail of criticism upon the Western. Leading the attack was the other third of the Western's own committee, William Jackson, who in addition to his position as a Western Railroad director, served as the Worcester Corporation's agent. Jackson complained that a station on Hathaway's farm (also called Washington Square) placed the Western's passenger depot almost a mile from the terminals of both the Norwich & Worcester and the Boston & Worcester railroads. The latter two lines expected to compete with the Providence and Stonington for a part of the Boston and New York travel. This, said Jackson, explained "the promptness and decision of the Norwich Corporation in the location of their passenger depot immediately in the vicinity of the Worcester."[22] Jackson maintained that it was vital, if the railroads hoped to capture the highly competitive long-distance New York to Boston business, that inconvenience of traveling be minimized and that cumbersome transfers be avoided. Even Jackson, however, writing as late as January 1837, assumed that passenger cars would not run through from one railroad to another.

The Worcester road's President Hale refused to sell the Western any land at Hathaway's farm unless the new corporation agreed to establish its passenger station on Main Street, next to the Worcester's terminal.[23] But both Jackson's and Hale's views fell on deaf ears. Even the town of Worcester's solid support for Hale's position did not impress Bliss, who felt that the town's views were of no consequence since its citizens had failed to subscribe for a single share of Western stock. The position that a Washington Square depot afforded a cheaper and shorter railroad carried the day, and on March 2, 1837, the Western's directors voted to bypass Worcester Center and to establish their passenger and freight stations at Hathaway's farm.[24] This did not end the dispute. The Boston & Worcester still refused to sell land to the Western, and property that abutted the farm had to be purchased at a comparatively high price. William Jackson, whom the legislature had just reappointed to the Western's board as a state director, angrily declined the position.[25] The town of Worcester held mass meetings to protest the Western's action. In fact as the years went on, Worcester's anger seemed to fester and grow, and the locals made many attempts to get the Western and the Worcester to share a joint passenger station in the center of town.[26]

But all efforts were to no avail, and the Worcester and Western passenger depots remained separated by nearly a mile of city until after the Civil War, when a union depot was built at

Washington Square. Despite the dire predictions, through passenger traffic did not suffer since the Worcester road finally relented and allowed the Western to connect with the B&W at the Hathaway's farm. Under the arrangement all through trains destined from Boston for points on the Western Railroad ran to the Washington Square station, which became known as the Lower Worcester Depot. Here crews removed the Worcester locomotives and hooked on a Western engine, which pulled the train onward. Therefore, from the first, the two roads interchanged both freight and passenger equipment. Only the local passengers suffered the inconvenience of changing stations, for all Norwich & Worcester service used a Main Street station as did all local trains of the B&W.

Springfield's experience was no less stormy, but the problems were of a different sort. The Western, as the pioneer line into the Connecticut River town, had no immediate need to coordinate its plans with other companies, and although the directors were interested in securing a site that would make possible a union station for the Western and the proposed Springfield and Hartford line, this consideration did not weigh heavily in the decision.[27]

By 1837 a sharp realization that railroads radically increased the worth of adjacent property replaced the indifference that characterized so many towns at the time the Boston and Worcester was surveyed. Although a minority of Springfield's citizens agreed with their Unitarian minister, William Peabody, that the tracks would "powerfully disfigure the village,"[28] most could think only of increased property values.

The town of Springfield stretched for about 5 miles along the Connecticut River's eastern bank. More than 70 per cent of its 7,000 people lived in a "village" located in the town's southern third. Nearly all the rest clustered about the factory development that the Dwights had promoted on the Chicopee River in the town's northern third. Between the two settlements lay open rolling farm land. No peculiar physical characteristics existed to force the roadbed into a definite channel. Although the engineers surveyed no less than thirteen different practicable routes through the town, there was soon agreement that the line ought to run as close to the main population center as possible so that "the railroad may not prove an injury instead of a benefit to a considerable portion of its owners who have contributed liberally towards its construction."[29]

The decision only set the stage for a bitter clash among various real estate speculators, all of whom seemed to want the depot to abut their property. And those who did not own suitable acreage engaged in a mad scramble to buy up every available plot that might conceivably include a station site. Even George Bliss, who should have known better, joined the rush, purchasing the 3½-acre Worthington estate, which lay directly on the path of one of the proposed routes, about a quarter of a mile north from the village center.[30] He did not expect to profit directly by land sales to the Western Corporation; indeed he offered space to the railroad at cost. The goal was to draw the depot into the vicinity of other property he owned. Meanwhile another large landowner proposed to sell the Western an acre on the southernmost line very near the village center.[31]

Besieged by offers, the directors hesitated, but on June 15, 1837, they decided to place the station a few hundred feet south of Main and Ferry streets. This location was less than ½ mile north of the center of Springfield village and within ¼ mile of the Worthington estate. The directors justified this route, which was almost 4 miles longer than that along the Chicopee's banks, by stating that they found it "inexpedient to diverge" further to the south and that this brought the tracks reasonably close to the main part of Springfield and still gave the railroad room to expand.[32] Although the company held to its decision, the controversy continued. The following year no less than a dozen mass meetings were held to get the railroad to change its depot location. The directors received a score of petitions to which more than 2,000 Springfield citizens attached their names urging particular sites. The directors' decision especially irked rival speculators, who accused George Bliss of serving his own interests. Later at a legislative hearing Edmund Dwight, a Western director through the entire period, substantiated the charges by affirming that Bliss was anxious to locate the depot near his own property.[33] Despite this turmoil, Springfield soon acquiesced to the railroad's location.

In reality the directors had made a sound move. The tracks came close enough to the old center to preserve and enhance property values there, but the rails did not come so near that they cut a large swath through the village proper. The location provided ample land for terminal facilities, yards, round houses, shops, and freight houses, and there was also room for other railroads and commercial development. However, the site did increase the total distance between Boston and Albany by nearly 4 miles, and it benefited a particular group of speculators.

Beyond the Connecticut loomed the Berkshire Mountains, challenging the Western with its toughest engineering problems. But even here route selection was no easy matter. Berkshire County, though united in its support of a railroad, was split into two rival forces, each determined that the trains should steam through their towns. Surveys disclosed two feasible routes. The northern was charted by James F. Baldwin in 1828. It crossed the Connecticut and ascended the Westfield River through the town of Westfield; then it passed "through Chester and up the valley of the Pontoosac turnpike to the summit in Washington; then through Hinsdale, Dalton, Pittsfield and Richmond to the state line in West Stockbridge."[34] The southern route, surveyed by the Western Railroad crews in 1836, diverged from the Baldwin line at Westfield and curved southward bypassing Pittsfield, but it included the thriving towns of Lee and Stockbridge on its way to the state line at West Stockbridge.

Throughout the first half of 1837 proponents debated the pros and cons of each line. Both surveys took nearly 63 miles to cover the distance between the Connecticut River and the state line; and the high point on the southern route, 1,400 feet above Springfield, was just 51 feet higher than the northern summit. Even the estimated cost of bridging and grading was nearly identical. The major difference, which caused the engineers to recommend the northern route, was that the southern line had more miles of steep grades and sharp curves than its northern counterpart. But even here statistical tables prepared by the engineering staff indicated that the difference was slight, and the official summary distorted the picture in favor of the northern line.[35]

Upon the decision rode the hopes of two burgeoning towns, Lee and Pittsfield. The railroad would bypass one of them, and the businessmen in each place feared that precious capital invested in the Western might turn out to aid the rival town. So sharp was this anxiety that Pittsfield citizens refused to subscribe to any Western stock unless they had the privilege of withdrawing their support if the tracks went south. Lee residents were more broadminded; they invested in $23,000 of stock with the hope that if the rails went north the burden might be shifted to Pittsfield.[36] In June 1837 the railroad's directors heard proponents in favor of both routes, but Pittsfield's champions were more aggressive. In a formal statement before the Western's board, Julius Rockwell, then speaker of the house in the Massachusetts Legislature, argued that the northern line's greater commercial potential demanded that the rails run through Pittsfield. He stressed that the Pomeroy Woolen Mills typified the industrial vigor of the area.[37] Lemuel Pomeroy, himself, worked behind the scenes, promising that if the tracks were laid on the northern line, Pittsfield would assume the stock held by the men of Lee and south Berkshire County.

Stockbridge's Theodore Sedgwick opposed his friend and associate Lemuel Pomeroy.[38] But neither Sedgwick's logic nor his rhetoric could match Pittsfield's economic power, and on June 15, 1837, Bliss informed Pomeroy that the Western would select the northern route provided that the towns along that line took over the $23,000 of stock owned by people in Lee and Stockbridge. Pittsfield went wild at this news, and the hills echoed to the thunder of cannon fire. Pomeroy left nothing to chance. Under his guidance the local bank opened stock subscription books. On June 24, a town meeting voted overwhelmingly to take fifty shares ($5,000) of Western stock. At the same time the people reached general agreement on the route through the village and granted a right of way across the new burial grounds.[39] The combination of municipal support and

Figure 15

The Western Railroad's *Superior*, built in the corporation's Springfield shops in 1859.

Figure 16

The Western Railroad's *Arizona*, built in the corporation's shops in 1866.

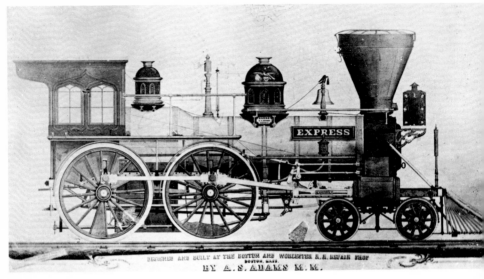

DESIGNED AND BUILT AT THE BOSTON AND WORCESTER R.R. REPAIR SHOP
BOSTON, MASS.
BY A. S. ADAMS M.M.

Figure 17

The Boston & Worcester's *Express,* a 28-ton coal-burning passenger
locomotive built in the corporation's own shops.

private subscription soon produced the required stock pledges, and the Western's directors voted on August 10, 1837, to build the railroad on the northern line.[40]

This completed the Western's route except for the portion that crossed New York State, although this was technically the responsibility of another corporation. Immediately after the Western assumed control of the New York section of the line in 1840, the corporation's engineer, George Whistler, surveyed the approximately 38 miles between the state line and Greenbush, which stood on the Hudson's eastern bank directly across the river from Albany. Fortunately the absence of any large towns or pressure groups between Massachusetts and the Hudson allowed engineering considerations to prevail. Whistler recommended that the tracks take advantage of the Hudson Valley's easy grades and run southeast from Greenbush 22 miles to Chatham Four Corners (Groat's), where it would join the Hudson & Berkshire Railroad. By the end of 1840 this segment was under contract, and the work was progressing rapidly. In the same year the Western's directors ordered their engineers to examine carefully the Hudson & Berkshire for the 16 miles between Groat's and the state line with a view toward using its tracks for joint operation. The engineers reported that the Hudson & Berkshire had such light rails, sharp curves, and steep grades that it was useless as a permanent connecting link. Therefore, in 1841, the directors ordered the building of a parallel line.[41]

The story of the Western's construction basically repeats that of the Boston & Worcester. Following the precedents established on the eastern road, the Western's management ordered the corporation's engineers to survey and locate the line; divide it into sections; and then supervise the building of each segment. As in the case of the Worcester, private firms bid for contracts to do the actual work. But the sheer size of the Western forced some significant changes. Construction took place in several stages, and some of the work progressed simultaneously. Work started on the first major division, the 55 miles between Worcester and Springfield in 1836, and the first train ran between those two towns on October 1, 1839. The Connecticut River bridge formed a project all by itself; it was not finished until July 4, 1841. Meanwhile, the Western's high command decided to speed the completion of its road by attacking the Berkshire Mountains from both sides. Taking advantage of the progress made by the Hudson & Berkshire, which started building in 1838 from Hudson to the Massachusetts line, the directors established a railhead at West Stockbridge and built eastward 11 miles to Pittsfield, where the first train arrived on May 4, 1841.[42] At the same time construction crews ferried engines, cars, and equipment across the Connecticut to begin work on the eastern slopes of the Berkshires. Progress was slow, but trains started service on the 28 miles of road directly west of the Connecticut (West Springfield to Chester Factories) in March 1841.

The following summer saw all effort directed toward closing the 35-mile gap between Pittsfield and Chester Factories; this was finally accomplished on October 4, 1841. The railroad in Massachusetts was now completed, and by transferring to the cars of the Hudson & Berkshire, passengers could travel the entire distance between Boston and the Hudson by train. On December 20, 1841, workmen put the final rails into place on the section of the Albany and West Stockbridge that connected Chatham Four Corners and Greenbush (Albany). The following day through train service commenced between Boston and Albany. This necessitated using the Hudson & Berkshire's rails from Chatham to West Stockbridge since this section of the Albany line was not finished until late in 1842.[43]

Between the time when the engineers finally located the route and the day when the first train ran through to Albany, the Western's management had to decide whether to follow the Worcester Corporation's example and build a heavy-duty, permanent system or to economize with light rails, minimal grading, and sharp curves. The combination of high costs and an acute capital shortage made the latter choice singularly attractive. In January 1837 the company's engineering staff recommended that long-term savings justified grading the line for a double track. But cost-conscious directors thought otherwise, and while they agreed that the railroad ought to be built in a solid, durable manner, they reasoned, since the "prospect of business upon the road for many years to come does not require and will not justify an immediate construction of . . . a double track," that ordinary grading should be for a single line only. But the board did order that all bridges (except that over the Connecticut River) and deep cuts should be made wide enough for two tracks.[44] Although this decision guided the laying of rails between Worcester and Springfield, the Western's shaky financial condition and the enormous cost estimates for building a railroad across the Berkshires caused the directors to consider cheaper construction west of the Connecticut. This sentiment would have prevailed had not George Whistler, who directed the survey between Springfield and Albany, convinced Agent Bliss and President Thomas B. Wales that flimsy construction was a false economy that would defeat the very purposes for which the Western was being built. Wales took the lead in directors' meetings and managed to thwart the laying down of what he termed a "two penny cow-path."[45]

Although the Western was but a single-track line, it was in every instance a fitting extension of the Worcester railroad. The Western's rails were laid on a bed "graded to a width of 20 feet in the cuts and 16 feet on the embankments."[46] The superstructure followed the Worcester's pattern, except that instead of 40-pound edge rails, the Western used "edge rail of the T pattern . . . weighing 56½ pounds to the linear yard."[47]

The major difference between the Worcester and the Western lay in the steepness of the grades. Here topography forced the engineers to abandon the Worcester's 30-foot-per-mile maximum rise. This gradient had to be doubled to build a railroad around Henshaw Ridge between Worcester and Springfield. But the Berkshires pushed previous problems into the shadows. In just 26 miles between Westfield and Washington the railroad had to climb nearly 1,400 feet, or to a point nearly three times higher than the Worcester's summit. To cross this range called for 18 miles of track with an inclination of 60 feet per mile or greater including 6 miles at 80 feet per mile.[48] By contrast, only 14 miles of the Worcester road had grades steeper than 20 feet per mile. From 1840 to 1867 this difference grew in importance, for it became the foundation of the Western's argument that high operating costs deserved a greater proportion of the Boston–Albany rates than a flat division on a mileage basis would allow.

The mountains were only one of the obstacles that increased operating expenses and necessitated a vast initial capital outlay. The tracks crossed the Connecticut River on a costly 1,260-foot truss bridge designed in accordance with William Howe's patent. This structure contained seven spans, each 180 feet in length supported by six hewn granite piers which had to be anchored to bedrock that rested under a layer of quicksand. The floor of the bridge was 30 feet above the water and was covered with tin.[49] Up the Berkshires' eastern slope the tracks followed the west branch of the Westfield or Pontoosac River, which they crossed no less than 21 times in the space of 13 miles. Nine of these bridges were stone arches, three of which had spans of 60 feet and soared as high as 70 feet above the water.[50] Construction started on this stretch in 1838; crews erected bridge abutments, embankments, and masonry walls at what the engineers thought were safe levels above the river. But a single freshet in the summer of 1839 washed away most of a year's work. Relocation pushed costs upward. Experience had shown the necessity of structures "of a more costly and permanent character." Stone arches of large openings required masonry of a superior nature, and it was also necessary "to resort to great depths in search of permanent rock foundations below the bed of the stream."[51] Furthermore the contractor was compelled to quarry and haul the stone from a distance over almost impassable roads.

At Washington summit the roadbed knifed through a mountain with a ½-mile-long cut that lay 55 feet below ground level and necessitated the removal of 100,000 cubic yards of rock.[52] The Berkshires' western side, while more gentle in slope, also required many large and expensive cuts and embankments. At Curtis summit, just west of the state line on the Albany and West Stockbridge, the tracks passed through the only tunnel, a short 548-foot bore.[53]

The need for supplies and materials was enormous. The company consumed rails at the rate of 100 tons per mile, a total of more than 16,000 tons, valued in excess of 1 million dollars.[54] American ironworks could not produce rails either in the quantity or at the price demanded by the burgeoning railroad industry. Thus like the Worcester, the Western Railroad turned to British suppliers. The directors imported the iron through the president's firm, Thomas B. Wales and Company, which received "one per cent upon the cost to the corporation of the iron rails in England."[55] Although Wales' firm bought no American rails, it did find satisfactory supplies of fishplates and iron spikes in Massachusetts which indicated that domestic iron makers were aware of the new opportunities and striving to meet them.[56]

The most attractive new fields for American industry were motive power and rolling stock. By nineteenth-century standards the Western Railroad was a giant enterprise. The company's engineering staff estimated that to establish a minimum service of two passenger and two freight trains daily between Worcester and Albany required fifteen passenger and twelve freight locomotives.[57] Aspiring industrialists rushed to meet this challenge. The Western's experience was quite different from that of the Worcester, four short years previously, when there were no suitable American locomotives.

The Western could send a committee to visit manufacturers in Rhode Island, Connecticut, New York, New Jersey, Pennsylvania, Delaware, and Maryland, as well as Massachusetts. Visibly impressed by the large number of would-be suppliers, the committee reported that, while adequate engines could be bought in any of the states visited, the first order for eight locomotives to operate the Worcester–Springfield division ought to be placed with the Locks and Canals Company in Lowell, Massachusetts. Strongly influencing the board, which accepted this recommendation, were the opinions of two men, William Jackson and George Whistler. Jackson, the Worcester Corporation's agent, praised the performance of his company's Lowell engine, which he maintained equaled if not surpassed the B&W's Philadelphia-made Baldwin steamers. Whistler, who held the position of engineer to the proprietors of the Locks and Canals Company before his connection with the Western, pointed out that local motive power construction allowed close supervision and custom adjustments that were not practicable on locomotives built in distant states.[58]

The year 1841 and the impending completion of the line from Springfield to Albany brought the Western's management to the brink of a motive-power crisis. The 10-ton engines delivered by the Locks and Canals Company performed well on the Worcester–Springfield division, but the directors knew that they were hopelessly inadequate to haul heavy freight up the prolonged inclines in the Berkshire Mountains. The railroad needed a dozen or more powerful engines. Locomotive builders throughout the United States were eager to fill the orders, for the combination of long distances and steep mountain grades provided a perfect proving ground for the new manufacturers; hence the directors found themselves literally flooded with offers to supply locomotives. George Whistler, anticipating the Western's requirements, ordered a large experimental 20-ton engine from the Locks and Canals Company, which commenced service as the *Massachusetts* in 1840. Whistler felt that the *Massachusetts* met the railroad's minimum needs but hoped that still better motive power could be found.[59]

Three rising new manufacturers each claimed that they had the answer. Philadelphia's William Norris, destined to become one of America's leading locomotive builders, took every possible measure to secure an order from the Western. In the summer of 1840 Norris sent his representative, Richard Imlay, to Massachusetts with an engine called the *America*, and asked that it be tested on the Western's tracks. The railroad immediately agreed, and in July 1840 three Western directors, Elias Hasket Derby, William Jackson, and John Henshaw, journeyed to Springfield to witness the *America* on trial against one of the road's Lowell engines, the *Suffolk*. This affair led to much controversy and bitterness. Jackson and Henshaw, backed by Whistler, reported that the Lowell's " 'Suffolk' gave [a] decided and unequivocal evidence of superiority."[60] However, E. H. Derby branded the trial "inconclusive" and proposed a new one. So anxious was Norris to secure another chance to show off his *America* that he promised to "procure freight for the engine independent of the receipts of the corporation and to pay the toll into its treasury."[61] Despite this generous offer the board spurned a second trial. Norris did not give up that easily.

176

Encouraged by Derby, who still thought the *America* a remarkable engine, the Philadelphian made a special trip to Boston in June 1841 to see whether he could procure an order for his works.[62]

The Boston firm of Hinkley and Drury also had high hopes of capturing the Western's business. Although it was destined to become one of the nation's foremost works, in 1841 this company had yet to sell its first engine. James Hinkley had founded the company to produce machinery and stationary steam engines.[63] Impressed by the expanding market for railroad equipment, he built an experimental locomotive, and in June 1841 he offered to demonstrate it on the Western.[64]

Whistler and the board found few of the offers attractive. Most, like the Hinkley, Norris, and Lowell engines, followed basic designs developed by England's Stephenson. These locomotives had horizontal boilers, and they relied for their power on from two to four large drive wheels. Whistler feared that such heavy engines would put too much pressure on their drive wheels which in turn would severely abuse the track. Baltimore's Ross Winans was the one builder who departed from Stephenson's pattern. Winans became associated with railroads in 1828, when he went to work for the B&O, where he formed a solid friendship with William Gibbs McNeill and George Whistler. In 1830 Winans collaborated with Peter Cooper in building the *Tom Thumb*. In 1835, in partnership with George Gillingham, he took over the management of the Baltimore and Ohio's shops and set out to establish a major locomotive works.[65]

Winans' early engines all followed the *Tom Thumb*'s basic design, that is they had vertical boilers, small drive wheels, and were made to negotiate sharp curves and steep grades. In 1837, Winans took out a patent on a locomotive that came to be called the "crab," which he claimed could move a train of 200 tons up grades of 82 feet per mile at the speed of 8 miles per hour.[66] George Whistler went to Baltimore to inspect the new engine and upon his return reported that Winans' experiment offered a solution to the Western's motive-power troubles. After a delegation had put the "crab" through a series of rugged tests on the Baltimore & Ohio's tracks, the directors finally decided the motive-power question. They had before them six concrete proposals to supply locomotives at prices ranging from $7,750 to $12,300 each.[67] Persuaded that the "crab" offered a unique chance to haul more freight faster, for less money, and at the same time to reduce track maintenance costs, they took the risk of a comparatively untried design. The board authorized an order for seven "crabs" and for three more passenger engines from the tried and true Lowell works.[68]

This decision did not satisfy Elias H. Derby, who at the next board meeting proposed that two engines be ordered from Mr. Norris.[69] The other directors, having just spent over $100,000 for motive power, refused to concur.[70] But within a year Winans' failure to deliver his full quota on time and better-than-expected business resulted in an urgent demand for motive power. In October 1842 the Western placed orders for one engine apiece with William Norris and Hinkley and Drury. At the same time the directors rejected further purchases from Lowell on the grounds that they were no longer competitive in price.[71]

Railroads like the Western proved an immediate stimulus to the nation's economy. An intense rivalry developed to supply the new systems, first with motive power and other rolling stock, later with iron rails and other items. Management faced the usual pressure of selecting the best products at the lowest cost without firm standards and while everything was experimental. The directors knew that the Western's success depended largely upon an advance in technology, and they tried to encourage the development of new and better locomotives. However, a program to underwrite technological development had perils. If the Winans engines failed, the board would be criticized for costly, foolish, and risky experimentation. Furthermore, standardization was the cornerstone of an effective maintenance program. Bliss made this point in his minority report opposing buying single locomotives from Hinkley and Norris. Neither purchase resulted in an improvement of technology, and each brought with it a host of special maintenance problems.[72]

The year 1841 saw Boston and Albany toast the inauguration

of full rail service between the two cities. On December 27, 125 dignitaries left the Massachusetts capital; they arrived in Albany that evening to attend a round of festivities. On December 29, 250 men of Albany partook of a similar celebration in Boston.[73] To Nathan Hale these events were a dream come true. His visionary scheme of the 1820s had become a 200-mile iron highway over which steam engines drew freight and passengers between Boston and Albany in less than a day.

But there had been many changes since Hale wrote his first editorial advocating a railroad to unite Massachusetts Bay with the Hudson. Plans for a state-owned system had given way to the formation of two separate private corporations.[74] At the route's eastern end stood the 44-mile Boston and Worcester, built entirely by private subscription to its stock. By 1841, its ownership as well as its direction lay concentrated in Boston. Built as the main "trunk" of a system that was to reach to Albany and Norwich, the Boston & Worcester soon developed interests and characteristics of its own. Its track ran through a thickly populated, heavily industrialized district, and the company catered to the needs of the region it served. It emphasized local passenger and freight services and the commuter business.

By contrast the Western Railroad's 156-mile line ran through a diverse area. It not only served the growing industrial centers of Palmer, Ludlow, Springfield, and Pittsfield, but it also spanned a wilderness to connect the Erie Canal with tidewater at Boston. From the first the Western found itself balancing two potentially contradictory but equally important interests: the hauling of local passengers and freight against the movement of through traffic from the Hudson to the Atlantic. The fact that the long-distance business remained important to the Western, but was peripheral to the Worcester, boded ill for a smooth relationship between the two corporations.

The Boston & Worcester entered the 1840s on a strong financial footing. It had no bonded debt, and its stock sold well above par.[75] The Western, however, was mired in a slough of uncertainty, for the financial troubles which had wrenched control of it from Hale's hands continued to stalk it. The stockholders, although largely centered in Boston, included a substantial minority from Springfield and Pittsfield, towns that demanded and got a significant vote in management. In addition the Commonwealth of Massachusetts held one-third of the company's stock. The railroad's owners clamored vainly for dividends, and the corporation's shares sold in the market at prices that sagged as low as 40 per cent of par value.[76] The Western also reeled under a bonded indebtedness of 5 million dollars, all of which the Commonwealth of Massachusetts or the city of Albany guaranteed. In 1841 doubt clouded the Western's ability to meet even interest payments. This led its management to insist that the Worcester road help by giving the Western the lion's share of the profits from the joint business.

This proposal split the two managements and engendered bitter fights for almost thirty years. Hale's system, deeply committed to a capital-improvement program geared to serve local needs along its tracks, declined to haul the joint traffic at low rates, especially since it claimed that the prospect of increased business from the Western had forced the outlay of huge amounts of capital to install the necessary double track, terminals, and yards required by the new traffic. The Western countered that the rugged nature of its line entitled it to special consideration.

A comparison of capital expenditures points up the difference between the two roads. The Worcester cost more per mile to build than the Western.[77] By 1843 the Worcester had spent a total of about $2,800,000 on its physical plant, an investment of approximately $60,000 per mile. Although the Western sank nearly $7,100,000 into its system, this was only $45,000 per mile. The public little understood these statistics because the Western's expenses were spectacularly visible. More than $3,250,000, or 45 per cent of its total outlay, went for roadbed, masonry, and bridges. By contrast but 25 per cent of the Worcester's capital went for those purposes. On the other hand, the Worcester's expenses lay hidden in land and terminals, which cost Hale's road in excess of $750,000, more than $100,000 above the total spent by the Western for the same items.

In its battle for rates the Western pointed to its steep mountain grades, which it said necessitated a big capital cost and vast operating expenses. But the Worcester insisted that its position as a terminal required huge investments in warehouses, yards, wharves, and land and that these, too, brought down upon the railroad extra operating expenses. In the years that followed, the public most often sympathized with the Western. The layman marveled at the line's costly stone arch bridges, deep cuts, and mighty embankments. He gazed awestruck at the two to four engines that thundered up the canyons pulling his train at a slow but sure pace across the mountain barrier, which for so long had thwarted commerce between Massachusetts and the Great West. To the public it was the Western that laid low the Berkshires, and the Worcester's argument that terminal costs were an equal expense fell on deaf ears.

CHAPTER IX

The Western Railroad in Crisis:
An Operating Man's Nightmare

IN 1842 GEORGE BLISS assumed the Western's presidency. If he entertained any hope of smooth running, it quickly faded, for his company was deep in the midst of problems unprecedented in the brief history of American railroading. The union of Boston and Albany at the end of 1841 transformed a local line into a major national artery. Suddenly traffic, or the threat of traffic, descended upon the Western before it was prepared to handle the load.

In 1842 the Western had several years of operating experience. Passenger service commenced in 1839 and early operation was similar to that on the Worcester. But nothing had prepared the Western for the stormy decade of the 1840s. Indeed at the beginning of Bliss's initial year as president, the Western seemed on the brink of total disaster: it still did not have a mail contract with the government; its Albany terminal was inadequate; its motive power was insufficient and unreliable; and worst of all, its safety record lay shattered by a series of spectacular wrecks.

The Western's early operations encountered a vital problem that plagued business leaders: the relationship between purely technical matters such as locomotive purchases and the unscientific realm of politics. The Western's operational crisis coincided precisely with a clash for control of the railroad by several powerful and determined interest blocs. The central issue was the setting of rates and fares. Warring factions attempted to turn wrecks, motive-power breakdowns, terminal inadequacies, and mail-contract squabbles into issues designed to weaken the administration of President George Bliss.

The Western's very magnitude made running trains more difficult than on the B&W. Although it was possible to time morning and afternoon movements between Boston & Worcester so that early runs were complete before later trains left their terminals, such practices were impossible on the Western. For example, the morning passenger train from Worcester to Albany started its run at 9:30 A.M.; it did not arrive in Greenbush (Albany) until 6:35 P.M. Initially the Western scheduled three trains a day each way (two passengers and one freight) between Worcester and Albany. This meant a total of twelve daily meets, or times when trains going in opposite directions passed each other.[1] Even assuming that there were no extra movements or work trains on the line, there was a scheduling problem on a single-track, unsignaled mountain system. Although the Western's management undoubtedly knew that safe operations demanded strict rules, only experience was to teach them how strict.

The twentieth century has become blasé about disasters. Although train, aircraft, and even automobile wrecks are headline news, there is a general acceptance of the maxim that accidents are the price of progress. Few newspaper subscribers are surprised to learn of several major disasters on the same day. That was not the case in Boston in the 1840s. Although ship mishaps were considered normal, no tradition prepared people for spectacular land wrecks. True, stages often overturned or smashed, but for the most part such accidents usually resulted in injuries rather than death and involved only a few people. By contrast, a single train carried hundreds, at speeds up to 30 miles an hour. The railroad disaster, with its potential to kill or maim scores, if not hundreds, held a special terror.

The Boston & Worcester's first few years set especially high safety standards: not a single major accident occurred involving a passenger train, and there was only one fatal freight wreck. Indeed accidents involving regularly scheduled trains on American railroads prior to 1840 were few, and the public soon came to regard the rails as an especially safe means of transportation.[2]

Events on the Western quickly modified that belief, for starting in the winter of 1840, there occurred a series of wrecks that startled not only Massachusetts but the entire nation. In February 1840 an engine killed a man at a crossing in West Brookfield.[3] In December of the same year, the engine *Massa-*

chusetts was approaching Springfield drawing nearly 40 freight cars. When the train reached the top of the hill that descended into the town, the engineer lost control, the cars gained momentum, and before the crew could apply the brakes, the train derailed and piled up in a twisted heap at the bottom of the incline. This wreck killed four crew members: the engineer, fireman, and two brakemen, all of whom left destitute families.[4]

Less than a year later in Westfield Township on October 5, 1841, there was a third and worse disaster. "The opposite [passenger] trains met, and the terrible consequences were immediately made known to the public. It appeared that the road had been opened but the day before [on Oct. 4] to the State line, [and] that the cars had run over the whole route [Worcester to the State Line at West Stockbridge] but once before the day of the accident."[5] This head-on collision killed a conductor and a passenger, seriously maimed eight others, and less critically injured nine more. All the injured were passengers except two members of the crew. Three months later, in February 1842 there was a fourth wreck. Frost twisted a section of track causing a freight locomotive to derail in the Berkshire Hills 8 miles from Pittsfield. Both the engineer and the fireman died in the wreckage.[6]

The public of the 1840s reacted with horror and disgust. The *American Railroad Journal and Mechanic's Magazine* editorialized:

> [as a result of the wrecks on the Western] public anxiety has been aroused, and inquiry is made as to what means are provided for the safe passage of trains. We have some recollection of having seen the rules and regulations for the . . . conduct of trains upon the Western Railroad . . . but there must be some fault in the regulations or in the mode of enforcing them. We are, for our own part, certain that such accidents are not necessarily attendant upon the railroad system, and that with proper care and precaution, most, if not all that has happened might have been avoided.[7]

Disaster brought the Western a host of problems. Since the railroad had no set procedures to compensate victims or to prevent future wrecks, the directors were forced to initiate policy. Immediately after the December 1840 Springfield freight pileup, a committee composed of William Jackson, John Howard, and John Lincoln began an investigation. The committee's attention focused primarily upon the four dead crewmen's dependents; each employee left a wife and children. The investigators determined that all four men had served the Western loyally. The directors on January 15, 1841, therefore, voted unanimously to make "monthly payments to the widows [of the employees] who were killed in the service of the corporation . . . for one year . . . in the same manner as if the deceased person remained in its employment."[8] This action followed the precedent already set by the Boston & Worcester, which granted a year's pay to the widow of engineer Hiram Bridges, who was killed in a freight wreck.[9] In neither instance was there overt public pressure to compensate the victims' families. And both corporations emphasized that their action was voluntary and stemmed from a moral rather than a legal obligation.

It took the spectacular head-on collision near Westfield, however, to bring a general examination of the Western's operating procedures. The startled directors did not wait for a public outcry to force action. They wanted to find the cause for the accident, to fix responsibility for it, and to prevent future incidents.

Within ten days the board committee on moving power, composed of John Howard, William Jackson, and John W. Lincoln, completed a report. The committee found a simple but deadly reason for the accident: the disregard of the company's fixed timetable. Conductor Warren, in charge of the eastbound train, was late arriving at Chester Village siding. The directors lamented:

> In conformity with the general order with which he had been furnished and the time sheet which he had then in his possession and which he had consulted on the route, he should have remained [at Chester Village] until the arrival of the [westbound] train. He must have known," the directors asserted, "by examining [his timetable] that if [the westbound] was then acting in conformity to the same order, that the trains [would] most certainly meet between Chester and

Westfield. [Since conductor Warren died in the wreck,] what motive he could have had in violating the provisions of an order of which he had been reminded by his brakeman can not . . . be known.[10]

The investigators concluded that there was laxness in distributing copies of new orders to the train crews and that the general control of the trains was too loose.

The committee on moving power recommended a sweeping study of train movements to include a detailed review of all operating procedures. The full board formed a new committee composed of Elias Hasket Derby, Nathan Carruth, Abraham Lowe, and Engineer George Whistler to draw up new operating rules. In the meantime the board ordered that the superintendent place baggage cars between the engines and the passenger cars instead of at the trains' rear as previously, a measure that might lessen the danger to passengers from head-on collisions. The board also specified that "no alteration in the time of running or mode of meeting and passing of trains shall take effect until after positive knowledge shall have been received at the office of the superintendent that orders for such change have been received and are understood by all concerned."[11]

On November 30, 1841, the special directors' committee to review the Western's organization and operating procedures made comprehensive recommendations, which the full board adopted. The directors' "Report on Avoiding Collisions and Governing the Employees" reveals a great deal about railroading in the early 1840s and about the problems that soon forced upon railroads the kind of managerial organization which later became the basis for the large-scale industrial corporations that arose after the Civil War.[12] Because railroads extended over vast distances and required absolute obedience of their workers and precise coordination of their various departments, the problems confronting railway management were closer to those of a modern-day concern with its far-flung integrated plants than to those of the pre-Civil War textile mills.

The directors attempted to end any ambiguities that might have led to past laxities. They fixed definite responsibilities

186

for each phase of the company's business, drawing solid lines of authority and command for the railroad's administration, maintenance, and operation. At the apex of power, just below the president, was the chief engineer, whose duties were soon to be assumed by the superintendent and who held ultimate responsibility for maintenance of track and structures. Under him the directors created three divisions, over each of which was a roadmaster charged with making the necessary repairs on track, roadbed, bridges, and buildings.[13] The company asked that each roadmaster keep a "journal of his operations" and make a formal monthly report to the engineer. Actively groping for ways to prevent further wrecks, the directors required that the roadmasters run handcars over "their respective divisions during the coming winter every morning before the arrival of the trains."[14]

The directors placed the authority for general administration of freight and passenger traffic, as well as maintenance of engines and rolling stock in the hands of the master of transportation at Springfield. And they created subordinate masters for each division. Reporting to these officials were the various station agents, who not only sold tickets and received freight but procured wood fuel for the locomotives as well.

The company's major shops at Springfield were supervised by the master mechanic, who in turn had deputies at various terminals and roundhouses along the line. As in the case of station agents, the master mechanic reported to the master of transportation.

Although the directors left much to the discretion of the administrators, they formulated careful and explicit rules for the operating men. As on the Worcester road the conductor had "sole charge of the train." He decided when and where to stop and when to start, and he was to report to the superintendent "any disobedience of the engineman." The new rules required that there should be at least three brakemen per train and that passenger trains should never have less than one to each car.

The directors minutely described the duties of the train-crew. Most rules focused on safety. A conductor attended "the brake of the first car in the train and his station while under way and not otherwise employed [was] on the platform outside the car and when he [requested] the engine to stop [he pulled] the check connected with the engine bell."

The conductor also had complete control over the brakemen, who at stops were to dismount and examine the wheel bearings of each car. If the train stalled, the conductor was to send a "brakeman to the nearest point for assistance with instruction to procure a horse if possible to enable him to proceed without any unnecessary delay." If the conductor expected to meet a train, he was "to send another brakeman forward with his signal, who [proceeded] with all possible dispatch till he [reached] the train expected with which he [returned] to his [own] train." If another train was following, the conductor sent another brakeman to meet it. At the terminal the regulations required the conductor to "proceed with the train to the car houses and there give his personal attention to the cleaning and preparation of the train for the next trip."

The engineman's activities were also carefully prescribed. "In descending grades higher than 60 feet per mile passenger trains [were] not to exceed 18 miles per hour and merchandise trains not over 10 miles per hour." All enginemen were to keep a sharp lookout on curves and were to ring the engine bell and then blow the whistle at intervals until the train had passed from a curve to a straight track. The bell and whistle were to be sounded simultaneously when the engine was within 80 rods of a crossing and to be kept ringing and blowing until the locomotive crossed the road. Although the engineman worked for the conductor while he ran the train, at the terminal he came under the master mechanic's supervision.

The directors had good reason to set their own house in order, for the public outcry demanding that something be done to make the trains safe was clearly audible on Beacon Hill. In fact, on January 17, 1842, the Massachusetts General Court ordered that its "Committee on Rail Roads and Canals . . . enquire into the cause of frequent accidents upon the Western." More ominously the legislature directed "that inquiry be made into the expediency of enacting such laws as will have a tendency to prevent recurrence of similar accidents."[15] And equally important for the company's management was the legislature's desire to determine whether the agents of the corporation were chargeable with negligence.[16]

The committee was faced with at least three possible courses of action: First, it could, after investigation, recommend a vote of confidence in the railroad's management and propose that no further action be taken by the General Court. Second, it could find managerial negligence and censure the directors, thus bringing pressure for voluntary reform. Third, the legislators could adopt the concept of state responsibility for the well-being of railway employees and passengers, a course that, although attractive politically, contained serious pitfalls. Massachusetts railroading, but ten years old in 1842, lay at the doorstep of technological revolution. Laws written to protect the people in the early 1840s might limit management's response to improved technology and in the long run could serve to delay the introduction of advanced safety devices or prevent realization of increased efficiency inherent in new methods.

The legislative committee wisely recognized that in theory it was in the railway's "own best interest, as well as their duty to the public, to guard, by all means in their power against accidents which endanger life and property."[17] Since any proper management would do this, the committee focused attention upon determining the fitness of the Western's executives. After a month of investigation the committee exonerated the directors from any taint of negligence. Inadequate rules governing employees may well have been a contributory cause to the accidents. But the report maintained that "the directors have been at great pains to collect and compare their rules with those of other similar companies in this country and in England with a view to adoption of those which would produce the greatest security."[18] The legislators felt that management had attempted to assess their rules after each accident and derive from experience new regulations more in accord with safe operation.

The final recommendation, approved by the General Court, opposed legislative assumption of responsibility for railway safety. In a classic argument for an unfettered management, the committee observed that the Western's directors adopt the regulations which their judgment, aided by experience, pronounces best. They employ men whom they suppose to be the best qualified to discharge the duties required of them; but everything human is fallible; and so long as we live among men, whether we ride or walk, or wake or sleep, we are exposed to accidents and casualties. And until there is evidence of a neglect to use every reasonable precaution to prevent accidents on the part of the directors . . . the committee are not prepared to recommend any action which may censure the directors in this matter. It is hoped that increased vigilance, and care will hereafter prevent the recurrence of the accidents which have so alarmed the community; but the committee cannot suggest any legal enactment which can aid in producing this desirable result.[19]

As the year 1842 wore on, the Western's safety record improved, and management's attention focused on a new and almost equally vexing crisis—motive power. The system's completion to Albany in December 1841 created, for the first time, substantial freight traffic. This increased business was not unforeseen. Indeed during the summer of 1841, several months before the railroad's completion, the directors furiously debated the purchase of locomotives to handle the forthcoming Albany-Boston freight traffic. On August 26, 1841, the directors placed an order with Baltimore's Ross Winans for seven powerful "crabs," freight engines of a radically new design, to be delivered by December 16, 1841.[20]

The Winans engines—wrapped in violent controversy even before the contract was signed—became one of the bitterest episodes in the Western's history. Although much of the acrimony stemmed from reasons unrelated to the locomotives' merits, there can be no doubt that they proved a costly failure. Although December 27, 1841, saw the inauguration of through services between Boston and Albany and Ross Winans' contract promised the delivery of all seven locomotives two weeks prior to that date, the new machines were not around to witness the great event. Indeed Winans' first engine, named the *Maryland* in honor of the state of its construction, did not run on the company's rails until January 1, 1842. The seventh and last engine arrived more than six months later on July 10, 1842.

And in order to achieve even this delivery schedule, Winans was forced to subcontract the construction of three locomotives to Baldwin and Vail's Philadelphia works.[21]

If all had gone well, Winans' tardiness might have been overlooked. Trouble developed, however, on the *Maryland's* first run when a low bridge knocked off the engine's smokestack. The obvious remedy of shortening the *Maryland's* chimney failed; this decreased the draught, and lowered the steam supply, thus rendering the locomotive unable to haul more than a fraction of its designed load. Shortly crews were out raising bridges all along the line from Worcester to Albany to accommodate smokestacks of the original length.[22]

Winans built his engines to burn coal, which made sense in Maryland where coalfields were nearby. But the Western found Massachusetts wood to be less expensive than Pennsylvania coal. Winans had assured the Western's chief engineer, George Whistler, that converting the locomotives to burn wood was a simple matter. This proved to be false, for even when the smokestacks were restored to their original height, the engines never produced enough steam.

Labor was also a problem. Two firemen had to stoke furiously to keep the steam up, while one easily did the job in the company's engines of equal size and power purchased from Lowell's Locks and Canals Corporation. One railroad official commented before a legislative investigating committee, "we have found it necessary, in order to secure the services of suitable men for these engines, to offer them increased pay [still] they . . . prefer the other [Lowell] engines."[23]

Winans' machines were also shoddy. "The causes of their failure are various," lamented the Western's newly appointed chief engineer, James Barnes, in 1843. "Parts of the engines have been found too weak, and have failed in consequence. The cog-wheels first broke. . . . The crank shaft has frequently broken, the connecting rods have broken, from defective materials, and most often one part breaking will lead to damage in other parts. . . . The pumps have not worked well."[24] His list seemed to go on endlessly.

In consequence the railroad could never depend on the crabs. The *Michigan's* record tells the doleful story. The locomotive made its initial run on January 26, 1842, and on this trip an overhead bridge 5 miles west of Springfield felled the smokestack. A broken blower sent the *Michigan* to the shops between January 31 and February 8. Two days later the locomotive went to Greenbush as a replacement for the *Maryland,* which was out of service due to a twisted spur wheel on its shaft. February 12 saw the *Michigan* break down again. This time it was in the shop for over six weeks until March 31. On April 14 the strap to the main connecting rod broke. And as the year went on, there was more of the same trouble.[25]

Statistics supported the verbal criticism. In 1843 the fifteen engines built by the Locks and Canals Corporation ran a total of more than 290,000 miles, and their repair cost about $13,500 for the year. By contrast Winans' seven locomotives ran less than 82,000 miles but their repair bill came to almost $12,000, or nearly the maintenance costs for the Lowell engines.[26]

A statistical comparison of operating costs also showed the Winans engines at a substantial disadvantage. In 1842 "estimated expenses per mile of running the . . . crab engines . . . as compared with the large Lowell engines, rating wood at $3 per cord and oil at $1 per gallon [with a] load [of] 25 cars over grades of 45 to 60 feet per mile" indicated that it cost 21 cents per mile for the Lowell engines and 35 cents per mile for Winans' locomotives.[27]

Unfortunately, during this critical period the Western lost the services of its chief engineer, George Whistler, who in May 1842 resigned to accept a commission from the Russian Czar to build the railroad between St. Petersburg and Moscow. It is true that the Western's completion through to Albany finished Whistler's major task; but when the chief engineer left, so went the crabs' staunchest ally. As late as April 1842 long after it was apparent that Winans' locomotives were failing, Whistler wrote "I first recommended them to be purchased, and I am full confident that when certain alterations are completed . . . they will prove to be better adapted to the economical running of the Western than any other engines I am acquainted with."[28]

But even before Whistler's departure there was substantial concern about Winans' engines. In February 1842 as a direct result of both the *Maryland's* troubles and Winans' tardy delivery, the directors voted to contract with the Locks and Canals Corporation to exchange an 11-ton passenger locomotive for a 20-ton freight engine.[29] This was absolutely necessary to maintain the road's freight service. In March 1842 after two or three crabs had arrived, one of the Western's directors, Dr. Abraham Lowe, felt that their poor performance might justify canceling the balance of the contract. Said Lowe to a fellow director, "Let us, while we can, recede, and make the best of a bad bargain."[30]

Although Winans delivered all seven engines, they were the last ever purchased by the Western from the Baltimore shops, even though Ross Winans went on to a distinguished and successful career building railway motive power. In August 1842 the Western placed orders for one freight locomotive each from Boston's Hinkley and Drury Works and Norris' Philadelphia shops. These additions would have been unnecessary had Winans' locomotives given satisfactory service.

Whistler's successor, James Barnes, began his duties in late 1842 after the Winans engines had all arrived. If Barnes had an open mind when he started, it did not take him long to close it. Although the new chief engineer admitted that the crabs might at least be modified to run adequately, he had no doubt that they were inferior to engines manufactured by other shops. In answer to the question whether, according to his experience, he would select locomotives from the Winans, Norris, or Lowell works, he said bluntly, "I should select the Lowell or the Norris engines."[31]

The crabs never did run well. By 1849 all seven had been scrapped, the *Maryland* being the first to meet the torch in 1847, barely five short years after her maiden trip. Ironically, the *Suffolk*, a 10-ton engine built by the Locks and Canals Corporation in 1839 to initiate service on the Western, was still rolling merrily along the company's tracks years after the crabs' demise. In fact the *Suffolk* ran until 1852, when it was sold to another railroad, where it had a long and productive life.[32]

The Western also suffered the consequences of poor planning for an Albany terminal. The Albany & West Stockbridge company's corporate title was misleading, for the road came no closer to Albany than Greenbush on the Hudson's eastern bank directly across from the capital city. For heavy freight, which in 1842 moved mainly by canal boat west of Albany, a rail terminus on the Hudson's eastern shore presented no problem since it was as easy to tow canal boats to docks on one side of the river as the other, provided that adequate facilities for the transfer of freight from water to rail were available.

For passengers and freight not associated with canal boats the Hudson proved a mighty barrier. Inadequate technology, lack of finances, and opposition from upriver interests made bridging the Hudson at Albany impossible. The only ways, therefore, to cross the river were by the bridge at Troy, which meant a 16-mile detour, or by ferry.

Unfortunately at the time the Western opened, it did not have proper facilities for canal boats, and it had made no arrangements for a company-owned ferry between Greenbush and Albany. The railroad had long-range plans for construction at Greenbush of an elaborate terminal for the direct interchange of freight between canal boats and rail cars. Meanwhile the corporation proposed to rely on the city of Albany's municipal ferry and temporary docks for canal interchange. This plan had obvious drawbacks since the railroad terminus was located ½ mile from that of the city ferry, thus burdening traffic with the added expense and inconvenience of carriage hire and truckage.

Worse yet, the municipal ferry proved totally inadequate to the system's need. The city ferry consisted of two boats, a 25-horsepower steamer, and an even smaller boat propelled by horses. During the first two months of 1842 ice and high water kept them out of service for thirty-three days, and passengers resorted to crossing the river on the ice, in row boats, or by the 16-mile detour via Troy. And the experience of past years indicated that there were many days in the spring and summer when the city boats stopped running for "want of power to stem the river current."[33]

By March 1842 it became obvious that the Western could postpone the purchase of its own boat no longer, and President Bliss recommended that his company buy a used steamer for sale in Albany. This boat, formerly used as a ferry in New York

City, would, after refitting with a new boiler, have twice the power of the Albany municipal ferry.[34] Although Bliss's proposal cost less than $20,000, the directors were split. Elias H. Derby agreed that the road must eventually run its own steamer, but he argued that an immediate outlay for a ferry would put too much of a strain on the financially ailing Western. Instead Derby proposed that the city of Albany change the terminus of its ferry to that of the Albany & West Stockbridge Railroad and then lease the entire operation to the railway. Derby's recommendation stemmed from his overwhelming desire to capture the Erie Canal's grain and flour trade for Boston. He demanded that the company's entire resources be focused upon constructing suitable facilities for canal boats. The old ferry could temporarily handle passengers and light freight, however inconvenient, Derby reasoned, whereas the high cost of handling grain and flour would keep the Erie trade of these items flowing down the Hudson to New York City. "My experience satisfies me," Derby wrote to Bliss, "that the greatest source of expense is the '*handling*' of merchandise, and with respect to it, I would as far as possible advocate the doctrine of 'touch not, taste not, handle not,' if dividends are desirable and packets are to be competed with."[35]

The directors overruled Derby's objections and purchased the ex-New York City ferry. On April 20, 1842, the corporation took a short-term lease on a city-owned dock near the Albany & West Stockbridge's own temporary terminal. Tracks were then extended to the leased wharves, and facilities were installed to accommodate both the new ferry, which went into service in the summer, and canal boats.[36]

Derby's warning, however, did not go unheeded, for the directors soon allocated over $100,000 for a permanent terminal on an island adjacent to the Greenbush shore. Completed in 1845, the freight house alone covered over 2½ acres, and it was reputedly the largest single building in the United States. Two tracks extended into the freight house and canal boats could dock along one side. Steam-powered machinery hoisted freight from the boats to the cars. Thirteen boats could be unloaded at one time. "A boat containing 500 barrels [of flour could] easily be discharged in two hours . . . indicating the ability

. . . for discharging merchandise to be 3,250 barrels per hour, [and] 32,500 per day of ten hours."[37]

Concurrent with the decisions on the Hudson River crossing, the directors found themselves engaged in a bitter dispute with the Postmaster General over carrying the United States mail. The public expected that the Western would replace the post coaches on the Worcester to Albany line, for speed alone dictated the change from road to rail. But the problem was not that simple. To the Post Office the Western Railroad was but a single link to two trunk mail routes, the first being that between New York City and Boston via Springfield and Hartford, and the second between Boston and Albany and thence to points west and north. Postal authorities demanded coordination between mail service on the Western and that of connecting carriers at Worcester, Springfield, and Albany. This meant that postal requirements would affect train schedules. Further, the Post Office had limited funds, and politics played an important part in their disbursement. Under both the Tyler and the Polk administrations the government favored southern and western states. The policy toward New England seemed to be to pay as little as possible. In all dealings with both the Worcester and the Western the word "subsidy" was never mentioned.

The Western Railroad began negotiations for mail contracts at a time when it was in desperate financial straits. In 1841 the company had a net operating income of slightly less than $50,000, a paltry sum compared with the annual $310,000 of fixed charges on the bonded indebtedness that the railroad faced starting in 1842.[38] Uncertain that operating income would provide sufficient funds to meet the fixed charges, the directors looked eagerly about for additional money. Their first thought was the Post Office Department.

Soon after train service commenced between Worcester and Springfield in October 1839, George Bliss, then acting as agent for the company, proposed that his railroad carry the Worcester–Springfield mail for the annual sum of $5,500. Burt, Billings & Co., which moved the mail in four-horse coaches six times a week for $3,000 per year protested, and the postal authorities rejected the railroad's offer on the grounds that the

196

cost was too high. Bliss, anxious to remove competing coaches, made a rapid counteroffer that lowered the railroad's price to $3,700. Finally on January 20, 1840, after negotiations that committed the railway to provide daily (except Sunday) mail service by horse to Leicester and Spencer, two towns served by stage but bypassed by the railroad, the postal authorities annulled the stage contract and gave it to the Western for $4,000 per year. Bliss maintained that the horse service to Leicester cost the railroad about $1,000 per year, which reduced the Western's mail income to but $3,000, or about the same as that received by the old stage line.[39]

The Western's first mail contract brought the corporation sound benefits. It ended competition, and since the mail was carried on regular passenger trains and involved no extra cars or employees, the $3,000 was nearly clear profit. In the spring of 1840, at the Post Office's request and at no additional compensation, the company provided exclusive mail cars in which a postal agent rode. This still involved no extra trains or schedule changes.[40] But the railroad's initial postal contract also established the dangerous precedent that the compensation paid to stagecoach operators for carrying the mail should be used as a yardstick for railway contracts.

The 1840 contract was but a temporary measure, and the impending completion of the Western to Albany brought new negotiations. Basically the Post Office wanted one mail train seven days a week and a second six days a week between Springfield and Worcester, and one mail train six days a week between Springfield and Albany. This bore little relation to the service required under the original contract. Not only did the Post Office demand Sunday service at a time when the railroad turned not a wheel on the Lord's Day, but it proposed that a mail train leave Springfield for Worcester daily at 3:30 A.M. This attempt to speed the New York and Boston mail required an extra locomotive assigned to an early morning train that would carry few, if any, passengers.

George Bliss was anxious for a new contract, and in April 1841 he went to Washington to bid on providing two daily mails, including the night run, between Springfield and Worcester, and on the Albany–Springfield mail, which would commence when the railroad was completed. Bliss asked $16,000 or $290 per mile per annum for the Worcester–Springfield mail. The Post Office rejected this and, to emphasize its displeasure, refused even to negotiate for the Springfield–Albany mail. Instead a four-year contract for that route was awarded to a stage company at $6,500 per annum.[41] This ended all negotiations and, although the Western's original contract expired in June 1841, the corporation continued to carry the mail, hoping that a future agreement would be retroactive. In January 1842 after the Western's completion to Albany, the Post Office dropped its request for a night mail and indicated that it wanted a new arrangement with both the Western and the Boston & Worcester.

Early in January 1842 in company with the Worcester road's David Henshaw, George Bliss went to Washington to negotiate a new contract. They worked out a joint approach. Both systems asked a flat $200 per mile per annum to carry the mails. For the Western this amounted to $31,000 per year. In addition, Bliss tried to negotiate an increased payment for the period from July 1841 through December 1841, the months when the Western carried the mail without a contract.

Bliss called on Postmaster General Charles A. Wickliffe during the evening of January 7. After waiting nearly an hour beyond the time of his appointment, Bliss was escorted into Wickliffe's office by the First Assistant Postmaster General, Major S. R. Hobbie, who aroused Bliss's ire by proclaiming that the Postmaster General was ready to decide the Western's case. Bliss retorted that he had "attended for the purpose of explaining [his] views of the case before asking a decision," but he added that he would still talk with Wickliffe.[42] Once inside, Bliss encountered a mind made up. The Postmaster General offered not the $200 per mile that Bliss wanted, but $150 per mile between Worcester and Springfield, and $100 per mile between Albany and Springfield. This came to $18,500 per year.[43] Bliss then inquired about payment for the six months of service already performed (July through December 1841) without a contract on the Worcester–Springfield route. The Postmaster General replied that he was willing to allow $356 above the old contract rate. Enraged, Bliss lost control of his temper, told the Postmaster General that "This is too small a game for me to play," and stalked out.[44] Meanwhile, David Henshaw, who had powerful friends in the Tyler administration, came to terms with the Postmaster General. The Worcester road received $188.88 per mile, all service to be rendered by the road's regular passenger trains, except for one special Sunday run.[45]

Back in Massachusetts Bliss felt that he could force the Post Office to bend to his will. The plan was simple: just refuse to carry the mail and thereby encourage the public to pressure the Post Office into accepting the railroad's terms. On January 31, 1842, at Bliss's urging the Western's directors instructed the company's superintendent "to prevent the transportation of mail matter for the Post Office Department or for their benefit, either directly or indirectly . . . so long as the corporation have no contract for carrying the mail."[46] This order merely ratified a *fait accompli*, for on January 25, the Western, to use Bliss's own words, "Threw out the mails."[47]

Bliss felt that he was on strong ground. He had printed in pamphlet form a letter to Postmaster General Wickliffe. In this broadside, which received wide distribution throughout the state, Bliss told of rude treatment accorded him by the Post Office and of its niggardly offers for compensation.[48] Simultaneously articles supporting the railroad's position, written under such pen names as "Common Sense," appeared in the Boston *Atlas* and other papers. Chief among Common Sense's arguments was that the Postmaster General believed "that the proper basis for all contracts for transporting the mail was the old stage rates."[49] This, implied Common Sense, proved the Postmaster General's lack of sympathy for the railroad. As final evidence of the Western's good faith, the directors offered to submit the entire question to a board of arbiters to be appointed by the governor or the legislature.[50]

To Mr. Bliss's surprise the Postmaster General was not helpless. Immediately Wickliffe dispatched an open letter to Bliss which found its way into the Boston press. Filled with sarcasm, Wickliffe matched Bliss point by point.

When I announced [my determination to pay only an additional $356 for the six months of mail service for July through December 1841,] you did remark that you would not accept it, 'It was too small a game,' a remark which would have been responded to by me but for a rule that I have always observed in official duties not to notice remarks of this character of those with whom I am called to act. Nor am I in the least offended that you should deem the reply worthy of record in your letter. . . . I declined the proposals for carrying the mail made by you between Worcester and Albany . . . because I thought them exorbitant. The citizens of Boston . . . upon an investigation of the facts . . . will see in the demand of $200 per mile, equal to $31,000 per year, an exaction to which it is neither the duty nor the interest of the Department to submit. Under your former contract you transported the mail from Worcester to Springfield for $72.72 per mile. You now demand $200 per mile. The Department offers you $150 per mile.[51]

The Postmaster General posed the argument on the narrowest financial terms. He demonstrated that the railroad would receive substantially more than had stagecoaches for transporting the Boston to Albany mail. The Post Office, he argued, was willing to double the compensation the Western had received for the Springfield–Worcester run. Wickliffe concluded, "The offer which your company has rejected was to pay you $150 per mile between Worcester and Springfield for [twice daily] service six times a week and $100 per mile for single service six times per week between Springfield and Albany equal to $18,250 per year. You ask $31,000. I am still anxious and willing to close the contract with your company," but he added, if you persist in your demand "for $200 per mile, I wish it distinctly understood that the Department cannot and will not pay it."[52]

Bliss's action in throwing the mails off the trains brought a quick response not only from the Postmaster General, but from the businessmen of Boston and the towns along the line. The Massachusetts Legislature immediately launched an investigation. The General Court found the basic cause for the dispute to be a simple quarrel over money. Concluded the legislators, "the corporation refused to carry the mail because the Postmaster General would not pay the price demanded and the public are suffering great inconvenience."[53] The General Court's entire analysis followed the Postmaster General's reasoning, not Bliss's; that is, it compared the compensation received by stage companies to that offered to the railroad. The legislators asked that the Western accept the Postmaster General's terms and resume mail service forthwith.

Faced with heavy pressure from all segments of state opinion, the directors capitulated. They promptly negotiated a contract with E. T. Bridge, a special agent of the Post Office Department. The Postmaster General won the major victory, for the railroad accepted $100 per mile for the Springfield–Albany service and $150 per mile for the Worcester–Springfield run. This meant that the company received the $18,250 that had been offered originally.[54] Further, the directors agreed "with great reluctance to the requisition of the Department to establish a Sunday mail . . . a measure (to say nothing of the additional expense it occasions) which does violence to the feelings of the community on the line of the road and prevents an observance of the Sabbath by many officers and servants of the company."[55] The Sunday service was included in the $18,250. The railroad, however, won a temporary victory on scheduling, for with the exception of the Sunday run, all mail was to be carried on regular trains. The Post Office agreed not to change mail schedules without the company's consent. Consequently on February 21, 1842, the Western Railroad ended its boycott and again carried the United States mail.[56]

Bliss had blundered badly. Animosity toward Postmaster General Wickliffe and a miscalculation of his influence with the Massachusetts public had led him into an open clash he could not win. Bliss succeeded only in illuminating the railroad's poor bargaining position. A threat to throw off the mails might have had some impact, but the act, coupled with the company's quick surrender, exposed the threat's emptiness. The dispute proved conclusively that a determined Postmaster General could force the railroad to carry the mails and that there was little that the corporation could do about unfavorable rates.

Bliss also failed to communicate to the public the complex points in the dispute. He maintained that the rates offered by Postmaster General Wickliffe had absolutely no relation to the cost or value of the service provided. Certain it is that the government made no effort to determine how much carrying the mail actually cost the railroad, nor did it evaluate the service in terms of enlarged capacity and greater speed. The Postmaster General was guided only by the government's ability to pay. The department received lump appropriations from Congress for mail transportation, and the Postmaster General had a comparatively wide latitude in making contracts with individual carriers. This allowed politics to influence decisions, and Wickliffe, a Tyler appointee and a Kentuckian, set rates that favored companies in the South and West. Bliss complained that many southern carriers and one system west of Albany on the route to Buffalo received as much as $300 per mile for mail routes no heavier than Worcester to Springfield.[57]

A second influence on early railroad mail rates was the tradition of payments to stage operators. This, Bliss argued, was largely irrelevant because rail service was faster, more frequent, and had many times the capacity of stages. Contracts proffered to the railroads committed them to carry for a lump sum all mail, regardless of the volume, for a fixed period of time. Although stage operators signed similar contracts, as a practical matter their space was strictly limited. Adding coaches was not feasible without extra compensation. Not only did one rail car carry more than a stage, but adding extra cars to a train was a simple matter.

It made little sense to compare, as the Post Office did, the cost of providing a limited, slow service by stage with that furnished by trains. And of course the Postmaster General thought nothing of asking for special schedules. The speed and capacity of trains entailed a substantial capital outlay for locomotives and cars (to say nothing of providing the railroad itself) and the labor costs of at least an engineer, fireman, conductor, and brakeman. The only way the railroad could overcome the stage line's cheaper capital expenditures and smaller labor costs was through speed and volume. In short, the railroad was a technological break-through offering the Post Office benefits equivalent to those conferred on the industrialist by mass production.

Figure 18

Chester W. Chapin, who became president of the Western Railroad in 1854, is discussed in Chapter XIII, "Chester W. Chapin and the Formation of the Boston & Albany."

Figure 19

Boston & Albany Railroad: Train crossing the Hudson River from Greenbush to Albany. From an engraving on a Boston & Albany stock certificate.

Bliss in his public arguments largely assumed the rails' superiority. His main concern was that his corporation receive adequate compensation for providing the capital outlays for the new service the rails offered. By focusing his argument on what the Western should receive, he missed an opportunity to educate the public to the true advantage of the railroad. Bliss could have said "Trains cost more to operate than stages, but they make it possible for an aggressive Postmaster General not only to give better service, but by exploiting the advantages inherent in the railroad, to increase volume to the point where postal rates can be lowered."

Bliss feared that the Post Office would soon be in a position to dictate important company policies such as scheduling. Because the Western in 1842 was not earning enough to pay the interest on its bonded indebtedness, he was reluctant to commit the company to operate special mail trains, unless adequate compensation was provided. From this standpoint, the February 1842 contract contained one minor victory for Bliss since it specified that all mail (except the one Sunday trip) would go on existing passenger runs.

The Post Office, however, was not content with unfavorable schedules. Boston merchants demanded that New York mail, originating in that city on the previous day should arrive in Boston by 9 A.M. for morning distribution.[58] The only way this could be accomplished was by a special night train leaving Springfield for Worcester between the hours of 2 A.M. and 3:30 A.M. Indeed the Postmaster General rejected Mr. Bridge's contract because it provided no such service. Instead he proposed that the Western be paid $150 per mile between Springfield and Worcester if a night train were added. Otherwise the compensation would be $100 per mile. On May 18, 1842, the directors agreed to an experiment; they added for a six-month trial period (May 1 through November 1) a train leaving Springfield at 3 A.M. to connect with the early morning Worcester road passenger. If this proved a financial failure, the Western kept the right to withdraw the train on November 1, 1842, and accept payment at $100 per mile.[59]

Experience proved Bliss's argument, for the night mail carried an average of only eight people between Springfield and

Worcester on each run. Passenger revenue amounted to less than $750 per month, and for this the engines and cars ran more than 3,300 miles. Bliss estimated that even these statistics misled since well over half the passengers would have taken the railroad's other trains had the night mail not run. He concluded that continued operation of the train would prove "onerous to the corporation," and the directors agreed to drop it, even though this act reduced the corporation's compensation from $150 to $100 per mile for the Springfield–Worcester mail run. Complaints by Boston merchants caused the Post Office to press the Western for restoration of the night mail in December 1842. This the company refused to do.[60]

Bliss, as long as he remained president, continued his tough stand toward the Post Office's demands. Although he dared not throw out the mails, he consistently refused to run night service. He also forced the company to drop its single special run, the Sunday Springfield–Worcester service. The Post Office retaliated by reducing payments to the corporation by one-seventh. In 1845 the Western's contract with the Post Office expired. Bliss complained that the government continued to favor systems south of New York at the expense of New England lines. Many southern roads, he reported, received as much as $237 per mile compared to the $134.57 per mile offered the Western.[61]

In 1845 Bliss again found himself unable to enter into a contract with the Post Office. But he agreed to accept $20,186 per annum from the government on an informal basis.[62] Bliss acted bravely, but his was a losing cause. Already the Western carried the mails at rates that he considered unfair and that were not based on what it cost to provide mail service or on a measure such as tons carried one mile. It was only a matter of time until the Post Office won the battle of service as well. Bliss left the company in 1846. Simultaneously the Western prospered, earning enough to pay both the interest on its bonded indebtedness and a substantial dividend. By 1847 the Western's total revenues exceeded $1,325,000, of which less than 2 per cent, or approximately $24,000, came from the mails.[63] Carrying the mails, which loomed as a significant activity during the Western's struggling early years, had become a minor affair. But pressure for better mail service continued from the business community and the general public.

Indeed clamor for superior service gave proponents of new railroad schemes such as that for a New York–Boston "Air Line" a major lever. In 1853 partly to forestall the Air Line, the Western and three connecting roads assumed a night mail leaving Boston at 7 P.M. and arriving in New York nine hours later.[64] Compensation for this was a mere 85 cents per mile run, unsatisfactory, but the Western's President William Swift deemed it essential to placate public opinion.[65] In December 1853 Swift entered into a formal contract with the Post Office Department, which acquiesced in most of the demands made ten years previously by Postmaster General Wickliffe. It included night and Sunday operation, and for this the Post Office paid the Western a lump sum of $26,000, only $8,000 more than the 1842 payment and still below the $31,000 Bliss had asked in 1841. Swift defended the contract because it satisfied the public demand for better mail service and thus deflated competitive schemes, especially those of that great "humbug," the New York–Boston "Air Line" Railroad.[66]

By holding firm, the Post Office found itself able to name its own price, and finally it was also able to pressure the Western into meeting its schedule requirements as well. All this was accomplished by public pressure, which became increasingly effective as competition rose and the mails represented a decreasingly small proportion of the company's total operation. In the pre-Civil War period the Post Office had no legal way to compel the railroads to carry the mail, but as Mr. Bliss's futile efforts proved, it needed none.

CHAPTER X

Low Fare or High? Elias Hasket Derby vs. William Jackson

As soon as the Western approached Albany, the problem of passenger fares and freight rates rose to the surface. Built to link one of America's most important seaports with the Erie Canal, the Western was to become an important carrier of through traffic. Although Boston had lost out to New York City in the race to export America's western agricultural products, there was in 1841 a substantial trade in these goods between the Erie's terminal and eastern Massachusetts via packets operating on the Hudson River and Long Island Sound. And the growth of industrial activity in and about Boston, which coincided with the Bay State's rural decline, ensured a continued increase in the movement of flour, grain, and meat from Albany to Boston.

Furthermore, the Western, connecting as it did with the Erie Canal's eastern terminus, had the potential to siphon away to Boston trade that had become a mainstay of New York City's phenomenal growth. Indeed, to some in New England the railroad seemed a final opportunity to give Boston its due in the competition with Manhattan. Rapid industrialization along the Western's entire line also gave promise of a substantial local business in which the railroad faced no water competition.

The Western, however, did not control the entire Boston to Albany route; the eastern end to Worcester lay under the domination of a separate corporation. This meant that all the through traffic and much of the local traffic was the joint business of the Western and the Boston & Worcester railroads.

The Western's directors in 1841 faced the difficult and complicated task of building a rate and fare structure that would divert much of the Erie Canal's traffic from New York City to Boston, capture the entire Albany–Boston water-borne trade, and please the local users along the line. In addition the structure would have to provide punctually for the high annual interest and sinking-fund charges of $310,000 guaranteed by the Commonwealth of Massachusetts and the city of Albany and also permit the Boston & Worcester Corporation to continue regular dividend payments of at least 6 per cent. To construct a rate and fare schedule to satisfy all these requirements proved impossible.

In November 1841 one fact was inescapable: the monetary returns for the Western's first two years of partial operation augured financial disaster. Although the railroad had a net operating income (receipts minus only the operating costs) of $50,000 in 1840, an increase in the number of miles run by trains from 94,000 in 1840 to 160,000 in 1841 was accompanied by a drop in the net operating income to $49,000.[1] In blunt terms this meant that despite greatly increased business, operating profits were stagnating. Even more alarming, the combined operating income from the first two years did not amount to one-third of the annual $310,000 needed to meet the fixed interest and sinking-fund charges. Until these mandatory payments were met, the corporation could not even consider paying a dividend on its 3 million dollars of capital stock. This grim outlook contrasted sharply with that of the Worcester Corporation, which had paid regular dividends since its first return in July 1835—the same month that its trains ran through on the completed line from Boston to Worcester.

Against this background the board met on November 11, 1841, to fix the rates and fares that would apply when the Western Railroad was opened for through traffic in late December. Although their decisions were not final or irrevocable, the debate recorded in the minutes and in the papers submitted by each director raised nearly every important issue.

The rate and fare argument of the Western occurred before any of the other major lines—the Erie, Baltimore & Ohio, and Pennsylvania—had pushed far enough westward from the Atlantic coast to tap a major source of traffic. The Western's directors had no precedents to guide them. The Western Railroad files give a unique insight into what must have been the first attempt in the United States to set charges for such a traffic, and the records give ample evidence that it was not preconceived theory or the example of practices elsewhere that molded action, but the specific problems confronting the railroad and the economic interests of the contestants in the debate.

Passenger fares generated the most passion. To those who saw the Western as a device to lure business from New York City, low fares seemed vital in attracting commercial men to Boston; initially this traffic seemed more important than freight. That had certainly been true on the Boston and Worcester, and for the first two years the Western's passenger earnings nearly doubled those from freight. The directors did not anticipate that freight revenues would equal those from passengers by 1843 and would far surpass them by 1845. There was also emphasis on flour, for that trade on the Erie Canal was enormous, and all of it went through the port of New York before it was exported or shipped on to Boston or other coastal cities. If the railroad could succeed in capturing that trade, the battle with New York could be won everywhere; flour became symbolic of the fight to attract to Boston all of the produce moving down the Erie to tidewater.

Each of the directors stood for the groups affected by the Western's charges and created theories to bolster their positions. Basically the directors split three ways: high fare, low fare, and a pragmatic group which admitted frankly that it was uncertain as to what kind of rate structure ought to be adopted.[2]

Leading the fight for low fares was Elias Hasket Derby, who regarded the Western Railroad as the "Erie Canal prolonged and improved."[3] Derby, one of seven sons of the great Salem India merchant of the same name, took his modest inheritance and moved to Boston to begin a career as a State Street lawyer. Although he never owned significant amounts of Western stock, Derby soon earned a reputation for his "money making talents" and as a "great speculator in railroads" and land.[4] Steeped in the glories of Massachusetts' maritime past, he spoke for those who again dreamed of Boston's commercial supremacy. In September 1841 he exclaimed, "Within the brief space of 60 days the great outlet of the Erie Canal itself will then pour its tribute into our city." The Western Railroad would free commerce "with the interior from the tribute it has thus far paid to another seaport, and bring to it, with the speed of the winds, the merchants of the West, without subjecting them [to] New York."[5]

Associated with Derby in the fight for low fares were two other Bostonians, P. P. F. Degrand and Nathan Carruth. Degrand, a Frenchman, early made his mark as a stockbroker and in 1834 helped found the Boston Stock Exchange, of which he was president from 1837 through 1839.[6] Degrand was quickly caught up in all sorts of financial adventures including investments in Boston port real estate. Characteristically at a celebration sponsored by a scheme to fill in part of Boston Harbor to create new dock and warehouse facilities, he toasted, "Speculation, the true magic of modern improvement, the mother of all such creations with which this country abounds."[7]

Nathan Carruth was a late arrival. Born of a poor family in North Brookfield, a town not too far from David Henshaw's birthplace in Leicester, Carruth, like the famous Jacksonian politician, came to Boston and engaged first in the drug and then the paint business. He later made a fortune in the Old Colony Railroad, but in 1841 he seemed still to be searching for a start.[8]

Those who hoped to take the Erie trade from New York faced a difficult contest indeed, for pitted against the 200-mile Boston to Albany railway was 150 miles of the Hudson River. Since the United States Supreme Court had struck down the Fulton–Livingston steamboat monopoly with the famous *Gibbons v. Ogden* decision in 1824, the Hudson River passenger business had been notoriously competitive. The monopoly attempted to maintain fares at $3, or about 2 cents per mile, for the Albany–New York City trip. Cornelius Vanderbilt, entering the trade with capital amounting to scarcely more than $30,000, soon proved that he could undercut the $3 fare and make a profit. In the battle Hudson fares fell to 50 cents, and finally passengers were carried free. The old monopolists could maintain a $3 fare only by buying off Vanderbilt with a $100,000 lump sum and an additional $5,000 annually. But as soon as Vanderbilt had been appeased, Uncle Daniel Drew arrived on the scene to repeat the Commodore's successful tactics. By 1840, the ex-steamboat monopoly had paid out over $250,000 in bonuses and was committed to at least $50,000 annually to keep competitors off the river and maintain an unstable $3 fare.[9]

Conditions were no different on the New York–Boston steamship route via Long Island Sound. Here boats plied between New York and Providence, Rhode Island, or Norwich, Connecticut, where rail connections were made for the remainder of the trip to Boston. When Vanderbilt allowed himself to be bought off by the Hudson monopolists, he merely transferred his activities to the Sound. By the mid-1830s the $8 New York to Providence fare had tumbled to $4, and between 1835 and 1836 competitive wars brought it down to a mere $1 so that a through New York–Boston passage including a ticket on the Boston & Providence Railroad cost but $2.50. In the 1840s competition worsened, and fares sagged for a brief time to $1.50 for the entire Boston–New York trip.[10]

Freight tariffs were equally competitive. In 1841, flour moved from Albany down the Hudson to New York City at rates that varied between $1.40 and $1.80 per ton. And the comparatively slow sailing vessels on the Boston–Albany run carried flour for $3 per ton.[11]

On the Hudson and the Long Island Sound the Western Railroad faced more than a simple contest between rail and water on the ground of pure economic efficiency. It was also a fight between a corporate giant with an enormous investment in stock and bonds and a waterway that attracted many. Water rates did not reflect the true cost of transportation but the competitive pressure of the instant, and they fluctuated violently as new enterprisers entered the struggle and lowered rates temporarily below costs. Although all operators hoped to raise charges to a profitable level, and indeed there were periods when agreements ended cutthroat rates, the ease of entry into the river and sound and the large supply of new men and capital ready to join the fray kept the water rates uneconomically low.

By contrast the Boston & Worcester escaped the vortex of destructive competition. It easily vanquished road haulers, had no threat from water, and the enormous capital costs of duplication and the clause in its charter endowing it with a thirty-year monopoly of the Boston–Worcester traffic prevented a rival railway. Therefore the Boston & Worcester was able to set rates that provided an ample return on its investment. In 1841 passengers traveling from Boston to Worcester paid a fare of $1.50 for 45 miles, which came to about 3.3 cents a mile. This contrasted sharply with the 2 cents a mile charged by the Hudson steamers at the monopoly's $3 Albany–New York fare. If the Boston & Worcester rate became the basis for the through charge to Albany, the fare would be at least $6.50, or more than double that on the Albany–New York steamers. If the Western and the Boston & Worcester were to compete at all with water, even for the Albany and Boston business, the rate per mile would necessarily have to drop below the 3.3 cents charged on the B&W. Only through fares of $4 to $3 (2 cents and 1.5 cents per mile) could possibly be competitive with even the Hudson's monopoly rate.

But the Boston & Worcester, waxing fat on an ever-increasing local business, looked with understandable coolness toward an arrangement that would push it into the competition, which it so far had been able to avoid. Setting competitive rates, even with the Hudson monopoly, meant that the B&W would get as its share for a Boston to Worcester passage between 65 cents and 90 cents instead of its customary $1.50. Thus it was not difficult to forecast the reaction of the Boston & Worcester to low-fare schemes. If the B&W had a choice—and its management consistently thought that it did—that company would vote against entering too far into the competitive wars of the Hudson River and Long Island Sound.

For the Western Railroad, however, the choice was not so simple; if it were not to become merely a local carrier, it had to face some water competition. The question, therefore, was not "to compete or not to compete," but rather one of degree. What divided the Derby's and the Degrand's from the other members of the Western's board was the belief that some diversion of business away from New York City was possible.

Elias Hasket Derby's proposed schedule of rates and fares was a sophisticated, but determined attempt to intrude the Western Railroad into the competitive struggle to capture traffic from the Erie's terminal to the seacoast. Although his most controversial suggestions centered on passenger fares, Derby also presented a complex and comprehensive rate structure for freight. Like all the directors, Derby recognized that winter curtailed or ended navigation; hence he followed custom in presenting two sets of figures, one relatively high for the winter period of reduced water traffic and a second low schedule for the competitive summer.[12]

Derby's passenger fare proposal included both the principle of winter and summer rates and discrimination between local and through traffic. For the winter (from November 21 through April 19) he asked that the first-class fare between Boston and Albany be $5, with second-class two-thirds of that amount. In the summer (April 20 through November 20) he recommended that the railroad challenge the Hudson River steamboats with a fare of $3 for the first class and $2 for the second class. This would have put first-class through rates at $1\frac{1}{2}$ cents per mile, quite a reduction when contrasted with the 3.3 cents charged by the Boston & Worcester. But Derby did not ask for a general passenger fare of $1\frac{1}{2}$ cents per mile, for he recommended that local fares be 3 cents per mile. This put the cost of the 50-mile Springfield–Pittsfield trip at $1.50, or one-half as much as the four times longer Boston to Albany run.

Derby piously maintained that he was a "low-fare man" through and through. He blamed discrimination between through and local traffic solely on the Hudson River competition, and he gave lip service to the principle that "in no instance should the [total] way charge exceed the charge for a longer distance." But Derby's heart lay unmistakably with the through, not the local traffic. "I deem it highly important," he argued, "to charge the through travellers at a lower rate than the way passengers in consequence of the extremely low rates between Albany and New York."[13] Ten years later Derby, still pushing for low rates on through Albany–Boston business, followed the logic of his position to its inevitable conclusion. In arranging a Hudson River–Boston tariff, he maintained, it was indispensable to refer to Albany–New York rates. As to the local business he would "get for it as high a price as it would afford."[14] Thus Derby advocated that the profits from local business should be used to establish rates that would lure the traffic of the Great West to Boston rather than New York.

Derby's freight tariff was less ambitious. Although he felt that the railroad would capture all the water-borne Albany–Boston commerce, he preferred to wait on the outcome of his low-fare passenger experiment before plunging the Western headlong into the race to divert the Erie's flow from New York to Boston. Prevailing Albany–Boston water tariffs shaped Derby's suggested rates. Investigation indicated that a combination of river and sound steamers and the Boston & Providence Railroad moved high-value freight between Albany and Boston in three days for $8.50 per ton. The slower sailing packets charged $3 per ton. Derby's winter and summer schedules divided goods into five different classes according to their value. This "strictly discriminating tariff" charged "each article as much as it will advantageously bear." The $7 per ton maximum charge for high-value through tonnage such as shoes and fruit would successfully defeat the steamboats, and a minimum of $3.50 per ton on bulky items such as flour would vanquish the packets. Here as in the passenger tariff the charges favored the through business at the expense of the local.

Although Derby designed his entire rate structure to thwart water competition, he presented his plan to the public in a series of newspaper articles and lectures as "the Low Fare System."[15] The theory was simple and rested on the concept that high volume brought the increased efficiency that would allow substantial rate reductions. Derby insisted that the railroad, if it would but lower its rates, could attract enough business to fill its half-empty cars, which could then move freight as cheaply as barges carried it over the Erie Canal.

Derby's arguments, backed with logic and loaded statistics, captivated the public. "Can a railroad transport goods at the same cost with a canal?" he asked rhetorically. "A few years since, the impression was, that this was impossible, but such has been the improvement in the power of the locomotive, in the strength of the rail, in the construction of depots and cars and of the track itself, that a well built railroad can transport the bulky articles of commerce as cheap as a canal."[16]

There followed elaborate statistics that categorized operating expenses from locomotive wood, to salaries and freight-car repairs and "proved" that the Western could move freight as cheaply as the Erie.

Derby's statistics misled. They omitted capital costs entirely, no small item on a line for which the fixed charges on the bonded indebtedness and sinking funds exceeded operating costs for a number of years even after the system's completion to Albany. Derby's omission could hardly have been accidental since he included interest charges in computing the cost of moving tonnage on the Erie Canal. His argument assumed constantly full trains and a line always running near capacity. Such examples might have been useful to aid thought about rate and fare structures in the abstract, and they certainly were useful in whipping up support for his schemes, but they bore only a passing relationship to the real problems facing the management of the Western Railroad.

At the opposite end of the spectrum from Elias Hasket Derby stood William Jackson of Newton, who championed high fares. Jackson, like Derby, did not take his stand for theoretical reasons. He spoke for the Worcester Railroad and its management and for the state legislature, which placed him on the Western's board with nearly unfailing regularity from 1836 through 1842.[17]

Jackson's concern for the Worcester was both official and private. Ironically, just as he was called upon to suggest fares for the Western, he was busily engaged in Newton's first major land subdivision, which depended for its success upon frequent and inexpensive rail commuter service. Largely at Jackson's urging, the Boston & Worcester directors established in 1843 special commuter trains, which ran "daily except Sundays, three times in each direction, between Boston and West Newton."[18] This service, which required the purchase of two engines and several cars, was available to Newtonites at substantially reduced rates. Sixty dollars per annum entitled a patron to unlimited rides.[19] Even if passengers used the trains only five times a week, this meant an annual savings of more than $150 over the regular fares. There was no opposition from William Jackson to this type of low-fare experiment.

Jackson was elected to the Worcester's board of directors from 1836 through 1839, and from 1838 to 1840 he served as the railroad's agent, the same position George Bliss filled in the Western Railroad until his elevation to the presidency in 1842. When Jackson spoke for the Boston & Worcester, he represented a different point of view from that taken by Nathan Hale when in the 1820s he first espoused the railroads as a way to revive Boston's faltering port. Hale had long since reconciled himself to Boston's decline as a seaport, and he now represented the new manufacturing class both in his actions as the railroad's president and in his capacity as a newspaper editor. Consequently, Derby's arguments about shifting the balance of the Erie's trade from New York to Boston did not sway Hale as they might have a decade earlier.

The Worcester management in 1841 possessed a highly successful local line. Traffic, both freight and passenger, was on the rise, as was income, which enabled the directors to pay regular dividends that never sank below 6 per cent on the par value of the company's stock. But Hale's road did not oppose cooperation with connecting roads or the handling of through traffic. Indeed, 1841 found the corporation making elaborate preparations to accommodate increased business from both the Western and the Norwich & Worcester. This included "the great enlargement of the depot grounds and buildings in Boston . . . an increased number of locomotives . . . passenger and freight cars," and the double-tracking of the entire 44 miles of main line.[20]

The Boston & Worcester financed its extensive improvement program by new stock sales. In 1841, the corporation increased its capital by $300,000, in the next year by $400,000, and in 1843 by an additional $200,000. Significantly, the entire $700,000 of stock created between 1841 and 1843 was sold at or above par and was purchased largely by those who already held the railroad's shares.[21] This is striking evidence that in the short space of ten years the Boston & Worcester had moved from the position of a speculative and risky venture whose shares could only be sold by arm-twisting and civic patriotism to that of a coveted blue-chip investment. This change cannot be overemphasized since Hale and future leaders came to regard the maintenance of at least a 6 per cent and preferably an 8 per cent dividend as one of their most important duties.

Derby's low-fare proposals demanded drastic reductions in the Worcester's passenger fares, the major source of revenue from which flowed the dividend payments so essential to the railroad's stock-enlargement program and to the interests of the widows, orphans, trusts, and other long-term investors who came to make up the majority of the system's stockholders. In addition to the joint passenger operations the B&W and the Western had begun in 1839, the Worcester had since December 24, 1840, operated joint through express trains between Boston and Norwich, where the cars connected with steamboats for New York City.[22] For the next few years joint business with the two connecting roads threatened to overshadow the passenger traffic originating and ending solely on the Boston & Worcester. By 1844 passenger-miles resulting from joint operations amounted to 4,370,000 compared with the 4,400,000 produced strictly on the Worcester road.[23] The corporation's directors, therefore, had good reason to see joint traffic providing the greater share of the business.

Unfortunately for the Worcester road, the Norwich & Worcester faced difficulties as serious as those of the Western. The Norwich, although it soon became a local road deriving most of its revenue from towns in the Quinebaug Valley, had in the early 1840s high hopes of becoming a major link in the Boston–New York business. In 1841 it chartered the steamship *Belle* to ensure regular boat service between its terminus at Norwich and New York City.[24] In 1843, the Norwich & Worcester extended its tracks 11 miles down the Thames River to Allyn's Point, where it reached permanently navigable water. The Boston & Worcester subscribed to $35,000 of the $100,000 of bonds issued to finance this extension.[25]

The Boston & Worcester's directors originally felt that the Norwich was in a prime position to capture a substantial part of the New York–Boston business and looked forward to sizable revenues from the joint operations. To help the Norwich meet competition, the directors decided on $1.25 as their share of the through tickets issued between Boston and points on the Norwich & Worcester. This constituted a reduction of one-sixth of the $1.50 passengers were charged to travel solely between Boston and Worcester, but it was exactly the concession the B&W had given the Western in 1839, when Hale's road started to sell joint tickets to points west of Worcester.

Brutal competition for the New York–Boston business on Long Island Sound soon forced the Norwich & Worcester to lower its fares, and in May 1841 the Norwich's desperate management asked the Boston & Worcester to take less than $1.25 for its share of a Boston–New York ticket. This Hale's road refused to do.[26] Instead the Boston & Worcester put its faith in a series of "peace conferences" held by the various Long Island Sound rivals. These meetings started in 1842, and the Worcester's interest in them continued until at least 1847. Each time, the conferees attempted to set uniform rates and limit competition to service alone. Although these agreements stopped cutthroat competition momentarily, it always revived when individual boatowners, following Vanderbilt's successful tactics against the Hudson monopoly, lowered rates.[27] The Boston & Worcester's final reaction to rate warfare on the Sound was to drop out of the struggle. The B&W simply refused to take less than $1 for its share, and by 1850 the Boston to New York route via Norwich was rapidly dying.

The Boston & Worcester directors reasoned that the only purpose for lowering fares was to meet uneconomic rate slashing. While this might have been necessary for the Norwich and also for the Western if it was to divert to Boston the business then going down the Hudson to New York, the Worcester management felt that rate warfare would ruin all concerned. Therefore Hale's road wanted through business only if it involved gentlemanly competition, for it was certain that there was enough noncompetitive traffic over the route between Boston and Albany to ensure a profitable business for both companies.

For the twenty-six years after 1841, the Boston & Worcester viewed the profits from its joint passenger business as a vital part of its program to maintain dividends. In 1841, the road had a net income of $148,000. It declared dividends of $152,000, an amount equal to 7 per cent of its capital.[28] Since dividend payments were so closely matched to the net income, the Worcester management felt that it could take no chances on

risky fare-reduction schemes, the failure of which would dev-
astate the company's treasury. And the board felt that large
cuts for the Western would force similar reductions in the joint
business with the N&W, which through 1845 was substantial.
The Boston & Worcester wanted only the *status quo*. To change
things was to jeopardize the company's capital improvement
program, the experimental commuter trains, and most important, the interests of the system's stockholders.

William Jackson never forgot that he also represented the
legislature, to which he owed his place on the Western's board.
Although members of the General Court might have conflicting
views about the Western's role, nearly all agreed that it should
never become a burden on the Massachusetts taxpayers. Any
default by the railroad on the annual $310,000 interest and
sinking-fund obligations would have immediately thrown these
charges on to the Commonwealth and the city of Albany. With
the corporation's net operating income in 1841 running at less
than one-third the amount necessary to pay the fixed charges,
there was growing apprehension in the legislature that the
railroad might require further state support. This fear worked
against risky, experimental low fares and caused Jackson to
moan as early as April 1841 that "the actual net [operating]
income of [the road so far] is not 2 per cent upon the outlay for
its construction."[29]

William Jackson's proposed rate structure, although less
complex than Derby's, had many of the same characteristics:
different tariffs for winter and summer, classes for freight according to value and bulk, and discrimination between the
long haul and the short haul. The basic difference lay dramatically exposed in the through passenger fares, for Jackson saw
no chance of diverting New York–bound passengers to Boston.
Whereas Derby suggested a winter fare of $5 and a summer
fare of $3 for first-class travel between Boston and Albany,
Jackson urged $10 in winter and $8 in summer, or failing that,
a standard year-round fare of $8. For local passengers Jackson
asked 4 cents per mile compared with Derby's 3 cents. As
payment to the Worcester railroad for its portion of joint tickets,
Jackson felt that it should receive between $1 and $1.25 in contrast with Derby's proposal of 70 cents.[30]

Jackson's freight tariffs were more complex than his passenger rates. Although he wanted no part of diverting flour from New York to Boston, he did hope that the railroad would carry most of that commodity then going via water between Albany and Boston. Consequently Jackson urged that flour be taken at $5.60 per ton in the winter and at $3.75 per ton in the summer. He agreed with Derby, however, that competition might force a rate of $3 per ton, and he felt that if the $3.75 rate failed, the lower charge should be tried.

Discrimination against local freight in favor of through shipments was unavoidable, Jackson argued, and it stemmed solely from water competition. Jackson also proposed that his corporation meet water competition at Springfield and Westfield, the only two inland places on the line with river or canal outlets. The resulting rate structure produced some peculiar results. Flour going but 50 miles from Albany to Berkshire Mountain points was to cost $5 per ton; that to Springfield or Boston, twice to four times as far, $3 to $3.75 per ton. Jackson admitted that inland towns might object, but he thought such complaints "groundless." Freight rates at these towns were historically higher than at Boston, Springfield, and Westfield, and as long as water transport remained a consideration, he thought this condition natural. Further, Jackson added, freight charges to inland places would not be "more than half what it has cost" by horse and wagon prior to the railroad.[31]

The basis for Jackson's fare structure, like Derby's was pragmatic, but the goals were different. Derby hoped his recommendations would open the way for a duel with New York City for the traffic of the West. Jackson rejected that idea as dangerous; his proposals aimed to ensure that the railroad would earn enough to pay its fixed charges and to do this without leaning too heavily on its neighbor, the Boston & Worcester.

The theory about setting rates and fares that emerges from Jackson's writing must be tempered by the realization that it is in part a reaction to Derby and an apology for his own interests. Jackson clashed head-on with Derby's claim that low rates produced profits. "It is not true," he argued, "[that on] the North River [Hudson] nor any other great thoroughfare, that the increase of the number of passengers in any considerable degree is attributable to low fare. On the contrary it is great numbers, produced by a great population that produces a low fare, and nothing but that can or will do it."[32] Jackson felt that in the thinly settled region between Albany and Worcester there was a limited quantity of traffic that normally moved along the Western's route and that would use the trains regardless of the rate structure. Low fares, he reasoned, would not increase this traffic enough to offset the losses caused by rate reduction, and entering into the Hudson competition was suicidal. Of course Jackson recognized that rails, by reducing the cost of travel and cartage, compared with stages and wagons, would eventually stimulate growth. Thus in the long run he agreed that fares would go lower, but this to Jackson would be a gradual trend, not one that could be initiated at the beginning of the Western's life.

The two keys to building rate and fare structures were the charges made by competition and the needs of the railroad's treasury. Therefore each road had to assess its own problems and set charges accordingly. Jackson stated that "a road costing $50,000 per mile should receive more than another costing but $20,000 per mile. The average cost of railroads [in the United States] will not probably be found to exceed $20,000 per mile, while the Western will be but very little less than $50,000."[33] This was simply another way of saying that the directors must fix rates that would pay for the capital used in the line's construction. Jackson also argued that the Western's steep grades required "double the power necessary on other railroads for carrying the same load."[34] These two claims—high capital costs and high operating costs—became the basis of the Western's policy of charging higher rates per passenger- and ton-mile than the Boston & Worcester, a policy to which Hale's road did not object, provided that the Worcester was allowed to charge what it considered necessary to its own interests.

Jackson felt that the railroad should meet competition when it had a chance of winning but should otherwise abstain. He argued that the directors must learn from the boatowners on the Hudson and the Sound. Their experience refuted the idea that profit is increased by low fares. "No boat company," he asserted, "has ever reduced the fare until driven to it by competition and on both routes [Hudson and Sound] the moment competition ceased the fare has gone up. With all their shrewdness and sagacity (no men have more of these characteristics than boat owners) and their superior opportunity of knowing what is to be expected from reduction, none of them have in any instance . . . put down fares to increase receipts or with expectation of anything but loss from it."[35] Of course Jackson was "high fare" only in relation to Derby, and in the matter of freight the two stood remarkably close together. Jackson, like Derby, hoped to see general benefits from the Western, but the man from Newton had no desire to court financial disaster by unnecessary competition.

Between the extremes of Jackson's high-fare proposals and the low charges advocated by Derby, Degrand, and Carruth stood the majority of the Western's directors.[36] Men like the Boston industrialist, Edmund Dwight, and his Springfield associate and banker, John Howard, or those from smaller towns along the line such as the Pittsfield merchant, Thomas Plunkett, agreed with Jackson that the Western must not be allowed to default on its debt or to slight its stockholders. At the same time they hoped for the lowest rates consistent with profitable operation. But none were so captivated by a single interest, as were Derby, Carruth, and Degrand, that they could not approach the entire issue with a large degree of flexibility. Most of them agreed with retiring President Thomas B. Wales, who when asked to suggest freight rates replied, "I am not . . . well prepared to give you positive answers, being entirely without the knowledge of the expense actually incurred in transporting a ton of merchandise per mile."[37] Wales felt that $6 should be the Boston–Albany first-class passenger fare and that local rides should vary between $3\frac{1}{4}$ and $3\frac{1}{2}$ cents per mile, but he was even willing to compromise on this.

Wales proposed this guide rule: "Freight should pay the whole expense of running the road and the income from passengers should go to pay the interest on the loans and the repairs of the road."[38] Only experience, however, would provide satisfactory data for final rates. Until such time as the Western had such data, the directors had to maintain an open mind.

The committee to which the directors assigned the task of

preparing a new rate and fare structure shifted the varying arguments and proposed a solution that satisfied neither the high- nor the low-fare advocates, but it came closer to Derby's position than to Jackson's. For the first-class passenger fares the committee recommended a $5.50 through rate between Albany and Boston. For freight it established three classes, placing merchandise in each according to its value. The through Albany–Boston rates were: $10 per ton for the first class, $8 per ton for the second class, and $6.50 per ton for the third class. Flour stood in a separate category; it was to be carried for $5 a ton between Albany and all stations east of Springfield, including Boston.[39]

The directors met to consider these recommendations on November 11, 1841. Nathan Carruth immediately advocated that the first-class through winter passenger fare conform with Elias Hasket Derby's initial recommendation of $5. This failed. William Jackson then moved that the through fare be $8, but his motion also lost. Next Springfield's John Howard proposed that the through fare be $6. On this question the eight directors present split evenly. The tie killed the motion, and the board then agreed to accept the committee's report with but insignificant variations.[40]

The decision of November 1841 settled nothing, for it fixed only the noncompetitive winter rates. In the spring of 1842 another navigation season would bring with it renewed business from the West down the Erie Canal and the Hudson River to New York City. Then would be the time of decision. The Western Railroad would either become a regional line, content to serve existing ways of life in New England, or it would act as a dynamic new force, rejuvenating the port of Boston and rededicating the city as a major emporium and exporter of western goods. If the Western Railroad failed to alter the basic trading pattern established by the opening of the Erie Canal, it would not be the fault of Elias Hasket Derby.

The Embattled Mr. Bliss

GEORGE BLISS took the Western's throttle on March 1, 1842, just one month before the railroad would again institute summer rates and fares. He, like Thomas B. Wales, the retiring president, had no fixed notions about railroad tariff structures. But Bliss came from Springfield, not from Boston, and his major goal had never been the restoration of Massachusetts' maritime glory. Nor did the Boston & Worcester's problems trouble him greatly.

Bliss desired to control the Western. Of course he wanted rates and fares that would bring prosperity and economic growth to the towns on the line and, in the bargain, increase the value of his own land along the tracks. And Bliss longed for the day when the corporation could raise his $3,000 a year salary. He recognized, however, that the Western's problem was not to placate various interest groups, but merely to survive. Above all else Bliss saw that financial collapse would endanger alike the corporation's stockholders, the Commonwealth, and his own presidential tenure.

Bliss received his office from the railroad's board of directors, which in turn was chosen by the private stockholders and the General Court. The president's position reflected their confidence, and conversely any insurgents attempting to dislodge him had only to convince the stockholders and the General Court.

In 1842 both groups were restless. Collecting assessments from the nearly 2,000 separate stockholders had been one of the most difficult and unpleasant tasks associated with building the line. As late as March 1841 the stockholders assumed that they would pay only $60 a share on stock that had a $100 par value. But an unfavorable market for Massachusetts scrip and the mountain of unpaid bills accumulated during the final construction days necessitated new capital. With the advice of

some of the most prominent shareholders, but against the protests of small shareholders who owned a majority of the stock,
the directors in January 1842 decided to assess the remaining
$40 per share, which amounted to more than $1,200,000. Therefore at the very time the new summer rates were under consideration, collectors were making reluctant stockholders pay
an additional $40 per share. That capped the years of frustra-
tion that began in 1837, when the first assessment had been
collected. Up to December 1841 the lack of dividends could be
explained by pointing to the unfinished line. But with Bliss's
administration the pressure for dividends mounted to an intensity that no management could long ignore.

The Commonwealth's interests were two-fold, for not only
did it own one-third of the Western's capital stock, but it had
loaned the railroad 4 million dollars of scrip. A predominantly
Whig legislature and Edward Everett, the Whig governor, initiated state aid in 1836. Governor John Davis, Everett's successor, continued the policy. There was, however, little party
controversy over the question until 1841, when Marcus Morton,
the perennial Democratic candidate for governor decided that
the Western's growing financial troubles would make a good
campaign issue. He represented rural Massachusetts, the small
freeholders, who still were a majority of the voters and whose
lands shouldered the burden of state taxes. Morton accused the
Whigs of endangering the Commonwealth's financial security.
They had changed a large annual surplus into a deficit, and the
Western Railroad's growing financial troubles, in which the
state was deeply involved, boded real disaster.[1]

Davis won in 1841, but November 1842 saw Morton unseat
the Whig governor by a narrow margin.[2] Morton's opening
speech before the legislature left no doubt about his views on
the Western Railroad:

> In assuming the government of the Commonwealth, we find
> its pecuniary affairs in an embarrassed condition. It is deeply
> involved in debt. Its credit is impaired. It has been compelled
> to sell its own notes under par, to meet its obligations.[3] It has
> become a partner in a joint stock company controlled by in-
> dividuals. Its stock will take from the earnings of the people
> more than fifty thousand dollars a year, without any present

prospect of a return in dividends. And it has also involved its fiscal abilities with numerous private corporations, upon whose ability and punctuality may depend the public faith and honor of the Commonwealth.[4]

Morton's emphasis on the Western's control by the private stockholders rather than the state coincided with his earlier views that the Commonwealth should have received control of the railroad's board of directors in return for public financial aid.

George Bliss saw the full implications of Marcus Morton's oration. Bliss, no stranger to politics, maintained membership in the General Court and leadership in the Whig Party throughout most of his Western Railroad career and for many years thereafter. In 1853 he became speaker of the house, just as he had been president of the senate in 1835. Bliss knew that the railroad's failure to meet the interest payments on the Massachusetts scrip meant disaster—for the Whig Party, which would continue to lose elections; for the private stockholders, who would lose control of the company and perhaps their investment as well; and for his own future. He therefore focused on one goal: the building of a secure financial foundation for the Western. In concrete terms this meant the prompt payment of the corporation's interest and sinking-fund obligations and the institution of a regular annual dividend of at least 6 per cent. Only these measures could remove the railroad from state politics and alleviate a widespread fear that Whig aid "had laid every farm in the Commonwealth under mortgage."[5]

Putting the Western's financial house in order was no easy task. The company's net operating income of $49,000 in 1841 fell far short of the $310,000 needed to meet the annual fixed charges. Bliss saw only two sources of revenue: the rates and fares collected by the Western Railroad and a subsidy of his company by the Boston & Worcester. Clearly, though, the setting of rates held the key to financial survival.

At the time of Bliss's election he had taken no stand on the high- and low-fare arguments raised by William Jackson and Elias Hasket Derby. But Bliss could avoid the issue no longer. After giving the matter considerable thought, he came to the same conclusion as Jackson: that there was a relatively stable

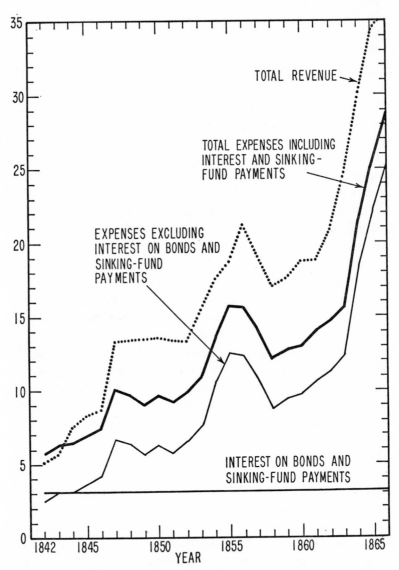

CHART I. Western Railroad: revenue and expenses, 1842–1866 (in hundred thousand dollar units). Compiled from Western Railroad Annual Reports to Stockholders 1842–1867.

passenger traffic between Albany and Boston, which the railroad would tap if its fares were lower than the traditional stage rates. He also felt that his company could not compete with Hudson River steamboats and thus lure New York–bound travelers toward Boston. Bliss, addressing the Western's board in May 1842, put it this way: "The extreme low price by water probably tempts a good many to take that course. This can only be met by a reduction on all through passengers, and it is extremely doubtful whether by a reduction . . . we should not lose more than we should gain."[6] Bliss, therefore, opposed lowering the summer Boston–Albany fare below $5, a stand that brought him into headlong clash with Elias Hasket Derby.

Bliss also came into conflict with the Boston & Worcester, which, he argued, should receive $1 or less as its share of the Boston and Albany through fare, even though the two systems kept the total charge to the passengers relatively high. If, for example, the through fare were $5, this would give the Western $4 or 2.56 cents per passenger-mile, and the Worcester $1, or 2.27 cents per passenger-mile. Bliss also demanded that the Worcester take less per passenger-mile for the joint local business. His theoretical justification was the Western's greater total capitalization and the higher operating costs caused by steep grades in the Berkshire Hills. Actually, as Nathan Hale soon pointed out, the Worcester's capital expenses were high because of terminal construction in Boston and because of double-tracking. In fact the capital invested in the Worcester per mile of road stood at $60,000 in 1843, compared with $45,000 per mile on the Western.

But theories had little to do with Bliss's position. His company in 1842 could not meet its annual fixed charges, while the Worcester paid dividends in excess of 6 per cent. As long as this condition remained, Bliss's request that the Western receive a higher compensation per passenger-mile on the joint through traffic received a grudging, if not an enthusiastic, approval from the Worcester's board.

The summer 1842 rate and fare structure that Bliss steered through the Western's board left the Worcester Road unhappy and enraged Elias Hasket Derby. The through Boston–Albany first-class passenger fare was reduced by a mere half dollar, from $5.50 to $5, which was clearly uncompetitive with the Hudson River traffic and far above the $3 fare Derby demanded. With a few minor exceptions local fares remained unchanged from the winter tariff.

A joint committee of Worcester and Western directors hammered out a compromise schedule for dividing receipts. Under heavy pressure the Worcester agreed to accept $1 as its share of tickets sold between Boston–Pittsfield and points west including Albany. The Worcester made it clear, however, that this arrangement was only a summer "experiment" and refused absolutely to take less than its customary $1.25 for joint tickets issued between Boston and points east of Pittsfield.[7]

Bliss and Derby worked together to produce a freight tariff that substantially reduced the through Boston–Albany charges. Their guiding principle was the diversion to the rails of as much as possible of the tonnage then moving via water between Albany and Boston. The new rate structure brought into sharp focus the contrast between the local and through traffic. In a joint statement, Bliss and Derby explained: "In order to control or compete with the transportation of merchandise through between Boston and Albany heretofore done principally by water at low rates, it was necessary materially to reduce the present through rates upon the railroad and at the same time for intermediate distances to keep as near the present rates as was practicable."[8]

The new summer tariff expanded the number of freight classifications from three to four. All through freight paid lower charges.[9] The vital through Boston–Albany flour rate fell from $5 per ton to $3.30, the exact charge customary on the Albany–Boston packet lines.[10] By July active water competition forced the railroad to adopt a $3 rate. Complaints from inland points, which were then paying more to move a ton of flour 50 miles than through shippers paid for the whole 200 miles between Boston and Albany, caused the directors to set the through rate as a maximum charge.[11]

The fall of 1842 brought the end of navigation and a new round of argument. Although the directors agreed to raise freight rates to the previous winter's level, they quarreled over a proposed increase in the through passenger fare to $6. Bliss,

Jackson, and the Worcester Railroad argued strongly for the raise, while Degrand, Derby, and Carruth demanded that the $5 rate be maintained. On November 29, the Western board voted five to four to raise the through fare to $6, or 3 cents per mile. At William Jackson's urging, intermediate charges were to be set as nearly as possible at 3 cents per mile. This act eliminated discrimination between through and local passenger traffic for the first time in the Western's history. Significantly, Derby, Degrand, and Carruth opposed this equalization.[12] The board's action was an important victory for both Jackson's high-fare position and the Boston & Worcester railroad, which again received $1.25 for its portion of a joint Boston-Albany ticket.

Bliss's cautious passenger-fare policy and the joint Bliss-Derby freight rates were moderately successful. The Western's gross revenues for 1842 topped a half million dollars, but the net operating income of $246,000 still fell short of the $310,000 needed to pay the annual interest and sinking-fund charges. If the $50,000 for the sinking funds were subtracted, the Western was but $14,000 short of meeting the required interest payments, which unlike the sinking-fund contributions could not be delayed. Fortunately the corporation's cash position, due to reserve capital and unspent receipts from the operation prior to the line's official completion in December 1841, allowed the railroad to meet crucial interest payments on time and gave the management another year in which to increase revenues to a level that could support the fixed charges.

Elias Hasket Derby's plans for low through passenger fares met defeat throughout 1842. On May 18, Derby made a desperate motion to reduce the through Boston–Albany summer fare to $4. Bliss's strong opposing argument carried the day, and Derby became convinced that only President Bliss's removal could clear the tracks for a low-fare experiment.[13] From the middle of 1842 onward Derby concentrated every effort toward forcing a trial of his low-fare scheme. His strategy focused upon winning over the private stockholders, who he hoped would at their annual meeting in February 1843 elect a slate of five directors favorable to low fares. He presented himself as the man who could turn the railroad into a profitable dividend-paying investment, and he blamed George Bliss for the Western's troubles.

In the fall of 1842, Derby seized a ready-made opportunity to exploit stockholder discontent. In September a substantial number of shareholders, still smarting from the final $40 per share assessment, presented a petition demanding interest upon "the installments paid by them up to the completion of the road."[14] This action coincided exactly with a directors' meeting held to determine the disposition of the railroad's net operating income.

At this meeting Derby, Carruth, and Degrand, the low-fare trinity, proposed that the net operating income earned prior to January 1, 1843, be used to pay a dividend. That the entire earnings for this period fell short of the fixed interest charges on the corporation's bonded indebtedness did not bother Degrand, who merely suggested that the interest charges accruing prior to January 1, 1843, be capitalized and charged to the construction account. Several hundred thousand dollars of unexpended capital in the railroad's treasury made this possible. Derby and Degrand's reasoning, which proved enormously popular with many stockholders, was that the years prior to 1843 were not representative of the Western's earning pattern. Both predicted soaring revenues for 1843 that would make it possible to meet the fixed charges and to pay a dividend.[15]

George Bliss was sympathetic to the stockholders' plan, but he categorically opposed any dividend until the railroad was able to meet its fixed charges. He recognized that if Derby's calculations proved incorrect, the result would be the elimination of the Western's cash surplus, the sole barrier that in 1842 had stood between the company and default on the interest payments. Indignantly Bliss took Derby to task, "[I] cannot believe," he lectured, "that any prudent association of men would so far hazard their reputation for correct business habits as to make their whole . . . expenses for the year a charge upon their associated capital, and divide their whole income among the associates."[16] The Western's board supported Bliss and voted to apply the entire net operating income prior to January 1, 1843, to meet the company's interest obligations.

The difference between earnings and the fixed costs ($14,000 in 1842), however, was charged to the construction account.[17]

Derby lost his battle, but he emerged from the clash as a champion of stockholder interests. The moral was clear: a vote against Bliss and for Derby and his supporters at the next shareholders' meeting was a vote for a dividend-minded management.

Although Derby attempted to woo stockholders by identifying himself with those pressing for early dividends, he balanced this with a systematic attempt to discredit President George Bliss. The Western Railroad had come within a few thousand dollars of meeting its fixed interest charges in 1842, the first year of through operation. That the corporation's income fell short, Derby argued, was due solely to Bliss's inept and perhaps corrupt management. Derby used every weapon at his command from the signed newspaper editorial to the surreptitious whispering campaign. In the *Boston Atlas* Derby stated his low-fare case, emphasizing that his policies would produce a volume of traffic great enough to sharply increase the net profit. But Derby's main attack concentrated not on low fares but upon the Western's operating crisis.

Over $80,000 had been expended on Ross Winans' worthless crab engines, Derby charged. Not only was this a waste of money, but the constant breakdown of Winans' crabs prevented the railroad from transporting much of the flour and other merchandise presented to it at the Albany terminal during the peak of the Erie's 1842 season. This forced tonnage onto rival packets, costing the Western much needed revenue. Derby blamed the Winans fiasco on George Bliss, the Westerns' agent in 1841, and on George Whistler, the corporation's erstwhile chief engineer, who was conveniently in St. Petersburg, Russia, and unable to defend himself. To substantiate the accusations, Derby referred to corporation records and memorandums, which revealed that Bliss and Whistler as members of the railroad's committee on moving power exercised a preponderant influence in the decision to purchase the Winans engines.

Derby had vigorously opposed the crab engines, advocating instead less expensive, but as fate willed it, highly successful

Table 2. *Joint passenger fares and division of revenues, 1839–1846:*
BOSTON & WORCESTER AND WESTERN RAILROADS

	FARES (1ST CLASS)[a]	WRR PROPORTION	WRR PROPORTION PER MILE (IN CENTS)	B&W PROPORTION	B&W PROPORTION PER MILE (IN CENTS)
Between Springfield and Boston					
Oct. 1, 1839, to April 1, 1840	$3.75	$2.50	$4.^{46}/100$	$1.25	$2.^{84}/100$
April 1, 1840, to Jan. 1, 1844	3.00	1.75	$3.^{12}/100$	1.25	$2.^{84}/100$
Jan. 1, 1844, to April 1, 1844	3.00	1.90	$3.^{39}/100$	1.10	$2.^{50}/100$
April 1, 1844, to Dec. 30, 1844	3.40	2.30	$4.^{11}/100$	1.10	$2.^{50}/100$
Dec. 30, 1844, to Jan. 1, 1846	3.15	2.05	$3.^{66}/100$	1.10	$2.^{50}/100$
Between Greenbush (Albany) and Boston (After the road was opened through.)					
Dec. 20, 1841, to April 1, 1942	5.50	4.25	$2.^{72}/100$	1.25	$2.^{84}/100$
April 1, 1842, to Dec. 15, 1842	5.00	4.00	$2.^{56}/100$	1.00	$2.^{27}/100$
Dec. 15, 1842, to April 12, 1843	6.00	4.75	$3.^{5}/100$	1.25	$2.^{84}/100$
April 12, 1843, to Dec. 1, 1843	4.00	3.00	$1.^{92}/100$	1.00	$2.^{27}/100$
Dec. 1, 1843, to Jan. 1, 1844	5.00	4.00	$2.^{56}/100$	1.00	$2.^{27}/100$
Jan. 1, 1844, to April 1, 1844	5.00	3.90	$2.^{51}/100$	1.10	$2.^{50}/100$
April 1, 1844, to Jan. 1, 1846	6.00	4.90	$3.^{14}/100$	1.10	$2.^{50}/100$

Source: George Bliss, *Historical Memoir of the Western Railroad* (Springfield, Mass., 1863), 162.
[a] Previous to April 1, 1840, way fares were about four cents a mile. From April 1, 1840, to April 1, 1844, three cents a mile. From April 1, 1844, to January 1, 1846, three and one half cents a mile. Second-class fares were two thirds of first-class fares.

locomotives from Philadelphia's William Norris. The Western's hurried order to Norris for a freight engine in the fall of 1842, while merchandise jammed the Albany terminal, seemed poetic justice. The implication was clear. If Derby's advice had been followed in 1841, there would have been no locomotive crisis. If his recommendation on rates and fares had been heeded, the Western's financial crisis would have been avoided.

Nor did Derby hesitate to remind his fellow directors and shareholders of the unfortunate Westfield collision. The damages, he emphasized, which amounted to more than $25,000, reduced the net operating income for 1842 by that amount.[18]

Next Derby attacked administrative waste. Annual salaries alone, he estimated, could be "reduced between fifteen and twenty thousand dollars."[19] Derby implied that Bliss used his office to line his pockets. Derby told a stockholders group how Bliss, in 1836, prior to assuming the Western's agency, charged the railroad $10 a day for work as a legal consultant. Derby gleefully recounted how the corporation paid Bliss, and then in 1837, upon the complaints of several directors, reevaluated Bliss's bills, allowed him $3 per day, and forced him to refund the difference.[20] At an unofficial stockholders meeting called by the low-fare faction, Derby charged that Bliss consistently used his directorship to inflate his own salary. An angry Bliss commented upon such an accusation:

"At that meeting as I hear from various sources, the Gentleman [Derby] who heads the ticket [for election to the board of directors in the 1843 election] brought forward and read sundry extracts from the records of the directors with which my name was connected, and among others a record of the votes given in March, 1837, when the salaries for the year were established. This was evidently done with a view to excite prejudice against me and to induce a belief that on that occasion I had voted to increase my own compensation [as agent of the Western Railroad]. I can see no other possible object in it. Whether this object was avowed, or not, I cannot say, at any rate the desired effect was projected, and I learn that from that time such a report has gained credence."[21]

Derby made it clear that Bliss had not reformed, for at a public meeting Derby read from the directors' minutes the result of a vote that set the president's salary, on March 1, 1842, immediately before Bliss's election to the presidency. A directors' committee had recommended a salary of $3,000 plus expenses for business travel. Mr. Derby moved that the president's expense account be eliminated and forced a roll-call vote. The minutes showed Bliss in favor of the expense account.[22] The charge stung Bliss, who referred to it as "an evident design of creating an impression that I had voted on a question in which I had an interest."[23]

More shocking to Bliss was the assertion that he had used "the patronage of [his] office to provide for family friends." Bliss retorted that there were over 400 men employed by the railroad and that "as of the returns of December last two of them are remotely allied to a member of my family by marriage and this is all. One of these," said Bliss, "is the Resident Engineer of the Albany [and West Stockbridge] Road who married a cousin of my wife and . . . was appointed to his present office . . . on the motion of Mr. Derby himself. The other case is that of my assistant and confidential office clerk; whose brother some thirty years ago was married to a sister of mine, since deceased."[24]

Derby's charges came to a climax in January 1843, just a few weeks before the annual stockholders' meeting, traditionally held in early February. His accusations produced two separate investigations. The corporation's shareholders initiated the first at a special meeting on January 10, 1843, called in response to a petition by the owners of 2,000 shares of stock. This meeting, although well attended by low-fare advocates, refused to act on a motion to instruct the directors to institute immediately a $4 passenger fare between Boston and Albany. Instead it named a committee of thirteen, headed by James Savage, a wealthy Boston lawyer, to investigate the corporation and to report to the regular annual meeting scheduled for February 8.[25]

One week later the Massachusetts General Court created a special joint committee under the chairmanship of Groton's George S. Boutwell of the house "to examine into the past management and present condition of the Western Railroad Corporation, with power to send for persons and papers."[26] For

Figure 20

The Boston & Worcester and Western promoted through freight business from Boston to the West, even as the bulky grain and flour traffic from the Erie Canal to Massachusetts Bay languished.

Figure 21

The Boston & Worcester's *Union*, a coal-burning passenger locomotive built by William Mason & Co., 1865.

more than six weeks Bliss and other railroad officials attended daily sessions. The problem of conducting two special probes of the same management simultaneously did not trouble the investigators, recalled Bliss ruefully, for the stockholders' committee met during the mornings and adjourned their proceedings in time for participants to attend the legislative committee's afternoon and evening sessions.[27]

The legislative committee made its report first, in late February 1843. Its investigation, although deeply concerned with Winans' locomotives, was wide-ranging and included an examination of alleged administrative waste and payroll padding. The committee concluded that although there had been no dishonesty, the purchase of Winans' engines "had been a most unfortunate one for the corporation." It censured the directors for assuming "too great a responsibility in the purchase of so large a number of engines, as they had not at the time been sufficiently tested . . . to justify an outlay of nearly eighty thousand dollars."[28] Furthermore, the committee agreed with Derby that the railroad's salaries were excessive and ought to be reduced. To emphasize this, the legislators resolved "That the State Directors of the Western Railroad Corporation are directed to use their exertions to reduce all excessive salaries, to abolish all useless offices, and to introduce and maintain a system of practical economy in the management of the road."[29]

If the legislators' report, with its damaging implications cheered Derby, the report of the stockholders' committee did not. Concentrating almost their entire effort on the Winans locomotives, the stockholders conducted a thorough, lengthy, and impartial investigation. After examining company records and holding prolonged interviews with directors and railroad operating men, the committee reported to the stockholders on February 8 that it needed more time. The annual election of directors was thus postponed. James Savage's committee made its final report on March 15, the day before the election of the new directors. The majority endorsed the railroad's experiment with Winans' radically different crabs and concluded "that the purchase of the engines was judicious." A minority, however, sharply condemned every aspect of the Winans locomotive experience.[30]

Derby's low-fare campaign, the attack against Bliss, the various investigations, and the corporation's precarious financial position combined to make the Western's annual meeting exciting. Unlike the great Massachusetts textile corporations, whose ownership was concentrated in a few great families, the Western's nearly 2,000 stockholders held but an average of 10 shares each, and no single investor had as much as 3 per cent of the stock. The annual meeting, therefore, when it finally opened in Boston's United States Hotel on March 15, assumed the character of a political convention. In all nearly 14,000 of 20,000 private shares were represented.

George Bliss arrived at the annual meeting tarnished but not discredited. The Western had a shaky but improving safety record; its locomotive crisis was still unsolved; and, worst of all, it was unable to meet even its fixed interest charges. Derby's campaign and catchy proposals certainly hurt, as did the president's high-handed and futile struggle with the Postmaster General over the mail contracts. But Derby's efforts convinced the public more than the railroad's owners.

The shareholders had followed the investigations closely, and a great many were convinced that the Western's difficulties stemmed from its newness. Bliss argued that any pioneer management was bound to make mistakes, but he insisted that if fares were maintained at current levels, the normal increase in traffic and in efficiency would soon make the Western pay. The stockholders' investigation helped Bliss, for it illuminated the extreme complexity and magnitude of opening the Western Railroad. But most important, the probe diffused the responsibility for the vital decisions, including purchasing the Winans engines. In short, it took the steam out of Derby's attempt to make Bliss a single cause for the Western's ills.

Under these circumstances, the stockholders' election did not produce a clear mandate. Only John Henshaw, David Henshaw's brother, who ran supported by retiring P. P. F. Degrand on a platform favorable to a limited low-fare experiment, got an almost unanimous endorsement. Henshaw received in excess of 13,000 of the nearly 14,000 shares voted. Next came Elias Hasket Derby with 7,600, followed closely by three anti-low-fare men, William Jackson, Jonathan Chapman, and George Bliss, each of whom had approximately 7,200 votes. The next three candidates, all unsuccessful and low-fare advocates, received between 7,000 and 6,900 votes each.[31] With the private directors split three to two in favor of Bliss's policies, the balance of power swung to the four state directors, Thomas Plunkett of Pittsfield, Edmund Dwight of Boston, Samuel C. Allen of Northfield, and John P. Tarbell of Pepperell.

When the newly constituted board met to select new officers for 1843 on March 21, it was badly split. George Bliss announced himself as a candidate for reelection. Edmund Dwight, who favored Bliss's rate policies, felt that the old president had lost much of his usefulness as a result of the strong attacks against him and his narrow vote of confidence by the shareholders. Dwight drew support for his own candidacy by promising to institute a low-fare experiment impartially if that were the board's will. Even so, four separate ballots were unable to produce a president, and the directors postponed action. The following day another vote failed. Even with so much at stake, Bliss felt that it was unethical to vote for himself, and consistently refused to do so. After the fifth ballot, recalled Bliss years later, "one of the candidates [Dwight] stated to the Board, that he considered there was an important principle involved in that election, and that he should cast a vote for himself. This his opponent declined to do. On the sixth ballot, Mr. Dwight was elected."[32]

The Western's new president had many of the prejudices and aims of his predecessor. Both were born of the Springfield elite and represented the rising new industrial class. Neither found a cause in Massachusetts' maritime decline. Yet there were significant differences. Bliss started life with a superior education but no money. Dwight, besides being well-educated, inherited a substantial part of western Massachusetts' largest fortune. Dwight moved to Boston in 1822 to become the partner of James K. Mills. Together they took a leading part in financing the Connecticut Valley's textile industry. By 1846 Dwight was estimated to be worth in excess of $600,000, and at his death in 1849 he left an estate of more than $1,500,000.[33] For Bliss the Western represented a full-time job on which he depended for most of his income. Bliss, therefore, combined policy making with the day-to-day responsibilities of the road's superintendent. Dwight, however, cared little for detail and consequently transferred the duties of the superintendent from the president to the chief engineer, James Barnes. Thus Dwight did not object to cutting the president's salary from $3,000 a year to $500.[34]

Under Dwight the presidency became more like that of the Western under Thomas B. Wales or of the Worcester under Nathan Hale. Dwight depended mostly on the advice of his superintendent for his knowledge of the railroad's problems, and he became concerned with these only as they affected broad policy. In contrast Bliss was a strong president who maintained a firm grasp on the railroad's entire operation and influenced nearly every aspect of it. When Bliss spoke, it was with the authority of actual experience.

For Dwight, as for Bliss, the major problem still involved producing enough revenue to meet the railroad's fixed charges. The rate and fare issue, therefore, remained paramount, and the opening of the 1843 navigation season forced an immediate decision. Derby still demanded a $3 through first-class passenger fare between Boston and Albany. But John Henshaw, and three of the state directors, Thomas Plunkett, Samuel C. Allen, and John Tarbell, while favorable to a low-fare experiment, shrank from so drastic a reduction and prevailed upon Derby to modify his demands.

On March 25, therefore, Derby moved that the first-class through passenger fare be $4. His motion passed by a five to four vote with the proviso that the Worcester Company agree to accept a comparable reduction for its share of the joint fare.[35] This the Worcester refused to do. Its directors replied that "a reduction of the rates of fare . . . below those which were charged during the last season would not tend to increase the number of passengers in proportion to the reduction of the rates and consequently . . . would be injurious to the stockholders of both roads, by diminishing the amount of income received."[36] The Worcester thereby served notice that it would not accept less than the $1 it got the previous summer for its portion of a first-class Boston to Albany ticket. If there was to be a low-fare experiment, the Western would have to go it alone. Bliss

238

made a final effort to block this by moving that the Worcester's stand made it inexpedient to reduce fares below those charged the previous summer. At this point Edmund Dwight went over to the low-fare side. He reasoned that a short experiment would do very little harm, and it might settle the whole issue once and for all. On April 7, 1843, under Dwight's leadership, the directors voted six to three to set the through fare at $4. This gave the Western $3 or 1.92 cents per mile and the Worcester $1 or 2.27 cents per mile.[37] This marked the first and only time that Hale's road ever received more per mile than the Western for the joint passenger business. But this did not make the $1 fare any more palatable to the Worcester management. Significantly, the Western's directors made only minor changes in the corporation's local passenger tariff.[38]

Freight rates under the new board of directors received a general modification, and although there was less acrimony than over passenger fares, the directors hotly debated the issue of discrimination against local freight. In an attempt to simplify the rate structure, the directors reduced the four classes of merchandise in the 1842 tariff to two. The new schedule moderately reduced costs for through freight: the charge per ton on the first class was set at $7 (compared with $9 and $6.50 for the first and second classes in 1842) and that for the second class at $4 (compared with $5 and $4 for the third and fourth classes in 1842). In a further attempt to lure large shipments from water to rail the directors fixed a 20 per cent discount for all quantities in excess of 3 tons. This, for example, enabled salted beef, pork, or fish to move between Boston and Albany at $3.20 per ton. Simultaneously to cushion the effect of the lower charges, the directors set special rates on items of high value or great bulk. The charge for domestic wool, for which freight represented an infinitesimal part of the product's value and of which the Western carried more than 6,500 bales between Albany and Boston in 1842, was set at $10 per ton, as was that for feathers and teazles.[39]

Flour rates continued to receive the most attention. Experience in 1842 proved that a through charge higher than $3 a ton would attract very little of that commodity away from traditional water routes. But the $3 rate brought to the Western nearly 8,600 tons of flour, which accounted for about one-fifth of all through freight moving between Albany and Boston in 1842.[40] And still more flour would have been transported if it had not been for the embarrassing motive-power breakdown at the height of the Erie's season. This success encouraged the directors to retain the $3 per ton rate. When in 1842 the corporation instituted this rate as an emergency measure to meet competition, the through charge became lower than some of those to intermediate points. Sharp protests by local interests quickly caused the railroad to fix the through rate as a maximum charge.

In 1843 Derby raised the entire issue again. He moved that the "charge on flour be 35¢ per barrel [10 barrels per ton] from Greenbush [Albany] to Boston and all points east of the Washington Summit [about 10 miles east of Pittsfield] and that a reduction of 5¢ per barrel be made on all quantities exceeding 100 barrels carried through to Boston . . . to meet the competition by water."[41] This placed Derby clearly on record favoring relatively high charges to intermediate stations. His major reason, of course, was to bring in the added money that could be realized by charging high rates to communities without water transportation. Derby hoped that revenue from local rates would support the experiment on through passenger fares. This type of discrimination was not feasible with passengers because if the through fare were lower than that to a local station, the railroad could do little to stop a passenger from buying a through ticket and getting off at a local stop. Frequent halts for wood, water, and to meet other trains made through limiteds that skipped local stations impossible.

Derby's flagrant discrimination against local shippers met hostility from the Pittsfield businessman and director, Thomas Plunkett, who proposed with the support of two other state directors, Samuel Allen and John Tarbell, who also came from interior Massachusetts, "that the price for carrying flour from Greenbush to the way stations should in no case exceed the price for carrying the same to Boston."[42] Although Derby's motion did not prevail unchanged, his concept did, and despite the objections of the three state directors the board set flour rates that flatly discriminated in favor of through traffic and actually made higher charges to move goods short distances than over the entire road. Under the new rate it cost $3 to move a ton of flour 200 miles from Albany to Boston and $3.40 to move that same ton if its destination were Springfield just 100 miles from Albany.[43]

The new rate and fare schedule gave Derby a limited trial of his low-fare system. As Bliss later wrote, "the operation of it was watched by all parties with much interest."[44] Actually the experiment was doomed from the start, for the $4 through fare was not competitive with the Hudson River steamboats, and it was only by tapping the large flow of travel from Albany to New York that the business between Albany and Boston could be increased spectacularly. To do this, however, required fares of $3 or less, and of all the directors only Elias Hasket Derby was willing to take such a daring gamble.

The end of 1843 found the Western Railroad still in deep financial trouble. Although the total number of through passengers had increased by nearly a third, it was difficult to attribute this to the low fare alone. Summarized Bliss, "the Annual Report of January, 1844, [compared] the business of 1842 [with 1843] claiming an advantage of the latter year. Such comparisons are unreliable unless all extraneous circumstances are considered. The year 1842," he argued, "was the first one of the opening through to Albany, and the business was done over fifteen miles of the Hudson & Berkshire Railroad, with its flat rail and high grades; and the traffic was not yet accustomed to a new channel."[45] It was certain, however, that the net operating income for 1843 had not shown a substantial increase, being only $269,000 as compared with $246,000 for 1842. It was possible to attribute most of the increase of about $24,000 to the $15,000 Dwight claimed he had saved as a result of his retrenchment campaign, which reduced salaries and eliminated supernumeraries.[46] The 1843 income equalled the required interest, but it still fell quite short of the $310,000 needed for the combined interest and sinking-fund payments. At the end of 1843 the railroad's first dividend seemed as far away as ever.

The Western's poor financial showing cooled shareholder support for the low-fare panacea. Derby himself sensed this, and he refused to be a candidate for reelection to the board of directors at the February 1844 annual meeting. In his stead stood Nathan Carruth. Interest waned considerably from the previous year, but even so, more than half of the railroad's shares were voted. The stockholders left no doubt where they stood. They soundly defeated both Nathan Carruth and John Henshaw, two of the nominees who had been associated with the low-fare experiment. George Bliss and William Jackson, both Derby's opponents, were returned to the board. In addition the stockholders elected three new men: George Pratt, a Boston merchant who in addition to holding 170 shares of Western stock had a substantial investment in the Boston & Worcester; Edward Austin, a Boston businessman; and Josiah Stickney, president of Boston's Market Bank. All opposed Derby's experiment.[47] The Commonwealth's directors included Edmund Dwight, Abraham Howland, James Russell, and Robert Campbell. Of the new state directors, Dr. Robert Campbell, a wealthy Pittsfield physician, was particularly significant, for he remained on the Western's board either representing the state or the private stockholders for twenty-two years—until the merger with the Boston & Worcester formed the Boston & Albany. Throughout his long tenure Dr. Campbell continued Thomas Plunkett's support of local traffic with greatly increased vigor.

When the new board of directors met on February 29 to select the railroad's officers for 1844, they elected Edmund Dwight president, who by prearrangement declined to accept the honor. The board thereupon unanimously chose George Bliss.[48] Bliss's joy at vindication must have been tempered by the troubles he inherited. Fixed charges and the clamor for a dividend still remained the basic issues. The company's financial ills also produced corollary problems. In response to the legislature's urging, the Dwight administration had cut salaries and wages. This not only touched Bliss, whose salary was set at $500, but the station agents and most other workers as well. At the start employees, feeling that the cuts were temporary, accepted them with good grace. But the prospect of a prolonged depression in wages was beginning to create unrest. In order to retain their highly competent engineer, James Barnes, who also had assumed the superintendent's duties, the board found it necessary to augment his salary by $500 to $2,500. In addition, salaries of the depot agents at Greenbush and Pittsfield and other responsible officials such as roadmasters were increased. Despite the board's hopes to the contrary, this stimulated expectations among the rank and file for a general raise, which the directors were not prepared to grant.[49]

The new administration immediately set about to revise the passenger-fare structure. Bliss felt that a differential between winter and summer fares made no sense for passengers once the idea of diverting New York–bound Hudson River steamboat traffic to Boston had been dropped. And as long as the railroad tariff was not excessively higher than the combined Albany-Boston steamboat charges, Bliss maintained that the Western's speed and convenience made the trains immune to Boston-Albany passenger competition via water. Thus the new fares instituted on April 1, which remained effective both winter and summer during Bliss's tenure as president, set the through Boston to Albany charge at $6, or 3 cents per mile, a full $2 higher than the 1843 experiment. The board also increased local passenger fares from 3 cents per mile to 3½ cents per mile, with the provision that the "way fare shall in no case exceed the through fare."[50] Negotiations fixed the Boston & Worcester's share of joint tickets to or from Boston and points on the Western at $1.10. Although this gave Hale's road 10 cents more per ticket on the Boston-Albany through traffic, it represented a 15-cent decrease on joint tickets between the Worcester and way stations of the Western. For the Worcester, therefore, the new fares had but a slight effect on revenues.

Bliss's administration continued the idea of winter and summer freight-rate variations since in this case the differential had originated not to divert traffic from New York City but to compete with the Albany–Boston water route. In general the 1844 freight tariffs remained the same as those for 1843. The Western depended for additional freight traffic upon new rail connections, which were opening on all sides; at Greenbush a line had been constructed to link the Western with Troy; at Pittsfield the Housatonic Railroad ran south to New

York City; at Springfield newly constructed railroads reached south to Hartford and New Haven, and plans were under way to build on to New York City and north to industrial Cabotville (Chicopee) with further construction proceeding up the Connecticut toward Northampton, Massachusetts. West of Albany the separate companies that were building an all-rail route between the Hudson and Buffalo, were beginning to cooperate in a joint freight business. In 1844 the New York Legislature removed the restriction that had prevented the Utica and Schenectady Railroad from carrying freight even during the winter, when there was no danger of competing with the Erie Canal. This action greatly increased the Western's winter freight traffic, which lagged badly when the Erie Canal closed down each fall.[51]

Under the Western's new passenger-fare structure, through traffic fell only slightly from 26,000 through tickets in 1843 to 24,000 in 1844. This supported William Jackson's theory that there was a relatively stable passenger flow between Boston and Albany that would use the railroad at any fare substantially below that on the old stagecoaches. Local traffic actually rose, but almost the entire increase came from second-class passengers, who paid two-thirds of the first-class fare.[52] But the important factor was the dramatic 21.5 per cent rise in gross passenger revenue from $275,000 in 1843 to $358,000 in 1844. Merchandise receipts went up even faster from $275,000 to $371,000, or by more than 34 per cent. This produced a net operating income of $439,000, which was within $100,000 of doubling the previous year's net operating income. For the first time the Western met its total fixed interest and sinking-fund charges, and there was substantially more than $100,000 that could be applied toward a dividend.[53] President Bliss's rate and fare policies had at last proved themselves.

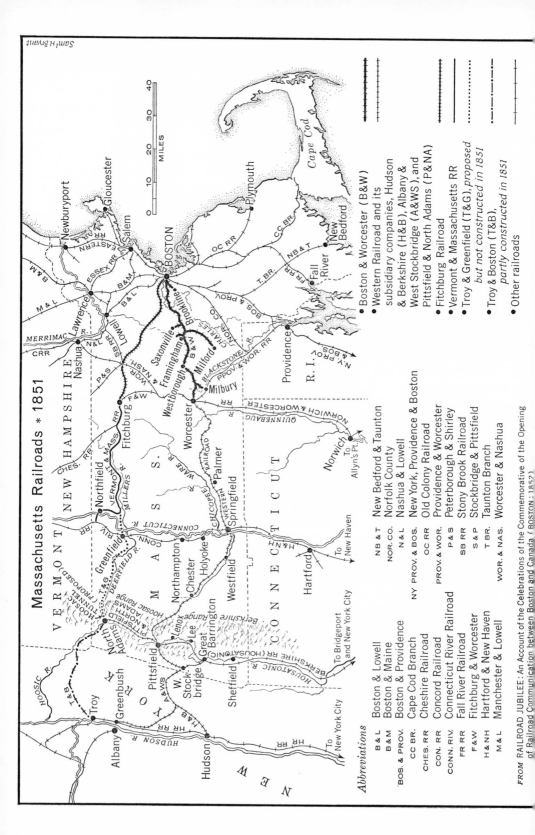

Massachusetts Railroads · 1851

Sam'l H. Bryant

MILES
0 10 20 30 40

Boston & Worcester (B&W)

Western Railroad and its subsidiary companies, Hudson & Berkshire (H&B), Albany & West Stockbridge (A&WS), and Pittsfield & North Adams (P&NA)

Fitchburg Railroad

Vermont & Massachusetts RR

Troy & Greenfield (T&G), proposed but not constructed in 1851

Troy & Boston (T&B), partly constructed in 1851

Other railroads

Abbreviations

B & L	Boston & Lowell	NB & T	New Bedford & Taunton
B & M	Boston & Maine	NOR. CO.	Norfolk County
BOS. & PROV.	Boston & Providence	N & L	Nashua & Lowell
CC BR.	Cape Cod Branch	NY PROV. & BOS.	New York, Providence & Boston
CHES. RR	Cheshire Railroad	OC RR	Old Colony Railroad
CON. RR	Concord Railroad	PROV. & WOR.	Providence & Worcester
CONN. RIV.	Connecticut River Railroad	P & S	Peterborough & Shirley
FR RR	Fall River Railroad	SB RR	Stony Brook Railroad
F & W	Fitchburg & Worcester	S & P	Stockbridge & Pittsfield
H & N	Hartford & New Haven	T BR.	Taunton Branch
M & L	Manchester & Lowell	WOR. & NAS.	Worcester & Nashua

FROM RAILROAD JUBILEE: An Account of the Celebrations of the Commemorative of the Opening of Railroad Communication between Boston and Canada (BOSTON : 1852)

CHAPTER XII

The Worcester Railroad Triumphant, 1844–1854

THE BOSTON & WORCESTER RAILROAD CORPORATION was a good investment. From the first year of its completion in 1835 until its merger with the Western in 1867, it never missed a dividend, and from 1837 onward it never paid less than 6 per cent per annum on the par value of its stock—often it paid 8, 9, and even 10 per cent. Neither financial panic nor war upset its fiscal stability. This was no accident, for the company was efficient, lacked competition, and served a densely populated industrial region. The Worcester's success formula was simple; it provided service at a moderate charge to the area in which it had an effective monopoly.

Its history up to 1850 was one of expansion. Capital, provided entirely by the sale of stock, grew from the original $1,000,000 in 1831 to $4,500,000 in 1850. By 1843 the entire main line from Boston to Worcester had been double-tracked, and by 1850 the road had built 23 miles of branch lines, equal to half the length of the main track. The Worcester invested more than $620,000 for roadbed and superstructure alone in its six branches.[1] It spent thousands more for locomotives and cars. Commuter service expanded substantially. In 1848 the company built the Brookline branch, predecessor to the Massachusetts Bay Transportation Authority's Riverside rapid transit line, to cater strictly to suburban passenger traffic.

The keynote, however, was caution. Through 1851 growth was gradual but constant. When particular ventures did not prove profitable, the management quickly curtailed them. Thus by the early 1850s the Boston & Worcester's physical growth stopped. Rugged competition ended the corporation's interest in providing through New York–Boston service via the Norwich & Worcester. Similarly, after 1850 the Boston & Worcester constructed no new branch lines, for it had learned that they made only marginal contributions to income.[2]

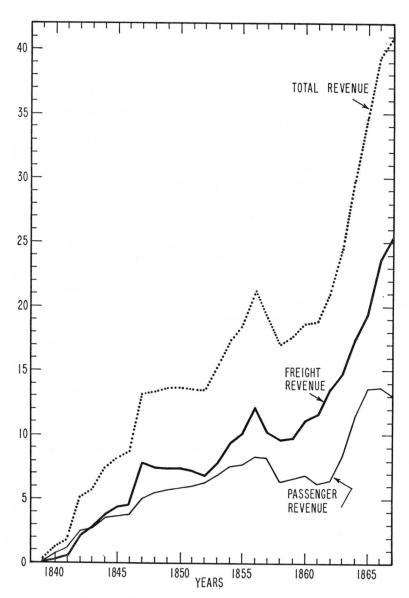

CHART II. Western Railroad passenger, freight, and total revenues, 1839–1867 (in one hundred thousand dollar units). Compiled from Western Railroad Annual Reports to Stockholders 1839–1868.

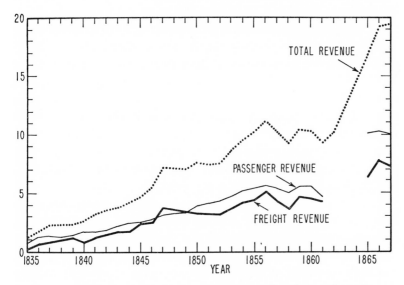

CHART III. Boston & Worcester passenger, freight and total revenues, 1836–1867 (in one hundred thousand dollar units). Compiled from Boston & Worcester Annual Reports to Stockholders 1835–1867.*

The year 1851 marked a change in policy—an end to expansion. Outstanding capital stock thereafter remained static.[3] The railroad lived off its existing physical plant, plowing back enough earnings to keep it in first-class condition. Gross revenues, which gained spectacularly during the period of capital growth, from $380,000 in 1834 to $760,000 in 1850, continued to rise, mainly because of flourishing local traffic on the main line even after the railroad stopped increasing its physical plant. Between 1850 and 1856, gross receipts rose from $760,000 to over $1,000,000. After 1856, however, partly because of the nationwide depression, gross receipts leveled off at about

* Data for a breakdown of freight and passenger traffic are not available for the years 1862–1864 because of the dispute with the Western Railroad. According to the B&W management the arbitration award in the dispute did not determine which part of the joint receipts were the result of freight traffic and which were from passenger traffic. Hence the B&W declined to make any official estimate. Manuscript data, however, indicate that during the disputed years passenger revenue ran well ahead of freight as had been the case for the previous years except for the period 1847–1849.

$1,000,000. The Civil War brought renewed prosperity, however, and receipts increased to a peak of $1,914,000 in 1867.

From 1850 through 1867 the Boston & Worcester continued its conservative fiscal policy. Rather than increase stock beyond $4,500,000 to fund the construction account, which amounted to over $4,900,000 in 1851, the directors created a short-term bonded indebtedness of $425,000, which they retired with money taken from the general earnings between 1851 and 1861. The directors preferred short-term debt to the creation of additional stock since bonds at 6 per cent interest drained revenues less than new stock at 8 or 9 per cent.[4]

Conservative financing, avoiding cutthroat competition on Long Island Sound and ending questionable expansion into unprofitable branches, enabled the Boston & Worcester in the 1850s and the 1860s to maintain a handsome dividend record. Through the early 1850s the company paid 7 per cent. During the panic years the rate fell to 6 per cent but rose to 8 per cent in 1860. From 1864 to 1867 the railroad paid a flat 10 per cent, the maximum allowed by its charter. This intense and constant concern for stockholder welfare determined the Worcester's behavior from 1844 through 1854.

The Boston & Worcester did not long hold the illusion that the Western Railroad would be a new source of lucrative freight and passenger business. During the Western's financially precarious first two years of through operation, 1842 and 1843, Hale's road had little choice but to cooperate by accepting a reduced share of the profits of the joint business. Hale wanted to prevent the alternative financial collapse and almost certain state take-over as much as Bliss.

By 1844, however, the Western's crisis was easing. Bliss's rate and fare structure provided the revenue to meet the fixed interest and sinking-fund requirements. As soon as the Western earned its operating costs and its fixed charges, the Boston & Worcester's attitude changed. To Nathan Hale and his directors the question was no longer one of preventing the Western's collapse but simply one of dispute between the stockholders of the two roads. Hale felt that if his company took a reduced share of the joint profits, the Boston & Worcester stockholders would be transferring money from their pockets to the Western's shareowners. Aside from the moral question involved, Hale feared that the B&W, with a rapidly expanding capital stock, could not afford a rate and fare structure that would force his corporation to carry passengers or freight at little or no profit.

The changing traffic pattern on the Western forced the issue to a head. In 1841 passenger business was the Western's major revenue source; freight income, only half that for passengers, was secondary. This seemed natural in the light of the Worcester's experience, in which passenger traffic had been the mainstay since the first day of operation. But the Western's opening through to Albany quickly changed the trend. By 1843 the freight income equalled the passenger income, and in 1844 it forged ahead. This swing continued until in 1847 freight revenue held a commanding lead, being $785,000 as against $502,000 for passengers.

Not only was freight important on the Western, but the line handled a different kind from the Worcester. On Hale's road most tonnage was high-quality merchandise; low-value commodities such as wheat and flour were insignificant. But on the Western, bulky agricultural products constituted a major part of the traffic. In 1843 and 1844, just one item, flour, carried at the Western's lowest rates, accounted for approximately one-fourth of all tonnage moved between Albany and Boston. By 1847, admittedly an unusual year due to the Irish potato famine, the Worcester and Western jointly moved 88,000 tons between Albany and Boston, of which more than 51,000 tons or approximately 60 per cent were flour.[5]

Nathan Hale in 1841 and 1842 worried that the Western's demand that the Worcester Railroad take a reduced share of the joint passenger revenue would jeopardize the Worcester's main source of profit. The Worcester road yielded reluctantly to the Western's pleas. But negotiations for a division of the freight income went smoothly at first since both corporations underestimated that traffic. But its rapid surge on the Western changed this. In 1844 the Worcester directors reviewed freight revenue trends and became alarmed. The statistics showed that there had been an increase above the previous year in the joint freight business of more than 604,000 ton-miles but that "there had been a diminution of about $4,000 in the compensation obtained for it."[6] The Worcester had carried one-fifth more freight but had received less revenue for doing so. Since the opening of the Western, argued the Worcester's directors, "the sum of $1,200,000 has been added to the capital stock of this corporation, nearly all of which has been expended in laying down a second track, enlarging the depot buildings and lands, and increasing the number of engines and cars for carrying on the enlarged business arising, and expected to arise from the union of this road with the Western Rail-road."[7] Despite increased activity, the Worcester had been forced to lower its dividends from 8 per cent in 1842 to 6 per cent in 1843 and to 6½ per cent in 1844. Thus in 1844 the Worcester management concluded that its corporation, now that the Western was moving toward financial stability, could no longer tolerate "hazardous" rate and fare experiments and must, in justice to its stockholders, be assured of a fair profit on all its traffic. In blunt language this meant that the Worcester wanted a greater, not a lesser, share of the joint revenue.

George Bliss, however, had girded himself to ask for further concessions. From 1844 onward he became convinced that the abandonment of Derby's low-fare system and increased passenger fares were insufficient to ensure a fair return upon the Western's capital. Bliss argued that his railroad faced unique obstacles that justified the Western's receiving substantially more per ton-mile and per passenger-mile on the joint traffic than the Worcester. He pointed to the steep grades across the Berkshire Hills which necessitated extra locomotives and fuel consumption, to the low population density between Albany and Springfield, to the expensive ferry across the Hudson, and to the severe water competition for the through traffic. Bliss asked the Worcester railroad to accept $1 as its share on through Boston–Albany passenger tickets (Hale's road raised its share to $1.10 at the abandonment of the low-fare experiment) and to enter into a new freight tariff agreement. In essence Bliss wanted to lower through freight rates to meet the Albany–Boston water competition, but he wanted the entire burden of the reduction to fall on Hale's road. This would have meant the end of the traditional prorata division of freight receipts and the institution of a split that would give the Western more per ton-mile than its counterpart. The Western's attempt to reach a new agreement with the Worcester's board of directors in early 1844 failed. Bliss reacted to the collapse of negotiations by requesting the Massachusetts Legislature to intervene.

The Worcester Corporation was in a strong position. Its charter gave it a thirty-year monopoly of rail traffic between Boston and Worcester and the absolute right to set rates and fares, subject only to the restriction that the General Court could regulate the toll after the first ten years if the dividends on the capital stock amounted to more than 10 per cent per annum. Since the Worcester's dividend record in 1844 had never exceeded 8 per cent, the legislature under the charter had no right to interfere.

Bliss considered three possible legislative moves. First, he pondered asking for authority to build a separate railroad from Worcester to Boston. This he rejected because it conflicted too dramatically with the Worcester's charter rights, and it was not practical since the Western had no capital to finance a Boston extension, nor was there a prospect that any could be raised for such a venture. Second, Bliss weighed asking the General Court to fix the rates and fares at which the Boston & Worcester would carry traffic to and from the Western. Third, Bliss considered applying for authority to run the Western's trains over the B&W tracks to Boston.

Bliss favored legislative action to set the rates and fares at which the Worcester would take the joint business. In January 1844 he presented such a petition to the General Court. This forced Bliss into an embarrassing position. As a capitalist and railroad president he was appealing to governmental authority to regulate railroad rates. Equally as disconcerting, the kind of regulation Bliss desired would not lower fares; it merely proposed transferring revenue from one company to another. His action stemmed not from the "public interest" or idealistic reform, but from the desperate desire to secure funds to pay dividends upon the Western Railroad's stock. The Western attempted to make its efforts appear in harmony with the Boston & Worcester's charter, of which it cited the fourteenth section, which read: "The Legislature may authorize any company to enter with another railroad, at any point of said Boston and Worcester, paying for the right of using the same, or any part thereof, such a rate of toll as the Legislature may from time to time prescribe."[8]

But Hale's road countered by charging that any attempt to fix rates on the Worcester tampered with the corporation's basic charter rights. The Worcester's directors quoted their charter's fifth section: "That a toll be and hereby is granted and established for the sole benefit of said corporation upon all passengers and property of all descriptions, which may be conveyed or transported upon said road, at such rates per mile as may be agreed upon and established from time to time, by the directors of said corporation."[9] The Worcester's directors conceded that the legislature had the power, at the time it chartered the Western, to authorize the new railroad to enter upon the Boston & Worcester, but they emphasized that the legislature did not grant such a right. "The two railroads were united," claimed the Worcester, "by mutual agreement of the two corporations, and . . . this corporation has made the expenditure of [$1,200,000 to accommodate the joint business] in the full faith that in making these expenditures, after the agreement had been made and executed for the union of the two roads, no act of the Legislature would be passed, which would change the relative rights of the two corporations, by taking away the toll granted for the sole use of one, and conferring it as a donation upon the other."[10] The legislature's only justification, maintained the Worcester's directors, for exercising its right to set rates under the Worcester charter's fourteenth article would be abuse of power by the corporation. But "such abuse has not been alleged, and it surely has not been practiced," asserted the directors. "On the contrary," they continued, the Boston & Worcester's rates are "materially lower than [those] on the Western Road itself; [and] they [the joint rates] are much lower than on any other class of customers of the Boston and Worcester Road."[11]

When Hale made his defense one of charter rights, he raised the ghost of the Charles River Bridge controversy. Stockholders in both roads preferred to avoid the corporate privilege issue.

The General Court, also wary of the dispute, referred Bliss's petition to its joint committee on railways and canals, whose chairman promptly urged that the matter be settled by arbitration.[12] With some trepidation both railroads acceded to the suggestion, and the two boards of directors jointly selected as arbitrators three eminent jurists, John M. Williams, Linus Child, and Charles H. Warren.

The jurists faced a difficult task in their search for a formula that would ensure a "fair" profit to all. Both corporations claimed that the rates proposed by the other were unremunerative and placed an onerous burden on their respective companies. The root of the trouble was that neither railroad based its rates and fares upon the cost of providing service. But accurate cost data were vital in the attempt to determine whether the Worcester could "profitably" carry freight at the rates Bliss desired. The entire tariff structure had been shaped by only one factor: competition. Until November 15, 1843, the Western did not even attempt the most elemental step in fixing costs: the allocation of charges between the freight and the passenger business.[13] And until the dispute, neither did the Worcester, whose first attempt at allocation in 1844 was both general and crude. In its written report, for example, the Worcester directors argued that "it is evident that the strain and wear upon the rails is greater from a heavy freight train, than from a passenger . . . ," but in their statistical summary they apportioned track upkeep equally between the two kinds of traffic.[14] In 1844 neither corporation kept the kind of records that enabled it to tell whether specific classes of freight were profitable.

Thus the jurists had to break new ground in an effort to fix more exactly the cost of doing business. Specifically they faced the Worcester's claim that it lost money on the transportation of flour. The arbiters had not only to isolate the freight from the passenger charges, but they had to separate from the general freight statistics those costs directly attributable to flour: extra motive power, cars, fuel, wages, terminals, warehouse facilities, and interest on capital. The jurists had no precedents to guide them. Carriers such as Pennsylvania's Reading fixed costs accurately on coal, but this commodity made up the majority of that corporation's business, while flour on the Worcester represented less than 10 per cent of the total tonnage, and it was seasonal. Considering both the lack of accurate data and the enormous number of variables, it is not surprising that the jurists' decision settled nothing but became a center for more dispute.

The arbiters held extensive hearings and on May 21, 1844, rendered their decision, which was binding on both parties until January 1845. The award upset Nathan Hale since the judges asserted that the "pecuniary situation of the Western Rail-road" should be a factor in determining charges made by the Worcester. The arbitrators concluded that under the then current tariff structure, the Worcester should receive a maximum of 2⅞ cents per ton-mile, which amounted to $1.26 per ton for the 44 miles between Boston and Worcester. This favored the Western on all but the lowest class of freight. But the ruling was not a total victory for Bliss's road since the arbiters accepted much of the Worcester's claim that even a prorata division (splitting rates in proportion to the mileage carried on each road) resulted in a loss on flour. Thus they awarded the Worcester 9 cents per barrel (90 cents per ton), which of the total summer charge of 30 cents per barrel ($3 per ton) between Boston and Albany actually gave Hale's road a greater sum per ton-mile than the Western. The jurists "proceeded upon the principle that they would not be justified, in compelling the Boston and Worcester . . . to carry any article over their road for a sum less than the actual cost of transportation."[15]

The arbitrators further aroused the Western's ire by refusing to tamper with the joint passenger-fare structure, which they concluded was already weighted heavily in favor of the Western. This left the Worcester free to take $1.10 as its share of all joint tickets on which the passenger traveled the full distance between Worcester and Boston. Under this division Hale's road received on the through Boston–Albany tickets 2.5 cents per mile, and the Western 3.14 cents per mile. The differential in the Western's favor was even greater for the local traffic.

Both railroads chafed under the arbiters' decision and

planned to abandon it as soon as possible. In December 1844 the Worcester Corporation took action that popularized its case and put the Western on the defensive; it lowered, as of January 1, 1845, its Boston to Worcester passenger fare from $1.50 to $1.25.[16] The reduction surprised and embarrassed Bliss's railroad because all joint tickets to and from way stations on the Western calculated the Boston-Worcester tariff at $1.50. But when the Worcester lowered its fare to $1.25, it became cheaper for the passenger to buy two separate tickets, one for the Worcester's portion and one for the Western. Therefore unless the Western lowered its own fares, it stood to lose considerable revenue, and the Worcester would gain since it would receive $1.25 for a separate ticket over its road as opposed to $1.10 for a joint ticket.

But the Western's loss was much greater than 15 cents. From Springfield to Boston under the old ticketing arrangement the charge was based on the following formula: $1.90 for the Western plus $1.50 for the Worcester portion, or $3.40 for the joint ticket. Under the award the Western paid the Worcester $1.10 and kept $2.30, or 40 cents more than the Western's local fare. But "if the passenger buys separate tickets [under the Worcester's new fares]," lamented Bliss, "we get only $1.90 our local fare."[17] Bliss concluded that the only way to salvage something was to lower joint fares so that there was no advantage to purchasing separate tickets. Thus as of January 1, 1845, the Western lowered its way tariff. The total Springfield–Boston fare, for example, dropped from $3.40 to $3.15. Under the traditional split, which the Worcester agreed to maintain, Hale's road received its usual $1.10 and the Western received $2.05. This was 15 cents better than the Western's local fare.

Hale's maneuver accomplished its purposes. It relieved the substantial pressure that was building for a fare reduction, but more important it established his corporation as the leader in reducing charges to the traveling public. Not only had the B&W lowered its own fares, but it had forced a reluctant Western management to take similar action. This was good strategy for a railroad facing a plea that its rate and fare structure be regulated to suit the pleasure of another corporation.

On January 14, 1845, the Boston & Worcester announced its

decision to terminate the freight portion of the arbitration agreement.[18] In an official statement the corporation charged that the award was offensive "because it gave to the Western Corporation a part of the income earned by us exclusively upon our road, and because the portion assigned to us, of the receipts for the transportation of merchandise upon our own road, in our own cars, . . . by our own agents, and at our cost and risk, was entirely inadequate, beyond the actual expense, to compensate this corporation for the capital which they had invested for the special accommodation of this branch of the business."[19] The B&W stated that it preferred a flat prorata division of the freight receipts.

The Worcester's action reenforced George Bliss's original conclusion that voluntary negotiation was insufficient to construct a satisfactory agreement. He therefore again turned to the legislature, asking it to prescribe the rates and fares. Bliss found the General Court icy. A majority of the legislative committee that heard the Western's plea flatly told him that they were "opposed to making any alteration in the Worcester charter . . . to make them carry the cars, passengers and merchandise of this company at prices to be prescribed by the Legislature."[20]

The lawmakers, however, tossed the Western a bone. In March 1845 they enacted a bill to "authorize the Western Railroad Corporation to enter upon and use the Boston and Worcester Rail-road." This measure specified that the Western would pay "therefore such rate of toll of compensation as the Legislature may, from time to time prescribe, or that may be fixed under any general law of the Commonwealth."[21] For Bliss this was a hollow victory indeed, for the act envisioned that the Western would run its own trains to Boston using only the Worcester's track. Even if arrangements could have been worked out to accommodate two railroads on the same rails, the Western would have had large new expenses for locomotives, cars, labor, and new terminals in Boston. But worst of all, although the act authorized the General Court to fix the payment to the Worcester for the use of its facilities, there was no provision to implement this clause. And the men on Beacon Hill made it clear that they had no intention of further action. Thus, if the Western were to run over the Worcester's tracks, the two managements had to come to a voluntary agreement as to the payment or go to court.[22]

On April 1, one week after the governor signed the new act, Bliss tried to pressure Nathan Hale into further negotiation, but feeling secure in his position, Hale did not even answer Bliss's communications. The Western's president thereupon moved, with the support of his board, to ask the Massachusetts Supreme Judicial Court to appoint commissioners to oversee the running of Western trains into Boston. The Boston & Worcester Railroad immediately employed legal counsel to block the Western.[23] Bliss recognized the futility of a drawn-out legal battle, "where, by the law's delays [the Western's case] was likely to be suspended indefinitely, without any decisive result."[24] Although the Western continued the court suit, this tactic had little more than a nuisance value.

The growing estrangement between the two railroads and the implications of Bliss's attack on the Worcester's charter rights alarmed prominent stockholders of both corporations who called a meeting on March 6, 1845, in Boston's United States Hotel. Speakers included the ubiquitous P. P. F. Degrand, Addison Gilmore, a major stockholder in both companies, and William Sturgis, a substantial investor in the Boston & Worcester and the Massachusetts textile industry. Toward the meeting's end Sturgis offered a motion, unanimously adopted, that a "committee of five be appointed to consult with the Directors of the Western and Boston and Worcester Railroad Corporations, and invite them to call a meeting of their respective stockholders," to consider uniting the two companies.[25] A joint committee representing both railroads was formed and began in June 1845 to plan the union of the two railroads.

The committee reported on December 17, 1845, to a special meeting of the Worcester's stockholders. It proposed that a new corporation be created to buy the outstanding shares of both companies. In this way the advocates of union hoped to sweep clean the slate, starting afresh, unencumbered by old rivalries. The major controversy centered about the valuation of the Western's and the Worcester's stock. "After taking into consideration the market value of the shares in the two Companies," concluded the committee, "and the general condition and prospects of the two Roads, they have come to the unanimous conclusion, that the property of the Boston & Worcester Railroad Company should be valued at twenty per cent per share above that of the Western."[26] The committee proposed that the new corporation purchase the Western's shares at par ($100 each) and the Worcester's at $120 per share. In practical terms, however, the merger advocates envisioned only a slight exchange of cash. They expected that the shareholders of both railroads would, in lieu of taking money, turn in their old shares for those of the new corporation. Under the proposed plan "each stockholder in the Western [would] receive for his shares . . . an equal number of shares in the new road. Each stockholder in the Boston and Worcester . . . would receive six shares in the new for every five in the present company."[27]

The terms met immediate hostility from William Sturgis, who felt that the Worcester had been undervalued, but the stockholders adjourned until mid-January 1846 without taking action.[28] At the January meeting Nathan Hale threw his full prestige against the merger. He agreed with Sturgis that the Worcester had been sold short, but significantly, he stressed the Western's burden of bonded indebtedness, its unhappy financial past, and its uncertain future. He argued that for the Worcester stockholders to accept union would be to throw away the almost certain prospect of perpetual 8 per cent dividends in return for stock of questionable merit. Reenforcing Hale's argument stood the dividend records of the two corporations: the Worcester's was nearly perfect, whereas the Western lacked but one year of negative perfection. In 1845, four years after its completion, Bliss's railroad paid its first dividends, 6 per cent on its capital stock. Hale's opposition ended the merger movement, and the dispute between the two railroads remained unresolved. Bliss favored returning to the General Court and again asking the legislators to fix the Worcester's charges for the joint traffic. He also suggested requesting authority for the Western to build a competing railroad from Worcester to Boston.

But Nathan Hale and his directors were not worried. The

General Court had refused the Western's pleas in the past, and it felt no more like revoking the Worcester's charter in 1846 than it had in 1845. Hale now moved to end Bliss's embarrassing attack. The Boston & Worcester directors let it be known that they would refuse to negotiate further if Bliss remained the Western's president.[29] Sensing that even the Western's own shareholders lacked the will for a continued fight, Bliss capitulated. He announced that he would not be a candidate for reelection to the Western's board of directors in 1846 for reasons of "ill health." Three other private directors, William Jackson, George Pratt, and Edward Austin, also declined to run. This cleared the way for a slate nominated by stockholders owning shares in both the Boston & Worcester and the Western corporations. The new group, headed by Addison Gilmore, a large Worcester stockholder and a former Worcester director, had Hale's full approval, and it was committed to an early settlement of the dispute between the two railroads. At their annual meeting the Western stockholders almost unanimously elected the nominees (Gilmore, Josiah Stickney, Stephen Fairbanks, John Howard, and Jonathan Chapman), and on February 17, 1846, Addison Gilmore became the fourth president of the Western Railroad.

The Western's new leader could hardly have been more different from his two immediate predecessors, Edmund Dwight and George Bliss, or for that matter from the Worcester's Nathan Hale. Addison Gilmore had humble beginnings. Born and raised in Vermont's Green Mountains he arrived in Boston penniless at twenty-one. He had no connections or friends and started as a handcart man. Like David Henshaw, Gilmore made his early capital in businesses that had the scorn of Boston's more respectable citizens. From pushcarts Gilmore moved to the drug business and from that into liquor.

From the first Gilmore engaged in the rough and tumble of the commercial world, and his reputation did not always emerge untarnished. A contemporary referred to him as "what Carlyle would call 'an heroic money maker.' "[30] Another sneered that Gilmore while the proprietor of a Boston spirits store added "rapidly to his fortune, by some speculating and an occasional winking at certain statutes, known as usury laws."[31]

But Gilmore's major reputation as a shrewd manipulator derived from his machinations in New Hampshire's Concord Railroad, of which he was president just before assuming the Western's leadership. To many, Gilmore's Concord exploits were shameful. Said one Bostonian:

> He laid aside the rum traffic, for iron rails and steam horses; went largely into the Concord Railroad, pitted the 'bulls' against the 'bears,' and in the course of a short time, *somehow,* the stock tripped and went down to a most disastrous figure for the original stockholders. Gilmore and his friends now entered the market, bought extensively, put him in [as] president of the road, the newspapers sang peans to his tact, talents, energy, and universal abilities in the way of railroad managing, and all other managing, and the tide at once set the other way until the stock realized its flood—went up to par; thus putting many a comfortable penny in pockets long before opened wide to catch them. Stock bought at $40 per share, touched $100 within a twelve-month.[32]

Addison Gilmore had two things in common with George Bliss: both believed in a strong presidency, and both saw railroads as a way to personal fortune. Bliss and Gilmore came closest together on their views of administration. Said Gilmore,

> Democracy will not answer in a Corporation of such magnitude as the Western Rail-Road, and nothing short of a monarchial government will. There must be one head, and that a clear, practical common-sense head. . . . When Directors become convinced that they do not possess such a President, they should be very careful not to mistake their duty, by endeavoring to supply the deficiency by their own labor, instead of electing a chief whom they would be willing to sustain. I believe that much injury is done in most of our Rail-Road Corporations, by the dabbling of directors in affairs of which they know nothing.[33]

Bliss and Gilmore were further apart on the question of railroads and their relationship to personal fortune. Bliss was a builder, cautious and conservative. He abhorred short-term speculation. When he bought lands, he did so with a view toward long-term gain. Bliss saw the Western as profitable in two ways. It would appreciate the value of lands that he had purchased adjacent to the tracks, and it would eventually pay its officers substantial salaries. Unfortunately the Western's financial crisis prevented Bliss from the realization of his aim of high pay in the corporation's service.

Bliss's record as a Western Railroad agent, director, and president in the decade between 1836 and 1846 was influenced greatly by his place in the Massachusetts community. He inherited, if not substantial wealth, his lawyer father's respect and standing and the realization that the honor long associated with his family had taken years to build but could be dissipated overnight if he did not keep faith with his fellow citizens. For Bliss, therefore, the railroad was not only a money-making scheme but a trust in which reposed the welfare of the stockholders and the community as a whole. From the Western's very inception Bliss saw the long pull. In the building years, he worked without scandal to give the company the finest physical plant possible.

After the system's completion, Bliss switched his focus from construction to operation and finance. He quickly recognized that rates and fares held the key to the railroad's financial survival. For Bliss a successful rate and fare policy was complex but clear. It would capitalize on the Western's ability to dominate the growing local trade, and it would seek to capture the through traffic normally moving between Albany and Boston. But the company would avoid plunging into the highly competitive Hudson River struggle by shunning any effort to divert the Erie Canal's flow from New York to Boston. Finally, Bliss felt that only a division of the joint Western–Boston & Worcester receipts that favored his company would enable it to prosper. Bliss contrasted the long and desperate struggle of the Western's early years with the Worcester's ease and concluded that his company deserved permanent special consideration in the apportionment of the joint revenue. He would not change his position, even though his other rate and fare policies were fast bringing the railroad financial security despite the Worcester's lack of concessions.

Addison Gilmore saw things differently. He was not a community leader, nor had he a vital concern for his image in western Massachusetts. Gilmore's interest in railroads was strictly financial. Like Bliss he demanded high salaries, but unlike his predecessor he succeeded. On February 24, 1846, the directors voted Gilmore an annual income of $5,000, or $3,500 more than Bliss received in 1845. Gilmore's strategy was simple; he merely stated that the Concord Railroad's presidency and a treasurership in a woolen mill which he was relinquishing paid him $5,000 and that he would not take the Western's presidency for less.[34] Of course, the corporation's 1845 profit made an increase in the president's pay possible.

But salary was minor to Gilmore's financial plans. He used his position to influence his corporation to purchase items from firms in which he had an interest. While Gilmore was president of the Concord Railroad, he made an agreement with the London iron exporting house of Thompson and Forman whereby he received a commission of 2.5 per cent on all orders placed with the firm for railroad iron. The Concord then gave the London exporters its business. When Gilmore assumed the Western's presidency, he continued his arrangement with Thompson and Forman. Within months a Western Railroad director's committee of which Gilmore was a member placed an order with Thompson and Forman for 2,000 tons of rails. Later the directors found out about Gilmore's arrangement and launched an investigation. Said an embarrassed Gilmore, "I am now satisfied that, in not stating [to the other directors] my position with Messrs. Thompson and Forman it was an omission which had it been stated would have been a great personal safeguard against an attack of my enemies—but I was not thinking of enemies."[35] The directors called the price for the rails in question "fair and legitimate" but concluded that the president's connection with the London house "was wrong."[36] In order to retain the confidence of the other directors, Gilmore promptly terminated his relationship with Thompson and Forman and paid over the $1,695 he had received in commissions as of December 1846 into the Western's treasury. In 1849 the directors returned Gilmore's conscience money to him with interest.[37]

In 1847 and 1848 the Western for the first time turned to an American rail manufacturer, the Tremont Iron Works in southern Massachusetts. In the two years the Tremont Works, in which Gilmore was heavily involved, delivered 3,500 tons of rails worth in excess of $235,000 before poor quality forced the Western to stop deliveries and again turn to British sources. Gilmore's profits from the rail transactions are unknown; but raised eyebrows among the other directors caused Gilmore some uneasy moments, and after 1848 he made no further rail sales to his company.[38]

Most important to Gilmore was stock speculation made possible by his inside knowledge of company policies. Unlike Bliss, Gilmore viewed not the long term but the short run. His quick and profitable maneuvers in the Concord prepared him for similar action in the Western. At the time he was elected, Gilmore already owned substantial stock: 200 shares worth $20,000 at par value. From 1846 onward Gilmore's holdings fluctuated rapidly to a peak of 409 shares (which made him the corporation's largest individual stockholder) in 1847, just before the raise in the Western's dividend from 6 per cent to 8 per cent. Less than a year later Gilmore held only 7 shares, but by 1849 he had over 350.[39]

It would be a mistake, however, to equate Gilmore with the railroad titans made infamous by their exploits in the Erie and the New York Central. Gilmore did not engage in stock watering, nor did he cause downward fluctuations in the dividend rate to lower stock prices. In fact none of his transactions were dishonest. He merely used his knowledge of dividend policies and made purchases and sales at appropriate times. By such methods, for example, Gilmore bought stock when it was selling for between $85 and $99 per share and sold it when it reached $126 per share several months later.

Gilmore's preoccupation with the short run left him little time or interest to develop the long-range view toward rates and fares which characterized Bliss's actions. In fact, there is little evidence that Gilmore had a detailed grasp of the problem. He inherited a railroad that was, thanks to Bliss's efforts, financially sound and growing stronger. In 1845, the last year of Bliss's administration, the Western's gross revenues amounted to more than $810,000, and the net operating income was more than $442,000. Any fear that the corporation would be unable to meet its total annual fixed charges of $310,000 was fast fading. Therefore Gilmore accepted the previous administration's basic rate and fare structure, making only minor changes to meet specific circumstances. Bliss's core policy, however, of reliance on local traffic, and the attempt to capture the Albany–Boston business while shunning any effort to divert the Erie's flow from New York City to Boston, remained unchanged.

The lack of a long-range financial overview and optimism induced by the Western's increasing prosperity made Gilmore the ideal man to conclude a bargain with the Boston & Worcester. Not surprisingly, therefore, Gilmore on the very day of his election to the Western's presidency got together with Nathan Hale and within a few hours the long-standing dispute between the two railroads was at an end. The agreement, which came to be known as "The Contract of 1846" was a triumph for the Boston & Worcester. Hale made minor concessions. On the through Boston–Albany first-class passenger fare, for example, the Boston & Worcester agreed to take $1 instead of the traditional $1.10 as its share, provided that the total fare was lowered from $6 to $5. This reduction, put into effect on April 1, 1846, was necessary to meet the combination river and sound steamer fares between Albany and Boston, which fell to ruinous lows due to severe competition in 1845 and 1846. But the Worcester won a major victory on freight. Although Hale made a slight concession by agreeing to pay the Western $2,000 per year toward the maintenance of its Greenbush–Albany ferry, the basic principle of a prorata division of the freight revenue for which the Worcester had long fought became the heart of the new agreement. In the words of the contract,

> It is . . . agreed that the receipts from the transportation of all joint merchandise shall be divided between the two corporations pro-rata according to the number of miles which each parcel is transported, with this exception, that after ascertaining the said pro-rata division, there shall be deducted from the proportion of the Boston & Worcester an amount equal to 12 cents per ton for every ton transported to or from places west of Springfield and the said amount shall be added to the pro-rata proportions of the Western Road.[40]

In effect this gave the Western a slight advantage on through freight, but preserved to the B&W a flat prorata split of the profitable local freight traffic between Worcester and Springfield. Hale felt so good about the contract that he gave a dinner in Boston's United States Hotel, to which he invited more than two hundred guests.[41]

Fortune smiled on Addison Gilmore. In 1847 tragedy and famine in Ireland brought prosperity to his railroad. Heavy demands for flour abroad not only boosted summer traffic in that commodity but created substantial winter business as well, for at the close of the navigation season the Western–Boston & Worcester route was the only feasible way to move stored flour from Albany to the Atlantic. As yet no competing rail route challenged it. And winter business was profitable since flour rates went up from the $3 per ton charged during the period of water competition to $5 per ton. In 1846 the railroad transported just over 20,000 tons of flour between Albany and Boston, and in 1847, more than 51,000 tons, which was an all-time high until the 1860s. When the flow of flour slackened, its loss was never felt because of the steadily increasing high-value local freight business generated by the growing industrial towns of Palmer, Springfield, Chicopee, Westfield, and Pittsfield.

Paced by freight, gross revenues climbed spectacularly. From $878,000 in 1846, they soared to over $1,300,000 in 1847. Despite a decrease in the transportation of flour during the following year, the increased local business kept revenues growing. They amounted to $1,330,000 in 1848. Net operating income increased similarly: from $465,000 in 1846 to $648,000 in 1847 and $679,000 in 1848. This made possible healthy dividends. The rate increased from 6 per cent in 1846, to 7 per cent in 1847, and 8 per cent in 1848.[42]

Addison Gilmore made his one big fare experiment early in his administration. In March 1846 he urged that the directors approve a special night express train between Albany and Boston. Gilmore felt that such a train, if it carried first-class passengers at $3 instead of the usual $5, might draw people electing to take Hudson and Sound steamers between Albany and Boston, which at times charged a total fare between $2 and $3 due to ruinous competition. To lessen the possibility that passengers bound for points such as Springfield or Pittsfield might attempt to buy through express tickets (which would be less than local fares) and get off at way stations, Gilmore proposed that the night express make no stops except for fuel and water and that these be made at obscure places along the route where it would be inconvenient for passengers to debark.[43]

The experimental express commenced on April 15, 1846; it made the 200-mile trip in slightly less than eight hours including stops. Six weeks later on May 31, Gilmore discontinued the low-fare flyer. Regretfully the president concluded that the express did not increase the total volume of traffic over the Western substantially, but merely diverted passengers from the regular day trains, which still charged a $5 fare between Boston and Albany. And the ban on way passengers proved only partly effective. A locomotive change at Worcester required a stop there, and many canny travelers bound from Albany to Worcester bought tickets to Boston, took the express and alighted in the yards during the engine change. Reported Gilmore, "The loss on tickets from Albany to Worcester . . . has been over 50 per cent."[44] Although Gilmore made several minor modifications of both the freight and passenger tariffs, the night express marked his only attempt to emulate the ideas of Elias Hasket Derby, and its purpose was not to divert passengers from New York to Boston but merely to help the railroad compete against the Albany–Boston water route. In the years that followed ruinous competition abated on both the Sound and the Hudson, and the railroad, which was a day or more faster than the boats, gained the major portion of the through Boston–Albany passenger traffic.

Booming business placed a strain upon the Western's single track and the meager equipment inherited from Bliss's administration, but the greatly increased revenue made new construction and equipment possible both by the sale of new stock and by plowing back profits into the system. Thus Gilmore's presidency marked a period of tremendous expansion. Between 1846 and 1850 the Western sold 1 million dollars of new stock, which increased the total paid in capital to 4 million dollars.[45] Between

1847 and 1851 this capital, together with some current earnings, went to construct over 45 miles of second track, which came within 10 miles of completing a double-track system between Worcester and Springfield. The new line, built in the most substantial manner, used rails weighing 70 pounds to the linear yard. This contrasted sharply with the original 40-pound rails used on the Boston and Worcester and the 56-pound rails used in the Western's initial construction. Equipment grew at an equally rapid pace. In 1847 and 1848 the Western purchased, mainly from Hinckley and Drury and the Taunton Locomotive Works, thirty-five 20-ton engines, which replaced the ill-fated Winans crabs and made it possible to retire some of the lighter 10-ton engines acquired from other builders. In 1846 the Western had forty-three engines; in 1850, sixty-five. And rolling stock similarly increased with heavier eight-wheel cars replacing the already antiquated four-wheeled stock.[46]

Gilmore also implemented a contract made during the last months of Bliss's presidency which pledged his corporation to operate the Pittsfield & North Adams Railroad, constructed in 1845 and 1846 under the Western's supervision for a separate company financed mainly by industrialists in Adams and North Adams. Under the agreement the Western leased and operated the new line for thirty years, paying a rent of 6 per cent annually on the Pittsfield and North Adams capital stock. The 18-mile railroad, which branched northward from the Western's main line 2 miles east of the Pittsfield station opened for traffic in the fall of 1846. Although the P&NA earned its operating costs, revenues fell short of the stipulated annual rent, which amounted to approximately $27,000. For three years a guarantee fund, put up by the North Adams industrialists to induce the Western to lease the P&NA protected Gilmore's line from loss. By 1850, however, the fund was exhausted and the Western sustained the small deficits. But the losses were more apparent than real, for the P&NA fed business to the Western's main line which more than compensated for the lack of revenue from the P&NA.[47]

Years of rough-and-tumble business activity took their toll of Addison Gilmore. In 1849 his health began to ebb, and only pressure from the Western's board kept him from retiring at the 1850 stockholders' election. After that Gilmore's strength continued to fail; and just before his departure for Europe on a vacation, he discovered that the system's trusted cashier, Addison Ware, had embezzled nearly $70,000. This brought added worry and an immediate investigation of the railroad's financial organization, which resulted in the establishment of an independent auditor of accounts to oversee all money collection.

Prior to Ware's defalcation Gilmore had decided that he would retire at the annual meeting in February 1851, but three months before this time death removed him from the scene. A few days earlier, Gilmore wrote a long justification of his reign. "When I commenced my official service as President of the Western Rail-Road, I possessed an iron constitution, and without reflection, applied myself day and night to its affairs. . . . Without stopping to reflect, energy and pride stimulated me to exertion, until at last I find myself scarcely able to crawl about."[48] But to Gilmore the results were worth the effort. "Gentlemen," he exuded, "I regard the success of the Western Rail-Road as almost beyond precedent. None but Mr. Degrand could have anticipated the results which are realized."[49] Summarizing his achievements, Gilmore argued, "It is well known, that prior to February, 1846, the Directors of the Road had been struggling with pecuniary embarrassments, and avoided all outlay not demanded by the most imperative necessity. They trusted to an increase of business, to enable them to pursue a different course. . . . During the last five years, the income of the Road has increased, so that we have been able not only to meet our ordinary expenses, but to make up much of the previous depreciation, and since July 1, 1847, we have made regular semi-annual dividends of 4 per cent each. . . . The fact is that the Corporation has been growing rich, and has been able to charge off almost any amount to expenses and still make remunerating dividends."[50]

Gilmore attributed this remarkable success to a united directorate that backed his policies. But the truth lay elsewhere. The real source of the Western's prosperity derived from the enormous increase of traffic, which the trains carried at the rate and fare structure that George Bliss spent so much effort evolving.

At first agricultural disaster in Europe swelled through freight, and by the time overseas agriculture recovered, local industrial growth beside the Western's tracks poured high-value merchandise onto the cars. And the Western Railroad, carefully avoiding the ruinous competition which characterized the traffic flowing down the Hudson to New York City, waxed strong on the business of its choice.

The directors picked William Swift, the West Point engineer who aided George Whistler during the Western's construction, to succeed Addison Gilmore. The new president, who ran the railroad for three years until February 1854, faced increasing difficulties. During his tenure gross revenues declined slightly, from $1,366,000 in 1850 to $1,339,000 in 1852, before they rose to $1,525,000 in 1853, Swift's final year. During his term expenses rose sharply, owing mainly to increased maintenance. This caused the net operating income to dip from $761,000 in 1850 to $683,000 in 1852 and to $746,000 in 1853. As a consequence the dividend rate fell from 8 per cent in 1851 to 7.5 per cent in 1852 and 6.5 per cent in 1853.[51]

The root of the trouble was competition. By 1851 the Western had ceased to be the only rail link between Boston and the western waters. In that year new systems opened to make it possible to reach the St. Lawrence River near Lake Ontario by a series of railroads running north out of Boston to Lowell, then up the Merrimack River to Concord, New Hampshire, and from there to White River Junction on the Connecticut River, and on to Rouses Point, New York, via Montpelier and Burlington, Vermont, and finally across the top of New York State to Ogdensburg, which hoped to build itself into a new Buffalo. A second route connected Boston with the upper Hudson at Troy. It ran circuitously from Boston to Fitchburg, Massachusetts, then to Bellows Falls, Vermont, and on to Rutland, before turning southward to Saratoga, Schenectady, and Troy. Neither route offered the Western effective competition, but they did skim off some through freight. Swift estimated that the new lines caused "a diminution in the gross receipts of the [first] six months [of 1852] of $40,706 as compared with those of 1851, and of $26,113 as compared with those of 1850."[52]

Swift saw the rapid multiplication of New England railroads creating a permanent and difficult problem. "Is it to be expected, by reasonable men," he asked rhetorically in December 1852, "that dividends at the rates received in former years when the business was less divided [between different railroads], can be continued, and the roads and their equipment fully maintained, if the ruinous practices recently introduced to obtain work for Rail-Roads at prices which all experience in this part of the country had proved to be inadequate to meet current expenses, deterioration, and a just return upon the capital employed, be continued?"[53] Specifically, Swift feared two proposed railroads. The first was an extension of the Fitchburg from its terminal city to Greenfield, Massachusetts, and from there to Troy, New York. This would provide the Western with direct and effective competition for the through Albany–Boston business. A second dangerous proposal was the so-called New York–Boston "Air Line," which was to run from Boston through southeastern Massachusetts to Hartford along what later became the Boston, Hartford and Erie Railroad. The Air Line would challenge both the Boston & Worcester and the Western for the growing through Boston–New York passenger traffic. In 1851 two through daily express trains ran between New York and Boston. They covered the distance of 240 miles in nine hours and used the tracks of four railroads: the Boston & Worcester, Western, New Haven & Hartford, and New York & New Haven.[54]

Swift saw the Western's potential problems clearly but seemed unable to create an over-all strategy to meet them. Instead he continued intact Gilmore's major policies. The contract of 1846 had been renewed almost unchanged in 1849, except that the Worcester was allowed to drop its $2,000 per annum subsidy of the Western's Greenbush–Albany ferry.[55] In April 1853 Swift again renewed it, yielding "with some reluctance . . . the 12¢ per ton which the Boston & Worcester had allowed to the Western . . . on all freight to and from points beyond the Connecticut river as a compensation for the [Western's] high grades."[56] This virtually gave to the Boston & Worcester the flat prorata division of the freight revenues it had long sought and marked the high point of the Western's

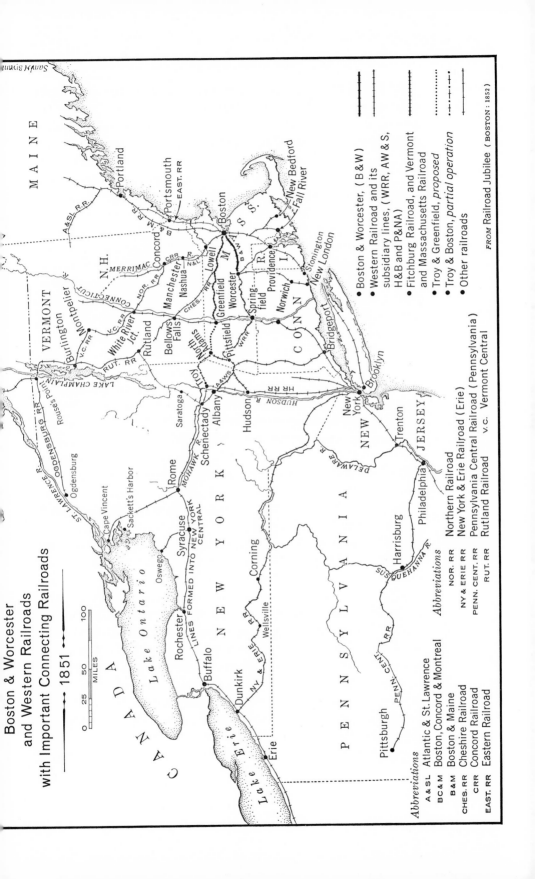

Boston & Worcester
and Western Railroads
with Important Connecting Railroads

— 1851 —

MILES
0   25   50   100

Abbreviations
A&SL Atlantic & St. Lawrence
BC&M Boston, Concord & Montreal
B&M   Boston & Maine
CHES. RR Cheshire Railroad
CRR   Concord Railroad
EAST. RR Eastern Railroad

Northern Railroad
New York & Erie Railroad (Erie)
Pennsylvania Central Railroad (Pennsylvania)
Rutland Railroad   v.c. Vermont Central

Abbreviations
NOR. RR
NY & ERIE RR
PENN. CENT. RR
RUT. RR

• Boston & Worcester, (B & W)
• Western Railroad and its
  subsidiary lines, (WRR, AW & S,
  H & B and P & NA)
• Fitchburg Railroad, and Vermont
  and Massachusetts Railroad
• Troy & Greenfield, *proposed*
• Troy & Boston, *partial operation*
• Other railroads

FROM Railroad Jubilee (BOSTON : 1852)

capitulation. Because of the stabilization of traffic, Swift halted, in line with Gilmore's dying advice, the construction of further double track.

Only in rare instances did Swift initiate bold new actions or plans. On December 26, 1852, the Western in conjunction with the three other railroads that made up the Boston–New York passenger route via Springfield and Hartford set out to demonstrate that the proposed Boston–New York Air Line was unnecessary. That afternoon a Western engine, the *Whistler*, pulling a mail car and a passenger coach left Boston's Beach Street Station. Less than six hours and 240 miles later the train arrived in New York. This remarkable speed run covered the Boston & Worcester's 44 miles in fifty-five minutes, and the 54 miles from Worcester to Springfield in fifty-nine minutes. Although motive power in the early 1850s could not pull a regular train at these speeds, Swift concluded that it "appears safe to assert that the land line via Springfield and New Haven can be run through . . . with four cars in seven hours [two hours less than the 1852 schedules], and in as short a time as any air line or other line which can be constructed between the two cities."[57]

Swift saw the Hudson River ferry between Greenbush and Albany as a major obstacle in attracting freight from points west of the Hudson. This was especially true since 1851 marked the end of the restrictions that limited or prevented the railroads west of Albany from carrying freight during the canal season. Thus for the first time a significant volume of rail freight from western New York State to New England became a possibility.[58] Swift was worried that rail bridges across the Hudson at and above Troy would make it easy to divert some through traffic, especially that from west of Schenectady, over the new lines to Massachusetts, which ran via Rutland, Vermont. "So long as there was no competition or competing line of railroads from the West to Boston," commented Swift, "the ferry was suffered as an evil almost unavoidable, but now that there is a continuous line or lines which exist by other routes (although circuitous) the evil is considered by the trading community as greater in magnitude than before."[59] Because the combined opposition of upriver Troy and some Albany property owners made the cause of a bill to bridge the Hudson at Albany hopeless in the New York Legislature, Swift proposed that the several roads that would benefit most from an all-rail crossing unite in constructing a tunnel.[60] Although New York State chartered a corporation for this purpose in 1852 and Swift became its president, engineering problems, lack of capital, and disunity doomed the tunnel.

Probably the most important departure from the past, was Swift's policy toward locomotive construction. In 1850 Wilson Eddy, a newly promoted master mechanic who ran the company's Springfield shops, convinced Addison Gilmore to permit the construction of a locomotive in the corporation's shops during slack periods. This involved no technical difficulties since the machinery required to repair engines was the same as that needed to build them. Eddy argued that local construction would ensure motive power specifically fitted for the Western's needs. He completed his first engine, appropriately named the *Addison Gilmore* in early 1851. The locomotive had two huge drive wheels 6 feet 9 inches in diameter. When the single drivers gave insufficient traction, Eddy rebuilt the *Addison Gilmore* into 4-4-0 (four leading wheels, four drive wheels, and no trailing wheels) which had four 6-foot drive wheels. Eddy's second engine, the *Whistler,* was similar to the rebuilt *Addison Gilmore*. It entered service in 1852, just in time to participate in the dramatic speed run between Boston and New York City.[61]

Gilmore authorized locomotive building as an experiment. Swift, pleased with the results, thought the Eddy machines the best on the system. In 1853 Swift made the practice of locomotive construction in the corporation's shops permanent. Economic factors were paramount in his decision. The railroad's construction of an engine a year, he asserted, would nearly equal the loss caused by the retirement of older locomotives, and the "machines can be finished at a very small advance upon the cost of material used in the construction, for an average number of some 24 hands have to be employed on the making of repairs in the machine shop, and when there is no particular press of work, a portion of the force is placed upon working on the engine."[62] This small beginning expanded into a major

272

operation, and soon the Western was building over half of its own locomotives. In the Western's final decade, from 1857 through 1867, the railroad added a total of forty-seven engines, of which twenty-eight came from its own shops.[63]

The era of Eddy locomotives marked a sharp contrast with the days just twenty years before, when the Boston & Worcester searched in vain for suitable American engines and was forced to rely on English imports. From 1833 onward, however, the trend in locomotive construction moved away from the mass-produced stock machine toward special units designed for particular operating problems. This favored the American builder and, on the larger railroads, home construction. Ultimately, American railroads came to possess a bewildering variety of engines, and in the days of consolidation this probably increased maintenance costs. For the Western, however, the home-built engines were a boon, for they meant the introduction of a large class, similar in design and familiar to the men in the repair shop. Most important, it regularized shop employment and therefore benefited both the workers and the railroad.[64]

Swift occupied the Western's presidency during a period of rapid transition in Massachusetts' railroad industry. But despite occasional dramatic moments, the Western changed little under his rule. Each year new railroads invaded the Western's territory, draining away traffic. And in the background lay the possibility of a second through railroad from Boston to the Hudson, running parallel to the Western just thirty miles to the north. Although Swift seemed to see clearly the problems that beset his system, he seemed powerless to meet them. In December 1853, he again renewed the Contract of 1846 in its modified form, which gave the Boston & Worcester most of the advantages.[65] At the annual meeting in February 1854 Swift stepped aside for Chester W. Chapin, who as a major stockholder was alarmed at the Western's apparent stagnation, which to him was symbolized in Swift's meek surrender to the Boston & Worcester.

CHAPTER XIII

Chester W. Chapin and the Formation of the Boston & Albany

CHESTER W. CHAPIN'S ELECTION to the Western's presidency in 1854 returned the railroad to a native Springfield man. Although its stockholders resided mainly in Boston, the Western almost from its inception had been a Springfield institution. The line's original need for state aid and the selection of George Bliss as agent and then president ensured the dominance of the Connecticut River city during the early years. Boston's Addison Gilmore temporarily interrupted Springfield's control, but even then the headquarters remained in the Connecticut Valley. Although President Swift, a Philadelphian, took up residence in Springfield, he remained an outsider.

Chapin, however, unlike Bliss and Dwight, did not descend from the elite. "To be a Dwight," a saying went, "is glory enough anywhere on the Connecticut River." To be a Swift and a West Pointer also carried prestige. But to be a Chapin, with neither ancestry nor education, meant rising the hard way, and certainly no resident in Western Massachusetts had had a more difficult road to fortune. Yet by 1851 Chapin was acknowledged as Springfield's richest man with assets in excess of half a million dollars.[1]

Chapin's early experiences shaped most of his later actions. Although he started as a trader without capital, ill health and the need of exercise caused him to take up stage driving. Before long, he had husbanded his earnings and purchased an interest in the lines that radiated from Springfield. Sensing new opportunities in steam navigation, in 1832 Chapin sold his stages and bought an interest in a steamboat running between Springfield and Hartford. Eventually he became sole owner of the Springfield and Hartford line and a firm friend of Cornelius Vanderbilt, whose ships served Hartford and New York. Chapin watched railroad expansion closely, and he soon recognized that the future belonged to the locomotive rather than the steamboat. Selling his boats, Chapin became the prime mover in railway construction from Springfield south to Hartford and north to Northampton. He became a director in the New Haven & Hartford Railroad, and in 1851 he became president of the Connecticut River Railroad. Starting in 1850, Chapin bought Western Corporation stock; by 1854, he held over 700 shares and was the railroad's largest individual stockholder.[2]

Chapin's view of railways differed fundamentally from that of his immediate predecessor. William Swift, an engineer by trade, was unable to grasp the economic revolution in transportation; he understood everything in terms of construction or oper-ational problems and therefore focused upon faster trains, bet-ter locomotives, and a tunnel under the Hudson. Swift viewed the Western as a fixed, developed institution rather than as the germ of a great railroad empire. Addison Gilmore's admin-istration undoubtedly colored Swift's thought. Under Gilmore, the Western changed from a risky investment to a blue-chip stock. Gilmore's main boast was that he raised the dividend to 8 per cent and placed his corporation in a position to maintain that rate indefinitely. During his administration the character of investors changed. The shares remained dispersed among a large number of holders. In 1846 there were approximately 2,000 stockholders, in 1854 more than 2,700. The average hold-ing per investor ranged from ten shares ($1,000) in 1846 to about 15 ($1,500) in 1854. But before Gilmore, the turnover was enormous. Of the 111 original stockholders who purchased 50 or more shares, only 12 still held stock in 1845. After Gilmore took control, however, investors tended to buy and hold shares. Of the 106 stockholders who held 50 or more shares when Gil-more became president in 1846, 58 still held them at his death. Thus the Western, like the Boston & Worcester before it, was becoming the preserve of the small but conservative investor who purchased the stock for the regular dividends it provided. The Western also became a favorite of institutions and trustees. A partial list of such investors in 1854 included the American Insurance Company, the Boston Athenaeum, the Boston Asylum and Farm School, the Boston Dispensary, the Hingham Bank, the Market Bank, the Merchants Bank, the Columbian Fire and Marine Insurance Company, the Gloucester Marine Insurance Company, the Lynn Mechanics Fire Insurance Company, the Massachusetts Congregational Charitable Society, the Massachusetts Society of the Cincinnati, the New England Mutual Marine Insurance Company, Harvard College, Hope Insurance Company, the Mount Auburn Cemetery, the Society for the Propagation of the Gospel, the Springfield Mutual Fire and Marine Insurance Company, Phillips Academy, and the United States Insurance Company. As years went on the stability of the stockholder list increased.[3] The Western's owners came to regard their shares almost like money in a savings bank. Their demand was for the *status quo*. Swift caught their mood when in 1852 he lamented the increase of rail mileage in New England, which he asserted merely divided a relatively stable business among more carriers and reduced profits, a fact to which he attributed a decline in the Western's dividend from 8 to 7½ per cent.[4]

Chester Chapin looked at the Western differently. His experience, which ranged from stages to boats and finally to railroads, made him aware of the revolution under way in the American transportation network. Chapin's capital came not from stability in the industry but through change and growth. Therefore Chapin welcomed expansion. He recognized that in 1854 railroads were just on the threshold of greatness, and he saw the Western not as a finished work but as a potential leader in the formation of a vast national system. Only by growth could its stockholders continue to profit from their investments.

At the time of the Western's completion in 1841, it was something of a wonder, a giant linking two of America's great cities separated by 200 miles of rugged terrain. West of the Hudson, canals ruled supreme; and those railroads under construction did not seem to challenge water transportation. By the 1850s, however, rails had proved themselves. Vast networks were beginning to form, and it took very little imagination to foresee a day when tracks would stretch from the Atlantic to the Pacific.

In New York State two great systems were emerging. In 1851, the New York & Erie Railroad, after eighteen frustrating years reached Lake Erie from its tidewater terminal at Jersey

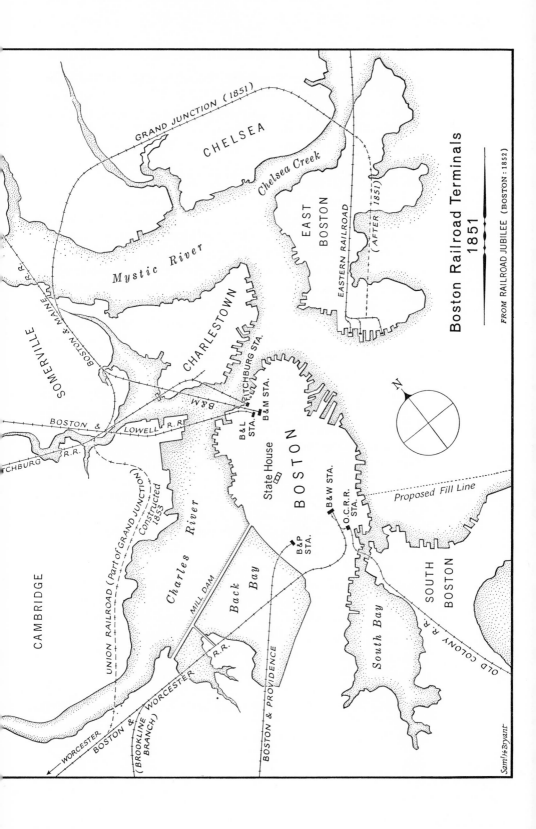

Boston Railroad Terminals
1851

FROM RAILROAD JUBILEE (BOSTON : 1852)

GRAND JUNCTION (1851)

CHELSEA

Chelsea Creek

EAST BOSTON

EASTERN RAILROAD

(AFTER 1851)

Mystic River

N

SOMERVILLE

BOSTON & MAINE R.R.

CHARLESTOWN

B&M

FITCHBURG STA.

B & M STA.

BOSTON & LOWELL R.R.

B & L STA.

State House

BOSTON

B & W STA.

O.C.R.R. STA.

Proposed Fill Line

CHBURG R.R.

UNION RAILROAD (Part of GRAND JUNCTION)
Constructed 1853

Charles River

MILL DAM

B & P STA.

CAMBRIDGE

Back Bay

R.R.

WORCESTER

BOSTON & WORCESTER
(BROOKLINE BRANCH)

BOSTON & PROVIDENCE

South Bay

SOUTH BOSTON

OLD COLONY R.R.

Sam'l G Bryant

City. The railroad directly challenged the Erie Canal for the freight moving from the Great Lakes to New York City. The Erie's completion forced New York to reappraise its policy toward the railroads that made up the through route between Buffalo and Albany, and on December 1, 1851, the legislature removed the restrictions designed to protect the state-owned Erie Canal from competition.[5] Thus the way opened for a vast expansion of rail freight moving from Lake Erie to the Western Railroad's terminal at Albany. In 1853, the ten separate railroad corporations linking Albany with Buffalo consolidated into the New York Central. This gave New York State a second trunk-line railroad from the Great Lakes to the Hudson River. There-fore, when Chapin took over the Western in 1854, he faced the problem of his company's relationship to the new Goliaths arising to the west. The New York Central's future was espe-cially crucial since as it drew more traffic away from the Erie Canal, it would become vital as a source of freight to the Western.

Chapin's road also faced a challenge closer to home. Under Gilmore and Swift the Western, scrupulously following Bliss's lead, avoided competition with the Hudson River by making scant effort to divert traffic from New York City to Boston. Further, after the initial business surge during the potato famine, the Western and the Worcester lost interest in the through Albany–Boston flour trade, which fell from a peak of more than 51,000 tons in 1847 to about 23,000 tons in 1854. The increase in high-value merchandise made hauling through flour, for which the railroad received its lowest rates, unattractive. If flour could have been carried without additional capital costs, the Western and the Worcester might have shown more interest. But the nature of the business required special prepa-ration. Flour was seasonal; it arrived in great bulk in the late summer and early fall. Its movement necessitated investments in extra cars and locomotives that would stand idle much of the year. And as local business grew, the single-track line be-tween Albany and Springfield, with its meticulously scheduled regular traffic, became less able to absorb a flood of extra business.

There was even less enthusiasm for carrying flour destined

Table 3. *Flour transported between Albany and Troy to Boston and way stations via the Western Railroad and alternative routes, 1842–1867*[a]

YEAR	TO BOSTON VIA WRR	TO OTHER STATIONS VIA WRR	TOTAL BARRELS VIA WRR	TOTAL BARRELS TO BOSTON FROM ALL SOURCES	TOTAL BARRELS EXPORTED FROM BOSTON
1842	85,986	86,124	172,110	—	—
1843	123,366	120,873	244,239	—	—
1844	154,413	142,990	297,403	—	—
1845	181,796½	146,386½	328,183	—	—
11 months in 1846	209,634	151,711	361,345	—	—
1847	513,851	188,649	702,500	—	—
1848	371,239	206,776	578,015	935,578	129,678
1849	327,694	262,471	590,165	1,026,309	153,933
1850	362,275	236,318	598,593	761,148	115,316
1851	267,073	189,570	456,643	773,512	177,346
1852	231,546	254,793	486,339	896,454	269,771
1853	264,474	207,330	471,804	935,962	382,305
1854	232,982	188,852	421,834	767,090	188,353
1855	340,108	212,937	553,045	1,012,929	159,084
1856	287,610	208,385	495,995	1,009,450	198,081
1857	198,870	207,390	406,260	1,049,023	184,597
1858	311,567	207,953	519,520	1,227,639	196,862
1859	265,779	182,131	447,910	1,049,186	164,875
1860	278,842	171,281	450,123	1,164,732	234,616
1861	594,005	254,964	848,969	1,433,999	389,730
1862	567,968	328,862	896,830	1,365,832	555,591
1863	538,310	436,697	975,007	—	—
1864	590,265	331,852	922,117	—	—
1865	363,844	332,489	696,333	—	—
1866	592,874	352,626	945,500	—	—
1867	634,881	327,591	962,472	—	—

Sources: WRR Annual Reports to Stockholders 1842-1867; and *Report of Commissioners upon the Troy and Greenfield Railroad and Hoosac Tunnel to His Excellency the Governor, and the Honorable Executive Council of the State of Massachusetts* (Boston, 1863), pp. 82, 86.

[a] Western Railroad faced only water competition until 1849. In 1850 the railroad from Troy via Rutland to Boston opened. In 1851 Ogdensburg route opened. In 1858 through freighting via Grand Trunk and Portland started. In 1860 the Providence and Erie Railroad opened.

for export at Boston. The Boston & Worcester lacked access to adequate port facilities. In the early years real estate promoters had lured it into Boston's South Cove, where dockage, although available, quickly became inadequate for ocean-going vessels. The Worcester had no rail connections with the new wharves and warehouses constructed across the harbor in Charlestown and East Boston. In 1853 the B&W took steps to link itself with East Boston; it underwrote $100,000 of bonds in the Grand Junction Railroad, a line already running from Somerville to East Boston. Under the arrangements tracks were to be constructed from the Boston and Worcester's main line in Brighton through Cambridge to connect with the Grand Junction in Somerville. In addition the Boston & Worcester was to receive a lease to wharf facilities in East Boston. Although construction crews soon had the necessary tracks in place, the Grand Junction Railroad, which from the first had been a tool of land speculators, collapsed financially. This threw a cloud over the Worcester's East Boston terminal property, and the corporation's directors found that to validate their lease, further financial aid to the Grand Junction would be necessary. Never enthusiastic about the bulky freight that came to their railroad from the Western, the Boston & Worcester directors refused to throw away good money after bad; instead of moving to resuscitate the Grand Junction, they went to court in an attempt to protect their "rights." Litigation dragged on for years, and weeds grew on the tracks connecting the B&W's main line with the Grand Junction. Not until 1869, after the formation of the Boston & Albany, did the plans for facilities adjacent to deep water in East Boston reach fruition. Meanwhile the Boston and Worcester kept its terminal in the South Cove, which denied direct rail connection to wharfage fit for ocean-going ships, thus requiring a costly, slow horse and wagon transfer of all freight from the trains to the ships.[6]

The Western's and the Boston & Worcester's freight policies produced the inevitable harvest of complaints. In the spring of 1854 the Albany Board of Trade launched an investigation. For Chapin its conclusions, published prominently in the city newspapers, made embarrassing reading. One substantial grievance was "the delay in getting flour and other articles over the

Western Railroad on board the cars at East Albany [Green-bush]. In some instances it has required three, four and five days and even a longer period to make a transhipment of a boatload of grain." The board found that the delay at the Western's terminal caused "purchasers of grain . . . to pay a cent per bushel more" for cargoes destined for the Western Railroad in addition to a demurrage of $6 to $12 per day for the idle canal boats. In the case of flour, delays at East Albany ranged from five to fifteen days. The board of trade's committee concluded "that the working machinery of the [Western] road has not been materially increased during the last four years, and consequently its rolling stock has been materially diminished."[7]

The Albany complaints supported the effort to build a competing railroad from Boston to Troy, New York, which would parallel the Western 20 to 30 miles to the north. Elias Hasket Derby and those interests associated with the port of Boston did not give up when Bliss emerged victorious in the battle to control the Western Railroad. Nor did Derby lose his interest in railroads. He just transferred his activities to another front.

After his defeat at the Western, Derby joined with a Fitchburg paper manufacturer, Alvah Crocker, the driving force behind the recently chartered Fitchburg Railroad. Together the two pushed the new system between Boston and Fitchburg in 1845. For both this was but a beginning; in 1844 at Crocker's urging the General Court chartered the Vermont and Massachusetts Railroad to extend westward from Fitchburg to Brattleboro, Vermont, with a branch to Greenfield, Massachusetts. Before it was completed in 1850, Greenfield on the Connecticut River 35 miles north of Springfield became the terminal.

Both Crocker and Derby then turned their attention toward building still further westward. For that purpose, and against the informal opposition of the Western Railroad, the legislature chartered the Troy & Greenfield to link the Vermont and Massachusetts with a line to be constructed from Troy, New York, to the Massachusetts-Vermont boundary near Williamstown in the Bay State's far northwest corner. The new roads, when finished, would open a second route from Boston to Erie's terminus 11 miles shorter than the Western's tracks.

The future, however, proved not to be easy for the Troy & Greenfield, for between the Connecticut River and the railroad's goal in northwestern Massachusetts stood Hoosac Mountain, the vast ridge that engineer Loammi Baldwin had in 1826 proposed piercing with a 4-mile tunnel as part of his abortive Boston–Hudson canal scheme. The Troy & Greenfield's promoters again revived the tunnel, but nothing of that magnitude had yet been built by man, and despite assurances that Old Hoosac was made of "soft" rock, prospective capital took flight at the very mention of the plan. Undaunted, Crocker and Derby, joined by P. P. F. Degrand, turned in 1851 to the General Court with a plea for the state to underwrite $2,000,000 in bonds.[8]

The Western railroad, cool toward the very idea of the Troy & Greenfield, bristled at the thought of state aid for it. President Swift immediately informed the legislature that his railroad opposed "any grant by the state which shall . . . enable a parallel road to be built within 20 miles of [the Western], a step highly injurious to the interests of the state as to the corporation."[9]

To counter Swift's opposition, Derby and his allies seized upon the Western's failure to divert the Erie Canal trade from New York City to Boston. Pamphlets appeared overnight, spreading wide and far the tales of disgruntled freight forwarders in Troy. Said Tillinghast and Company, Troy commission merchants, "We have [often] been unable to ship [over the Western] for some days after the receipt of orders and have sometimes been obliged to cart flour back into store returned from the depot for want of cars."[10] Another Troy merchant, James Hooker, wrote that the Western's inadequacies "many times" subjected him to "very serious inconvenience and loss. In 1847, 1848, and 1849 in forwarding flour, I had to wait for cars from three to ten days . . . and [I] now [in 1851] find the same difficulties."[11] Troy's Ide, Coit & Company stated that "the inconvenience has been at times so great that we have declined freight for that [the Western] route, preferring others."[12]

The Bliss rate policy and Gilmore's accommodation to the Worcester's interests in the Contract of 1846 stood at the root of the Western's inadequate service to the movers of bulky freight. In effect, prospering on local business, the Western under Gilmore and Swift had opted out, not only of the competitive struggle waged on the Hudson for the Albany–New York traffic, but of the trade in bulky freight, mainly flour and grain, moving between Albany and Boston as well. Thus after an initial effort to end packet competition, the Western lost interest, and water retained a vital part in the movement of flour and grain from Albany to Boston during the 1840s and 1850s.[13]

Derby, in his attack on the Western, graciously absolved management of any blame. Instead he asserted that high grades and a circuitous route made the Western inherently unsuited for diverting traffic from the Hudson to Boston.[14] Derby capped his reasoning with statistics, invoking the testimony of none other than the Western's William Swift. Derby addressed the legislature:

> He tells us that 2-1/2 cents per ton mile or $5 from Albany to Boston is the average cost of transportation [on the Western]. This has been . . . the average freight charge on the Western from its opening to the present time. How much margin an average charge of $5 and an average cost of $5 leaves for profit you can determine for yourselves; according to my arithmetic the balance is nothing. The dividends of the Western Railroad, so far as freight has contributed to it then, have been derived from the local trade, and not from the through business.[15]

Derby argued, using the Western's own figures, that its traffic, being local, would therefore not be adversely affected by the Troy & Greenfield. Speaking before the General Court Derby asked,

> Now what is the through tonnage of the Western Railroad compared with the whole business to be done? I have here the report of the Western Railroad Corporation printed for the stockholders in January last [1856], in which the through tonnage . . . is set down at 88,000 tons. The canals and the Central Railway of New York carry to and from the Mohawk Valley nearly 4,000,000 tons annually, but the Western Railroad, laid down to connect the Mohawk with the seaport of

Boston transports but 88,000 tons! . . . Why gentlemen, the entire local and through transportation of the road together amounted very nearly to 400,000 tons. The through business of the road is little more than one-fifth of its entire business.[16]

The Troy & Greenfield's proponents left no doubt as to their line's superiority. Compared with the 200-mile long Western, the tunnel route was shorter, needing only 189 miles to cover the distance from Boston to the Hudson. But most important, the tunnel took the rails through, not over, the mountains, making possible the use of faster and heavier trains. These advantages, asserted Derby, meant the difference between success and failure in the struggle to divert to Boston the trade of the Great West. Experience after the tunnel was finished in 1875 gave scant support to Derby's arguments. The line, lacking good connections westward, never became a major passenger route, but it did carry substantial freight. By 1895 over 60 per cent of the commodities exported from Boston came through the tunnel. But rates lower than those on the rival Boston & Albany never did materialize. Operating expenses on the tunnel line did not differ from those on the old Boston & Worcester and Western route, and the Hoosac had a much higher bonded debt.[17]

The Western Railroad used every weapon at its command to defeat state aid to the Troy & Greenfield. Legislators from Springfield and other towns along the Western delayed action in the General Court for three years. In 1853, during a state constitutional convention, the Western, which itself had benefited from state aid, vainly attempted to force into the Massachusetts constitution a provision prohibiting the state from underwriting loans to private corporations.[18]

The Western's efforts failed. In 1854, Derby and his friends won the day. The legislature voted to guarantee $2,000,000 of the Troy & Greenfield's bonds. Although this was but the beginning (the Hoosac Tunnel would require twenty-one years and more than $14,000,000 of state aid before it was completed), the General Court's action placed the state of Massachusetts for a second time behind the construction of a railway alleged to be the key to winning the western trade for Boston.[19]

Chapin, a strong leader in the tradition of Bliss and Gilmore, clearly recognized that the Western could not meet the challenges of railroad consolidation and effective competition with old policies. Chapin, therefore, focused on three major objectives. First he desired to extend his railroad's control westward beyond the Hudson to Buffalo. He also strove to build up the Western's physical plant by the addition of over 110 miles of second track and more rolling stock. Finally he sought to change the relationship Gilmore had constructed between the Western and the Boston & Worcester.

Immediately after his election Chapin tried to buy control of the newly formed New York Central. The time was propitious, for prior to Vanderbilt's purchase of the system in 1868, the Central had a modest capital of but $23,000,000, and its shares sold freely at about 80 per cent of par.[20] Because the Central's stock was widely dispersed among many investors, Chapin felt that the railroad could be controlled with less than $9,000,000. Of this he commanded about $1,000,000 through his own resources and those of Springfield financial institutions to which he had access. For the rest he depended upon outside capital.

Chapin tried in vain to interest State Street in his plans. Failing himself, Chapin asked his good friend James Colt, the leading Berkshire County lawyer and later a justice on the Massachusetts Supreme Judicial Court, to make a further attempt to interest Boston in the New York Central's purchase. Writing years later, Charles Francis Adams, Jr., pointed up the problem:

> Both the mission and the messenger singularly illustrated the separation which then existed between the main artery of Boston's commerce and Boston's financial and business men. So far from being able to effect a combination to carry out a great scheme, the Springfield president of the Western Railroad Corporation did not even know how to put himself in communication with the men who were necessary to make up the combination. Mr. Colt was a lawyer. The business in hand, however, was one to be transacted not with lawyers or judges, but with bankers and men of business and capital.[21]

Inevitably Colt failed, and Chapin sadly gave up his dreams of controlling the Central.

Chapin, however, could not and would not give up his other

Table 4. *Sources of capital, 1866 and 1868 compared:*
BOSTON & WORCESTER AND WESTERN RAILROADS

	WESTERN RAILROAD, 1866		BOSTON & WORCESTER, 1866
Stock			Stock, private $4,500,000
Private	$5,710,000		
State	1,000,000		
		$ 6,710,000	
Bonds			
State	4,000,000		
Albany	1,000,000		
		5,000,000	
		$11,710,000	

	WESTERN RAILROAD, 1868		BOSTON & WORCESTER, 1868
Stock			Stock, private (capital paid-in) $5,000,000
Paid-in, private	$7,000,000		
Paid-in, state	1,000,000		
Issued to old shareholders on a prorata basis without payment of money	2,000,000		
		$10,000,000	
Bonds			
State	4,000,000		
Albany	1,000,000		
		5,000,000	
		$15,000,000	
Total value of sinking funds to retire Massachusetts and Albany bonds, as of 1867		$ 3,611,164.92	

objectives. A double-track line from Worcester to Albany was vital. Much of the bottleneck which delayed flour and grain shipments, thus providing steam for the Western's critics, resulted from congestion on the 100 miles of single track between Springfield and Albany and the 10 miles of single line still remaining between Worcester and Springfield. The prospect of competition from the Troy & Greenfield made the increased efficiency of double-track operation even more imperative. Although it was true, as Elias Hasket Derby had asserted, that the Western prospered mainly from the local business, much of the selected through traffic that it did carry was highly profitable. For the 88,000 tons transported "through" in 1855 (which equalled one-fifth of the total freight volume) the Western received in excess of $350,000, or more than a third of its total freight revenue. This was business the Western could ill afford to give to another railroad. "I can plainly see," wrote William Jackson to Chapin in 1854, "that the interests of your stockholders will call more loudly for that second track, after the completion of the Hoosick [sic] Tunnel than they do now."[22] Jackson reasoned that the elimination of delays caused by a single track would augment locomotive capacity by 20 per cent and would reduce the need for additional rolling stock by an even greater amount. Increased capacity, better safety, more efficient use of motive power and cars, lower operating costs—these were the lures of a double track.

Money was the big problem. Chapin estimated that the entire cost of the 110 miles of second track would be about $1,500,000.[23] Previously Addison Gilmore had financed the construction of 45 miles of double track and other needs through the creation of new shares. During Gilmore's administration the Western's capital stock rose by $2,150,000, or from its original $3,000,000 to a total of $5,150,000. But less buoyant expansion and the stabilization of gross revenues and net profits during his final three years caused Gilmore to reject further capital increases and halt construction of the double track. Swift followed Gilmore's thinking, and since gross revenues and profits continued to be relatively stable, Swift increased neither the system's double track nor its capital. Chapin faced a difficult situation. Potential competition from the

Hoosac Tunnel route demanded a double track, but the rail-road's position in the money market was poor. Between 1855 and 1857 inflation in the national economy and high profits in speculative ventures, many of which collapsed in the panic of 1857, adversely affected the price of conservative securities. In 1855 and 1856 the Western's stock returned 7 per cent and sold at prices ranging from a low of 87 per cent to a high of 98 per cent of par value. With the Western's stock selling below par, a new stock offering was not possible. And interest rates above 6 per cent made a bond issue unattractive.

Consequently Chester Chapin recommended that the Western finance its expansion by borrowing from the growing sinking funds established to retire the Western's government guaranteed bonds issued between 1838 and 1841.[24] These funds in 1855 amounted to more than $1,500,000. Chapin argued that money could be borrowed from the funds at 6 per cent, better terms than could be had on the "feverish" open money market. Chapin's scheme did not find favor with the committee of the railroad's stockholders to which it was referred. Francis B. Hayes, Ingersoll Bowditch, and J. J. Dixwell felt that the sinking funds must be kept separate from the fortunes of the railroad. They emphasized that the funds protected the stockholders as well as the bondholders, ensuring that the Western would not be "overwhelmed at the maturity of the debt."[25]

Blocked from using the sinking funds, Chapin decided to attempt bond sales. Backed by a vote of the stockholders at a specially called meeting, the Western's president presented in April 1855 a petition asking the General Court to authorize $1,500,000 of new state scrip. Although the legislature refused to guarantee further Western railroad securities, it did vote on May 21, 1855, to allow the Western to create $1,500,000 of bonds for which the railroad was solely responsible. Since the domestic market was unfavorable, the Western attempted to dispose of the securities through the London financial house of George Peabody and Company. This failed, for the English financiers proved unable to sell the bonds at the stipulated 6 per cent.[26]

Chapin's inability to raise money through bond or stock sales, despite the Western's urgent need, focused his attention upon the Boston & Worcester Railroad. Chapin knew that a cardinal policy of one of his predecessors, George Bliss, had been that the Boston & Worcester should aid the less fortunate Western by giving the latter railroad the lion's share of the profits from the joint freight business. Bliss clung to this policy and it proved his downfall. Addison Gilmore had capitulated to the Worcester, and the Contract of 1846 and its later revisions divided freight revenues upon a prorata basis, which gave to each system equal revenue per ton-mile. The contract had worked as long as the Western prospered, but the threat of competition and the renewed financial crisis revived the conditions that had caused Bliss to ask for more than a prorata division of the joint freight profits. In 1855 Chapin suddenly "discovered" that the Contract of 1846 had been "misinterpreted." The Western's president charged that through an "error" the Worcester Railroad had long received "a much greater share than [it] was entitled to by the the fair construction of the [Contract of 1846]."[27]

The Western's president thus reopened the old controversy. If it had been feasible, Chapin would have proposed an immediate union of his company with the Boston & Worcester. The advantages were clear, for consolidation would reduce the overhead of both roads, enable a more aggressive policy toward the through traffic, and most important, make available the Worcester's earnings for the construction of the desired second track.

But the Worcester was no more disposed to merger in 1855 than it had been in 1846. Although Nathan Hale had retired from the presidency in 1849, his influence still remained strong. His successors, Thomas Hopkinson, who presided from 1849 until his death in 1856, and Ginery Twichell, who ran the road during its final decade from 1857 through 1867, both opposed union. Like Chapin, Twichell was a self-made man who started his career as a post rider and a stage driver. But he was never able to break free of his Worcester County origin.[28]

Thomas Hopkinson and Ginery Twichell saw the same basic objections to union as did Hale. Despite a temporary decline in the Worcester's dividends to near 6 per cent from 1855 through 1859, due to the short-term bonded indebtedness contracted in support of the system's mildly unsuccessful branch-line expansion, the Boston & Worcester's long-range outlook seemed brighter than the Western's. After 1860, the B&W would have no significant indebtedness, and the entire net profits could be directed toward dividends. And the road stood secure from effective competition. The Western, on the other hand, not only had an enormous bonded indebtedness, but faced the prospect of sharp competition for the through traffic after the completion of the Hoosac Tunnel.

The Worcester's management also felt that union would eliminate their jobs since it seemed certain that in any merger the larger Western would be dominant. In addition Twichell sympathized with local opposition. His native city of Worcester, proud of its status as a terminal, feared that a unified railroad would be less responsive to its interests. In fact most towns along the Worcester Railroad felt the same way.

The Western's cancellation of the Contract of 1846 in November 1855 to take effect on June 1, 1856, initiated a long, bitter fight. Chapin's demand that the Worcester pay to the Western money allegedly owed because of the "incorrect" interpretation of the Contract of 1846 came as a surprise. After much argument Chapin agreed to limit the Western's "claims" for past damages to the years of his presidency, 1854 and 1855. A neutral arbitrator, F. B. Crowninshield, a Boston lawyer and president of the Old Colony Railroad, in April 1856 supported the Worcester's interpretation. Chapin, however, refused to sign a new contract until the Worcester agreed to terms that were strikingly close to those of Bliss a decade before.

The dispute dragged on into 1857, when the legislature, mainly at the Western's urging, passed a law which provided that connecting railroads must haul each other's traffic and that if no agreement were reached voluntarily, commissioners appointed by the state supreme judicial court would fix the rates. This opened the way for endless litigation. The first commissioners under the new law, James W. Brooks, Holmes Hinkley, and Waldo Higginson, sat during December 1857. More than three months later, in March 1858, they ruled in favor of the Worcester. The Western immediately appealed to the supreme court, asking that the commissioners' award be set aside. This delayed the final decision until December 1860, when the judges ruled against the Western.[29]

Frustrated by the court, the Western in 1860 again turned to the legislature. This time Chapin asked for a statute that specifically embodied his concepts of rate division. Simultaneously, to bolster his case, Chapin hired Benjamin Peirce, Harvard University's Perkins Professor of Astronomy and Mathematics, who "proved scientifically" that the Worcester's interpretation of a prorata split of the joint freight revenues was unfair. Wrote Peirce to a committee of Western directors,

> It is apparent then that the carriage of this joint freight is most unequally profitable to the two roads upon this principle of division [the traditional split derived from the Contract of 1846], and that it is worth twenty four per cent more to the Worcester than to the Western Railroad. It is quite possible, indeed, that this work may be profitable to the Worcester Railroad, while it is of insignificant value, or even a loss to the Western Railroad; if the profits which accrue from it to the Western Railroad are just, those derived by the Worcester must be excessive. I can not understand how such an unequal compensation of services can be consistent with the public interests.[30]

Unimpressed by the professor's highly theoretical argument, the legislators bowed to backstage maneuvering by the Worcester's friends, and the Western's bill quietly died without even coming to a vote. After years of argument, litigation, and frustration Chester Chapin seemed no closer to victory than on the day he assumed the Western's presidency.

But the 1860s brought dramatic changes. The Civil War revitalized the Western. Overnight, traffic increased. By 1863 swelling profits made possible a 10 per cent dividend—a rate the corporation maintained with ease through its final year in 1867. Prosperity provided funds for the double track. At first Chapin cautiously financed construction from current income. But the rising price of the Western's shares, which never sold below par from 1860 through 1867, soon made stock offerings attractive. In 1865, therefore, the Western created 5,150 ($515,000) new shares. Other increases soon followed, raising the Western's total paid in capital in 1867 to 80,000 shares worth $8,000,000 at par value.[31] By 1866 the 110 miles of single track that Chapin inherited had been reduced to 40, and by the end of 1867 the entire line from Worcester to Albany had a double track.[32]

The crush of business and cooperation between the three railroads most interested—the Western, New York Central, and Hudson River Railroad—finally overwhelmed Troy's opposition to a railway bridge across the Hudson at Albany. In 1865, the three railroads jointly formed a special bridge corporation in which the Western invested $125,000, more than one-third of the required capital.[33] By the end of 1866, the cumbersome ferry between Greenbush and Albany was only a memory, and trains rolled across the Hudson on a brand new span built according to Howe's design.

In the 1860s the spectacle of two of Massachusetts' greatest corporations constantly waging a bitter war against each other began to tell against both, but especially against the Boston & Worcester. The Twichell management won in court, but the public dispute over the rate and fare policies began to expose the tacit assumptions of Bliss, Gilmore, and Hale. Specifically it became embarrassingly clear that the tariff structure for the through traffic discouraged the grain and flour trade and eschewed any competition with the Hudson River for the trade of the Great West. This was not a revolutionary discovery, but never before had the public realized how little effort the Western and the Boston & Worcester had made to tap the traffic of the Erie Canal.

Chapin had no more desire to divert the Erie's trade than had Bliss, whose rate and fare policies the Western still maintained. Chapin's main concern was for the future, the day when the Hoosac tunnel would be completed and when competition would start whether the Western liked it or not. Meanwhile Chapin did little to halt the idea that it was the Worcester, not the Western, which kept the trade of the West from Boston.

Josiah Quincy, Jr., a former Western Railroad treasurer deeply involved in Boston wharf property, decried the great failure to win the Erie's trade for Boston. Speaking in 1866 before the Boston Board of Trade, Quincy underscored statistically the Worcester's lack of concern for the growing freight traffic arriving in Albany from the West. "During the last ten years," he emphasized, "the Western railroad have added 212 freight cars to their equipment, and the Worcester railroad not one. During the same time the New York Central, which is one of the continuations of this line, have added 2,095 to theirs and increased its business 400 per cent while that of the Western has increased by 62."[34]

Quincy blamed excessive rates for the failure to capture the Erie's traffic. But perhaps because he knew in his heart that no capitalists would risk rushing into competition with the Hudson River, he proposed that the state exercise its option to buy the Boston & Worcester and the Western, and then lease the combined lines to the city of Boston. Quincy claimed that a municipally run system could reduce rates and fare sufficiently to win the grain and flour trade. But Quincy thought the export trade and the profits arising from it important. To achieve his aims, he cared not whether the railway lost money. "The City of Boston is not entering into a speculation for profit," he lectured. "Whatever the corporation lose the city and the people will gain ten times over in the increase of taxable values of their property and the decrease of the price of all the necessities of life."[35]

Quincy's scheme had little support, but his criticism reflected a growing feeling that the Commonwealth and the city of Boston suffered from the separation between the Boston & Worcester and the Western. As early as 1862, the Boston Board of Trade, called upon to act as a referee in the continuing dispute between the two lines, became "convinced that consolidation, as recommended with singular unanimity by a committee of the two corporations in 1845, is the only measure which can insure permanent harmony and give certain and adequate protection to the distinctive business of Boston."[36]

Chapin, too, favored consolidation. But the Worcester's steadfast opposition made such a movement impossible until the 1860s, when the situation changed. In 1861 the Worcester road's thirty-year monopoly of rail traffic between its terminal cities expired, and the Western acquired the economic power to build a competing railroad between Worcester and Boston.

In January 1863 the Western's board instructed Chapin to petition the legislature to allow "it to extend its line of railroad to Boston."[37]

The Worcester stockholders, alarmed by the pressure from the board of trade and the Western's threatened extension, voted at their annual meeting in February 1863 to establish a committee to explore terms of union.[38] Working with a similar committee of the Western's stockholders, the Boston & Worcester's committee reported in October 1863 that they had agreed upon the details of a merger and had applied to the General Court for a law authorizing the union. The Boston & Worcester's management, however, still opposed any action that would end the corporation's separate existence and worked discreetly to defeat the measure in the General Court. Charles Beck, a member of the joint legislative committee on canals and railroads, which killed the bill later, wrote that among the major objections to it was the impossibility of properly compensating the Worcester's shareholders for their property.[39]

Chester Chapin's road, deep in the midst of capital expansion necessary to finish the double track and the Hudson River bridge, allowed the merger proposal to drop temporarily. But in 1867, with the second track and the Hudson bridge completed, Chester Chapin would wait no longer. That year, therefore, the legislature, under heavy pressure from the Western and the Boston Board of Trade, passed a law increasing the Western's capital by $3,850,000 and granting it the right to build tracks into Boston if terms for consolidation were not arranged within four months. The Worcester stockholders, noting the Western's prosperity, no longer had a fear of merger, and they wanted to avoid the prospect of a new railroad to Boston. The only question was the terms. The agreement, which took effect in 1868, created a new corporation, the Boston & Albany Railroad, whose capital equalled the combined shares of the old corporations. The holders of Western stock merely exchanged it for shares in the new corporation on a one for one basis. The Boston & Worcester stockholders also received one share in the Boston & Albany for each one held in the Worcester, but as a sop they got an extra $10 in cash for each share exchanged.[40]

The Worcester's "bonus" was more apparent than real, for Chester Chapin just before the merger took an action he was accused of learning from Cornelius Vanderbilt. Chapin caused 20,000 shares (par value $2,000,000) of unissued stock to be distributed without payment among the Western's shareholders. This amounted to three new shares for each ten held in the company, or a bonus of about $40 per share if the dividends were kept at the current level.[41] Josiah Quincy, intent on lowering grain and flour rates, accused Chapin of stock watering, that is, creating shares which paid into the railroad's treasury no capital, but upon which full dividends were maintained.[42] Chapin took issue with Quincy, claiming that the capital thus created merely rewarded the stockholders for the years of "slack" dividends prior to the Civil War, when net profits had been diverted to constructing a double track or to the sinking fund, which was worth nearly $3,000,000 in 1867.

Chapin's idea of creating new shares differed considerably from those of Vanderbilt, who in his first two years as the New York Central's leader created more than $30,000,000 (at par value) of watered stock.[43] Recognizing that such large-scale additions would depress the value of the shares, Chapin, who was a director of the New York Central, stated to Vanderbilt after he unveiled his plans: "Commodore, this is a pretty large scheme, but I doubt if you can continue to pay 8 per cent dividend upon the increased capital."

"How much can we pay?" asked Vanderbilt.

"Perhaps 6 per cent" came the reply.

"Well that is enough for any investor who obtains his capital as easily as this," retorted the Commodore.[44] The idea of creating new stock in such quantities that it depressed the value of the old horrified Chapin as it did every one of the leaders who had constructed both the Western and the Boston & Worcester, including even Addison Gilmore.

The Boston & Albany Railroad started life as Massachusetts' wealthiest corporation. But those who expected the new company to win for Boston the Erie's trade were doomed to disappointment. Some realists assessed the problem and agreed with Charles Francis Adams that Boston's hopes were "built upon 'the fallacy that steam could run uphill cheaper than water could run down.' "[45] It was true indeed that Boston faced disadvantages in the competition for the western trade. Not only did the rugged Berkshires block the route between Albany and Boston, but New York City was 58 miles (out of 980) closer to Chicago than Massachusetts' capital. Yet significant though these difficulties were, Chester Chapin would not have ascribed Boston's failure solely to its geographic position.

As it stood for its total life, the Boston & Albany had a relationship to the New York Central comparable to that which the Boston & Worcester had with the Western. The Albany's neighbor to the west, the New York Central, faced severe competition and could afford to grant the B&A only a very small part of the revenues from the joint traffic moving from the interior to the seacoast. As an appendage at one end of the trunk Boston to Chicago route, the B&A had little power to influence through rates, which were made in New York by directors controlling the whole line of rails from the Hudson to Chicago. In setting rates between East and West an extra 58 miles came to mean little. Indeed the New York Central competed very well with the Pennsylvania Railroad, which was 60 miles shorter. Backed by a highly profitable local traffic and ownership of the Central, as Chapin had desired in the 1850s, the Albany might have made a strong bid for the western trade. Alone, however, the Boston & Albany, like the Worcester road before it, turned from its visions of a through carrier and became an institution dedicated to local traffic, dividends for the shareholders, and preservation of its identity.

CHAPTER XIV

Conclusion

WHEN NATHAN HALE proposed a railway from Boston to Albany in the 1820s, not a single mile of track existed in the United States. The industrial revolution was still in its infancy. Yet four decades later, when the Boston & Worcester and the Western merged to form the Boston & Albany, the driving of the golden spike on the nation's first transcontinental line was but a year away. In a short forty years railroads had grown from visionary schemes to vast corporate giants that dwarfed any other previous economic enterprises.

It is certain, however, that the men who started the Worcester and the Western did not know what they were creating. Railroads to Nathan Hale, Thomas B. Wales, and George Bliss were not institutions in themselves but merely a means to stimulate other economic activities such as Boston's traditional commercial life or the new Chicopee River cotton factories. Railroads, like lighthouses, post roads, and city streets, were an essential public service, which was the proper responsibility of the Commonwealth as a whole.

Paradoxically, Massachusetts' railroad development, when it did occur, was predominantly generated by private enterprise with the state playing little more than a passive role. Despite the grand designs for a public network presented to the General Court in the late 1820s, it is significant that such plans were always advanced by small but vocal private economic interests such as speculators in Boston wharf property or Pittsfield factory owners. The Massachusetts General Court, controlled by a combination of small farming communities and declining seaport towns, most of which would not benefit directly from railroad development, simply refused to initiate any state network. The legislature was reluctant to back railroads, not because it had scruples against government enterprise, but rather because of the overriding fear that railroads would be unprofitable and that the resulting tax burden would fall heavily on those who would receive no benefits.

The Commonwealth's refusal to initiate railway construction and the subsequent success of the private ventures set the pattern for continued private development. But, though the state did not initiate or shape the Massachusetts network, the government's role cannot be ignored. Railroads differed substantially from other private enterprises. Factories, stores, and warehouses needed no special charters, but railroads required the power of eminent domain, which was the gift of the state alone.

More than any other factor, the Commonwealth's reluctance to incur the taxation that would have resulted from unprofitable government railroads fixed the early relationship between the private corporations and the state. Had individuals not been willing to risk their capital, transportation development in Massachusetts would have been greatly delayed. Private money was attracted because railroads were ancillary to other ventures such as Lowell factories and because the state was willing to grant favorable charters.

Private builders faced the legislature from a position of strength. In return for hazarding their money, they wanted and got a thirty-year monopoly of all traffic along their routes as well as full power to set rates. The state gave the managers nearly complete freedom, but it was careful to guard against any abuses that would hurt vested economic groups. Thus the legislature minutely prescribed the eminent domain procedures, and it carefully protected investors from unsound or corrupt practices. Charter restrictions made it virtually impossible to issue stock without receiving paid in capital to the full par value of the certificates. Legislation made railroad financial records part of the public domain. Finally the General Court made periodic investigations of the honesty of the managements.

Even when private corporations proved that railroads were profitable, the Commonwealth allowed its fear of financial loss to dominate its relationship with the Western and Worcester railroads. The state's purchase of Western Railroad stock and its loan of credit to the corporation was done in a manner that avoided any taxation. And the state directors, instead of pressing for low rates, became committed to policies designed to protect the Commonwealth's financial interests. In fact the legislature's directors voted for rates and fares that would produce a maximum net operating profit. Significantly those interests that attacked the railroad's management and attempted to lower through tariffs spent their energies trying to influence the private shareholders rather than the state.

The Commonwealth continually avoided actions that would interfere with management's freedom. Despite strong pressure from George Bliss and other influential Whig politicians, the legislature refused to set the rates at which the Worcester would take freight and passengers from the Western. The General Court deliberately avoided setting safety standards for the Western Railroad, even after a series of disastrous wrecks had shaken public confidence in the line's management. And it defeated measures that would have given the state a majority of the Western's directors in return for the loan of the public credit. The state's one move to influence rates came through its support of the Hoosac tunnel route. The primary effort here, however, was not to set rates but to lower them through fostering competition.

In summary, the state did not initiate railroads. Nor did it interfere in the operation and management of the lines. The state did, however, act in limited support of private capital through a loan of the public credit. But the Commonwealth's main interest remained the protection of private property, whether that property was real estate that might be damaged through the misuse of eminent domain or whether it was money invested in railroad stock. Nothing better illustrates the relationship between the state and the corporation than the Western's public directors, whose actions cannot be distinguished from those of their private counterparts.

More significant than the relations between the railroads and the state were the changes the Western brought about in the nature of management. The first presidents, Nathan Hale of the Worcester and Thomas B. Wales of the Western, considered railroads secondary to their other interests. Neither regarded them as profitable enterprises in themselves, and certainly neither foresaw the day when railway corporations would dwarf all other economic ventures. The early executives did not realize that railroads required new managerial techniques unknown to either Boston's merchant princes or the rising textile entrepreneurs. The Western, measured by any standard except by those of the railroads completed in the 1850s, was a giant enterprise. By 1842, its 160 miles of main line had absorbed more than $7,000,000, and by 1854 its capital was $10,000,000. By contrast even the Erie Canal, which was more than 360 miles long, cost only $7,000,000; and only the biggest industrial concerns had as much capital as $500,000. Even in 1850 in textiles, the most advanced segment of industry, only forty-one American factories had a capitalization of $250,000 or more.[1]

Traditionally merchants had used the bonds of kinship and friendship to cement far-flung ventures. The formal organizational structures characteristic of twentieth-century businesses were then unknown. Before 1860 even the largest manufacturing corporations had only one or two factories, normally located in a single place. Thus the manager of a cotton mill could view his entire establishment in an hour or two and found no need for elaborate systems to supervise subordinates.

At the time of its completion in 1841, the Western Railroad was one of the two longest railroads in the United States (only the Baltimore & Ohio had more miles of track) and the only one of any length to have a major source of traffic. Most other systems, like the Boston & Worcester, barely exceeded 40 miles in length and were of a size that one person could properly oversee. But the Worcester's managerial system failed to produce the discipline needed for safe operation on the Western. The disasters of the early 1840s and the resulting operational crisis forced the line's president, chief engineer, and directors to devise new managerial methods, substituting bureaucracy for kinship and friendship. The Western's new multidivisional structure, which drew clear and formal lines of authority and responsibility between the president and the superintendent and the lowest carsman and depot agent and which simultaneously instituted a series of elaborate reports that enabled valuable data to flow upward from the operating men to top

299

management, received widespread publicity. It is significant that the Baltimore & Ohio Railroad, usually thought of as the nation's "railroad university," and the Pennsylvania, which has been regarded as the source of major managerial innovations, both lagged far behind the Western in adopting a new type of management. The B&O for example did not discard a plan of organization that resembled that used on the Boston & Worcester during the first few years until 1847. The Baltimore road, although long in miles, did not until later years connect two points between which flowed a heavy traffic. The old type of organization was therefore adequate for it. The managerial reforms on the Erie which became the foundation of those on the Pennsylvania were not adopted until after 1850. Indeed the managerial system of the Western bore a striking resemblance to those that later emerged on the Erie, Pennsylvania, and Baltimore & Ohio in the 1850s and 1860s. Thus the Western Railroad marks the real start of modern business administration since practices worked out on the railroads were adopted by industrial corporations toward the end of the nineteenth century.[2]

The professionalization of management increased the powers and prestige of the president and superintendent while diminishing those of the directors and the stockholders. This was especially true in a corporation like the Western, in which the stockholders numbered more than a thousand and in which they had little time or opportunity to study the mass of data upon which the decisions of the president and superintendent were based.

For the Western the presidency of George Bliss marked a transition from a railroad dominated by men who were interested primarily in nontransportation activities to the start of a professional management. Those leaders who followed George Bliss and Nathan Hale, starting with the Western's Addison Gilmore and the Worcester's Thomas Hopkinson, made railroading a career.

In the 1840s the managers of both the Worcester and the Western became subject to strong pressures from various and diverse interests. On both systems the stock was widely dispersed, largely held by small capitalists and trustees who demanded regular annual dividends of at least 8 per cent. The railway users presented a variety of conflicting demands. On both lines the local exceeded the through business. On the Worcester commuter, short-haul passenger, and intraline freight dominated. On the Western local freight was most important, but the through freight and passenger traffic produced enough revenue to be essential to the line's prosperity. On both railroads the local clashed with the through traffic—those passengers and commodities the railroads carried from Albany to Boston in competition with waterways. If the Western and the Worcester were to win for Boston the business of the Erie Canal and the Great West, they would have had to carry through tonnage at very low rates. Such a policy might have caused higher charges on local traffic, which was immune from either rail or water competition.

Aside from the various economic pressure groups, geographic factors strongly influenced the management of both roads. Until the 1860s the Worcester always occupied the position of strength. It tapped a densely populated region, it lacked water competition, and its charter protected it from the construction of rival railways. For the Worcester's management, decisions were relatively simple. Catering to local demands meant a substantial profit, while an attempt to win the Erie's business would have endangered dividends and caused higher local rates.

The Western's problems were more complicated. It could survive neither on the local nor on the through traffic alone; its salvation lay in a careful balance between the two. The Western's policy to attempt to capture the freight and passenger business that normally flowed between Albany and Boston but ignore the traffic that gravitated down the Hudson to be exported at New York City alienated the Boston mercantile community, which supported the construction of a new railroad from Massachusetts Bay to Troy, New York.

The Western's essential weakness accounts for its fights with its shorter neighbor. In the beginning George Bliss demanded that the Worcester road take a reduced share of the profits of the joint business—a plea that would have forced the Worcester to absorb most of the burden of competing with the Albany–Boston water route. Only the phenomenal growth of industry in central and western Massachusetts in the 1840s and 1850s and the corresponding increase in local traffic made possible the amicable relationship between the Worcester and the Western from 1846 through 1854. During the Gilmore and Swift administrations the Western wrote off all attempts to divert the Erie's flow to Boston, and it lost interest in the bulky grain trade between Albany and Boston as well. But the Western carried enough high-value through traffic and local business to earn a large profit. It was the threat of competition in the form of the state-financed Hoosac Tunnel route that caused Chester Chapin to break the Contract of 1846 and renew the fight started by George Bliss.

The histories of the Boston & Worcester and the Western railroads, therefore, began with both corporations subordinate to the economy that spawned them and ended when the two systems combined to become the Commonwealth's wealthiest and most powerful enterprise. As early as the 1840s both railroads had become primarily profit-making ventures and were controlled by professional managers whose primary aim was to produce an annual dividend of at least 8 per cent. The common goal of both managements, however, did not produce harmony; indeed it did quite the opposite, for the divergent geographic positions of each system and their differing susceptibilities to competition ensured that they would view the through business from opposite vantage points. Only in the 1860s, when the Western enjoyed a sustained prosperity that built up its local traffic, improved its physical facilities, eliminated its bonded indebtedness, and made easy the sale of new capital stock, was merger possible. And even then, union depended upon an accident of fate which saw the Western's new-found strength coincide with the termination of the Worcester's thirty-year monopoly, thus opening the way to the construction of a competing road.

There can be little doubt that the welfare of the stockholders, which paralleled that of the local users, shaped the rate and fare structures of both the Western and the Worcester. The port of Boston never controlled the two lines or exercised a decisive influence in their policies. Not only did the mercantile group own little railroad stock, but they were a minority in a Commonwealth that had shifted its interests from shipping to industry. Direct attacks on the Western or Worcester by those proposing that the lines enter the highly competitive struggle to control traffic moving from the West to the Atlantic found no favor with the stockholders or the Commonwealth, which aside from its interest in the Western's earnings because of its heavy stake in the road's financial structure, instinctively withdrew from any measures that assaulted the rights of private property. But Boston's merchants, supported by much of northern Massachusetts, did procure state aid for a second transregional line. While neither the Western nor the Worcester changed its attitude about diverting the Erie's flow from New York to Boston, the threat of a competing railroad caused Chester Chapin to bring the entire Boston-to-Albany railroad under one management. Thus weakness and competition led to consolidation.

The over-all impact of the two railroads on the economy and life of Massachusetts can hardly be overestimated. The most discussed aspect was management's refusal to attempt to divert to New England the traffic of the Erie Canal and the Boston's consequent failure to rival New York City. Had Boston money purchased the New York Central as Chapin suggested in the 1850s, the fate of the Massachusetts capital might have been different. Without trackage west of Albany, however, even the combined Western and Worcester systems were helpless in luring the traffic of the West to New England. Thus the Boston & Albany in the 1860s had exactly the same relationship to the Central that the Worcester had had to the Western, and the newly created corporation had every incentive to emphasize local traffic and to avoid reversing the long-established policies regarding the highly competitive through business.

Despite their failures the railroads had many positive influences on Massachusetts life. The Boston & Worcester changed urban living; its commuter trains made possible new suburban patterns; in fact the railroad created two of Boston's satellite communities, Newton and Brookline, which forever ended their status as country towns. The railroads also stimulated large-scale industrial production in the Connecticut Valley and made significant factories possible in Berkshire and Worcester Counties. By accelerating industrial and urban growth and by linking the farm to the city, the railroads shaped agriculture and transformed much land along their lines from a decadent backwater into prospering dairy farms and market gardens. And the railroads' success created new wealth and a new and safe form of investment.

Only slightly less dramatic than the development of new towns and cities were the railroad's other influences on the Massachusetts economy. In the 1830s the Commonwealth's large-scale industrial efforts were confined almost exclusively to cotton mills. The railroads, however, opened a national market and stimulated the mass production of an endless variety of new products. Worcester, which became the Bay State's second city, rose not through textiles but through the manufacture of machinery, wire, tools, and other diverse items. Equally as important, the railroads themselves became a major market. Their needs for rolling stock brought into being suppliers such as Boston's Hinkley and Drury Locomotive Works and caused Osgood Bradley's Worcester factory to forsake carriage building for car building.

The railroads' iron requirements stimulated the development of large-scale mills. At the time the Worcester was constructed, American ironmasters produced chiefly for blacksmiths, stovemakers, and the molders of pots and pans. American iron production was, therefore, widely scattered and on a small scale, sufficient for locomotive building and rolling stock, but unable to fill the orders for hundreds and thousands of tons needed for rails. Although both the Worcester and the Western relied on English rails during their construction, they soon turned to domestic sources.[3]

American manufactures entered the rail-making business through the reworking of scrap railroad iron. By 1853 the Western was replacing 20 miles of worn rails annually; and it sent its scrap iron to the Rensselaer Iron Company's works at Troy, and the Bay State Company's mills in South Boston to be cut up and rerolled. Ironically, the use of scrap, originally imported from Great Britain in the form of new rails, made American mills competitive with the English for the first time.

The first forty years of the Boston-to-Albany railroad coincides with the beginning of the industrial era in the American economy. The Boston & Worcester and the Western mark the ascendancy of private over state enterprise and illustrate the enormous complexity in the relationship between such ventures and the diverse economic interests of a mature economy.

In 1867, the private enterprise, which in the 1830s most Massachusetts citizens thought essential but financially risky, had become the Commonwealth's most powerful corporation. The weakness of the early years had led the state to grant special concessions to the railroad managements. The attack on corporate privileges that arose in the 1830s in connection with the Charles River Bridge made the Boston mercantile community, which suffered most from the railroads' rate policies, but which also had increasing investments in chartered companies, reluctant to attack the two railroads directly.

Yet in 1867, Massachusetts was still changing. Small farmers and merchants were losing their power to large corporations and urban masses, the latter, of course, caring little for corporate rights. Thus it is not surprising that the railroad which had demonstrated so much vitality and which had worked such far-reaching changes on nearly every aspect of the Massachusetts economy became the target of increasing attacks and that by the end of the century the railroads' managements were subject to rigorous government control. Indeed to many in 1867 the Boston & Albany was so large and powerful that no force, save that of the state itself, seemed adequate to protect the Commonwealth's other economic interests.

Appendix A. Western Railroad receipts and expenses, 1839–1867

YEAR	PASSENGERS	MERCHANDISE	MAILS, ETC.	TOTAL	EXPENSES	BALANCE OF RECEIPTS	MILES RUN
3 months in							
1839	$ 13,472.94	$ 4,136.21	—	$ 17,609.15	$ 14,380.64	$ 3,228.51	—
1840	70,820.79	38,359.78	$ 3,166.82	112,347.39	62,071.72	50,275.67	94,404
1841	113,841.85	64,467.14	4,000.00	182,308.99	132,501.45	49,807.54	160,106
1842ᵇ	266,446.83	226,674.61	19,566.84	512,688.28	266,619.30	246,068.98	397,295
1843	275,139.64	275,696.19	23,046.68	573,882.51	303,973.06	269,909.45	441,608½
1844	358,694.00	371,131.84	23,926.88	753,752.72	314,074.20	439,678.52	499,968
1845	366,753.02	420,717.30	26,009.83	813,480.15	370,621.25	442,858.90	530,201
11 months in							
1846	389,861.42	459,365.18	29,191.29	878,417.89	412,679.80	465,738.09	573,956
1847	502,321.92	785,345.66	37,668.48	1,325,336.06	676,689.75	648,646.31	819,010
1848	551,038.43	745,909.76	35,120.10	1,332,068.29	652,357.11	679,711.18	804,492
1849	561,575.25	745,393.81	36,841.51	1,343,810.57	588,323.58	755,487.99	730,491
1850	590,743.74	740,493.53	35,015.47	1,366,252.47	607,549.36	761,964.32	768,764
1851	603,207.05	714,362.92	36,324.36	1,353,894.63	597,756.20	756,138.43	774,609
1852	615,480.87	685,062.85	39,329.37	1,339,373.09	656,687.17	683,194.92	848,002
1853	693,290.01	786,215.87	45,718.04	1,525,223.02	778,487.92	746,736.00	947,382
1854	756,502.91	924,973.32	82,468.03	1,763,944.26	1,045,241.19	718,703.07	989,432
1855	763,037.32	1,007,992.84	87,831.59	1,858,861.75	1,236,659.74	622,202.01	1,021,630
1856	812,880.08	1,207,788.61	95,151.36	2,115,820.05	1,228,219.46	887,600.59	1,027,018
1857	808,977.37	1,007,185.62	94,179.49	1,910,342.48	1,084,118.55	826,223.93	959,103
1858	637,042.25	968,516.38	94,734.97	1,700,293.60	890,930.40	809,363.20	944,951
1859	679,121.23	986,305.00	101,641.90	1,767,068.13	936,920.12	830,148.01	1,020,054
1860	690,991.87	1,101,118.64	89,240.21	1,881,350.72	993,096.30	888,254.42	1,114,091
1861	613,365.08	1,164,320.23	116,882.65	1,894,567.96	1,081,571.17	812,996.79	1,234,018
1862	634,656.44	1,351,862.20	109,403.86	2,095,922.50	1,111,358.20	984,564.30	1,257,201
1863	837,610.50	1,479,874.21	118,227.43	2,435,712.14	1,207,006.90	1,228,705.24	1,275,929
1864	1,143,318.31	1,739,796.12	111,884.31	2,994,998.74	1,818,141.71	1,176,857.03	1,439,223
1865	1,366,565.25	1,926,220.48	138,798.37	3,431,584.10	2,204,925.58	1,226,658.52	1,358,514
1866	1,379,684.03	2,394,313.85	158,019.41	3,932,017.29	2,525,226.58	1,406,790.71	1,660,062
1867	1,303,990.21	2,522,125.92	260,591.50	4,086,707.63	2,837,411.77	1,249,295.86	1,840,291

Source: Western Railroad Annual Reports to Stockholders, 1839–1868.

ᵃ Expense statistics exclude interest on bonded debt or sinking-fund payments, which amount to $310,000 each year.

ᵇ First year of opening through to Albany.

Appendix B. Western Railroad: number of through and way passengers, 1842–1867

YEAR	THROUGH PASSENGERS			WAY PASSENGERS			TOTAL 1ST CLASS	TOTAL 2ND CLASS	GRAND TOTAL
	1ST CLASS	2ND CLASS	TOTAL	1ST CLASS	2ND CLASS	TOTAL			
1842	15,890	2,680½	18,570½	148,500	23,366	171,866	164,390	26,046½	190,436½
1843	19,987	6,608	26,595	140,425	33,945½	174,370½	160,412	40,553½	200,965½
1844	17,016½	7,314	24,330½	140,868½	55,058½	195,927	157,885	62,372½	220,257½
1845	13,401½	5,791	19,192½	144,723	59,717½	204,440½	158,124½	65,508½	223,633
11 months in									
1846	21,033	8,799½	29,832½	165,196	70,635½	235,831½	186,229	79,435	265,664
1847	23,678	10,621½	34,299½	264,444½	89,567	354,011½	288,122½	100,188½	388,311
1848	21,647	12,084	33,731	287,480	84,403	371,883	309,127	96,487	405,614
1849	20,440	13,311	33,751½	319,202	82,851	402,053	339,642½	96,162	435,804½
1850	23,575	11,744½	34,319	416,915ᵃ	79,082½	495,997½	440,490ᵃ	90,827	531,317ᵃ
1851	23,074	10,897	33,971	377,874	68,059	445,933	400,949	78,956	479,905
1852	29,946	5,487	35,433	401,907	59,953	461,860	431,853	65,140	497,293
1853	31,804	6,363	38,167	561,312	56,714	618,027	593,116	63,078	656,194
1854	46,968	7,667	54,635	486,679	56,245	542,924	533,647	63,912	597,559
1855	50,829½	9,237½	60,067	485,474	47,836	533,310	536,303½	57,073½	593,577
1856	55,840½	7,405½	63,246	511,926	46,523	558,449	567,766½	53,928½	621,695
1857	51,155	8,223	59,378	519,167	50,509	569,676	570,322	58,732	629,054
1858	42,591	5,046	47,637	442,412	41,865	484,277	485,003	46,911	531,914
1859	42,284	1,967	44,251	516,467	17,052	533,519	558,751	19,019	577,770
1860	39,105½	2,568½	41,674	563,738½	12,470	576,208½	602,844	15,038½	617,882½
1861	30,930½	3,099½	34,030	514,733½	14,376½	529,110	545,664	17,476	563,140
1862	32,634	2,863	35,497	512,005	10,545½	522,550½	544,639	13,408½	558,047½
1863	53,983½	2,259½	56,243	644,895	9,319	654,214	698,878½	11,578½	710,457
1864	71,195	2,770½	73,965½	851,729	11,020½	862,749½	922,924	13,791	936,715
1865	80,021	1,003	81,024	929,267	82½	929,349½	1,009,288	1,085½	1,010,373½
1866	70,959½	570	71,529½	975,307		975,307	1,046,266½	570	1,046,836½
1867	66,712½		66,712½	961,508½		961,508½	1,028,221		1,028,221

Source: Western Railroad Annual Reports to Stockholders, 1842–1868.
ᵃ There appears to be an error in the number of way passengers reported for 1850.

Appendix C. Western Railroad: number of tons transported, 1846–1867

YEAR	WESTWARD			EASTWARD			TOTAL TONS MOVED	EQUIVALENT TONS CARRIED ONE MILE	EQUIVALENT TONS CARRIED OVER THE WHOLE ROAD
	THROUGH FROM BOSTON TO ALBANY	ALL OTHER TONNAGE	TOTAL GOING WEST	THROUGH FROM ALBANY TO BOSTON	ALL OTHER TONNAGE	TOTAL GOING EAST			
1846	8,358	40,251	48,609	36,403	81,382	117,785	166,394	15,748,223	100,950
1847	11,962	56,554	68,516	88,438	117,737	206,175	274,691	28,037,628	179,728
1848	10,808	68,610	79,418	63,667	122,457	186,124	265,542	24,656,129	158,052
1849	14,222	67,506	81,728	58,217	133,663	191,880	273,608	25,307,146	162,289
1850	12,390	60,430	72,820	60,900	127,549	188,449	261,269	25,206,308	161,579
1851	13,731	57,855	71,593	47,057	132,116	179,173	250,766	23,304,050	149,385
1852	14,989	67,436	82,425	44,386	141,242	185,628	268,053	23,724,070	152,078
1853	20,317	89,729	110,046	59,018	155,764	214,787	324,833	28,153,554	180,471
1854	20,991	89,088	110,079	55,874	189,100	244,974	355,053	32,284,823	206,954
1855	22,808	95,908	118,716	65,839	213,494	279,333	398,049	35,541,725	227,832
1856	33,054	104,698	137,752	62,517	218,401	280,918	418,670	38,605,615	247,472
1857	25,544	93,723	119,267	40,041	218,199	258,240	377,507	31,286,514	200,555
1858	18,383	103,582	121,965	56,245	259,686	315,931	437,896	33,043,106	211,815
1859	22,673	115,794	138,467	60,795	249,083	309,878	448,345	33,299,566	213,459
1860	24,350	147,788	172,138	66,355	267,054	333,409	505,547	43,311,064	277,635
1861	20,295	106,974	127,269	111,272	269,638	380,910	508,179	47,924,408	307,208
1862	22,785	136,521	159,306	113,040	315,158	428,198	587,504	51,994,206	333,296
1863	30,933	147,432	178,365	104,776	380,786	485,562	663,927	53,808,561	344,927
1864	27,256	144,944	172,200	116,288	394,372	510,660	682,860	57,749,666	370,190
1865	29,173	164,451	193,624	87,254	412,876	500,130	693,754	54,190,069	347,372
1866	43,991	219,543	263,534	140,191	480,839	621,030	884,564	75,650,824	484,941
1867	61,630	219,025	280,655	162,638	491,312	653,950	934,605	84,534,424	541,887

11 months in

Source: Western Railroad Annual Reports to Stockholders, 1846–1867.

Appendix D. Comparison of stock prices and rates of dividends, 1835–1867: BOSTON & WORCESTER AND WESTERN RAILROADS

	HIGHEST MARKET PRICES		LOWEST MARKET PRICES		RATES OF DIVIDEND IN PERCENTAGE POINTS—EACH 6 MONTH PERIOD[a]	
YEAR	B&W	WRR	B&W	WRR	B&W	WRR
1835	114	—	90¼		2	
1836	107	83	81½	81½	4	—
1837	100	83½	74	74	5–3	—
1838	105½	80	92	77	3–3	—
1839	109	88	100¾	78¾	3–3½	—
1840	111½	82	103	78	3–3	—
1841	110¾	85½	104¾	75	3–3	—
1842	113¾	80½	109	40⅛	4–4	—
1843	119	59¾	107	40¾	3–3	—
1844	121	92	110½	51¾	3–3½	—
1845	122½	104½	116½	90½	4–4	3–3
1846	118	100	110½	85	4–4	2–3
1847	126	114¾	111½	99	4–5	3–4
1848	118	110	106½	96¾	5–4½	4–4
1849	107	107	98½	100½	4–3	4–4
1850	104	105¼	91¾	100¼	3–3	4–4
1851	106¼	107¼	98	99½	3½–3½	4–4
1852	107¾	107½	98	99½	3½–3½	4–3½
1853	105	102¼	100¼	97	3½–3½	3–3½
1854	102	100¼	89½	89	3½–3½	3½–3½
1855	95½	98	86½	87	3–3	3½–3½
1856	90	94	81	87¼	3½–3	3½–3½
1857	91½	100	74½	87½	4–3	4–4
1858	101	108	78	91	3–3	4–4
1859	103	111	91¾	103	3–3	4–4
1860	112¾	117	102½	107	4–4	4–4
1861	114¼	116½	100¼	105¾	4–4	4–4
1862	132½	147	107	111	4–4	4–4
1863	150¼	171	127	140	4–4	4–4
1864	160	170	135	139	5–5	5–5
1865	140	150¼	118	122	5–4½	5–4
1866	127¾	149¼	127¾	132½	5½–5	6–5
1867	150	170	139	134	5–5	5–5

Sources: George Bliss, *Historical Memoir of the Western Railroad* (Springfield, Mass., 1863) 157; and Joseph G. Martin, *Seventy-three Years of the Boston Stock Market from January 1, 1798, to January 1, 1871 (Boston, 1871)*, 74–79.

[a] Dividends calculated as a percentage of the par value of the stock which was for both the B&W and the WRR $100 a share.

Appendix E.   Boston & Worcester Railroad: Receipts, expenses and dividends, 1834–1866

YEAR	GROSS RECEIPTS FROM ALL SOURCES	EXPENSES, NOT INCLUDING INTEREST	AMOUNT PAID IN DIVIDENDS	RATE (%)	WHEN PAID
1834–1835	$ 161,806.95	$ 85,533.28	$ 25,000	2	July 1835
1836	183,189.03	103,674.69	50,000	4	March 1836
1837	209,261.31	119,062.49	75,000	5	Jan. 1837
			45,000	3	July 1837
1838	212,325.03	93,492.97	51,000	3	Jan. 1838
			51,000	3	July 1838
1839	231,807.18	126,384.83	51,000	3	Jan. 1839
			59,500	3½	July 1839
1840	267,547.41	140,441.00	51,000	3	Feb. 1840
			54,000	3	July 1840
1841	310,807.87	162,998.58	54,000	3	Jan. 1841
			60,000	3	July 1841
1842	349,206.67	168,509.51	92,000	4	Jan. 1842
			92,000	4	July 1842
1843	383,367.10	206,641.42	81,000	3	Jan. 1843
			81,000	3	July 1843
1844	428,437.34	233,273.92	81,000	3	Jan. 1844
			101,500	3½	July 1844
1845	487,455.53	249,729.50	116,000	4	Jan. 1845
			116,000	4	July 1845
1846	554,712.46	283,876.11	116,000	4	Jan. 1846
			120,000	4	July 1846
1847	722,170.32	381,985.63	140,000	4	Jan. 1847
			175,000	5	July 1847
1848	716,284.11	381,917.42	175,000	5	Jan. 1848
			157,500	4½	July 1848
1849	703,361.15	405,551.05	168,000	4	Jan. 1849
			135,000	3	July 1849
1850	757,946.79	377,041.08	135,000	3	Jan. 1850
			135,000	3	July 1850
1851	743,922.60	393,687.03	157,500	3½	Jan. 1851
			157,500	3½	July 1851
1852	758,819.47	409,740.26	157,500	3½	Jan. 1852
			157,500	3½	July 1852
1853	887,219.87	455,528.01	157,500	3½	Jan. 1853
			157,500	3½	July 1853
1854	952,895.28	594,528.56	157,500	3½	Jan. 1854
			157,500	3½	July 1854

(*continued on next page*)

YEAR	GROSS RECEIPTS FROM ALL SOURCES	EXPENSES, NOT INCLUDING INTEREST	AMOUNT PAID IN DIVIDENDS	RATE (%)	WHEN PAID
1855	1,008,004.90	603,542.89	135,000	3	Jan. 1855
			135,000	3	July 1855
1856	1,108,781.90	671,719.87	157,500	3½	Jan. 1856
			135,000	3	July 1856
1857	1,019,148.70	612,686.42	180,000	4	Jan. 1857
			135,000	3	July 1857
1858	923,223.63	570,929.36	135,000	3	Jan. 1858
			135,000	3	July 1858
1859	1,067,070.73	565,434.51	135,000	3	Jan. 1859
			135,000	3	July 1859
1860	1,045,683.01	606,398.88	180,000	4	Jan. 1860
			180,000	4	July 1860
1861	928,932.79	520,338.40	180,000	4	Jan. 1861
			180,000	4	July 1861
1862	1,006,129.82	515,825.72	180,000	4	Jan. 1862
			180,000	4	July 1862
1863	1,202,654.05	714,296.29	180,000	4	Jan. 1863
			180,000	4	July 1863
1864	1,471,985.08	984,520.45	225,000	5	Jan. 1864
			225,000	5	July 1864
1865	1,697,164.10	1,160,100.47	225,000	5	Jan. 1865
			202,500	4½	July 1865
1866	1,914,729.54	1,424,528.21	247,500	5½	Jan. 1866
			225,000	5	July 1866
			225,000	5	Jan. 1867

Source: Boston & Worcester Annual Reports to the Stockholders, 1834–1867.

BIBLIOGRAPHY

A. Primary Sources

1. UNPUBLISHED MANUSCRIPT MATERIAL

Boston & Worcester Railroad, Minutes of the Directors' and Stockholders' Meetings, 1832–1867; Dividend Records, 1835–1867; together with Stock Ledgers and miscellaneous other records including a good collection of freight tariffs, letter books, and legal documents for the years 1832–1867. This material is part of the Boston and Albany Collection at the Baker Library of the Harvard Business School, Boston.

John P. Cushing Manuscripts, 1832–1882. Includes 6 volumes and one box with detailed accounts of this Boston merchant's investments. Material held in the Baker Library of the Harvard Business School, Boston.

Oriental Bank Collection, 1835–1845. Includes material on the South Cove Corporation. Held by the Baker Library, Harvard Business School, Boston.

Western Railroad, Directors' Minutes, 1835–1867; Minutes of the Stockholders' Meetings (Corporation Records), 1835–1867; Clerk's File, 1835–1867 (this invaluable file contains many letters in and out of the President's office, numerous reports of special Director's Committees on questions such as rates, fares, and equipment purchases, monthly reports by the president and superintendent on earnings, traffic, etc., and other miscellaneous documents); Administrative Files; Stock Journals, 1835–1867; Dividend Records, 1845–1867; letter books, freight tariffs, engineer's reports, and other miscellaneous account books, legal documents, etc. This material is part of the Boston & Albany Collection at the Baker Library of the Harvard Business School, Boston.

2. GOVERNMENT DOCUMENTS

An Act in Addition to the 39th Chapter of the Revised Statutes of Turnpike, Rail-Road and Canal Corporations. Mass. Senate Document 55, March 1836.

An Act to Establish the Boston, Providence and Taunton Rail Road Corporation. Mass. House Document 57, session 1829–1830.

An Act to Establish the Massachusetts Rail Road Corporation. Mass. House Document 4 (1830).

An Act to Incorporate the Franklin Rail Road Company. Mass. House Document 35, session 1829–1830.

An Act Relating to Rates of Freight on Railroads. Mass. Senate Document 102, April 1850.

Andrews, Israel D. *Communication from the Secretary of the Treasury, Transmitting, in Compliance with a Resolution of the Senate of March 8, 1851, the Report of Israel D. Andrews, Consul of the United States for Canada and New Brunswick, on the Trade and Commerce of the British North American Colonies and upon the Trade of the Great Lakes and Rivers; Also, Notices of the Internal Improvements in Each State of the Gulf of Mexico, and the Straits of Florida, and a Paper on the Cotton Crop of the United States.* Washington, D.C.: Beverley Tucker, Senate Printer, 1854.

Annual Reports of the Boston and Worcester Railroad to the [Massachusetts] Legislature, 1834–1867. (Filed with other Massachusetts railroad reports and printed as *Annual Reports of the Railroad Corporations in the Commonwealth of Massachusetts*)

Annual Reports of the Western Railroad to the [Massachusetts] Legislature, 1837–1867. (Filed with other Massachusetts railroad reports and printed as *Annual Reports of the Railroad Corporations in the Commonwealth of Massachusetts*)

Bigelow, John P. *Statistical Tables: Exhibiting the Condition and Products of Certain Branches of Industry in Massachusetts, for the Year Ending April 1, 1837. Prepared from the Returns of the Assessors.* Boston: Dutton and Wentworth, 1838.

DeBow, J. D. B. *Statistical View of the United States, Embracing Its Territory, Population, White, Free Colored, and Slave— Moral and Social Condition, Industry, Property, and Revenue; the Detailed Statistics of Cities, Towns, and Counties, Being a Compendium of the Seventh Census [1850]; to Which Are Added the Results of Every Previous Census, Beginning with 1790, in Comparative Tables, with Explanatory and Illustrative Notes, Based Upon the Schedules and Other Official Sources of Information.* Washington, D.C.: Beverley Tucker, Senate Printer, 1854.

An Exposition of Facts and Arguments in Support of a Memorial to the Legislature of Massachusetts by Citizens of Boston and Vicinity in Favor of a Bank of Ten Millions. Mass. Senate Document 30. Boston: Dutton and Wentworth, 1836.

The Inaugural Addresses of the Mayors of Boston, vol. I: *From 1822 to 1851.* Boston: Rockwell & Churchill, 1894.

Laws of the Commonwealth of Massachusetts Passed by the General Court at Their Session Which Commenced on Wednesday the Fourth of January and Ended on Thursday the Twentieth of April, 1837. Boston: Dutton and Wentworth, 1837.

Laws of the Commonwealth of Massachusetts Passed at the Several Sessions of the General Court Beginning May, 1831, and Ending March, 1833. Boston: Dutton and Wentworth, 1833.

Lincoln, Levi. *Speech of His Excellency Levi Lincoln, before the Two Branches of the Legislature, in Convention, June 6, 1827.* Boston: True and Greene, 1827.

————. *Message of His Excellency Levi Lincoln, Communicated to the Two Branches of the Legislature, January 2, 1828.* Boston: Dutton and Wentworth, 1828.

————. *Speech of His Excellency Levi Lincoln, Delivered before the Two Branches of the Legislature in Convention, June 2, 1828.* Boston: Dutton and Wentworth, 1828.

————. *Message of His Excellency Levi Lincoln Transmitted to Both Branches of the Legislature, January 7, 1829.* Boston: True and Greene, 1829.

————. *Speech of His Excellency Levi Lincoln, before the Honourable Council and Both Branches of the Legislature, May 30, 1829.* Boston: True and Greene, 1829.

————. *Message of His Excellency Levi Lincoln Communicated to the Two Branches of the Legislature, January 6, 1830.* Boston: Dutton and Wentworth, 1830.

Memorial and Report of the Western Rail-Road Corporation [for a Loan of the Credit of the State], Mass. Senate Document 8, January 13, 1838.

Morton, Marcus. *Address to the Legislature, 1843.* Mass. House Document 3 (1843).

Petition of the Western Rail Road Corporation for the Establishment of a Bank to Aid in Constructing Their Road. Mass. Senate Document 16, January 1836. Boston: Dutton and Wentworth, 1836.

A Report to Aid the Construction of the Western Railroad. Mass. House Document 17, February 3, 1838.

Report of the [Massachusetts] Board of Commissioners for the Survey of One or More Routes for a Railway from Boston to Albany. Mass. Senate Document 5. Boston: Dutton and Wentworth, 1828.

Report of the Board of Directors of Internal Improvements of the State of Massachusetts on the Practicability and Expediency of a

Rail-Road from Boston to the Hudson River and from Boston to Providence, Submitted to the General Court, January 16, 1829. To Which Are Annexed, the Reports of the Engineers, Containing the Results of Their Surveys, and Estimates of the Cost of Constructing a Rail-Road, on Each of the Routes Selected. With Plans and Profiles of the Routes. Boston: Press of the Boston Daily Advertiser, 1829.

Report of the Commissioners of the State of Massachusetts on the Routes of Canals from Boston Harbour to Connecticut and Hudson Rivers. Boston: True and Greene, 1826.

Report of the Commissioners upon the Troy and Greenfield Railroad and Hoosac Tunnel to His Excellency the Governor, and the Honorable Executive Council of the State of Massachusetts, February 28, 1863. Boston: Wright and Potter, 1863.

Report Concerning Statistical Information in Relation to the Western and Other Rail Roads. Mass. Senate Document 28, February 5, 1838.

Report on the Construction of the Western Rail-Road. Mass. House Document 32, February 27, 1839.

Report of the Joint Committee to Investigate the Application of the Western Rail-Road for State Aid. Mass. Senate Document 35, February 24, 1841.

Report of the Joint Committee on Rail-Roads and Canals on the Causes of Frequent Accidents on the Western Rail-Road. Mass. Senate Document 55, February 18, 1842.

Report on the Western Rail-Road. Mass. Senate Document 65, January 18, 1842.

Transportation of the Mails. Mass. Senate Document 47, February 1842.

The Tunnel Hearing in 1854, A Brief Report of the Evidence of the Petitioners for a Loan to the Troy and Greenfield Railroad Company of Two Millions, before a Joint Committee of the Legislature of Massachusetts. Boston: Thurston, Torry and Emerson, 1854.

3. RAILROAD DOCUMENTS

Annual Reports of the Directors of the Boston and Worcester Railroad Corporation to the Stockholders, 1832–1866.

Annual Reports of the Directors of the Western Railroad Corporation to the Stockholders, 1836–1866.

Answer of the Troy and Greenfield Rail Road to the Memorial of the Western Rail Road, 1851. Boston: A. Forbes, 1851.

Appendix of the Minority Report of the Investigating Committee of the Western Railroad Corporation. n.p., March 1843.

A Brief Statement of Facts in Relation to the Western Rail-Road. n.p., January 15, 1838.

A Brief Statement of Facts in Relation to the Western Rail-Road. n.p., February 1839.

A Brief Statement of Facts in Relation to the Western Rail-Road. n.p., February 6, 1841.

Hoosac Tunnel, the Memorial of the Western Railroad Corporation Relating to the Application of the Troy and Greenfield Railroad for a State Loan of Two Millions of Dollars. Boston: Eastburn's Press, 1853.

A Letter to the Majority of the Joint Committee of the Legislature on the Affairs of the Western Rail Road, with Some Additional Testimony Proposed by the President of the Corporation. Boston: Eastburn's Press, 1843.

Proceedings of the Annual Meeting of the Western Rail Road Corporation, Held by Adjournment in the City of Boston, March 12, 1840, Including the Report of the Committee of Investigation, Appointed by the Stockholders. Boston: Dutton and Wentworth, 1840.

Proceedings of the Convention of the Northern Lines of Railway, Held at Boston in December, 1850, and January, 1851. Boston: J. B. Yerrinton & Son, 1851.

Proceedings of the Western Rail-Road Corporation, December 12, 1838, Including an Address to the People of the Commonwealth of Massachusetts on the Application for an Additional Loan of the State Credit. Boston: James Munroe and Company, 1838.

Proceedings of the Western Rail-Road Corporation, January 27, 1841, Including an Address to the People of the Commonwealth of Massachusetts, on the Application for an Additional Loan of the State Credit. Boston: Dutton and Wentworth, 1841.

Proceedings of the Western Rail-Road Corporation, January 21, 1842, Including an Address to the People of the Commonwealth of Massachusetts on the Application for a Restoration of the Original Privileges of the Corporation, and for other Measures Calculated to Sustain the Credit and Promote the Interest of the State, to Which is Added a Letter from the Agent of the Corporation to the Postmaster General. Boston: Dutton and Wentworth, 1842.

Proceedings of the Western Rail-Road Corporation, November 23, 1837, Including an Address to the People of the Commonwealth of Massachusetts on the Application for a Loan of the State Credit. Boston: Dutton and Wentworth, 1837.

Proceedings of the Western Railroad Corporation, with a Report of the Committee of Investigation, 1843. Boston: Freeman and Bolles, 1843.

Report of a Committee of Directors of the Boston and Worcester Rail-Road Corporation, on the Proposition of the Directors of the Western Rail-Road to Reduce the Rates of Fare and Freight on the Two Rail-Roads. With the Correspondence on that Subject. Boston: Samuel N. Dickinson, 1840.

Report of the Committee of the Stockholders of the Western Railroad Corporation Appointed at the Annual Meeting in February, 1851, to Examine into the System of Accountability in the Collection and Disbursing Departments; and Also the Condition and Value of the Property of the Corporation; Submitted to the Stockholders at Their Annual Meeting, February, 1852. Boston: Eastburn's Press, 1852.

Report of the Committees of the Boston and Worcester and Western Rail Road Corporations on the Subject of Uniting the Two Rail Roads. Also the Report of a Committee of the Stockholders of the Boston and Worcester Rail Road Instructed to Inquire into the Pecuniary Condition and Property of the Boston and Worcester and Western Rail Roads with Several Statements Appended Thereto. Boston: Eastburn's Press, 1846.

Report of the Executive Committee of the Subscribers for Procuring a Survey of the Western Rail-Road. n.p., July 7, 1835.

Report of the Delegation to Albany to the Stockholders of the Western Rail Road Corporation, May 12, 1840. Boston: Dutton and Wentworth, 1840.

Report of the Engineers of the Western Rail Road Corporation, Made to the Directors in 1836–7. Springfield, Mass.: Merriam, Wood & Co., 1838.

Reports of the Engineers of the Western Rail Road Corporation Made to the Directors in 1838–9. Springfield, Mass.: Merriam, Wood & Co., 1839.

4. OTHER PRIMARY SOURCES

American Railroad Journal, 1832–1844.

Appleton, William. *Selections from the Diaries of William Appleton, 1786–1862.* Boston: Privately printed, 1922.

The Aristocracy of Boston; Who They Are and What They Were;

Being a History of the Business Men of Boston for the Last Forty Years, By One Who Knows Them. Boston, 1848.

Baldwin, Christopher Columbus. *Diary of Christopher Columbus Baldwin, 1829–1835.* Worcester, Mass.: The American Antiquarian Society, 1901.

Beck, Charles. *On the Consolidation of the Worcester and Western Railroads.* n.p. [1864?].

Beech, E. D. *The Hoosac Mountain Tunnel; Speech of Hon. E. D. Beech of the Senate, on the Bill Providing for a Loan of the Credit of Massachusetts to the Amount of Two Millions of Dollars to the Troy and Greenfield Railroad, in the Senate, April 11, and 12, 1851.* Boston: Eastburn's Press, 1851.

Blau, Joseph L., ed. *Social Theories of Jacksonian Democracy: Representative Writings of the Period 1825–1850.* New York: The Liberal Arts Press, 1954.

Bliss, George. *Historical Memoir of the Western Railroad.* Springfield, Mass.: Samuel Bowles & Co., 1863.

Boston *Atlas,* 1841.

Boston Board of Trade. *Report of the Select Committee of the Board of Trade on the Controversy between the Boston and Worcester and Western Railroads, August, 1862.* Boston: Wright & Potter, 1862.

————. *Sketch of the Report of the Committee of the Boston Board of Trade, Appointed on the 19th of May, 1854, to Examine into the Subject of the Transportation of Merchandise from Boston to the West.* Boston: Moore & Crosby, 1854.

Boston *Courier,* 1827–1832.

Boston *Daily Advertiser,* 1826–1850.

Boston *Transcript,* 1834.

Boston and the West. Boston: A. Forbes, 1851.

Cary, Thomas G. *Speech of T. G. Cary on the Use of the Credit of the State for the Hoosac Tunnel in the Senate of Massachusetts, May 18, 1853.* Boston: J. M. Hewes & Co., 1853.

Chandler, Peleg W. *Argument in Favor of the Proposed Consolidation of the Western and Worcester Railroad Corporations, before the Committee on Railways and Canals, March 16, 1864.* Boston: Geo. C. Rand & Avery, 1864.

Chickering, Jesse. *A Statistical View of the Population of Massachusetts from 1765 to 1840.* Boston: Charles C. Little and James Brown, 1846.

A Citizen of New York (pseud.), *Hoosac Tunnel.* Boston: A. Forbes [1851?].

Clapp, Otis. *A Letter to the Hon. Abbott Lawrence and the Hon. Robert G. Shaw on the Present Condition and Future Growth of Boston.* Boston: John Wilson & Son, 1853.

Clark, Peter. *A Letter to Thomas Whittenmore, Esquire, President of the Vermont and Massachusetts Railroad upon the Cost of Tranportation between Boston and Troy.* Boston, 1853.

Crane, Edward. *Abstract of An Address by Edward Crane, Esq., on the Subject of Transportation at the Green Room, State House, February 13, 14, and 18, 1868.* Boston: Wright & Potter, 1868.

Derby, Elias H. *The Argument of E. H. Derby, Esq., in Favor of a State Loan to the Vermont and Massachusetts Railroad Co. before the Joint Committee on Railways and Canals of the Legislature of Massachusetts.* Boston: Dutton and Wentworth, 1855.

———. *Boston: Commercial Metropolis in 1850, Her Growth, Population, Wealth, and Prospects, As Originally Published in Hunt's Merchant's Magazine for November, 1850.* Boston: Redding and Co., 1850.

———. *A Brief Review of the Speech of Hon. Thomas G. Cary, a Senator from Suffolk County, against the Loan of State Credit for the Hoosac Tunnel, May, 1853.* Boston: Damrell & Moore, 1853.

———. *The Troy and Greenfield Railroad, Argument of E. Hasket Derby, Esq., Delivered Feb. 29, 1856, before a Joint Special Committee of the Legislature of Massachusetts in Behalf of the Troy and Greenfield Railroad Company: Petitioners for a State Subscription to their Stock.* Boston: Bazin and Chandler, 1856.

Derby, John Barton. *Political Reminiscences, Including a Sketch of the Origin and History of the "Statesman Party" of Boston.* Boston: Homer & Palmer, 1835.

Field, Alfred R. *The Hoosac Tunnel Route Compared with the Western Railroad.* Lowell, Mass.: Stone & Huse, 1866.

Fiske, Oliver. *Address Delivered Before the Worcester Agricultural Society, October 8, 1823: Being Their Anniversary Cattle Show and Exhibition of Manufactures.* Worcester, Mass.: William Manning, 1823.

Forbes, A., and J. W. Greene. *The Rich Men of Massachusetts: Containing a Statement of the Reputed Wealth of About Fifteen Hundred Persons, with Brief Sketches of More Than One Thousand Characters.* Boston: W. V. Spencer, 1851.

[Hale, Nathan.] *Remarks on the Practicability and Expediency of Establishing a Rail Road on One or More Routes from Boston to the Connecticut River.* Boston: William L. Lewis, 1827.

320

————. *Remarks on the Practicability and Expediency of Rail Roads from Boston to the Hudson River, and from Boston to Providence.* Boston: William L. Lewis, 1829.

Haupt, Herman. *Closing Argument of H. Haupt on Behalf of the Troy and Greenfield Railroad Co. before the Joint Special Committee of the Senate and House of Representatives of Massachusetts at a Public Hearing on Thursday, March 6, 1862: Including His Reply to Ex-Governor Boutwell, the Counsel of F. W. Bird, and other Memorialists in Opposition.* Boston: Wright & Potter, 1862.

————. *The Rise and Progress of the Hoosac Tunnel: Or the Way to Prosperity: Which Consists in Doing Right and Speaking Truth, A Review of the "Decline and Fall," in a Letter to F. W. Bird.* n.p., April 14, 1862.

Henshaw, David. *Letters from David Henshaw to the Boston Morning Post, on the Western Rail-Road and the Greatly Beneficial Effects of Internal Improvements.* Boston: Beals and Greene, 1839.

This Highly Important Report upon the Finances and Internal Improvements of the State of New York, 1838, Is Reprinted for the Benefit of the Friends of the Western Rail Road. Boston: Dutton and Wentworth, 1841.

Hoosac (pseud.), *The Troy and Greenfield Rail Road, Cost of the Tunnel.* Boston: A. Forbes, 1851.

The Hoosac Tunnel, A Brief Report of the Hearing of the Troy and Greenfield Railroad Company [in 1853] Petitioners for a Loan of Two Millions before a Joint Special Committee of the Legislature of Massachusetts. Boston: Thurston, Torry and Emerson, 1854.

Jackson, William. *A Lecture on Rail Roads, Delivered on January 12, 1829, before the Massachusetts Charitable Mechanic Association,* 2nd ed. Boston: Henry Bowen, 1829.

Loring, Thomas. *Speech of Thomas Loring, Esq., of Hingham in the House of Representatives of Massachusetts, March 20, 1839, upon the Bill Granting Farther Aid in the Construction of the Western Rail-Road.* Boston: Ezra Lincoln, 1839.

"Our First Men": A Calendar of Wealth, Fashion and Gentility: Containing a List of Those Persons Taxed in the City of Boston, Credibly Reported to Be Worth One Hundred Thousand Dollars with Biographical Notices of the Principal Persons, rev. ed. Boston, 1846.

Proceedings of a Public Meeting of the Inhabitants of Worcester, August 28, 1847, upon the Subject of the Passenger Depot of

Western Railroad in Worcester. Worcester, Mass.: Henry J. Howland, 1847.

The Railroad Jubilee: An Account of the Celebration Commemorative of the Opening of Railroad Communication between Boston and Canada, September 17th, 18th, and 19th, 1851. Boston: J. H. Eastburn, 1852.

Report of the Directors of the Boston Water Power Company. Boston: Boston Water Power Company, 1834.

Quincy, Josiah, Jr. *Cheap Food Dependent on Cheap Transportation: An Address Delivered before the Boston Social Sciences Association, January 14, 1869, by Josiah Quincy [Jr.], Its President.* Boston: J. H. Eastburn's Press, 1869.

————. *The Railway System of Massachusetts: An Address Delivered before the Boston Board of Trade, by Hon. Josiah Quincy, Nov. 19, 1866,* Boston: Mudge & Son, City Printers, 1866.

[Sedgwick, Theodore], Berkshire (pseud.), *Brief Remarks on the Rail Roads Proposed in Massachusetts.* Stockbridge, Mass.: Charles Webster, 1828.

South Cove Corporation, *Annual Reports of the Board of Directors to the Stockholders, 1835–1845.*

Tufts, George A. *Address, Delivered before the Worcester Agricultural Society, October 12, 1825: Being Their Seventh Anniversary Cattle Show and Exhibition of Manufactures.* Worcester, Mass.: Charles Griffin, Printer, 1825.

Walker, James. *Report to the Directors of the Liverpool and Manchester Railway on the Comparative Merits of Locomotive and Fixed Engines, as a Moving Power;* Robert Stephenson and Joseph Locke, *Observations on the Comparative Merits of Locomotive and Fixed Engines as Applied to Railways;* Henry Booth, *An Account of the Liverpool and Manchester Railway,* Philadelphia: Carey and Lea, 1831.

Washburn, Emory. *Speech of Emory Washburn, of Worcester, Delivered in the House of Representatives of Massachusetts, February 14, 1838, on the Bill to Aid the Construction of the Western Rail Road.* Springfield, Mass.: Merriam, Wood & Co., 1838.

Williams, Stephen K. *Reports of Cases Argued and Decided in the Supreme Court of the United States,* vol. IX. Newark, New York:, Lawyers Co-operative Publishing Company, 1883.

B. *Secondary Sources*

Adams, Charles Francis, Jr. *Railroad Legislation*. Boston: Little, Brown and Company, 1868. [Reprinted from *The American Law Review*.]

Anderson, George Baker. *Landmarks of Rensselaer County, New York*. Syracuse, N.Y.: D. Mason & Company, 1897.

Baker, George Pierce. *The Formation of the New England Railroad Systems: A Study of Railroad Combination in the Nineteenth Century*. Cambridge, Mass.: Harvard University Press, 1937.

Barber, John Warner. *Historical Collections: Being a General Collection of Interesting Facts, Traditions, Biographical Sketches, Anecdotes, &c., Relating to the History and Antiquities of Every Town in Massachusetts, with Geographical Descriptions. Illustrated by 200 Engravings*. Worcester, Mass.: Dorr, Howland & Co., 1841.

Bidwell, Percy Wells. *Rural Economy in New England at the Beginning of the Nineteenth Century*, Transactions of the Connecticut Academy of Arts and Science, vol. XX, New Haven, Conn., 1916.

———, and John I. Falconer. *History of Agriculture in the Northern United States, 1620–1860*. Washington, D. C.: Carnegie Institution, 1925.

Bowen, Francis. *Memoir of Edmund Dwight*, n.p., n.d. [Reprinted from Barnard's *American Journal of Education* for September 1857.]

Bradbury, Anna R. *History of the City of Hudson, New York, with Biographical Sketches of Henry Hudson and Robert Fulton*. Hudson, N.Y.: Record Printing and Publishing Co., 1908.

Bradford, Alden. "Commercial Sketch of Boston with Statistical Facts, and Notices of Eminent Merchants," *Hunt's Merchant's Magazine and Commercial Review* 1:124–135 (August 1839).

Brown, Robert R. "Pioneer Locomotives of North America," *Railway and Locomotive Historical Society, Bulletin* 101 (October 1959), 7–76.

Carlson, Robert E. "British Railroads and Engineers and the Beginnings of American Railroad Development," *Business History Review* 34:137–149 (Summer 1960).

Carter, James G., and William H. Brooks. *A Geography of Massachusetts: for Families and Schools. Embracing 1. A Topographical View of the Towns of Each County, with Sketches of Their History. 2. A General View of Each County. 3. A General View of the State. Its Natural Features, History, and Internal Improvements; and of the Employments of the People, Their Education, Religion, and Government.* Boston: Hilliard, Gray, Little, and Wilkins, 1830.

Chandler, Alfred D., Jr. *Strategy and Structure: Chapters in the History of Industrial Enterprise.* Cambridge, Mass.: The M.I.T. Press, 1962.

Chandler, Alfred D., Jr., and Stephen Salsbury. "The Railroads: Innovators in Modern Business Administration," in Bruce Mazlish, ed. *The Railroad and the Space Program: An Exploration in Historical Analogy.* Cambridge, Mass.: The M.I.T. Press, 1965.

Charlton, E. Harper. *Railway Car Builders of the United States and Canada, Interurbans Special 24.* Los Angeles: Interurbans, 1957.

Copeland, Alfred Minot, ed. *"Our County and Its People," A History of Hampden County, Massachusetts,* vol. II. n.p.: The Century Memorial Publishing Company, 1902.

Crane, Ellery B. "The Boston and Worcester Turnpike," *Proceedings of the Worcester Society of Antiquity,* XVII, 1901, pp. 585–598.

Cutler, U. Waldo. "Backward and Forward along the Old Worcester Turnpike," *The Worcester Historical Society Publications,* new series, 2:58–61 (April 1936).

Darling, Arthur B. *Political Changes in Massachusetts, 1824–1848: A Study of Liberal Movements in Politics.* New Haven, Conn.: Yale University Press, 1925.

Field, David Dudley, ed. *A History of the County of Berkshire, Massachusetts: In Two Parts. The First Being a General View of the County; the Second, An Account of the Several Towns.* Pittsfield, Mass.: Samuel W. Bush, 1829.

Fisher, Charles E. "The Hinkley Locomotive Works," *Railway and Locomotive Historical Society Bulletin* 25 (May 1931), 6–11.

———. "Whistler's Railroad: The Western Railroad of Massachusetts," *Railway and Locomotive Historical Society Bulletin* 69 (May 1947), 5–102.

Fishlow, Albert. *American Railroads and the Transformation of the Ante-Bellum Economy.* Cambridge, Mass.: Harvard University Press, 1965.

Goodrich, Carter. "American Development Policy: The Case of

Internal Improvements," *Journal of Economic History* 16:449–460 (December 1956).

——, ed. *Canals and American Economic Development*, New York: Columbia University Press, 1961.

——. *Government Promotion of American Canals and Railroads 1800–1890*. New York: Columbia University Press, 1960.

Green, Mason Arnold. *Springfield 1636–1886: History of Town and City Including an Account of the Quarter-Millennial Celebration at Springfield, Massachusetts, May 25 and 26, 1886*. Springfield, Mass.: C. A. Nichols & Co., 1888.

Guild, William. *A Chart and Description of the Boston and Worcester and Western Railroads; in Which is Noted the Towns, Villages, Stations, Bridges, Viaducts, Tunnels, Cuttings, Embankments, Gradients, &c., The Scenery and Its Natural History, and Other Objects Passed by This Line of Railway*. Boston: Bradbury & Guild, 1847.

Handlin, Oscar, and Mary Flug Handlin. *Commonwealth: A Study of the Role of Government in the American Economy: Massachusetts, 1774–1861*. New York: New York University Press, 1947.

Harlow, Alvin F. *Steelways of New England*. New York: Creative Age Press, 1946.

Hartz, Louis. *Economic Policy and Democratic Thought: Pennsylvania, 1776–1860*. Cambridge, Mass.: Harvard University Press, 1948.

Hayward, John. *A Gazetteer of Massachusetts, Containing Descriptions of All the Counties, Towns and Districts in the Commonwealth; Also of Its Principal Mountains, Rivers, Capes, Bays, Harbors, Islands, and Fashionable Resorts. To Which are Added, Statistical Accounts of Its Agriculture, Commerce and Manufactures; with a Great Variety of Other Useful Information*, rev. ed. Boston: John P. Jewett & Co., 1849.

Heath, Milton Sydney. *Constructive Liberalism: The Role of the State in Economic Development in Georgia to 1860*, Cambridge, Mass.: Harvard University Press, 1954.

Hidy, Ralph W. *The House of Baring in American Trade and Finance: English Merchant Bankers at Work, 1763–1861*, Cambridge, Mass.: Harvard University Press, 1949.

Hill, Benjamin Thomas. "The Beginnings of the Boston and Worcester Railroad," *Proceedings of the Worcester Society of Antiquity*, XVII, 1901, 527–576.

Hill, Hamilton Andrews. *Trade and Commerce of Boston* [Reprinted from a *Professional and Industrial History of Suffolk County,* vol. II, 1894] (Boston, 1894).

Hodge, Charles L. "Economic Beginnings of the Boston and Albany Railroad, 1831–1867," in *Facts and Factors in Economic History.* Cambridge, Mass.: Harvard University Press, 1932, 446–469.

Holland, Josiah Gilbert. *History of Western Massachusetts: The Counties of Hampden, Hampshire, Franklin, and Berkshire. Embracing an Outline or General History of the Section, an Account of Its Scientific Aspects and Leading Interests and Separate Histories of its One Hundred Towns,* 2 vols. Springfield, Mass.: Samuel Bowles and Company, 1855.

Howell, George Rovers, and Jonathan Tenny, eds. *Bi-Centennial History of Albany: History of the County of Albany, New York for 1609 to 1886 with Portraits, Biographies and Illustrations.* New York: W. W. Munsell & Co., 1886.

Hurd, D. Hamilton, ed. *History of Worcester County, Massachusetts, with Biographical Sketches of Many of Its Pioneers and Prominent Men,* 2 vols. Philadelphia: J. W. Lewis & Co., 1889.

Jacobus, Melancthon W. *The Connecticut River Steamboat Story.* Hartford, Conn.: The Connecticut Historical Society, 1956.

Kelly, Ralph. *Boston in the 1830's and the "William Penn."* New York: The Newcomen Society of England, American Branch, 1947.

King, Moses, ed. *King's Handbook of Springfield, Massachusetts: A Series of Monographs, Historical and Descriptive.* Springfield, Mass.: James Gill, 1884.

Kirkland, Edward Chase. *Men, Cities, and Transportation: A Study in New England History, 1820–1900,* 2 vols. Cambridge, Mass.: Harvard University Press, 1948.

Kistler, Thelma M. *The Rise of Railroads in the Connecticut Valley,* Smith College Studies in History, vol. XXIII, nos. 1–4, October 1937–July 1938.

Knowlton, Evelyn H. *Pepperell's Progress: History of a Cotton Textile Company, 1844–1945.* Cambridge, Mass.: Harvard University Press, 1948.

Lane, Wheaton J. *Commodore Vanderbilt: An Epic of the Steam Age,* New York: Alfred A. Knopf, 1942.

Lincoln, William. *History of Worcester, Massachusetts, from Its Earliest Settlement to September, 1836, with Various Notices Relating to the History of Worcester County.* Worcester, Mass.: Moses D. Phillips and Co., 1837.

Lively, Robert A. "The American System: A Review Article," *The Business History Review* 29:81–96 (March 1955).

Loring, James Spear. *The Hundred Boston Orators Appointed by the Municipal Authorities and Other Public Bodies from 1770 to 1852: Comprising Historical Gleanings, Illustrating the Principles and Progress of Our Republican Institutions.* Boston: John P. Jewett and Company, 1852.

Lothrop, Samuel Kirkland. "Memoir of Hon. Nathan Hale, LL.D.," *Proceedings of the Massachusetts Historical Society* 18:270–279 (1881).

Martin, Joseph G. *Martin's Boston Stock Market: Eighty-eight Years from January, 1798, to January, 1886.* Boston, 1886.

———. *Seventy-three Years of the Boston Stock Market from January 1, 1798 to January 1, 1871.* Boston: Published by the author, 1871.

Martin, Margaret E. *Merchants and Trade of the Connecticut River Valley, 1750–1820.* Smith College Studies in History, vol. XXIV, nos. 1–4, October 1938–July 1939.

Meyer, Henry Balthasar. *History of Transportation in the United States Before 1860.* Washington, D.C.: Carnegie Institution, 1917.

Morison, Samuel Eliot. *The Life and Letters of Harrison Gray Otis, Federalist, 1765–1848,* 2 vols. Boston: Houghton Mifflin Company, 1913.

———. *The Maritime History of Massachusetts, 1783–1860.* Boston: Houghton Mifflin Company, 1921.

Munsell, Joel. *The Annals of Albany,* 10 vols. Albany: published by various companies between 1850 and 1859.

North, Douglass C. "Comments on Stuart Bruchey's Paper," *Explorations in Entrepreneurial History, Second Series* 1:159–163 (Winter 1964).

———. *Growth and Welfare in the American Past: A New Economic History.* Englewood Cliffs, N.J.: Prentice-Hall, Inc., 1966.

Parker, Amasa J., ed. *Landmarks of Albany County, New York.* Syracuse, N.Y.: D. Mason & Co., 1897.

Pierce, Harry H. *Railroads of New York: A Study of Government Aid, 1826–1875.* Cambridge, Mass.: Harvard University Press, 1953.

Porter, Kenneth Wiggins. *The Jacksons and the Lees: Two Generations of Massachusetts Merchants, 1765–1844,* 2 vols. Cambridge, Mass.: Harvard University Press, 1937.

Quincy, Josiah. *A Municipal History of the Town and City of*

Boston During Two Centuries, from Sept. 17, 1630 to Sept. 17, 1830. Boston: Charles C. Little and James Brown, 1852.

Roberts, Christopher. *The Middlesex Canal, 1793–1860.* Cambridge, Mass.: Harvard University Press, 1938.

Rubin, Julius. *Canal or Railroad? Imitation and Innovation in the Response to the Erie Canal in Philadelphia, Baltimore, and Boston. Transactions of The American Philosophical Society,* New Series vol. 51, part 7. Philadelphia: The American Philosophical Society, November 1961.

Sagle, L. W. "Ross Winans," *Railway and Locomotive Historical Society Bulletin* 70 (August 1947), 7–17.

Salsbury, Stephen. "Private Enterprise in Massachusetts: The Beginnings of the Boston and Albany Railroad, 1825–1842," unpub. diss. Harvard University, 1961.

Schlesinger, Arthur M., Jr. *The Age of Jackson.* Boston: Little, Brown and Company, 1946.

Shlakman, Vera. *Economic History of a Factory Town: A Study of Chicopee, Massachusetts,* Smith College Studies in History. vol. XX, nos. 1–4, October 1934–July 1935.

Smith, J. E. A. *The History of Pittsfield, Massachusetts, from the Year 1800 to the Year 1876.* Springfield, Mass.: C. W. Bryan & Co., 1876.

Smith, Samuel Francis. *History of Newton, Massachusetts, Town and City from Its Earliest Settlement to the Present Time, 1630–1880.* Boston: The American Logotype Co., 1880.

Spalding, Robert Varnum. "The Boston Mercantile Community and the Promotion of the Textile Industry in New England, 1810–1865," unpub. diss. Yale University, 1963.

Spofford, Jeremiah. *A Gazetteer of Massachusetts: Containing a General View of the State, with an Historical Sketch of the Principal Events from Its Settlement to the Present Time, and Notices of the Several Towns Alphabetically Arranged. With a Map of the State.* Newburyport, Mass.: Charles Whipple, 1828.

Stevens, Frank Walker. *The Beginnings of the New York Central Railroad: A History.* New York: G. P. Putnam's Sons, 1926.

Sumner, William H. *A History of East Boston: with Biographical Sketches of Its Early Proprietors and an Appendix.* Boston: J. E. Tilton and Company, 1858.

Taylor, George Rogers. *The Transportation Revolution, 1815–1860.* New York: Holt, Rinehart, 1951.

————, and Irene Dorothy Neu. *The American Railroad Network, 1861–1890.* Cambridge, Mass.: Harvard University Press, 1956.

Temple, Josiah Howard. *History of Framingham, Massachusetts, Early Known as Danforth's Farms, 1640–1880, with a Genealogical Register.* Framingham, Mass.: the town of Framingham, 1887.

————. *History of the Town of Palmer, Massachusetts, Early Known as the Elbow Tract: Including Records of the Plantation, District and Town, 1716–1889.* Springfield, Mass.: Clark W. Bryan & Co., 1889.

Thomson, Thomas Richard. *Check List of Publications on American Railroads before 1841. A Union List of Printed Books and Pamphlets, Including State and Federal Documents, Dealing with Charters, Bylaws, Legislative Acts, Speeches, Debates, Land Grants, Officers' and Engineers' Reports, Travel Guides, Maps, etc.* New York: The New York Public Library, 1942.

Vose, George Leonard. *A Sketch of the Life and Works of George W. Whistler, Civil Engineer.* Boston: Lee and Shepard, 1887.

Ward, Andrew Henshaw. "Hon. David Henshaw," in *Memorial Biographies of the New England Historic Genealogical Society,* vol. I:1845–1852, 483–499.

Ware, Caroline F. *The Early New England Cotton Manufacture: A Study in Industrial Beginnings.* Boston: Houghton Mifflin Company, 1931.

Washburn, Charles G. *Industrial Worcester.* Worcester, Mass.: Davis Press, 1917.

Weise, Arthur James. *History of the City of Troy, from the Expulsion of the Mohegan Indians to the Present Centennial Year of the Independence of the United States of America, 1876.* Troy, N.Y.: William H. Young, 1876.

————. *Troy's One Hundred Years, 1789–1889.* Troy, N.Y.: William H. Young, 1891.

Whitford, Noble E. *History of the Canal System of the State of New York, together with Brief Histories of the Canals of the United States and Canada,* 2 vols. Albany, N.Y.: State of New York, 1906.

Willis, Henry A. *The Early Days of Railroads in Fitchburg.* Fitchburg, Mass.: Sentinel Printing Company, 1894.

Winsor, Justin, ed. *The Memorial History of Boston, Including Suffolk County, Massachusetts, 1630–1880,* 4 vols. Boston: James R. Osgood and Company, 1881.

Abbreviations Used in Notes

A&WS   *Albany & West Stockbridge Railroad*

B&O   *Baltimore & Ohio Railroad*

B&W   *Boston & Worcester Railroad*

CF   *Clerk's File*

Dir. Rec.   *Directors Minutes*

Div. Rec.   *Dividend Records*

WRR   *Western Railroad*

Preface

1. Oscar Handlin and Mary Flug Handlin, *Commonwealth* . . . (New York, 1947), 3.
2. *Ibid.*, 4.

CHAPTER I. *The Economic Revolution in Massachusetts, 1830*

1. Boston *Daily Advertiser*, June 8, 1929.
2. J. D. B. DeBow, *Statistical View of the United States* . . . *Compendium of the Seventh Census [1850]* . . . (Washington, D.C., 1854), 97.
3. Noble E. Whitford, *History of the Canal System of the State of New York* . . . (Albany, N.Y., 1906), I, 15.
4. Boston *Daily Advertiser*, January 17, 1830, described the Pennsylvania project as a canal to run from Columbia to Pittsburgh, a distance of 322 miles, with an 80-mile railroad to link Columbia and Philadelphia.
5. *Boston Daily Advertiser*, June 8, 1829.
6. Jesse Chickering, *A Statistical View of the Population of Massachusetts from 1765 to 1840* (Boston, 1846), 15–34.
7. Samuel Eliot Morison, *The Maritime History of Massachusetts, 1783–1860* (Boston, 1921), 151-153.
8. *Ibid.*, 79.
9. Chickering, *Population of Massachusetts*, 16.
10. DeBow, *Compendium of the Seventh Census*, 192; Hamilton Andrews Hill, *Trade and Commerce of Boston* (Boston, 1894), 90.
11. John P. Cushing Manuscripts, 1832–1882 (Baker Library, Harvard Business School, Boston), vol. IV, unpaged.
12. Morison, *Maritime History of Massachusetts*, 188-189.
13. *Ibid.*, 191.
14. For Erie Canal traffic statistics, see Whitford, *Canal System of the State of New York*, I, 947-951.
15. Morison, *Maritime History of Massachusetts*, 213.
16. Beverly declined from 4,608 in 1810 to 4,073 in 1830; Ipswich from 3,569 in 1810 to 2,949 in 1830; Marblehead from 5,900 in 1810 to 5,149 in 1830. Chickering, *Population of Massachusetts*, 16.
17. Morison, *Maritime History of Massachusetts*, 308-313.

18. Israel D. Andrews, . . . *Report . . . On the Trade and Commerce of the British North American Colonies and upon the Trade of the Great Lakes and Rivers . . .* (Washington, D.C., 1854), 771-772.

19. The dollar value of Massachusetts imports shows an almost continual decline starting with the year 1822, while New York State's generally rose from 1822 to 1830. DeBow, *Compendium of the Seventh Census,* 186-187.

20. Boston *Courier,* December 1, 1828.

21. Caroline F. Ware, *The Early New England Cotton Manufacture . . .* (Boston, 1931), 138.

22. *Ibid.,* 61.

23. *Ibid.,* 138, 146; *The Aristocracy of Boston . . .* (Boston, 1848) 3-4, 22-23; *"Our First Men:" A Calendar of Wealth, Fashion and Gentility . . .* (Boston, 1846), 45.

24. Joseph G. Martin, *Martin's Boston Stock Market . . .* (Boston, 1886), 90.

25. Morison, *Maritime History of Massachusetts,* 151; Ware, *Early New England Cotton Manufacture,* 301-302.

26. Martin, *Martin's Boston Stock Market,* 90.

27. Chickering, *Population of Massachusetts,* 15-34; DeBow, *Compendium of the Seventh Census,* 193.

28. *"Our First Men,"* 44; Ware, *Early New England Cotton Manufacture,* 320-321.

29. *Aristocracy of Boston,* 4; Ware, *New England Cotton Manufacture,* 320.

30. Samuel Eliot Morison, *The Life and Letters of Harrison Gray Otis . . .* (Boston, 1913), II, 288-289.

31. Cushing Manuscripts, vol. IV, unpaged.

32. Josiah Quincy, *A Municipal History of the Town and City of Boston During Two Centuries . . .* (Boston, 1852), 285.

33. Chickering, *Population of Massachusetts,* 15-35.

34. Percy Wells Bidwell, *Rural Economy in New England at the Beginning of the Nineteenth Century* (New Haven, 1916), 303-305, 317; Percy Wells Bidwell and John I. Falconer, *History of Agriculture in the Northern United States 1620–1860* (Washington, D.C., 1925), 133-136.

35. *Report of the Board of Directors of Internal Improvements of the State of Massachusetts on the Practicability and Expediency of a Rail-Road from Boston to the Hudson River and from Boston to Providence, Submitted to the General Court, January 16, 1829 . . .* (Boston, 1829), 32.

36. Bidwell, *Rural Economy in New England*, 261-262; D. Hamilton Hurd, ed., *History of Worcester County, Massachusetts* (Philadelphia, 1889), II, 1593-1594.

37. Timothy Dwight, writing of nearby Hampshire County, as quoted in Bidwell, *Rural Economy in New England*, 370.

38. William Lincoln, *History of Worcester, Massachusetts from Its Earliest Settlement to September, 1836* . . . (Worcester, Mass., 1837), 246.

39. Hurd, *Worcester County*, II, 1673.

40. Towns in decline included Brookfield, Grafton, Holden, Sterling, and Uxbridge. Chickering, *Population of Massachusetts*, 20–22, 34.

41. Oliver Fiske, *Address Delivered Before the Worcester Agricultural Society, October 8, 1823: Being Their Anniversary Cattle Show and Exhibition of Manufactures* (Worcester, Mass., 1823), 4-5; Bidwell, *Rural Economy in New England*, 328-329.

42. The main source for plaster of Paris was Nova Scotia. Price quotations may be found in the Boston *Daily Advertiser*, May 3, 10, and June 14, 1830. Freight rate data are from the Boston *Courier*, December 8, 1828.

43. George A. Tufts, *Address, Delivered Before the Worcester Agricultural Society, October 12, 1825: Being their Seventh Anniversary Cattle Show and Exhibition of Manufactures* (Worcester, Mass.: 1825), 10-11.

44. Fiske, *Address*, 11.

45. *Report of [Mass.] Board of Directors of Internal Improvements, January 16, 1829*, 34.

46. Charles G. Washburn, *Industrial Worcester* (Worcester, Mass., 1917), 23–24.

47. John P. Bigelow, *Statistical Tables* . . . (Boston, 1838), 170-171.

48. *Ibid.*

49. A. Forbes and J. W. Greene, *The Rich Men of Massachusetts* . . . (Boston, 1851), 142; Washburn, *Industrial Worcester*, 44, 82.

50. Bigelow, *Statistical Tables*, 169.

51. Washburn, *Industrial Worcester*, 44, 82, 145.

52. *Ibid.*, 111.

53. In 1837 Worcester County manufactured 89,310 scythes, 124,710 axes, 1,934 plows; the value of its firearm production was $52,475, and the value of its wire production $56,770. Bigelow, *Statistical Tables*, 172.

54. *Ibid.*

55. Washburn, *Industrial Worcester*, 31.

56. Oscar Handlin and Mary Flug Handlin, *Commonwealth* . . . (New York, 1947), 118-120.

57. Lincoln, *History of Worcester*, 339-340.

58. *Ibid.*, 372.

59. Chickering, *Population of Massachusetts*, 23–24.

60. Josiah Gilbert Holland, *History of Western Massachusetts* . . . (Springfield, Mass., 1855), I, 389.

61. For a detailed account of the Dwights, see Margaret E. Martin, *Merchants and Trade of the Connecticut River Valley, 1750–1820* (Northampton, Mass., 1939), 94-99, 209-210; Mason Arnold Green, *Springfield, 1636–1886* . . . (Springfield, Mass., 1888), 358.

62. Moses King, ed., *King's Handbook of Springfield, Massachusetts* . . . (Springfield, Mass., 1884), 296.

63. Francis Bowen, *Memoir of Edmund Dwight* (n.p., n.d.), 6-7; Vera Shlakman, *Economic History of a Factory Town* . . . (Northampton, Mass., 1935), 29-30.

64. Bowen, *Memoir of Edmund Dwight*, 9.

65. Green, *Springfield*, 359–360; King, *King's Handbook*, 296.

66. Green, *Springfield*, 358.

67. Holland, *History of Western Massachusetts*, II, 45.

68. *Ibid.*, 45-46; Shlakman, *Economic History of a Factory Town*, 26.

69. Shlakman, *Economic History of a Factory Town*, 26.

70. The amount actually subscribed was only $500,000.

71. Shlakman, *Economic History of a Factory Town*, 27-28.

72. Rates to Boston from Connecticut Valley points were about $20 per ton, and to Hartford $5 per ton. The total cost per ton from Springfield to New York was $10. *Report of [Mass.] Board of Directors of Internal Improvements, January 16, 1829*, 32.

73. The capital stock of the Massachusetts corporation was only $300,000; the rest was spent on the Connecticut portion. Holland, *History of Western Massachusetts*, I, 428; Boston *Courier*, February 24, 1828.

74. See the article "To the Mechanics" in the Boston *Courier*, December 8, 1828.

75. For the hazards of steamboat travel between the Connecticut Valley and New York City, see Melancthon W. Jacobus, *The Connecticut River Steamboat Story* (Hartford, Conn., 1956), 52-57.

76. David Dudley Field, ed., *A History of the County of Berkshire, Massachusetts* . . . (Pittsfield, Mass., 1829), 1–36.

77. *Ibid.*, 10-11.

78. *Ibid.*, p. 87; Chickering, *Population of Massachusetts*, 28.

79. Field, *History of the County of Berkshire*, 91-92.

80. Chickering, *Population of Massachusetts*, 27-28.

81. [Nathan Hale,] *Remarks on the Practicability and Expediency of Rail Roads from Boston to the Hudson River, and from Boston to Providence* (Boston, 1829), 27-28.

82. J. E. A. Smith, *The History of Pittsfield, Massachusetts, From the Year 1800 to the Year 1876* (Springfield, Mass., 1876) 472-479.

83. *Report of [Mass.] Board of Directors of Internal Improvements, January 16, 1829*, 31-32.

84. Smith, *History of Pittsfield*, 508-509.

85. *Ibid.*, 464, 472, 477, 509.

86. *Ibid.*, 508-514.

87. Jacobus, *Connecticut River Steamboat*, 6-7, 27-33.

88. DeBow, *Compendium of the Seventh Census*, 192.

89. Arthur James Weise, *History of the City of Troy . . .* (Troy, N.Y., 1876), 129.

90. George Baker Anderson, *Landmarks of Rensselaer County, New York* (Syracuse, N.Y., 1887), 252.

91. Arthur James Weise, *Troy's One Hundred Years, 1789–1889* (Troy, N.Y., 1891), v.

92. Amasa J. Parker, ed., *Landmarks of Albany County, New York* (Syracuse, N.Y., 1897), 96.

93. Anna R. Bradbury, *History of the City of Hudson, New York . . .* (Hudson, N.Y., 1908), 187.

94. Anderson, *Landmarks of Rensselaer County*, 77-78.

95. *Ibid.*, 238, 256-257.

96. *Report of [Mass.] Board of Directors of Internal Improvements, January 16, 1829*, p. 28.

97. A quintal equals 100 pounds, a barrel probably about 200 pounds. For the trade statistics see Joel Munsell, *Annals of Albany* (Albany, N.Y., 1850–1859), X, 389.

98. *Ibid.*

99. For complete statistics on Worcester–Providence trade in the year 1830 see Boston *Daily Advertiser*, March 10, 1831.

100. Boston *Courier*, July 28, 1828.

101. Prices for the trip varied. One line offered daily-except-Sunday service to New York via Providence for $5 with the meals extra. Dinner on board the boat was 50 cents, breakfast and tea were 33 cents. Boston *Courier*, July 15, 1830. Prices for the Hudson trip also varied: the fare on board the "North America" was $2, with

breakfast and dinner $1 extra. Other steamers charged $2, meals included. Boston *Courier*, July 28, 1828.

102. Boston *Courier*, July 15, 1830; Munsell, *Annals of Albany*, X, 389.

103. [Hale,] *Rail Roads from Boston to the Hudson*, 38.

104. *Ibid.*

CHAPTER II. *The Issue of State Aid*

1. Harvey H. Segal, "Cycles of Canal Construction," in Carter Goodrich, ed., *Canals and American Economic Development* (New York, 1961), 179. For a general review of the whole state-aid question, see Robert A. Lively, "The American System: A Review Article," *The Business History Review* 29:81-96 (March 1955).

2. Carter Goodrich, "American Development Policy: The Case of Internal Improvements," *Journal of Economic History* 16:450-451 (December 1956). See also Carter Goodrich, *Government Promotion of American Canals and Railroads, 1800–1890* (New York, 1960), 265-297.

3. Douglass C. North, *Growth and Welfare in the American Past: A New Economic History* (Englewood Cliffs, N.J., 1966), 100.

4. The above quotations from Douglass C. North, "Comments on Stuart Bruchey's Paper," *Explorations in Entrepreneurial History, Second Series*, 1:162 (Winter 1964).

5. H. Jerome Cranmer, "Improvements without Public Funds: The New Jersey Canals" in Goodrich, *Canals and American Economic Development*, 157.

6. Louis Hartz, *Economic Policy and Democratic Thought: Pennsylvania 1776–1860* (Cambridge, Mass., 1948); and Milton Heath, *Constructive Liberalism: The Role of the State in Economic Development in Georgia to 1860* (Cambridge, Mass., 1954).

7. Hartz, *Economic Policy*, 289.

8. Heath, *Constructive Liberalism*, 281.

9. Julius Rubin, *Canal or Railroad? Imitation and Innovation in the Response to the Erie Canal in Philadelphia, Baltimore, and Boston, Transactions of the American Philosophical Society, New Series*, Vol. 51, Part 7, 1961 (Philadelphia, Pa., 1961).

10. *Ibid.*, 9.

11. *Ibid.*, 78, 94.

12. Albert Fishlow, *American Railroads and the Transformation of the Ante-bellum Economy* (Cambridge, Mass., 1965), 260, asserts that "There is little reason to suppose that the rapid rise of ante-

bellum manufacturing in the 1840's evoked, except in a general way, the construction of railroads, or that it depended crucially upon completion of the rail network." Railroads were not essential to early New England industrial development, particularly cotton mills. Factories in the Merrimack Valley were well established before the railroad appeared and could have continued to grow without it. Fishlow's argument, however, that industrialism did not spur railroad construction in Massachusetts, Maine, and New Hampshire is unfounded. His reasoning is not based upon an analysis of who promoted railroads or of who supplied the capital for their construction and why (which seems the only logical way to settle the issue) but upon the thesis that alternative forms of transportation could have and, in some isolated cases he cites, did supply the wants of New England factories. Fishlow makes no attempt to analyze systematically how much of the cotton mill traffic in the Merrimack Valley the railroads did carry or what percentage such traffic was of the railroads' total traffic. The fact that Lowell mills could have done without rail transport in 1845 (p. 245) does not prove that the millowners lacked enthusiasm for railroad building. The Boston & Lowell was the creature of the Lowell textile millowners who built it to serve their factories. Furthermore Robert Varnum Spalding's unpublished doctoral dissertation "The Boston Mercantile Community and the Promotion of the Textile Industry in New England, 1810–1865" (Yale University, 1963) demonstrates the decisive role played by textile mill promoters in railroad building up the Merrimack to Manchester, New Hampshire.

Fishlow views the Boston & Worcester and the Western Railroad in the light of Boston's attempt to link itself with the West (p. 240). In doing so, he merely accepts the traditional interpretation in Edward Chase Kirkland's *Men, Cities, and Transportation . . .* (Cambridge, Mass., 1948), which he cites.

Fishlow's approach to this problem despite its veneer of mathematical precision is based on faulty logic. His case is not supported by statistics gathered after a widespread search, nor does he use a valid conceptual framework. His thesis about factory owners and their position on railroads is based upon deductive reasoning which flows from an irrelevant major premise. He argues merely that because factories could have existed without railroads, industrial leaders did not promote railroads. This could be true, but it does not logically follow, and the case of the Boston to Albany line does not support it. Only by looking at the promotion and building of the railroads can this question be answered.

337

13. Samuel Eliot Morison, *The Life and Letters of Harrison Gray Otis*, . . . (Boston, 1913), II, 240, 243.

14. John Hayward, *A Gazetteer of Massachusetts, Containing Descriptions of All the Counties, Towns and Districts in the Commonwealth* . . . , rev. ed. (Boston, 1849), 417.

15. Daniel Webster was one of the lawyers for the Charles River Bridge Corporation; see Arthur M. Schlesinger, Jr., *The Age of Jackson* (Boston, 1946), 324-325. Harrison Gray Otis was one of the shareholders in the same bridge. Morison, *Harrison Gray Otis*, II, 241; Oscar Handlin and Mary Flug Handlin, *Commonwealth* . . . (New York, 1947), 210.

16. See the opinion of Chief Justice Taney for the Court in *Reports of the Cases Argued and Adjudged in the Supreme Court of the United States in the January Term, 1837*, Richard Peters, X, 536-551, reprinted in Stephen K. Williams, *Reports of Cases Argued and Decided in the Supreme Court of the United States* (Newark, N.Y., 1883), vol. IX.

17. This problem emerged in the attempt to charter a railroad from Boston to Lowell. In the winter 1830 session of the General Court a

> bill for incorporating [the Boston & Lowell Railroad] intended to secure the property in this road from being destroyed (by the construction of another on precisely the same rout [sic], whenever it should be found by the experience of this company and others that another road could be made with some improvements and at less expense) was struck out by the House of Representatives, and as the petitioners were not inclined to take a charter on terms which would subject them to all the expense of making the experiment of building the first rail road without any chance of profit from it, the bill was withdrawn. A similar provision in favor of the proprietors was struck out of all other rail road bills which passed at the last session, and in consequence, as was fully anticipated, nobody has been disposed to subscribe to the stock.

Boston *Daily Advertiser*, June 10, 1830.

18. James G. Carter and William H. Brooks, *A Geography of Massachusetts* . . . (Boston, 1830), 184; Boston *Daily Advertiser*, May 14, 1830.

19. Boston *Daily Advertiser*, January 12, 1831.

20. Levi Lincoln, *Speech of His Excellency Levi Lincoln, Delivered before the Two Branches of the Legislature in Convention, June 2, 1828* (Boston, 1828), 13. Levi Lincoln, *Speech of His Excel-*

lency Levi Lincoln, before the Honourable Council and Both Branches of the Legislature, May 30, 1829 (Boston, 1829), 14-17.

21. See the Boston *Daily Advertiser* for January 23, 1829, and June 11, 13, 15, and 16, 1831.

22. Christopher Roberts, *The Middlesex Canal, 1793–1860* (Cambridge, Mass., 1938), 28-30, 41-43, 179-182.

23. *Ibid.*, 183.

24. *Ibid.*, 152-153. Note that the Middlesex Canal terminated in Charlestown and that to reach Boston a transfer of goods to wagons was necessary. See also Boston *Daily Advertiser*, June 10, 1830.

25. Jeremiah Spofford, *A Gazetteer of Massachusetts . . .* (Newburyport, Mass., 1828), 252.

26. U. Waldo Cutler, "Backward and Forward along the Old Worcester Turnpike," *The Worcester Historical Society Publications*, new series, 2:59-60 (April 1936).

27. Ellery B. Crane, "The Boston and Worcester Turnpike," *Proceedings of the Worcester Society of Antiquity* 17: 593–594 (1901).

28. George Bliss, *Historical Memoir of the Western Railroad* (Springfield, Mass., 1863), 3-4.

29. *Ibid.*, 5.

30. *Ibid.*

31. *Ibid.*

32. Charles Francis Adams, Jr., "The Canal and Railroad Enterprise of Boston," in Justin Winsor, ed., *The Memorial History of Boston . . .* (Boston, 1881), IV, 114.

33. Noble E. Whitford, *History of the Canal System of the State of New York . . .* (Albany, N.Y., 1906), I, 79.

34. Winsor, *History of Boston*, IV, 114-115.

35. *Ibid.*, 115.

36. Kirkland, *Men, Cities, and Transportation*, I, 81; D. Hamilton Hurd, ed., *History of Worcester County, Massachusetts . . .* (Philadelphia, 1889), II, 1602.

37. Boston *Daily Advertiser*, November 17, 1825; [Nathan Hale,] *Remarks on the Practicability and Expediency of Establishing a Rail Road on One or More Routes from Boston to the Connecticut River* (Boston, 1827), 45-46.

38. Winsor, *History of Boston*, IV, 117-119; [Hale,] *Rail Road from Boston to the Connecticut*, 4-5.

39. [Hale,] *Rail Road from Boston to the Connecticut*, 5.

40. *Ibid.*, 5, 7.

41. Bliss, *Memoir*, 5.

42. *Ibid.*, 6.

43. Details about Hale's life unless otherwise footnoted are taken from Samuel Kirkland Lothrop, "Memoir of Hon. Nathan Hale, LL.D.," *Proceedings of the Massachusetts Historical Society* 18: 270-279 (1881).

44. Hale originally subscribed for 100 shares of stock in the Boston & Worcester, but by the time the first dividend was declared on July 10, 1837, he held but two shares. Later he held none. See: B&W, Dir. Rec., I, 19-29; and B&W, Div. Rec., I, unpaged.

45. Lothrop, *Proceedings of the Massachusetts Historical Society* 18:275 (1881).

46. In 1830 Hale strongly supported protariff Nathan Appleton for Congress. Hale editorialized that although tariffs were unwise in principle, they could not in 1830 be radically changed without doing great harm to industry which had come to depend upon them. Boston *Daily Advertiser*, October 15, 1830; Boston *Courier*, March 31, 1828.

47. [Nathan Hale,] *Remarks on the Practicability and Expediency of Rail Roads from Boston to the Hudson River, and from Boston to Providence* (Boston, 1829), 39-40.

48. Boston *Daily Advertiser*, July 19, 1830; for a counter argument see the Boston *Courier*, July 26, 1830.

49. Boston *Courier*, March 31, 1828.

50. Boston *Daily Advertiser*, September 2, 1830.

51. James Spear Loring, *The Hundred Boston Orators Appointed by the Municipal Authorities and Other Public Bodies, from 1770 to 1852* . . . (Boston, 1852), 567; John Barton Derby, *Political Reminiscences, Including A Sketch of the Origin and History of the "Statesman Party" of Boston* (Boston, 1835), 143; and Andrew Henshaw Ward, "Hon. David Henshaw," in *Memorial Biographies of the New England Historic Genealogical Society*, vol. I, 1845–1852 (Boston, 1880), 497.

52. J. G. Harris to George Bancroft in 1838, cited by Arthur B. Darling, *Political Changes in Massachusetts, 1824–1848* . . . (New Haven, Conn., 1925), 176; J. B. Derby, *Political Reminiscences*, 71.

53. Loring, *Hundred Boston Orators*, 566.

54. A. Forbes and J. W. Greene, *The Rich Men of Massachusetts* . . . (Boston, 1851), 133; Ward, in *Memorial Biographies*, I, 483; Darling, *Political Changes*, 15.

55. Darling, *Political Changes*, 225-226.

56. Ward, in *Memorial Biographies*, I, 486-487.

57. *Ibid.*, 485.

58. Darling, *Political Changes*, 49-51.

59. *Ibid.*, 135-136.

60. *Ibid.*, 225-227.

61. Ward, in *Memorial Biographies*, I, 496.

62. David Henshaw, "Remarks upon the Rights and Powers of Corporations, and of the Rights, Powers, and Duties of the Legislature Toward Them," in Joseph L. Blau, ed., *Social Theories of Jacksonian Democracy: Representative Writings of the Period 1825–1850* (New York, 1954), 163.

63. Boston *Courier*, August 9, 1830.

64. The detail on William Jackson, unless otherwise noted, comes from the excellent description of his life in Samuel Francis Smith's, *History of Newton, Massachusetts . . .* (Boston, 1880), 783-786, also see 312.

65. The Newton Bank was incorporated in 1848, and Jackson served as its president from 1848 until 1855. See *Ibid.*, 759-760, 785.

66. William Jackson, *A Lecture on Rail Roads, Delivered January 12, 1829 . . .* 2nd ed. (Boston, 1829), 4.

67. [Hale,] *Rail Roads from Boston to the Hudson River*, 24.

68. David Dudley Field, ed., *A History of the County of Berkshire, Massachusetts* (Pittsfield, Mass., 1829) 272.

69. J. E. A. Smith, *The History of Pittsfield, Massachusetts, from the Year 1800 to the Year 1876* (Springfield, Mass., 1876), 382.

70. [Theodore Sedgwick, writing under the name "Berkshire"], *Brief Remarks on the Rail Roads Proposed in Massachusetts* (Stockbridge, Mass., 1828), 15-16.

71. J. E. A. Smith, *History of Pittsfield*, 521.

72. For an account of the opening of the Baltimore & Ohio Railroad, see Boston *Daily Advertiser*, May 24, 1830, and January 10, 1831.

73. Interest in the Liverpool and Manchester Railway was so great that official documents connected with it, including the engineer's reports and articles by Robert Stephenson, had immediate American editions. This account is taken from *An Account of the Liverpool and Manchester Railway* by Henry Booth, Treasurer to the Company, which was appended to the *Report to the Directors of the Liverpool and Manchester Railway on the Comparative Merits of Locomotive and Fixed Engines as a Moving Power* by James Walker, and *Observations on the Comparative Merits of Locomotive and Fixed Engines as Applied to Railways* by Robert Stephenson and Joseph Locke (Philadelphia, 1831), 124. Note that

Walker's report was printed by Hale in the Boston *Daily Advertiser*, November 25, 1829.

74. Walker, *Report to the Directors of the Liverpool and Manchester Railway*, 126-153.

75. Boston *Daily Advertiser*, November 23, 1829.

76. The only illustrations (advertisements excepted) which appeared in the Boston *Daily Advertiser* for the years 1829, 1830, and 1831 were of steam locomotives in the June 17, 1830, edition.

77. Boston *Daily Advertiser*, November 25, 1829.

78. *Ibid.*, December 9, 1829.

79. *Ibid.*, January 2, 1830.

80. *Ibid.*, April 15, 1831.

81. [Hale,] *Rail Road from Boston to the Connecticut*, 65.

82. *Ibid.*, 61-62.

83. Boston *Daily Advertiser*, March 14, 1829.

84. *Ibid.*, October 24, 1828.

85. *Ibid.*, November 19, 1828.

86. *Message of His Excellency Levi Lincoln Communicated to the Two Branches of the Legislature, January 6, 1830* (Boston, 1830), 6.

87. J. E. A. Smith, *History of Pittsfield*, 528-529.

88. In February 1829 a group of prominent Massachusetts citizens, mostly Bostonians, petitioned the legislature for state aid to a railroad leading toward the Connecticut River. The names included the Dwights, Harrison Gray Otis, Israel Thorndike, Joseph Coolidge, Amos Lawrence, Joseph Lee, John T. Apthorp, and Henry Sargent. Boston *Daily Advertiser*, February 16 and 26, 1829.

89. *Ibid.*, February 26, 1829, and February 2 and May 11, 1830. Note that William Sturgis represented Boston in the lower house of the General Court for the political year 1829–1830 and constantly voted for state aid to a western railroad. For Otis's views as expressed in his inaugural speeches as mayor of Boston see, for the year 1829, Josiah Quincy, *A Municipal History of the Town and City of Boston During Two Centuries* . . . (Boston, 1852), 280-286; for the years 1830 and 1831 see *The Inaugural Addresses of the Mayors of Boston*, vol. I: *From 1822 to 1851* (Boston, 1894), 139, and 159-160.

90. Men like William Foster, a leading advocate of free trade; Andrew Allen, a stationer; Joseph Coolidge, a China trader; and Robert Shaw, a dealer in South European goods, supported a railroad before they were investors in industry, largely on the ground that it would help maintain Boston's commercial advantages. See

the Boston *Daily Advertiser,* February 26, 1829; *The Aristocracy of Boston* (Boston, 1848), 3, 13, 30–31; and *"Our First Men": A Calendar of Wealth, Fashion and Gentility* (Boston, 1846), 22; for the town meeting, see the Boston *Daily Advertiser,* February 11, 1829.

91. [Hale,] *Rail Road from Boston to the Connecticut,* 38-40.

92. Jackson, *Lecture on Rail Roads,* 32.

93. *Ibid.,* 35.

94. *Ibid.*

95. Editorial from the Haverhill *Essex Gazette,* reprinted in the Boston *Daily Advertiser,* December 8, 1829.

96. Berkshire [Sedgwick], *Brief Remarks,* 14.

97. Boston *Daily Advertiser,* January 7, 1830.

98. Bliss, *Memoir,* 6–9.

99. *Ibid.,* 9.

100. *Ibid.,* 10–11; see also Lincoln, *Speech Delivered June 2, 1828,* 7-12.

CHAPTER III. *The Rejection of State Initiative*

1. Royal Makepeace represented Cambridge in the lower house of the General Court during the years the railroad was under consideration; William Foster, a wealthy Bostonian, had an interest in the import-export business, and was a zealous free trader; see *"Our First Men": A Calendar of Wealth, Fashion and Gentility . . .* (Boston, 1846), 22. Thomas W. Ward was the Boston representative of the House of Baring. See *"Our First Men,"* 46. Edward H. Robbins was described as a wealthy man who secured his fortune by real estate speculation; see *The Aristocracy of Boston . . .* (Boston, 1848), 30.

2. George Bliss, *Historical Memoir of the Western Railroad* (Springfield, Mass., 1863), 12-13.

3. For a breakdown on the prorailroad and the antirailroad vote in the General Court, see the Boston *Courier,* June 16, 1828. For the representation in the legislature, see the Boston *Daily Advertiser,* January 12, 1831.

4. Levi Lincoln, *Message of His Excellency Levi Lincoln Transmitted to Both Branches of the Legislature, January 7, 1829* (Boston, 1829), 14-15.

5. *Report of the Board of Directors of Internal Improvements of the State of Massachusetts on the Practicability and Expediency of a Rail-Road from Boston to Providence, Submitted to the General Court, January 16, 1829* (Boston, 1829), 54-55.

6. *Ibid.*, 26.

7. *Ibid.*, 22-24.

8. Nothing influenced Hale's views on railroads more than the Liverpool and Manchester Railway, which owned all vehicles from the first. This was mainly because established cartage companies on the turnpikes and canals refused to make satisfactory contracts with the railroad. When the Liverpool and Manchester went into operation in 1830, there was much anguish from the old companies, especially the stage companies and other highway carriers. Hale printed much of this controversy in his paper. Significantly nearly all of it presented but one side, that of the Liverpool and Manchester. Boston *Daily Advertiser*, April 27, 1831.

9. The actual figure given was $16,434.77 per mile. *Report of the [Mass.] Board of Directors of Internal Improvements, January 16, 1829,* 17.

10. *Ibid.*, 40-41.

11. *Ibid.*, 46.

12. This freight rate for flour included a toll of 1/2 cent per ton-mile or a total of $1 for the 200 miles between Boston and Albany. This charge was to be for the use of the rails only and to pay the interest on the investment and the repairs on the track. The rest, or from $1.59 to $1.97, was to pay for the vehicles (in the case of the report horses and wagons), fuel, labor, etc. *Ibid.*, 22-23.

13. Traffic estimate of the Board of Internal Improvements. Note the importance of local trade both in volume and in projected revenue.

TERMINAL POINTS	TONS	MILES	TOLL (CENTS PER MILE)	REVENUE
Between Albany and Boston	28,902	200	½	$ 28,902
Between Berkshire and Albany	13,855	40	2	11,084
Between Berkshire and Boston	4,618	150	2	13,855
Between Hampden and Boston and Albany	12,855	95	2	24,424
Between Hampshire and Boston and Albany	13,689	95	2	26,009

Between Franklin and Boston and Albany	4,929	95	2	9,365
Between Worcester and Boston	14,000	40	2	11,200
Between Vermont, Connecticut, and Boston and Albany	10,000	95	2	19,000
Totals	102,848			$143,839

Passengers (estimated equal to 23,475 through trips
that would yield a revenue of 1 cent per mile)   46,950

$190,789

Source: *Report of the Board of Directors of Internal Improvements of the State of Massachusetts on the Practicability and Expediency of a Rail-Road from Boston to Providence, Submitted to the General Court, January 16, 1829* (Boston, 1829), 40.

14. *Report of the [Mass.] Board of Directors of Internal Improvements, January 16, 1829*, 22-23.

15. *Ibid.*, 43-51.

16. *Ibid.*, 48.

17. *Ibid.*, 73.

18. The actual figure given amounted to $3,254,876.46 for the entire line from Boston to Albany. New York promised to cooperate with Massachusetts by passing legislation allowing the Bay State to build and control the portion of the line that was to run through New York. *Ibid.*, 17. For the action of New York State, see the Boston *Daily Advertiser*, March 6, 1829.

19. Boston *Daily Advertiser*, March 6, 1829.

20. *Ibid.*, May 1, 1829; January 12, 1831.

21. *Ibid.*, May 26, 1829; January 12, 1831.

22. William Jackson, *A Lecture on Rail Roads, Delivered January 12, 1829 . . .*, 2nd ed. (Boston, 1829), 24-25.

23. Justin Winsor, ed., *The Memorial History of Boston . . .* (Boston, 1881), IV, 122.

24. Boston *Courier*, July 14 and September 17, 1830.

25. *Essex Register*, as quoted in the Boston *Daily Advertiser*, May 28, 1829.

26. *Hampshire Gazette*, April 1, 8, 1829, as quoted in the Boston *Daily Advertiser*, April 11, 13, 1829.

27. *Hampshire Gazette*, April 8, 1829, as quoted in the Boston *Daily Advertiser*, April 11, 1829.

28. Levi Lincoln, *Speech of His Excellency Levi Lincoln before the Honourable Council and Both Branches of the Legislature, May 30, 1829* (Boston, 1829), 11-12.

29. Boston *Daily Advertiser*, June 13, 1829.

30. Worcester *Massachusetts Spy*, June 17, 1829, as quoted in the Boston *Daily Advertiser*, June 19, 1829.

31. *Berkshire Journal* article, as quoted by the Boston *Daily Advertiser*, September 24, 1829.

32. Boston *Daily Advertiser*, February 1, 1830; see also *An Act to Establish the Massachusetts Rail Road Corporation*, Mass. House Document 4 (1830), 1-2. This bill also proposed to establish a second Massachusetts railroad with a capital of $600,000, one-third of which was to be subscribed by the Commonwealth. This second company was to build a line from Boston to Providence.

33. Boston *Daily Advertiser*, January 22, 1830.

34. *Ibid.*

35. *Ibid.*

36. *Ibid.*, January 26, 1830.

37. *Ibid.*, January 28, 1830.

38. The vote on the railroad bill.

	VOTE FOR THE RAILROAD	VOTE AGAINST THE RAILROAD
Coastal counties:		
Essex	6	41
Suffolk (Boston)	53	—
Norfolk	21	6
Plymouth	7	19
Bristol	—	31
Barnstable (Cape Cod)	1	17
Dukes	1	1
Nantucket	—	5
Inland counties:		
Middlesex	25	28
Worcester	17	51
Franklin	—	27
Hampshire	2	28
Hampden	15	12
Berkshire	14	18

Source: Boston *Daily Advertiser*, February 2, 1830.

Note: Norfolk gave strong support to the bill because the measure included state aid for the Boston & Providence Railroad, which would run the entire length of the county.

39. Boston *Daily Advertiser*, February 2, 1830.

40. Northampton *Courier*, as quoted in the Boston *Daily Advertiser*, February 15, 1830.

41. Boston *Daily Advertiser*, February 2, 1830.

42. Carter Goodrich, *Government Promotion of American Canals and Railroads, 1800–1890* (New York, 1960), 79.

43. Boston *Daily Advertiser*, February 2, 1829.

44. Boston *Courier*, July 17, 1830.

45. *Ibid.*, July 13, 1830.

46. George Blake was a prominent Boston politician. President Jefferson had appointed him United States district attorney in Boston, an office he kept until Jackson removed him. Blake's brother earned a fortune as a ship captain and later by investing in the Calcutta and Sicily trade. *Aristocracy of Boston*, 6-7; Boston *Courier*, July 13, 1830.

47. James Spear Loring, *The Hundred Boston Orators Appointed by the Municipal Authorities and Other Public Bodies, from 1770 to 1852* . . . (Boston, 1852), 350-351.

48. Boston *Courier*, July 13 and August 3, 1830.

49. *Ibid.*, August 10, 1830.

50. Lemuel Shaw, who was soon to become chief justice of the Supreme Court of Massachusetts, favored a western railway, but he "did not think that a rail road was a city project in any way." He strongly urged Boston not to venture into municipal support of internal improvements. Although there is little doubt that eventually legal blocks could have been removed from Boston's proposed subscription to a railroad, the fact that such important and respected men as Shaw opposed the action as unconstitutional cast a cloud over the whole affair and indicated that securing municipal aid would be a lengthy and bitter process. Boston *Courier*, August 3, 1830.

51. Boston *Daily Advertiser*, July 12, 1830.

52. This group included many Lowell industrialists who would also back the railroad to the West. Among this group were John Lowell, George W. Lyman, Edmund Munroe, and George W. Pratt —all of whom took shares in the Boston & Worcester Railroad. See: Winsor, *History of Boston*, IV, 122; also B&W, Dir. Rec., I, 19-29.

53. Boston *Daily Advertiser*, May 11 and June 30, 1830.

54. *Ibid.*, May 11, 1830.

55. *Ibid.*, January 20, 1831.

56. *Ibid.*, March 16, 1831.

57. *Ibid.*

CHAPTER IV. *The Boston & Worcester Charter: A Triumph of Private Interest*

1. For a general view of the national trend away from government enterprise to private or mixed government and private works in the period from 1825 to 1850, see Carter Goodrich, *Government Promotion of American Canals and Railroads 1800–1890* (New York, 1960), 255-291.

2. Unless otherwise noted, all quotations and references are to the Charter of the Boston & Worcester, approved by Governor Levi Lincoln on June 23, 1831. A copy of this document may be found in the B&W, Dir. Rec., I, 3-16.

3. Joseph G. Martin, *Martin's Boston Stock Market . . .* (Boston, 1886), 110.

4. For the troubles of the Liverpool and Manchester resulting from its policy of a single ownership of all engines and cars, see the Boston *Daily Advertiser*, April 2, 27, and May 3, 1831.

5. Charles Francis Adams, Jr., *Railroad Legislation* (Boston, 1868), 4. Adams argued that the legislators in 1830 saw little difference between a railroad and a turnpike.

6. B&W, Dir. Rec., III, 23-24.

7. *Eleventh Annual Report of the Directors of the Western Rail-Road Corporation, to the Stockholders, February, 1846* (Boston, 1846), 34.

8. Boston *Daily Advertiser*, July 27, 1830.

9. *First Report of the Directors of the Boston and Worcester Rail-Road Corporation to the Stockholders, together with the Report of John M. Fessenden . . .* (Boston, 1832), 34-35.

10. Ellery B. Crane, "The Boston and Worcester Turnpike," *Proceedings of the Worcester Society of Antiquity 1900–1901*, 17: 593-594; Christopher Roberts, *The Middlesex Canal 1793–1860* (Cambridge, Mass., 1938), 30.

11. In the winter 1830 session the General Court chartered three private railway corporations: The Franklin Railroad (to Vermont); the Massachusetts Railroad (to the Western boundary of the state); and the Boston, Providence and Taunton. All proved abortive because investors found the charters unacceptable.

12. Boston *Daily Advertiser*, June 10, 1830.

13. *An Act to Incorporate the Franklin Rail Road Company*, Mass. House Document 35, session 1829–1830, see section ten.

14. *An Act to Establish the Boston, Providence and Taunton Rail*

Road Corporation, Mass. House Document 57, session 1829–1830, see section five.

15. *[First] Report of the Directors of the Boston and Worcester Rail-Road Corporation to the Stockholders, together with the Report of John M. Fessenden,* 23-24.

16. The Liverpool and Manchester, said Hale, paid a dividend of 9 per cent per annum, and it was limited by its charter to pay not more than 10 per cent, and Parliament had the power to reduce its toll immediately if its profits exceeded 10 per cent per annum. Boston *Daily Advertiser and Patriot,* April 2, 1832.

17. *Report of the Board of Directors of Internal Improvements of the State of Massachusetts on the Practicability and Expediency of a Railroad from Boston to Providence, Submitted to the General Court, January 16, 1829* (Boston, 1829), 73.

18. Boston *Daily Advertiser and Patriot,* September 1, 1832.

19. The original charter was a bit vague on the procedures of eminent domain. On March 11, 1833, the governor signed "An Act in Addition to an Act to Establish the Boston and Worcester Rail-Road," which specified the measures outlined above. On March 25, 1833, the general court made these procedures applicable to all railroad corporations in the Commonwealth. See *The General Laws of Massachusetts, 1833,* chap. 187, "An Act for Defining the Rights and Duties of Railroad Corporations in Certain Cases"; also the Boston *Daily Advertiser and Patriot,* April 6, 1833. For an excellent account of railroad land purchasing, see *The Fourth Annual Report of the Directors of the Western Rail-Road Corporation, to the Stockholders* (Boston, 1839), 29-31. These laws did not give a railroad unlimited power to take land anywhere but only along a route between terminal cities specified in the charter. The width of the right of way was limited to 5 rods, plus the land necessary for cuttings, embankments, and procuring stone, or protecting the right of way from flooding, etc.

20. The railroad to Albany was built by three separate corporations: the Worcester Corporation from Boston to Worcester, the Western Railroad Corporation from Worcester to the Massachusetts state line, and the Albany & West Stockbridge Corporation from the state line to Albany. Two corporations beyond Worcester were necessary because a railroad running through New York State had to have a charter issued by that state. At all times, however, the Albany & West Stockbridge was a creature of the Western and was controlled by it, having only a separate corporate existence to meet legal requirements.

21. Charles F. Adams, Jr., in an article originally published in the *American Law Review* in 1867, presented an interesting analysis of the charters of the Boston & Worcester and the Western railroads. Adams's interpretation was strongly colored by the fact that he was arguing for a general change in railroad charters. Adams took a stand against legislative "meddling," and in his attempt to show that the charters of the Worcester and the Western in their restrictions on dividends work against the interest of the state, he asserted that the early railroad charters actually came from the same mold as the English railroad charters, especially that of the Liverpool and Manchester. Actually Adams failed to note that although the form of the early English charters was brought over, the restrictions contained in the English charters were greatly modified or vitiated entirely. Where the Liverpool and Manchester charter allowed Parliament to regulate the British company's rates every year to make certain that they never produced more than the maximum dividend of 10 per cent, the charters of the Worcester and the Western allowed the corporations to operate for ten years before they were subject to any dividend or rate restrictions. Furthermore, even then state regulation was to occur only at ten-year intervals. These generous provisions in the Massachusetts charters were not accidental but were the result of strong pressure by those who had abandoned the idea of state railroad construction and who were then trying to interest private investors in railroad building. See Adams, *Railroad Legislation*, 1-24. Edward Chase Kirkland, *Men, Cities, and Transportation* . . . (Cambridge, Mass., 1948), I, 118, follows Adams's interpretation almost uncritically. To support his thesis, Kirkland cites the Boston & Lowell's charter, which allowed the legislature to reduce tolls every four years if the profits from these tolls gave the stockholders more than a 10 per cent per annum profit. The Boston & Lowell's charter was not only the first issued to a Massachusetts railway but also the least liberal.

CHAPTER V. *The Construction of the Boston & Worcester*

1. William Appleton, *Selections from the Diaries of William Appleton, 1786–1862* (Boston, 1922), 38.

2. Directors were elected by the stockholders each June and served for a term of one year. For the first two years the board consisted of seven members, but in June 1833 it was enlarged to nine.

3. Note that William Jackson also served as agent for the Boston & Worcester during its construction period.

4. Eliphalet Williams was a member of the Boston Common Council from 1827 to 1829, and in 1829 he served as its president; Josiah Quincy, *A Municipal History of the Town and City of Boston During Two Centuries* . . . (Boston, 1852), 339-341. For Williams's link with Appleton, see the Boston *Daily Advertiser,* October 25, 1830. The City Bank had one of the largest capitalizations of any bank in Boston; in 1832 it became the Boston representative of the Baring Brothers; see: Ralph W. Hidy, *The House of Baring in American Trade and Finance* . . . (Cambridge, Mass., 1949), 110.

5. For Sturgis's views on corporate responsibility see the Boston *Daily Advertiser,* March 3, 1830. In 1836 Sturgis's partner, John Bryant, served on the Boston & Worcester's board.

6. George Morey was made clerk to the board of directors from the date of organization and remained in that position until June 1845; *"Our First Men": A Calendar of Wealth, Fashion and Gentility* . . . (Boston, 1846), 33.

7. A. Forbes and J. W. Greene, *The Rich Men of Massachusetts* . . . (Boston, 1851), 167.

8. By an act passed in 1833 the Worcester railroad stockholders were given authority to increase the capital of their corporation by an additional million dollars for a total capital of $2,000,000. The first new stock under this act was not created until 1835. *Laws of the Commonwealth of Massachusetts Passed at the Several Sessions of the General Court Beginning May, 1831, and Ending March, 1833* (Boston, 1833), 453-454.

9. *[First] Report of the Directors of the Boston and Worcester Rail-Road Corporation to the Stockholders, together with the Report of John M. Fessenden* . . . (Boston, 1832), 38.

10. Appleton, *Selections from the Diaries,* 38.

11. Data on the subscribers and the shares they took come from the complete list of the original subscribers found in B&W, Dir. Rec., I, 19-29.

12. The following list includes all those taking 100 shares or more: A. J. Allen, 100; Samuel Appleton, 163; William Appleton, 100; George Bangs & Co., 100; Joshua Blake, 100; Chandler & Howard, 100; Joseph Coolidge, 164; Daniel Denny & Co., 100; Edmund Dwight, 100; Eldridge & Nickerson, 100; David Ellis, 163; John W. Fenno, 100; Arthur French, 100; Nathan Hale, 100; David Henshaw, 100; Patrick Jackson, 100; Russel Jarvis, 100; George Kuhn, 100; A. & A. Lawrence and Co., 164; Edward Munroe, 100; C. C.

Nichols, 100; Harrison Gray Otis, 163; A. W. Paine, 100; George Parkman, 100; Sanborn & Nichols, 100; Henry Sargent, 100; Thomas R. Sewall, 200; Robert G. Shaw, 163; Isaac Stevens, 100; William Tuckerman, 100; H. & E. Upham, 100; Thomas B. Wales, 100; Daniel Webster, 163; Lot Wheelwright, 163; Lot Wheelwright, Jr., 100; Whitwell, Bond & Co., 164; J. D. Williams, 163; Henry Williams, 100; and S. Williams & Co., 100.

13. Boston *Daily Advertiser and Patriot,* January 24, 1833.

14. B&W, Div. Rec., vol. I, dividend of July 10, 1835, unpaged. These records provide a full list of all stockholders and the number of shares held at the time of each dividend; B&W, Stock Ledger "A," 165; Appleton, *Selections from the Diaries,* 40; Kenneth Wiggins Porter, *The Jacksons and the Lees: Two Generations of Massachusetts Merchants, 1765–1844* (Cambridge, Mass., 1937), I, 769.

15. B&W, Div. Rec., vol. I, Dividends of July 10, 1835, and March 1, 1836.

16. Boston *Daily Advertiser and Patriot,* August 31, 1835.

17. The shift of stock from Boston to New York can be traced in B&W, Stock Ledger "A," 315, 317, 319, 320. Particularly active in New York was the firm of John Ward and Company, which handled over 1,800 shares. Also important were A. H. Dorr & Co., and Shipman and Corning. John Ward served as registrar of Boston & Worcester stock in New York until March 1835. Leonard Corning followed him for a few months, and then Corning was replaced by Lewis Forman, who received a salary of $700 a year; see B&W, Dir. Rec., II, 10, 73–74, 134. In 1837 R. H. Winslow handled the bulk of the Worcester stock sold in New York; see B&W, Dir. Rec., II, 273. Winslow was appointed formal stock registrar in place of Lewis Forman on July 8, 1839; see B&W, Dir. Rec. III, 144–145.

18. R. H. Winslow served on the board of directors from June 1836 to June 1842, when he was dropped in favor of a Massachusetts resident, Nathaniel H. Emmons. During his time as a director Winslow seldom attended board meetings and almost never took an active part in the direction of the road. An exception to this were debates over the dividend, which he did attend. He voted for a high dividend rate.

19. *[First] Report of the Directors of the Boston and Worcester Rail-Road Corporation to the Stockholders, together with the Report of John M. Fessenden,* 3–6. When Fitchburg began to agitate for a railroad in 1835, Hale in the Boston *Advertiser* advocated that such

a road could easily be built as a branch to the Worcester road, leaving the main line at Westborough. Boston *Daily Advertiser and Patriot,* October 5, 1835.

20. Since Cape Cod blocked fast steamboat travel between Boston and New York City, there was great interest in an all-land or a combination land-rail route to New York which could save many hours over the all-water New York–Boston route. Hale saw three main possibilities: train between Boston and Providence, then steamer to New York (this was already being done with steamers and stages in 1831); train from Boston to Norwich via Worcester, then steamer to New York; and finally an all-rail route via Worcester, Springfield, and Hartford.

21. Edward Chase Kirkland, *Men, Cities, and Transportation . . .* (Cambridge, Mass., 1948), I, 121.

22. Robert R. Brown, "Pioneer Locomotives of North America," *Railway and Locomotive Historical Society Bulletin* 101 (October 1959), 14–17; *[First] Report of the Directors of Boston and Worcester Rail-Road Corporation to the Stockholders, together with the Report of John M. Fessenden,* 29–31.

23. Note that since 1832, that part of Needham through which the railroad was constructed has become the town of Wellesley.

24. *[First] Report of the Directors of the Boston and Worcester Rail-Road Corporation to the Stockholders, together with the Report of John M. Fessenden,* 20–31.

25. Report of the Directors of the Boston and Worcester Rail-Road presented at a Special Meeting of the Stockholders held on the 18th of January 1833 printed in full in the Boston *Daily Advertiser and Patriot,* January 21, 1833.

26. By February 2, 1835, land costs amounted to $122,324.58. This did not include damages later paid to the Boston Water Power Company or expenses necessary in Boston for expanded terminal facilities; see Third Annual Report of the Directors of the Boston and Worcester Rail Road Corporation to the Legislature, February 2, 1835, printed in full in the Boston *Daily Advertiser and Patriot,* February 9, 1835. By November 30, 1843, total land damages paid for the main line only (this included damages incurred for the construction of a second track, making the entire main line double track) totaled $365,934.21; see *Twenty-First Annual Report of the Directors of the Boston and Worcester Railroad Corporation for the Year Ending November 30, 1850* (Boston, 1851), 22.

27. Josiah Howard Temple, *History of Framingham, Massa-*

chusetts, Early Known as Danforth's Farms, 1640–1880 . . . (Framingham, Mass., 1887), 376–377, and 740.

28. A full discussion of various approaches to Boston is found in the Report of the Directors of the Boston and Worcester Rail Road, Presented at a Special Meeting of the Stockholders held on the 18th of January, 1833, printed in full in the Boston *Daily Advertiser and Patriot,* January 21, 1833.

29. *"Our First Men,"* 40; *First Annual Report of the Board of Directors of the South Cove Corporation to the Stockholders, Submitting the Report of their Agent and the Treasurer's Account to which are Annexed the Act of Incorporation and the By-laws,* 2nd ed. (Boston, 1835), 3.

30. The actual terms were that the South Cove Corporation was to guarantee to the Worcester railroad 100,000 square feet of land (43,560 square feet to the acre) with a 150-foot frontage on navigable water, at a rate not to exceed 35 cents a foot; see Report of the Directors of the Boston and Worcester Rail Road presented at a Special Meeting of the Stockholders held on the 18th of January, 1833, printed in full in the Boston *Daily Advertiser and Patriot,* January 21, 1833. Note that 2 acres were not nearly enough for the terminal. Eventually the railroad purchased several times that much, at market price.

31. Boston *Daily Advertiser and Patriot,* February 17, 1835; B&W, Dir. Rec., I, 210–212.

32. Edward Stanwood, "Topography and Landmarks of the Last Hundred Years," in Justin Winsor, ed., *The Memorial History of Boston* . . . (Boston, 1881), IV, 34.

33. An excellent summary of the arguments used by the Water Power Company against the Boston & Worcester is found in the *Report of the Directors of the Boston Water Power Company for 1834* (n.p.; n.d), 24–26. Actually, the whole case probably came about because the Boston Water Power Company saw a chance to get a substantial money settlement from the railroad. Indeed the Directors' Records of the Boston & Worcester Railroad indicate that the Water Power Company might have agreed to a large cash settlement. The Boston & Worcester directors, however, felt that the entire damage could be compensated for by enlarging the basins to make up for the land taken by the railroad fills. The Water Power Company refused to agree to this and started injunction proceedings to prevent the railroad from going across the basins. In other words the suit represented a sort of blackmail to get

the company to agree to a hasty cash settlement and not to resort to the board of county commissioners. Eventually after many years of litigation a cash settlement was reached. See B&W, Dir. Rec., I, 160.

34. B&W, Dir. Rec., II, 158.

35. The Second Annual Report of the Directors of the Boston and Worcester Railroad to the Legislature on February 5, 1834, printed in full in the Boston *Daily Advertiser and Patriot,* February 7, 1834; *Report of the Directors of Boston and Worcester Rail Road to the Stockholders at their Third Annual Meeting,* June 2, 1834, 3–4.

36. *[First] Report of the Directors of the Boston and Worcester Rail-Road Corporation to the Stockholders, together with the Report of John M. Fessenden,* 32; *Annual Reports of the Railroad Corporations in Massachusetts, 1838,* Mass. Senate Document 33 (1838), 52. William Guild, *A Chart and Description of the Boston and Worcester and Western Railroads . . .* (Boston, 1847), 27.

37. Report of the Directors of the Boston and Worcester Rail Road to the Stockholders at their Annual Meeting, June 3, 1833, printed in full in the Boston *Daily Advertiser and Patriot,* June 5, 1833; Second Annual Report of the Directors of the Boston and Worcester Railroad to the Legislature, February 5, 1834, printed in full in the Boston *Daily Advertiser and Patriot,* February 7, 1834.

38. *Ibid.*

39. Third Annual Report of the Directors of the Boston and Worcester Rail Road Corporation to the Legislature, February 2, 1835, printed in full in the Boston *Daily Advertiser and Patriot,* February 9, 1835.

40. Fessenden was undecided as to the merits of Stevens' edge rail, which weighed 79-1/5 tons to the mile, as compared with a lighter flat rail that weighed only 15-2/3 tons per mile. See: *[First] Report of the Directors of the Boston and Worcester Rail-Road Corporation to the Stockholders, together with the Report of John M. Fessenden,* 33.

41. Second Annual Report of the Directors of the Boston and Worcester Railroad to the Legislature, February 4, 1834, printed in full in the Boston *Daily Advertiser and Patriot,* February 7, 1834.

42. *Ibid.*

43. B&W, Dir. Rec., II, 5.

44. Originally the job of purchasing lands and arranging the contracts for building the road went to the superintendent, Colonel Amos Binney. Unfortunately Binney died late in 1832, and his

duties devolved on a new officer, the agent, who was William Jackson. In December 1834 a new superintendent, James F. Curtis, was appointed, but his job was not to build, but to operate the railroad; see The Report of the Directors of the Boston and Worcester Railroad Presented at a Special Meeting of the Stockholders, January 18, 1833, printed in full in the Boston *Daily Advertiser and Patriot,* January 21, 1833; and B&W, Dir. Rec., I, 251–252.

45. Carmichael and Co. and Carmichael, Fairbanks and Co., contractors, had charge of these sections. A total of $25,000 was given them in addition to the original contract agreement, to enable them to finish the job; see B&W, Dir. Rec., I, 232, and II, 57.

46. [Nathan Hale,] *Remarks on the Practicability and Expediency of Establishing a Rail Road on One or More Routes from Boston to the Connecticut River* (Boston, 1827), 6; *The Report of the Directors of the Boston and Worcester Rail-Road Corporation to the Stockholders, together with the Report of John M. Fessenden,* 32–33.

47. Report of the Directors of the Boston and Worcester Rail Road, presented at a Special Meeting of the Stockholders, January 18, 1833, printed in full in the Boston *Daily Advertiser and Patriot,* January 21, 1833.

48. The least expensive locomotive bought by the Worcester Railroad was that built by Col. Stephen Long for $4,500. But most of the initial locomotives, whether English or American, cost $6,000 each. The first three Stephenson engines cost $6,000 apiece as did the one from the Mill Dam Foundry in Boston. Engines ordered from the Locks and Canals Machine Shop in Lowell in July 1836 and from Baldwin in April 1837, cost $7,000 each. See B&W, I, 157; II, 215; and the Third Annual Report of the Directors of the Boston and Worcester Rail Road Corporation to the Legislature, February 2, 1835, printed in full in the Boston *Daily Advertiser and Patriot,* February 9, 1835.

49. The Worcester was built to today's American standard gauge, 4 feet 8½ inches.

50. B&W, Dir. Rec., I, 194–195; II, 72, 222; Brown, *Railway and Locomotive Historical Society Bulletin* 101 (October 1959), 23–24.

51. All other early locomotives on the Boston & Worcester used wood fuel. Wood became standard on all New England railroads for the first few decades. For details of the argeements with Long, see B&W, Dir. Rec., I, 157, 178.

52. *Report of the Directors of the Boston and Worcester Rail*

Road, to the Stockholders at their Third Annual Meeting, June 2, 1834, 5.

53. At first the Worcester directors threatened to sue Long to get the money back which they had advanced him, but they ended up selling the locomotive to the Boston & Providence. Brown, *The Railway and Locomotive Historical Society Bulletin* 101 (October 1959), 24; B&W, Dir. Rec., I, 230–231, 260; II, 64.

54. B&W, Dir. Rec., II, 71–72, 76, 106.

55. Second Annual Report of the Directors of the Boston and Worcester Railroad to the Legislature, February 5, 1834, printed in full in the Boston *Daily Advertiser and Patriot,* February 7, 1834. The initial local orders were for two cars each from Kimball and Davenport of Boston and Osgood Bradley of Worcester. B&W, Dir. Rec., I, 197–199. This was the first of many orders from Osgood Bradley, who became one of the leading American railroad car builders. His factory eventually became the Worcester division of Pullman-Standard. E. Harper Charlton, *Railway Car Builders of the United States and Canada, Interurbans Special 24* (Los Angeles, 1957), 55–57.

56. *Reports of the Andover and Wilmington, Boston and Lowell, Boston and Providence, Boston and Worcester, and Taunton Branch Rail Road Corporations, 1836,* Mass. Senate Document 49 (1836), 33; *Annual Reports of the Railroad Corporations in Massachusetts, 1838,* Mass. Senate Document 33 (1838), 22; *Report of the Directors of the Boston and Worcester Rail-Road Corporation to the Stockholders, together with the Report of John M. Fessenden,* 35.

57. The following is a comparison of the estimated and actual costs of the single-track railroad between Boston and Worcester including the cost of terminals, shops, land, roadbed, rails, engines, and cars, but excluding any costs for building branch lines or for double tracking other than that needed for passing in the normal single-track operation. The year 1838 is chosen since most of the actual construction expenses for the original line had been paid out, however, the estimates for land costs are not accurate since there were still large charges yet to be assessed against the road for damages to the Boston Water Power Company and for taking land to raise Tremont and Washington Streets in Boston. After 1838, however, the railroad started on a large capital expansion program including double tracking and several branch lines, plus additional terminal facilities in Boston to accommodate the business produced by the construction of the Western Railroad between Worcester and Albany.

357

	ESTIMATES, 1832	APPROXIMATE COSTS, JANUARY 1, 1838
For track, roadbed, and bridges	$803,422.82	$1,086,073.07
For land	23,156.04	173,764.08
For engines and cars	35,000.00	135,389.35
For depots, shops, and other buildings	—	147,644.97
For engineers and other expenses	24,335.00	126,405.00
Totals	$885,913.86	$1,670,476.47

Source: The figures for the estimated 1832 costs come from the *[First] Report of the Directors of the Boston and Worcester Rail-Road Corporation to the Stockholders, together with the report of John M. Fessenden . . .* (Boston, 1832), 35. The 1838 figures are taken from *Annual Reports of the Railroad Corporations in Massachusetts, 1838,* Mass. Senate Document 33 (1838), 51–52.

58. *Thirty-third Annual Report of the Directors of the Boston and Worcester Railroad Corporation for the Year ending November 30, 1862* (Boston, 1863), 12.

59. Boston *Evening Transcript,* April 4, 1834.

60. On the date Baldwin first saw the train, the cars ran only as far as Needham. Christopher Columbus Baldwin, *Diary of Christopher Columbus Baldwin, 1829–1835* (Worcester, Mass., 1901), 316.

61. *Ibid.,* 355.

62. Benjamin Thomas Hill, "The Beginnings of the Boston and Worcester Railroad," *Proceedings of the Worcester Society of Antiquity 1900–1901,* XVII (1901), 563.

63. Boston *Daily Advertiser and Patriot,* July 6, 1835.

64. *American Popular Library* for 1835, quoted in Hill, *Proceedings of the Worcester Society of Antiquity 1900–1901,* XVII, 560–562.

CHAPTER VI. *Running the Boston & Worcester,*
1834–1842

1. Boston *Daily Advertiser and Patriot,* January 31, 1835.

2. An exception to this was Nathan Hale, who as president received a salary of $2,000 a year. He spent much of his time on the railroad and became familiar with operational problems as well as those affecting broad policy. When Superintendent Curtis died unexpectedly in 1839, Hale assumed the post of acting superin-

tendent until a new man could be found for the job. B&W, Dir. Rec., III, 119, 145.

3. Invaluable for understanding the early operation of the Boston & Worcester is a "Report upon the Locomotive Engines and the Police and Management of the Several Principal Rail Roads in the Northern and Middle States," made in 1838 to Louis McLane, then President of the Baltimore & Ohio Railroad. The part of this report dealing with the Boston & Worcester is reprinted in full in Ralph Kelly, *Boston in the 1830's and the "William Penn"* (New York, 1947); for the part dealing with the agent and superintendent, see pp. 28–29.

4. B&W, Dir. Rec., I, 190–191.

5. *Ibid.*, III, 46.

6. *Ibid.*, III, 67–69; Kelley, *Boston in the 1830's*, 28.

7. The conductors were an exception. Because of their responsible position both in running the trains and in collecting the fares, they received a yearly salary of $600. Enginemen received $2 per day; firemen and brakemen $1 per day. Kelly, *Boston in the 1830's*, 27–28, 32.

8. Benjamin Thomas Hill, "The Beginnings of the Boston and Worcester Railroad," *Proceedings of the Worcester Society of Antiquity, 1900–1901*, XVII, 550.

9. *Report of the Directors of the Boston and Worcester Rail Road, to the Stockholders at their Third Annual Meeting, June 2, 1834*, 4.

10. From an advertisement in the Boston *Daily Advertiser and Patriot*, November 15, 1834.

11. Boston *Daily Advertiser and Patriot*, May 2 and August 19, 1835. For the freight carried, see Kelly, *Boston in the 1830's*, 25.

12. Running times from Worcester for passenger trains.

A TRAIN FROM WORCESTER TO	HOURS	MINUTES
Westborough	—	40
Hopkinton (Ashland)	1	10
Framingham	1	20
Natick	1	40
Needham (Wellesley)	2	—
Angiers (Newton Corner)	2	20
Boston	2	45

Source: Ralph Kelly, *Boston in the 1830's and the "William Penn"* (New York, 1947), 31.

13. Advertisement in the Boston *Daily Advertiser and Patriot*, July 7, 1835.

14. Kelly, *Boston in the 1830's*, 31.

15. B&W, Dir. Rec., II, 273.

16. The railroad paid all medical and other expenses of the dead engineer, and made a $500 payment, equal to about a year's pay to the widow. See B&W, Dir. Rec., III, 74–75.

17. The Norwich–Boston via Worcester through boat train started on December 24, 1840. Although the departure from Boston could be reliably scheduled, the trip from Norwich was often two or more hours late; see B&W, Dir. Rec., III, 270.

18. *Ibid.*, II, 275.

19. Superintendent Curtis had proposed that a double track be laid between Natick and Hopkinton as early as August 31, 1835 (B&W, Dir. Rec., II, 65), but the directors did not order this improvement made until the pressure of the increased traffic from both the Western and the Norwich & Worcester made this move an absolute necessity; see B&W, Dir. Rec., III, 107–108.

20. Boston *Daily Advertiser and Patriot*, March 11, 1835.

21. *Ibid.*

22. Kelly, *Boston in the 1830's*, 25.

23. *Ibid.*, 25, 33.

24. B&W, Dir. Rec., I, 223–224.

25. Boston *Daily Advertiser and Patriot*, September 22, 1834.

26. The Worcester management boasted that it had been ahead of the law in the adoption of safety regulations. See: *Annual Reports of the Rail-Road Corporations of Massachusetts 1837*, Mass. Senate Document 43 (1837), 28–29; for the state law, see: "An Act in Addition to an Act for Defining the Rights and Duties of Rail Road Corporations in Certain Cases," signed and approved by the governor on April 8, 1835, printed in full in the Boston *Daily Advertiser and Patriot*, April 22, 1835.

27. In 1836 the General Court refused to pass a bill which proposed that 'whenever by reason of snow, ice, or other cause, any railroad corporation shall not be able to transport passengers upon their road, they shall without additional charge furnish all reasonable facilities for conveyance of persons between the termini of their road." *An Act in Addition to the 39th Chapter of the Revised Statutes of Turnpike, Rail-Road, and Canal Corporations*, Mass. Senate Document 55 (March 1836), 2; a notable exception was section 8 of "An Act Concerning Railroad Corporations" passed April 19, 1837. This provided that "no railroad be permitted to run upon their road any train of cars moved by steam power for the transportation of passengers unless there be placed upon the train

one trusty and skilful brakeman to every two cars in said train." See: *Laws of the Commonwealth of Massachusetts Passed by the General Court, at their Session which Commenced on Wednesday the Fourth of January and Ended on Thursday the Twentieth of April, One Thousand Eight Hundred and Thirty-seven* (Boston, 1837), 254–257.

28. [Nathan Hale,] *Remarks on The Practicability and Expediency of Rail Roads from Boston to the Hudson River* (Boston, 1829), p. vii.

29. *[First] Report of the Directors of the Boston and Worcester Rail-Road Corporation to the Stockholders, together with the Report of John M. Fessenden,* 20.

30. Boston *Daily Advertiser and Patriot,* August 19, 1835.

31. It is difficult to give exact statistics for passengers during the early years since the Boston & Worcester published only scanty figures in its annual reports both to the stockholders and to the legislature. It is doubtful that the railroad kept a record of the total passengers during the first few years. This was partly because nearly half the money was collected by the conductors in the cars. During the final six months of 1836 for example the railroad sold 31,880 tickets at the stations which represented a revenue of $39,576.11. During the same period the conductors took in on the cars $36,611.05, but they apparently kept no record of the number of passengers this represented. Significantly many of the stations nearest Boston had no agents to sell tickets, indicating possibly that the latter amount may represent considerably more than 31,000 passengers. See: Kelly, *Boston in the 1830's,* 26. Further, When the railroad started to give estimates of the passenger traffic in its reports the initial reports confuse the "number of passengers transported" with the "number of passengers transported over the whole road." However, starting in the late 1840s the legislature specified that all railroads would report the exact number of passengers carried, plus the number of passengers moved one mile (passenger miles).

32. Boston *Daily Advertiser and Patriot,* July 16, 1835.

33. Many church groups strongly opposed Sunday trains, and the railroad received a large number of petitions against Sunday operation; B&W, Dir. Rec., II, 13, 21. The board, backed by the stockholders who voted down Sunday trains at a meeting on April 27, 1836 (B&W, Dir. Rec., II, 127–128), continually refused to institute regular Sunday service. But as early as July 1837 the post office combined with the Boston commercial interests prevailed on

the board to run one train a day each way between Boston and Worcester to carry the mail; B&W, Dir. Rec., II, 246. In October 1835 the directors voted to cut one round trip a day from the schedule, but they restored it with the summer rise of passenger traffic on June 27, 1836; B&W, Dir. Rec., II, 76, 147.

34. B&W, Dir. Rec., II, 182, 214; III, 22–23, 32.

35. Kelly, *Boston in the 1830's*, 26.

36. *Annual Reports of the Rail-Road Corporations in the State of Massachusetts for 1844* (Boston, 1845), 32.

37. William Guild, *A Chart and Description of the Boston and Worcester and Western Railroads* . . . (Boston, 1847), 10–11.

38. In 1837 the total number of passenger cars was 24; the total number of freight cars (not including work equipment), 106; Kelly, *Boston in the 1830's*, 26. For revenue statistics, see *Annual Reports of the Rail-Road Corporations in the State of Massachusetts for 1838*, Massachusetts Senate Document 33 (1838), 22.

39. *Annual Reports of the Rail-Road Corporations in the State of Massachusetts for 1844* (Boston, 1845), 25–29.

40. *Annual Reports of the Rail-Road Corporations in the State of Massachusetts for 1841* (Boston, 1842), 20.

41. *[First] Report of the Directors of the Boston and Worcester Rail-Road Corporation to the Stockholders, together with the Report of John M. Fessenden*, 9–20.

42. Kelly, *Boston in the 1830's*, 26.

43. B&W, Dir. Rec., III, 57.

44. The railroad adopted in 1837 a rate of $6 per carload for cows, sheep, etc., moving from Worcester to Boston and $5 from Framingham to Boston. There was a charge of $8 per car from Boston to Worcester. See: Printed Freight Tariff of the B&W dated November 7, 1837.

45. B&W, Dir. Rec., II, 24.

46. Boston *Daily Advertiser and Patriot*, November 15, 1834, and April 23, 1835; *[First] Report of the Directors of the Boston and Rail-Road Corporation to the Stockholders, together with the Report of John M. Fessenden*, 20; B&W, Dir. Rec., II, 4, 48; WRR, CF, 1837, No. 15.

47. Boston *Daily Advertiser and Patriot*, August 12, 1835.

48. B&W, Div. Rec., vol. I, dividends of July 10, 1835 and March 10, 1836; B&W, Dir. Rec., II, 180.

49. B&W, Dir. Rec., II, 210; III, 122.

50. Passenger revenue, 1836–1840.

YEAR	REVENUE	COMMENTS
1836	$120,792.24	(fare increased November 1836)
1837*	123,331.80	(full year of fare increases)
1838*	112,032.43	(full year of fare increases)
1839	122,495.92	(fare decreased, April 24, 1839; on October 1, 1839, the Western Railroad opened from Worcester to Springfield)
1840	170,855.95	(full effects of increased business from the Western and the fare decrease)

Source: Statistics compiled from the *Annual Reports of the Railroad Corporations in the State of Massachusetts* for the years 1836, 1837, 1838, 1839, and 1840.

* Years of panic.

51. B&W, Dir. Rec., II, 236–237.

52. In April 1843 under the influence of William Jackson, Newton's real estate developer, the B&W established special commuter trains to Newton, and it set a price of $60 a year for unlimited rides on the special trains. B&W, Dir. Rec., V, 7–8.

53. "Ton" unless otherwise defined will represent 2,000 pounds, rather than the "long ton" of 2,240 pounds. The initial charge from Boston to Westborough was $2.50 per ton. This rate stimulated so little traffic that the directors on March 10, 1835, lowered it to $2 per ton. See Boston *Daily Advertiser and Patriot*, November 15, 1835; and B&W, Dir. Rec., II, 4.

54. B&W, Dir. Rec., II, 48.

55. *Ibid.*, 225–226; see also printed Boston & Worcester freight tariff, dated November 7, 1837.

56. Sample freight rates per ton (Tariff of November 7, 1837).

STATION	FROM BOSTON TO WORCESTER	EASTWARD TO BOSTON	SPECIAL RATES FOR COAL FROM BOSTON
Worcester	$3.50	$3.00	$3.00
Grafton	3.00	2.70	2.60
Westborough	2.50	2.25	2.35
Southborough	2.25	2.00	2.00
Hopkinton	2.00	2.00	1.80
Framingham	2.00	2.00	1.60

Source: Printed Boston & Worcester freight tariff, November 7, 1837.

57. The average price per ton of anthracite coal delivered in Boston between 1835 and 1838 was $7.50. *Report and Bill Relating to the Coal Mines of the State*, Mass. House Document 33 (March 1839), 10.

58. Percy Wells Bidwell and John I. Falconer, *History of Agriculture in the Northern United States, 1620–1860* (Washington, D.C., 1925), 219.

59. B&W, Dir. Rec., III, 32, 96.

60. From 1840 on the road made many special contracts for season tickets on passenger trains at concession rates. B&W, Dir. Rec., III, 248; IV, 59, 61, 71, 76.

61. *An Act Relating to Rates of Freight on Railroads*, Massachusetts Senate Document 102 (April 1850), 3–4.

62. *Annual Reports of the Rail-Road Corporations in the State of Massachusetts for 1843*, Massachusetts Senate Document 19, (1844), 63–64. The railroad also negotiated many short-term loans ranging from $20,000 to $90,000. This was especially common when the company needed large amounts of cash for items such as dividend payments. B&W, Dir. Rec., II, 94.

63. The committee was composed of Nathan Hale, Eliphalet Williams, and George W. Pratt. B&W, Dir. Rec., II, 39.

64. *Ibid.*, 44–46.

65. *Ibid.*

66. *Ibid.*, 97–101.

67. Voting for the dividend (3): Hale, Williams, and Winslow. Against (6): Henshaw, Denny, Bryant, Morey, Jackson, and Hammond. B&W, Dir. Rec., II, 157–158.

CHAPTER VII. *Financing the Western Railroad*

1. Boston *Daily Advertiser and Patriot*, July 9, 1835.

2. Castleton was a town on the Hudson 9 miles below Albany. On May 5, 1836, the New York Legislature changed the name from the Castleton & West Stockbridge to the Albany & West Stockbridge, giving the new corporation the right to construct the railroad from Greenbush (directly east across the Hudson from Albany) to the Massachusetts state line. George Bliss, *Historical Memoir of the Western Railroad* (Springfield, Mass., 1863), 21–22.

3. J. E. A. Smith, *History of Pittsfield*, 533.

4. Lemuel Pomeroy to Julius Rockwell, July 18, 1835, quoted in *ibid.*, 533–534.

5. Bliss, *Memoir*, 29.

6. *Ibid.*, 25–26. For the contemporary view of railroads and the growth of commercial cities both in the United States and Europe, see the Boston *Daily Advertiser and Patriot*, October 27, 1835.

7. Springfield *Gazette,* as quoted in the Boston *Daily Advertiser and Patriot,* January 31, 1835.

8. Other Western Railroad advocates included William B. Calhoun, long one of Springfield's representatives in the lower house of the General Court; George Ashmun, a lawyer and politician; Charles Stearns, a speculator in Springfield real estate; and Justice Willard, another lawyer-politician. See Bliss, *Memoir,* 23.

9. Boston *Daily Advertiser and Patriot,* March 7, 1835.

10. For the details of this fund and its expenditure, plus the proposals for its eventual repayment, see WRR, CF, 1836, no. 8.

11. Bliss, *Memoir,* 24–25.

12. *Ibid.,* 25.

13. A full report of this meeting is reported in the Boston *Daily Advertiser and Patriot,* July 9, 1835.

14. *Ibid.,* August 19, 1835.

15. Bliss, *Memoir,* 22–23.

16. Boston *Daily Advertiser and Patriot,* August 19, 1835.

17. *Ibid.*

18. *Ibid.,* August 24, 1835.

19. *Ibid.,* September 15, 1835.

20. Boston *Daily Advertiser and Patriot,* October 8 and 9, 1835.

21. A. Forbes and J. W. Greene, *The Rich Men of Massachusetts* ... (Boston, 1851), 137.

22. Boston *Daily Advertiser and Patriot,* September 24, 1835.

23. As the years went on Quincy became more and more an advocate of low rates for grain; see Josiah Quincy, Jr., *Cheap Food Dependent on Cheap Transportation* . . . (Boston, 1869), especially 7–20.

24. William Appleton wrote in December 1836 that short-term notes of the first class would bring 2 per cent per month and that such money was in great demand. William Appleton, *Selections from the Diaries of William Appleton, 1786–1862* (Boston, 1922), 50. For dividends in the textile industry, see Joseph G. Martin, *Martin's Boston Stock Market* ... (Boston, 1886), 90.

25. Boston *Daily Advertiser and Patriot,* October 9, 1835.

26. Justin Winsor, ed., *The Memorial History of Boston* . . . (Boston, 1881), IV, 131.

27. *Ibid.*

28. The data for the number and distribution of stockholders are based upon an analysis of the complete list of original subscribers found in WRR, Stock Journal, 1836, vol. B-7.

29. Note also that in addition to Nathan Appleton's 100 shares, Samuel Appleton subscribed 50 shares as did William Appleton. *Ibid.* The full list of those taking 100 shares or more is as follows: *Boston and suburbs:* Nathan Appleton, 100; Benjamin Bussey, 100; James Hobart, 100; A. & A. Lawrence & Co., 150; William Lawrence, 100; James K. Mills & Co., 200; Edmund Munroe, 100; The Palmer Co., 100; Thomas H. Perkins, 100; Thomas Sewall, 100; Robert G. Shaw, 100; Israel Thorndike, 100; Waterson, Pray & Co., 100; Whitwell, Bond & Co., 150; John D. Williams, 100. *New York City:* John Crumby, 100. *Springfield:* D. & J. Ames, 200; George Bliss, 100; Jonathan Dwight, 100; and Henry Sterns, 100.

30. The original nine directors were George Bliss, Justice Willard, Thomas B. Wales, Edmund Dwight, Henry Rice, Francis Jackson, William Lawrence, Josiah Quincy, Jr., and John Henshaw.

31. Bliss, *Memoir,* 35.

32. WRR, Dir. Rec., I, 4.

33. By 1839 the legislature had passed acts that loaned the credit of the state to the Eastern Railroad, the Nashua & Lowell, the Boston & Portland, and the Norwich & Worcester, as well as the Western. A brief summary of the Whig policy of public aid to railroads can be found in Arthur B. Darling, *Political Changes in Massachusetts, 1824–1848* . . . (New Haven, Conn., 1925), 255–257.

34. WRR, CF, 1836, no. 19.

35. *Ibid.;* also Bliss, *Memoir,* 31–32.

36. *Ibid.;* prominent on the bank side were Thomas H. Perkins, Thomas B. Wales, Henry Lee, George Bond, Henry Rice, Ozias Goodwin, and William Loring. *An Exposition of Facts and Arguments in Support of a Memorial to the Legislature of Massachusetts by Citizens of Boston and Vicinity in Favor of a Bank of Ten Millions,* Mass. Senate Document 30 (1836), 1–6. For the railroad's proposal for a Bank of Five Millions, see *A Petition of the Western Rail Road Corporation for the Establishment of a Bank to Aid in Constructing Their Road,* Mass. Senate Document 16 (1836), 10–11.

37. Justice Willard to Ellis G. Loring, February 16, 1836, WRR, Administrative File, case 3.

38. *First Annual Report of the Directors of the Western Rail-Road Corporation, with the Act of Incorporation, The Act in Aid of the Western Rail-Road and By-Laws* (Boston, 1836), 24; also, Bliss, *Memoir,* 32–33.

39. Edward Chase Kirkland, *Men, Cities, and Transportation* . . . (Cambridge, Mass., 1948), I, 130. Besides the money from the

Maine lands, Massachusetts in 1844 appropriated to the fund $75,000 received by the Commonwealth as a result of the Webster-Ashburton Treaty; see Josiah Gilbert Holland, *History of Western Massachusetts* . . . (Springfield, Mass., 1855), I, 421–422.

40. WRR, Div. Rec., vol. V., dividend of January 2, 1854.

41. The initial $10 was paid in two assessments of $5 each.

42. Bliss, *Memoir,* 35.

43. *Ibid.,* 44.

44. The Western's board postponed the fourth assessment on May 9, 1837, and the fifth assessment on October 17, 1837. In both cases collection ran into 1838. WRR, Dir. Rec., I, 87, 99.

45. WRR, CF, 1838, no. 51.

46. WRR, Dir. Rec., I, 87–88.

47. Emory Washburn, *Speech . . . on the Bill to Aid the Construction of the Western Rail Road* (Springfield, Mass., 1838), 6.

48. Draft Copy of the Western Railroad's "Address to the Commonwealth," November 23, 1837, WRR, CF, 1837, no. 45.

49. WRR, Dir. Rec., I, 40–44.

50. Washburn, *Speech,* 7.

51. WRR, CF, 1837, no. 45.

52. Washburn, *Speech,* 17–18.

53. Bliss, *Memoir,* 41.

54. All the following references are to the "Act to Aid the Construction of the Western Rail Road" (February 1838), reprinted in its entirety in the *Third Annual Report of the Directors of the Western Rail Road Corporation to the Stockholders* (Boston, 1838), 17–20.

55. The most complete printed account of the sinking funds is a chapter: "Origin and Progress of the Western Railroad and the Albany and West Stockbridge Railroad Sinking Funds" in Bliss, *Memoir,* 133–146. There are two difficulties with this account. First, it was written in 1862 and hence does not cover the final decade and a half of their histories; and second, it minimizes the unsuccessful battle of the Western's management in the 1850s to change the ground rules for investing the funds in order to allow the trustees to invest the money in the securities of the Western itself.

56. For the specific types of investments allowed, see Bliss, *Memoir,* 134.

57. Note that the loss on the scrip was charged to the construction account as an expense of building the road, while all money received from the sale of scrip above par was put into the sinking fund. See *Seventh Annual Report of the Directors of the*

Western Rail-Road Corporation to the Stockholders, January, 1842, Comprising a Copy of the Sixth Report to the Legislature (Boston, 1842), 16; also WRR, CF, 1842, no. 116.

58. The status of the sinking fund payments is recorded in the Annual Reports of the Western Railroad. See the *Eighth Annual Report . . . February 8, 1843* (Boston, 1843), 43–44; *Ninth Annual Report . . . January, 1844* (Boston, 1844), 39; and the *Tenth Annual Report . . . February, 1845* (Boston, 1845), 9–10.

59. See "Valuation of the Sinking Funds from December 1, 1854 to January 1, 1871," WRR, Administrative File, case 3.

60. *Sixth Annual Report of the Railroad Commissioners [Massachusetts] January, 1875* (Boston, 1875), part II, 22.

61. WRR, CF, 1838, no. 18.

62. For a copy of the agreement signed by the Barings and the Western see WRR, CF, 1838, no. 20.

63. *Fifth Annual Report of the Directors of the Western Rail-Road Corporation to the Stockholders, February 12, 1840* (Boston, 1840), 17–19.

64. WRR, Stockholders' Minutes, I, 57–60; also WRR, CF, 1838, no. 51.

65. Bliss, *Memoir*, 46.

66. *Ibid.*, 45–47.

67. WRR, Dir. Rec., I, 166–167.

68. *Brief Statement of Facts in Relation to the Western Rail-Road, February 6, 1841* (n.p., n.d.), 11.

69. *Ibid.*, 10.

70. Anna R. Bradbury, *History of the City of Hudson, New York* . . . (Hudson, N.Y., 1908), 181.

71. Note that Harry H. Pierce, *Railroads of New York* . . . (Cambridge, Mass., 1953), 116, refers to the city of Albany as "lending its money" to the Albany & West Stockbridge. Actually Albany lent its credit rather than its money. This is an important distinction. The former implies that Albany actually raised the money through taxes or direct borrowing and paid it over to the Albany & West Stockbridge, when in fact the city never did any more than print notes which it agreed to pay if the Albany & West Stockbridge did not meet the obligations. Albany, like Massachusetts, took every precaution to insure that the city's taxpapers would never have to pay a cent. In this Albany was successful.

72. There was only $30,000 in A&WS stock outstanding, and this was bought out by the Western in 1840, using money raised by the sale of Albany scrip. WRR, Dir. Rec., II, 215.

73. Bliss, *Memoir*, 48–50; "The Permanent Contract of Transportation [of the Western] with the Albany and West Stockbridge Rail-Road Company" is printed in the *Seventh Annual Report of the Directors of the Western Rail-Road Corporation to the Stockholders, January, 1842, Comprising a Copy of the Sixth Report to the Legislature* (Boston, 1842), 19–24.

74. *Brief Statement of Facts in Relation to the Western Rail-Road, February 6, 1841*, 7.

75. *Proceedings of the Western Rail-Road Corporation, January 27, 1841; Including an Address to the People of the Commonwealth of Massachusetts, on the Application for an Additional Loan of the State Credit* (Boston, 1841), 3–4.

76. *Ibid.*, 6, 7, 9.

77. The "Act to Complete the Construction of the Western Rail-Road" is reprinted in the *Seventh Annual Report of the Directors of the Western Rail-Road Corporation to the Stockholders, January, 1842*, 27–29.

78. Bliss, *Memoir*, 65.

79. WRR, Dir. Rec., I, 219–220; Treasurer Josiah Quincy, Jr.'s, Report to the Board on the Sale of the Massachusetts and Albany Scrip, dated February 9, 1842, WRR, CF, 1842, no. 23.

80. *Ibid.*

81. *Seventh Annual Report of the Directors of the Western Rail-Road Corporation to the Stockholders, January, 1842*, 14–15.

82. WRR, Dir. Rec., II, 32–33; WRR, CF, 1842, no. 5.

83. WRR, Dir. Rec., II, 35–36.

84. The results of the auctions including the names of the buyers and the amount purchased are recorded in WRR, CF, 1842, no. 130.

85. Treasurer's Report on Finances, WRR, CF, 1842, no. 116.

86. Note that the interest charges on the $4,000,000 of Massachusetts Scrip was 5 per cent, while that on the $1,000,000 of Albany Scrip was 6 per cent.

87. *Eighth Annual Report of the Directors of the Western Rail-Road Corporation to the Stockholders, Presented February 8, 1843, Comprising a Copy of the Seventh Report to the Legislature* (Boston, 1843), 27–28.

CHAPTER VIII. *Rails Across the Mountains*

1. Charles E. Fisher, "Whistler's Railroad: The Western Railroad of Massachusetts," *Railway and Locomotive Historical Society Bulletin* 69 (May 1947), 88.

2. George Bliss to James Savage, February 25, 1843, WRR, Administrative File, case 3.

3. *Ibid.*

4. *Ibid.*

5. George Bliss, *Historical Memoir of the Western Railroad* (Springfield, Mass., 1863), 151–152.

6. Mason Arnold Green, *Springfield, 1636–1886* . . . (Springfield, Mass., 1888), 366.

7. *Ibid.*

8. George Bliss to James Savage, February 25, 1843, WRR, Administrative Accounts, case 3.

9. WRR, Dir. Rec., I, 25; Fisher, *Railway and Locomotive Historical Society Bulletin* 69 (May 1947), 87; Robert E. Carlson, "British Railroads and Engineers and the Beginnings of American Railroad Development," *Business History Review* 34:147–149 (Summer 1960). Also, George Leonard Vose, *A Sketch of the Life and Works of George W. Whistler, Civil Engineer* (Boston, 1887), 16–17.

10. Justin Winsor, ed., *The Memorial History of Boston* . . . (Boston, 1881), IV, 40.

11. WRR, Dir. Rec., I, 17–21.

12. *Ibid.*

13. *Ibid.*, 27–31.

14. Whistler came in first to share the salary and duties of the Chief Engineer, William Gibbs McNeill, but then when Captain Swift resigned in July 1839, Whistler took over the job of resident engineer, which gave him the main responsibility for locating the railroad across the Berkshires. *Second Annual Report of the Directors of the Western Rail-Road Corporation to the Stockholders* (Boston, 1837), 3; also Fisher, *Railway and Locomotive Historical Society Bulletin* 69 (May 1947), 25.

15. For the data on the Worcester-Springfield route, see Bliss, *Memoir*, 34–35; *Second Annual Report of the Directors of the Western Rail-Road Corporation to the Stockholders* (Boston, 1837), 4–10; *Fourth Annual Report of the Directors of the Western Rail-Road Corporation to the Stockholders, February 13, 1839* (Boston, 1839), 21–23; and William Guild, *A Chart and Description of the Boston and Worcester and Western Railroads* . . . (Boston, 1847), 31–35.

16. Nathan Hale to the Directors of the Western Railroad, February 15, 1837, WRR, CF, 1837, no. 15.

17. *Ibid.*

18. William Jackson to George Bliss, January 2, 1837, WRR, CF, 1837, no. 1–b.

19. At the time the Worcester Corporation fixed its depot site, the Western's charter had not been activated, and by terms of the Western's Charter the Worcester's directors controlled the Western Railroad until the charter was activated.

20. WRR, Dir. Rec., I, 53–63.

21. William Jackson argued that there would be a saving of less than $9,000 to the Western by putting all the facilities at Hathaway's farm. This he maintained did not furnish a good reason for the separation of the Worcester and Western passenger depots. See William Jackson to George Bliss, January 2, 1837, WRR, CF, 1837, No. 1–b.

22. *Ibid.*

23. Nathan Hale to the Directors of the Western Railroad, February 15, 1837, WRR, CF, 1837, No. 15.

24. WRR, Dir. Rec., I, 73–74.

25. *Ibid.,* 73.

26. *Proceedings of a Public Meeting of the Inhabitants of Worcester, August 28, 1847, upon the Subject of the Passenger Depot of the Western Railroad in Worcester* (Worcester, Mass., 1847), 5–15.

27. William Jackson to George Bliss, January 2, 1837, WRR, CF, 1837, no. 1–b.

28. William B. O. Peabody to Mrs. Stephen Pearse, December 7, 1835, WRR, Administrative File, case 3.

29. WRR, Dir. Rec., I, 88–90; also WRR, CF, 1837, nos. 28, 29.

30. Bliss, *Memoir,* 36–37, 151–152; also WRR, CF, 1838, no. 40.

31. Bliss, *Memoir,* 37.

32. WRR, Dir. Rec., I, 91–92.

33. Most of these petitions are still preserved in the records of the Western Railroad. A careful check of the names against the property owned by the petitioners indicates that in most cases people wanted the railroad to locate the depot as near their land as possible. WRR, CF, 1837, nos. 33, 34, 35, 38, and in the year 1838, nos. 26, 29, 30, 31, 32, 33, 34, 35. For the charges made against Bliss, see Bliss, *Memoir,* 152.

34. *Second Annual Report of the Directors of the Western Railroad Corporation to the Stockholders* (Boston, 1837), 16.

35. An example of the distortion is a table comparing the grades of the northern and southern lines. This table gives the number of miles with a grade above 71.57 feet per mile as 16.6 miles on the

south route, and 8.9 on the north. If the comparison had read "number of miles with gradients of 71 feet per mile or over" the figures would have read 16.6 for the southern line and 15.6 for the northern route! See: *Third Annual Report of the Directors of the Western Rail-Road Corporation to the Stockholders* (Boston, 1838), 9.

36. If the Western did not run on the southern route, Lee wanted to be free to reinvest its money in the proposed Housatonic Railroad, which was to link Pittsfield with Bridgeport, Connecticut. This line was to run through Lee and give the town its much needed connection with the outside world. WRR, CF, 1837, no. 30.

37. J. E. A. Smith, *The History of Pittsfield, Massachusetts, from the Year 1800 to the Year 1876* (Springfield, Mass., 1876), 595; see also a paper read by Julius Rockwell before the Western's Board of Directors on June 14, 1837, WRR, Administrative File, case 3.

38. WRR, Dir. Rec., I, 90–92.

39. Smith, *History of Pittsfield*, 536–540.

40. WRR, Dir. Rec., I, 96.

41. Bliss, *Memoir*, 51–52.

42. Full rail service over the Hudson & Berkshire between Hudson and West Stockbridge opened in October 1841.

43. The Western made a contract with the H&B that allowed the Western to operate its trains over the H&B between West Stockbridge and Chatham while that portion of the Albany & West Stockbridge was under construction. Since the H&B rails were too light to permit the Western's regular engines to use the H&B track, the Western purchased special light locomotives to provide this service. This made it possible for the same car to run through from Boston to Greenbush after December 20, 1841; see Bliss, *Memoir*, 65.

44. WRR, Dir. Rec., I, pp. 66–67.

45. Vose, *George W. Whistler*, 22.

46. Deep cuts were 30 feet wide, and high embankments 26 feet. This was in line with the policy that all masonry and expensive work should be made wide enough to allow for a double track. *Annual Reports of the Rail-Road Corporations in the State of Massachusetts for 1842* (Boston, 1843), 13.

47. *Ibid.*

48. For exact tables of the Western's gradients, see *Eighth Annual Report of the Directors of the Western Rail-Road Corporation to the Stockholders, Presented February 8, 1843* (Boston, 1843), 10–11.

49. The Western had 48 wooden bridges with a total length of 1 mile 812 feet. The Albany & West Stockbridge had 17 wooden

bridges with a total length of 1,474 feet. In addition the two railroads had 12 major stone arch bridges, all in the Berkshire Mountains; *ibid.*, 14–15; The Connecticut River bridge alone cost $131,612. See Guild, *Chart and Description*, 49.

50. *Eighth Annual Report of the Directors of the Western Railroad Corporation to the Stockholders, Presented February 8, 1843* 14.

51. *Sixth Annual Report of the Directors of the Western Railroad Corporation to the Stockholders, February 10, 1841* (Boston, 1841), 13–14.

52. Guild, *Chart and Description*, 58.

53. *Ibid.*, 71.

54. *Annual Reports of the Rail-Road Corporations of the State of Massachusetts for 1842* (Boston, 1843), 17, 20.

55. After May 14, 1840, Bates and Co. imported the iron upon the same terms as Thomas B. Wales; see Dir. Rec., I, 120–123, 208.

56. WRR, Dir. Rec., I, 154.

57. WRR, CF, 1841, no. 67–f.

58. WRR, CF, 1838, no. 41.

59. Fisher, *Railway and Locomotive Historical Society Bulletin* 69 (May 1947), 82.

60. WRR, Dir. Rec., I, 195–196, 232–234.

61. *Ibid.*, 239–240.

62. William Norris to William Jackson, July 6, 1841, WRR, CF, no. 55.

63. Charles E. Fisher, "The Hinkley Locomotive Works," *Railway and Locomotive Historical Society Bulletin* 25 (May 1931), 6–8.

64. WRR, CF, 1841, nos. 53, 54, 54–b.

65. L. W. Sagle, "Ross Winans," *Railway and Locomotive Historical Society Bulletin* 70 (August 1947), 7–12.

66. WRR, CF, 1841, nos. 67, 67–a.

67. These builders offered engines at the following prices: William Norris, $7,750; Baldwin & Vail, $8,000; Locks and Canals, $10,000; Ross Winans, $11,000; Hinkley and Drury, $9,500; and Rogers, Ketchum and Grosvenor (Patterson, N.J.), $12,300. WRR, CF, 1841, no. 67.

68. Also purchased were two light Winans engines for the temporary operation over the rails of the Hudson & Berkshire between West Stockbridge and Chatham. WRR, Dir. Rec., I, 300.

69. WRR, Dir. Rec., I, 306–307.

70. Norris did not take his defeat gracefully. E. H. Derby and Norris both accused Whistler of placing orders to help his former

employer, the Locks and Canals Corporation; see undated (but probably 1842) statement of John W. Lincoln regarding the Winans engine controversy and the role of Whistler in the affair; this document is in the Clerk's File for 1842. Also WRR, Dir. Rec., II, 38; WRR, CF, 1842, no. 64; and Fisher, *Railway and Locomotive Historical Society Bulletin* 69 (May 1947), 40-45.

71. The Norris and Hinkley price was $7,600, and the Locks and Canals price was $10,000. WRR, Dir. Rec., II, 158–159; WRR, CF, 1842, no. 118.

72. Derby, on the contrary, felt that the Norris engines were not only cheaper but an improvement over any engine then on the road. For Bliss's position, see WRR, CF, 1842, no. 119.

73. Bliss, *Memoir*, 66.

74. Except for legal purposes the Albany & West Stockbridge should be considered part of the Western Railroad.

75. Joseph Martin, *Martin's Boston Stock Market* . . . (Boston, 1886), 101.

76. *Ibid.*

77. In the following table, note that the Western's expenditure

Relative capital investments of the Western and the Boston & Worcester, 1843.

ITEM	WESTERN AND THE ALBANY & WEST STOCKBRIDGE	BOSTON & WORCESTER
Grading, masonry, bridges, etc.	$3,271,595.07 (46.5%)[a]	$ 695,169.74 (25%)
Superstructure	1,298,237.49 (18.5%)	922,433.41 (34%)[b]
Depot and terminal facilities	307,237.32 (4.5%)	393,786.32 (14%)
Land	327,757.64 (4.5%)	365,934.21 (13%)
Engines and cars	467,427.04 (6.5%)	257,217.95 (8.5%)
Engineering costs	239,970.51 (3.0%)	158,354.17 (5.5%)
Miscellaneous and interest	1,174,865.07 (16.5%)	— (—)
	$7,087,190.14	$2,792,895.80
Approximate cost per mile	$45,000	$60,000

Sources: *Eighth Annual Report of the Directors of the Western Rail-Road Corporation to the Stockholders, February 8, 1843* (Boston, 1843), 17–20; *Twenty-First Annual Report of the Directors of the Boston and Worcester Railroad Corporation for the year ending November 30, 1850* (Boston, 1851), 22.

[a] Approximate percentage of each system's capital spent on each item.

[b] Note that the large amount spent by the B&W for superstructure is a result of complete double tracking of the line.

(including that for the A&WS) of $7,087,190.14 falls short of its total capitalization of $8,000,000. This is for two reasons: first, the loss from selling the state and city bonds at a discount and, second, a desire of the management to hold some money in reserve to purchase additional equipment as needed.

CHAPTER IX. *The Western Railroad in Crisis: An Operating Man's Nightmare*

1. Data from timetable published in *Report of the Joint Committee on Rail-Roads and Canals on the Causes of Frequent Accidents on the Western Rail-Road,* Mass. Senate Document 55, dated February 18, 1842, 16–18.

2. *American Railroad Journal & Mechanics Magazine,* September 15, 1841, 161.

3. *Report of Frequent Accidents on the Western,* Mass. Senate Document 55 (1842), 3–4.

4. WRR, Dir. Rec., II, 244–245; WRR, CF, 1841, no. 2.

5. *Report of Frequent Accidents on the Western,* Mass. Senate Document 55 (1842), 5.

6. *Ibid.,* 7–8.

7. *American Railroad Journal & Mechanic's Magazine,* September 15, 1841, 161.

8. WRR, Dir. Rec., I, 247; WRR, CF, 1841, no. 2.

9. B&W, Dir. Rec., III, 270.

10. WRR, CF, 1841, no. 74.

11. WRR, Dir. Rec., I, 305-306.

12. Alfred D. Chandler, Jr., *Strategy and Structure: Chapters in the History of the Industrial Enterprise* (Cambridge, Mass., 1962), 21-24.

13. The three divisions: Worcester–Springfield; Springfield–Pittsfield; Pittsfield–Albany.

14. This and the following quotations from: WRR, CF, 1841, no. 104.

15. *Report of Frequent Accidents on the Western,* Mass. Senate Document 55 (1842), 1.

16. *Ibid.,* 7.

17. *Ibid.*

18. *Ibid.*

19. *Ibid.,* 8–9.

20. Charles E. Fisher, "Whistler's Railroad: The Western Railroad

of Massachusetts," *Railway and Locomotive Historical Society Bulletin* 69 (May 1947), 41.

21. *Report on the Western Railroad Corporation,* Mass. House Document 65, dated February 1843, 7; Fisher, *Railway and Locomotive Historical Society Bulletin* 69 (May 1947), 41.

22. George Bliss, *Historical Memoir of the Western Railroad* (Springfield, Mass., 1863), 75.

23. *Report on the Western Rail-Road Corporation,* Mass. House Document 65 (1843), 25.

24. *Ibid.,* 23.

25. Fisher, *Railway and Locomotive Historical Society Bulletin* 69 (May 1947), 42.

26. *Ninth Annual Report of the Directors of the Western Rail-Road Corporation to the Stockholders; and the Eighth Report to the Legislature* (Boston, 1844), 29, 36.

27. *Report on the Western Rail-Road,* Mass. House Document 65 (1843), 9.

28. George Whistler to George Bliss, April 20, 1842, WRR, CF, 1842, no. 62.

29. WRR, Dir. Rec., II, 51-52.

30. *Report on the Western Rail-Road,* Mass. House Document 65 (1843), 7.

31. *Report on the Western Rail-Road,* Mass. House Document 65 (1843), 26.

32. Fisher, *Railway and Locomotive Historical Society Bulletin* 69 (May 1947), 82–83.

33. WRR, CF, 1842, no. 58.

34. WRR, Dir. Rec., II, 66.

35. Elias Hasket Derby to George Bliss, March 7, 1842, WRR, CF, 1842, no. 58.

36. WRR, Dir. Rec., II, 93; WRR, CF, 1842, no. 59.

37. *Fourteenth Annual Report of the Directors of the Western Rail-Road Corporation to the Stockholders* (Boston, 1849), 13; William Guild, *A Chart and Description of the Boston and Worcester and Western Railroads . . .* (Boston, 1847), 80–81.

38. *Thirteenth Annual Report of the Directors of the Western Rail-Road Corporation to the Stockholders* (Boston, 1848), 6.

39. WRR, CF, 1842, nos. 22, 25.

40. WRR, CF, 1842, no. 11.

41. WRR, CF, 1842, no. 19.

42. WRR, CF, 1842, no. 11.

43. WRR, CF, 1842, no. 25.

44. WRR, CF, 1842, no. 11.

45. WRR, CF, 1842, no. 19; B&W, Dir. Rec., IV, 137.

46. WRR, Dir. Rec., II, 45.

47. Bliss, *Memoir*, 67.

48. WRR, CF, 1842, no. 11.

49. WRR, CF, 1842, no. 25.

50. WRR, Dir. Rec., II, 41.

51. C. A. Wickliffe to George Bliss, January 29, 1842, WRR, CF, 1842, no. 25.

52. *Ibid.*

53. *Transportation of the Mails*, Mass. Senate Document 57, dated February 1842, 2–3.

54. WRR, CF, 1842, no. 48.

55. WRR, Dir. Rec., II, 59-61.

56. WRR, CF, 1842, no. 48.

57. WRR, CF, 1842, no. 19.

58. WRR, CF, 1842, no. 132.

59. WRR, Dir. Rec., II, 104–106.

60. President Bliss's Fifth Monthly Report to the Directors, WRR, CF, 1842, no. 87; WRR, Dir. Rec., II, 177.

61. WRR, Dir. Rec., II, 344-348; WRR, CF, 1845, no. 47.

62. WRR, CF, 1846, no. 30.

63. Note that the statistics shown in the annual reports for "Mails, &c." are misleading since they also include express revenue, which soon began to rival the amount received from the mails.

64. A similar service was provided from New York to Boston.

65. WRR, CF, 1853, no. 12.

66. WRR, CF, 1853, no. 31.

CHAPTER X. *Low Fare or High? Elias Hasket Derby vs. William Jackson*

1. *Thirteenth Annual Report of the Directors of the Western Rail-Road Corporation to the Stockholders* (Boston, 1848), 6.

2. The terms "low fare" and "high fare" must be used with some caution. Hereafter, unless otherwise specified, they will refer to through traffic only, for as it will quickly become apparent those advocating "low fares" were little interested in local traffic and did not hesitate to keep local rates relatively high since this had the effect of subsidizing lower through charges.

3. Boston *Atlas*, September 28, 1841.

4. *"Our First Men": A Calendar of Wealth, Fashion and Gentility* . . . (Boston, 1846), 20; for specifics on how Derby profited from one railroad, the Fitchburg, see Henry A. Willis, *The Early Days of Railroads in Fitchburg* (Fitchburg, Mass., 1894), 13–16.

5. Boston *Atlas,* September 28, 1841.

6. Joseph Martin, *Martin's Boston Stock Market* . . . (Boston, 1886), 152.

7. William H. Sumner, *A History of East Boston* . . . (Boston, 1858), 500.

8. A. Forbes and J. W. Greene, *The Rich Men of Massachusetts* . . . (Boston, 1851), 166.

9. Wheaton J. Lane, *Commodore Vanderbilt* . . . (New York, 1942), 51-62.

10. *Ibid.,* 63-84.

11. Report of the Western Railroad Committee on Freight Rates and Passenger Fares, November 11, 1841, WRR, CF, 1841, no. 79; William Jackson to George Bliss, September 24, 1841, WRR, CF, 1841, no. 79.

12. The source for Derby's recommendations is E. H. Derby to George Bliss, September 25, 1841, attached to WRR, CF, 1841, no. 79.

13. *Ibid.*

14. *Proceedings of the Convention of the Northern Lines of Railway, Held at Boston in December, 1850, and January, 1851* (Boston, 1851), 113.

15. Forbes and Greene, *Rich Men of Massachusetts,* 24.

16. Boston *Atlas,* October 5, 1841.

17. Except for the years 1838 and 1839.

18. *Annual Reports of the Railroad Corporations in the Commonwealth of Massachusetts for 1843* (Boston, 1844), 64.

19. B&W, Dir. Rec., V, 7-8.

20. *Annual Reports of the Railroad Corporations in the Commonwealth of Massachusetts for 1841* (Boston, 1842), 18; and *Annual Reports of the Railroad Corporations in the Commonwealth of Massachusetts for 1842* (Boston, 1843), 64-65.

21. *Annual Reports of the Railroad Corporations . . . for 1841,* 18; *Annual Reports of the Railroad Corporations . . . for 1842,* 64; *Annual Reports of the Railroad Corporations . . . for 1843,* 63.

22. B&W, Dir. Rec., III, 270.

23. Exact passenger mile statistics: solely on the Boston & Worcester, 4,421,000; to and from the Western Railroad, 2,535,000; to and from the Norwich & Worcester, 1,847,000. See *Annual Reports*

of the Railroad Corporations in the Commonwealth of Massachu-setts for 1844 (Boston, 1845), 41.

24. B&W, Dir. Rec., IV, 20–21.

25. B&W, Dir. Rec., V, 16; also *Annual Reports of the Railroad Corporations . . . for 1843*, 64.

26. B&W, Dir. Rec., IV, 36; 54.

27. For the Boston & Worcester's part in the peace efforts, see B&W, Dir. Rec., IV, 205–206; V, 130–131, 262–265.

28. *Annual Reports of the Railroad Corporations . . . for 1841*, 20–21.

29. WRR, CF, 1841, no. 31.

30. William Jackson to George Bliss, September 24, 1841, ap-pended to WRR, CF, 1841, no. 79.

31. *Ibid.*

32. William Jackson's Majority Report on Rates of Fare, April 6, 1841, WRR, CF, 1841, no. 31.

33. *Ibid.*

34. *Ibid.*

35. *Ibid.*

36. There were only nine Western Railroad directors at any one time, but owing to changes at the annual election in February 1842, there were a total of twelve different directors for the years 1841 and 1842.

37. Thomas B. Wales to George Bliss, October 6, 1841, attached to WRR, CF, 1841, no. 79.

38. *Ibid.*

39. Report of the Western Railroad Committee on Freight Rates and Passenger Fares, November 11, 1841, WRR, CF, 1841, no. 79.

40. WRR, Dir. Rec., II, 1–19.

CHAPTER XI. *The Embattled Mr. Bliss*

1. Arthur B. Darling, *Political Changes in Massachusetts, 1824–1848* . . . (New Haven, Conn., 1925), 277.

2. *Ibid.*, 270.

3. This is a reference to P. P. F. Degrand's sale of the Common-wealth's 5 per cent scrip at rates which yielded 6 per cent, an act necessitated by 6 per cent Federal securities.

4. Marcus Morton, *Address to the Legislature*, Mass. House Document 3 (1843), 15. Note that of the $5,000,000 total of Massa-chusetts scrip issued to various railroad corporations, four-fifths, or $4,000,000, was for the benefit of the Western Railroad.

5. Everett to Ruggles, November 28, 1849, quoted in Oscar Handlin and Mary Flug Handlin, *Commonwealth* . . . (New York, 1947), 228.

6. President Bliss's 3rd Monthly Communication to the Board of Directors, May 18, 1842, WRR, CF, 1842, no. 70.

7. B&W, Dir. Rec., IV, 155-156; WRR, Dir. Rec., II, 82–87.

8. WRR, CF, 1842, no. 56.

9. The first-class through rate was reduced from $10 per ton to $9. The *first class* included the following articles and all others not specified in other classes or in special rates and all articles or parcels of less than 1,000 pounds in one consignment by and to the same party: bales, boxes, and packages of imported dry goods, baskets, bonnets, boots and shoes, brooms, cocoa, chocolate, corks, cannon, clocks, drugs not specified in other classes, empty casks, eggs, fancy goods, furs, hats, indigo, ivory, tinware, jewelry, medicines, mustard, muskets and small arms, pelts, saddlery, seeds not in other classes, spices, teas, twine, wax, whalebone, whips, umbrellas, and hops. The *second class* through rate was reduced from $8 to $6.50 per ton. It included butter, bottles, sheet and manufactured copper, cotton waste, coffee, ducks, fresh fish, shellfish, glass, glassware, ginger, grass seed, hardware, hams, hemp in bales, horns, hoofs, hides, leather, wrought marble, oranges, lemons, pineapples, paper, paints, pepper, fresh provisions, rattan and cane, foreign spirits, steel, sperm candles, starch, white sugar, tin, wires, children's fancy wagons in boxes, domestic woolens, and woolen ware packages. The *third class* was reduced from $6.50 to $5 per ton. It included apples, tanners bark, bread, brimstone, bones, window blinds, chairs, carriages, and wood in shapes, bedsteads, cordage, cheese, tallow candles, cement, pig copper, cotton, domestic cottons from manufacturers, dye woods, earthen and crockery ware in crates, flour and meal to and from stations not named in special rates, pressed hay, straw and fodder, wrought iron, junk, lard, molasses, nails, naval stores, sperm, olive oil, oil cake, rags, rice, brown sugar, bleaching salts, shot, domestic spirits, soap, turpentine, tobacco, tallow, woods (mahogany, imported cedar, cherry, black walnut), and water. The charge for the new *fourth class* was set at $4 per ton. The fourth class included pot and pearl ashes, bran, bricks, beans, beef, pork and fish in casks, beer, cider, corn in bags or casks, coal, charcoal, copperas, clay, flax seed, grain in casks or bags, dried fish, grindstones, hooks and hoop holes, and pig and cast iron, pig sheet, pipe, lead, lime, and lumber not in the third class, marble in blocks and slabs, plaster, peas, roots, salt in casks, bags or boxes; staves, sand,

salt petre, stones, slate, tiles, timber wood, vinegar. WRR, CF, 1842, no. 56.

10. Circular to freighters dated May 2, 1842, WRR, Administrative File, case 3.

11. WRR, CF, 1842, no. 96.

12. WRR, Dir. Rec., II, 168-170; WRR, CF, 1842, no. 124.

13. WRR, CF, 1842, no. 70; WRR, Dir. Rec., II, 109, 116.

14. Petition to the Directors of the Western Railroad by George Pratt and other Stockholders, WRR, Administrative File, case 3.

15. WRR, Dir. Rec., II, 151-157; WRR, CF, 1842, no. 110.

16. WRR, CF, 1842, no. 111.

17. WRR, Dir. Rec., II, 172; WRR, CF, 1842, no. 129.

18. WRR, CF, 1842, no. 110; *Eighth Annual Report of the Directors of the Western Rail-Road Corporation to the Stockholders* (Boston, 1843), 27.

19. *Report on the Western Rail-Road,* Mass. House Document 65 (1843), 12.

20. George Bliss to J. Savage, February 25, 1843, WRR, Administrative File, case 3.

21. *Ibid.*

22. WRR, Dir. Rec., II, 68–70.

23. Bliss to Savage, February 25, 1843, WRR, Administrative File, case 3.

24. *Ibid.*

25. WRR, Stockholders' Minutes, I, 106–111.

26. *Report on the Western Rail-Road,* Mass. House Document 65 (1843), 3.

27. George Bliss, *Historical Memoir of the Western Railroad* (Springfield, Mass., 1863), 72.

28. *Report on the Western Rail-Road,* Mass. House Document 65 (1843), 11.

29. *Ibid.*, 41.

30. Bliss, *Memoir,* 76.

31. WRR, Stockholders' Minutes, I, 116–118.

32. Bliss, *Memoir,* 79; WRR, Dir. Rec., II, 201–203.

33. *"Our First Men": A Calendar of Wealth, Fashion and Gentility* . . . (Boston, 1846), 21; A. Forbes and J. W. Greene, *The Rich Men of Massachusetts* . . . (Boston, 1851), 25.

34. WRR, Dir. Rec., II, 197–202, 213, 235, 245–246, 315.

35. Allen, Derby, Henshaw, Plunkett, and Tarbell for; and Dwight, Bliss, Jackson, and Chapman against, WRR, Dir. Rec., II, 226–227.

36. B&W, Dir. Rec., IV, 269.

37. WRR, Dir. Rec., II, 236–240.

38. They set the Boston–Pittsfield rate at $3.75, a reduction of 75 cents, and the Albany–Worcester fare at $4, a reduction of 85 cents. The $3 Boston–Springfield fare remained the same, as did all others.

39. WRR, Dir. Rec., II, 217–227, and the railroad's printed tariff dated April 10, 1843, in the WRR collection at the Baker Library.

40. *Ninth Annual Report of the Directors of the Western Rail-Road Corporation to the Stockholders; and the Eighth Report to the Legislature* (Boston, 1844), 12.

41. WRR, Dir. Rec., II, 217–227.

42. *Ibid.*

43. *Ibid.;* and printed Western Railroad Tariff for April 10, 1843.

44. Bliss, *Memoir*, 80.

45. *Ibid.*

46. *Ninth Annual Report of the Directors of the Western Rail-Road Corporation to the Stockholders*, 14.

47. WRR, Stockholders' Minutes, I, 118–127.

48. WRR, Dir. Rec., II, 330–335.

49. WRR, Dir. Rec., II, 359–364.

50. WRR, Dir. Rec., II, 339, 343–344, 348.

51. *Tenth Annual Report of the Directors of the Western Rail-Road Corporation to the Stockholders* (Boston, 1845), 17–18.

52. Statistics: 140,000 local first-class tickets in both 1843 and 1844; 34,000 local second-class tickets in 1843 compared with 55,000 in 1844. Bliss, *Memoir*, 166.

53. *Tenth Annual Report of the Directors of the Western Rail-Road Corporation to the Stockholders*, 16.

CHAPTER XII. *The Worcester Railroad Triumphant, 1844–1854*

1. The Boston & Worcester branches: Millbury, Milford, Saxonville, Newton Lower Falls, Brookline, and Framingham Center.

2. In 1859 the B&W leased the 14-mile Agricultural Branch line to Marlboro and provided both freight and passenger service over it.

3. In 1867, $500,000 additional capital stock was created and sold as part of the railroad's premerger strategy.

4. B&W, Dir. Rec., VII, 85–86; and *Thirtieth Annual Report of the Directors of the Boston & Worcester Railroad Corporation* (Boston, 1860), 5.

5. Statistics for freight revenue and tonnage drawn from various *Annual Reports of the Western Railroad Directors to the Stockholders, 1840–1848.*

6. *Annual Reports of the Railroad Corporations in the Commonwealth of Massachusetts for 1844* (Boston, 1845), 26.

7. *Ibid.,* 31.

8. *Tenth Annual Report of the Directors of the Western Rail-Road Corporation to the Stockholders* (Boston, 1845), 24.

9. *Annual Reports of the Railroad Corporations . . . for 1844,* 43.

10. *Ibid.,* 44.

11. *Ibid.*

12. *Ibid.,* 35.

13. WRR, Dir. Rec., II, 296–297.

14. *Annual Reports of the Railroad Corporations . . . for 1844,* 28–29.

15. See report of the arbitrators, printed in full in the *Tenth Annual Report of the Directors of the Western Rail-Road Corporation to the Stockholders,* 34.

16. B&W, Dir. Rec., V, 161.

17. Bliss to the Western Railroad Directors, January 1, 1845, WRR, CF, 1845, no. 1; WRR, Div. Rec., III, 35–36.

18. B&W, Dir. Rec., V, 166–167.

19. *Annual Reports of the Railroad Corporations in the Commonwealth of Massachusetts for 1845* (Boston, 1846), 30.

20. Bliss to the Western Railroad Directors, March 13, 1845, WRR, CF, 1845, no. 27.

21. Act produced in full in the *Eleventh Annual Report of the Directors of the Western Rail-Road to the Stockholders* (Boston, 1846), 33.

22. Bliss to the Western Railroad Directors, April 2, 1845, WRR, CF, 1845, no. 32.

23. *Ibid.;* B&W, Dir. Rec., V, 196.

24. George Bliss, *Historical Memoir of the Western Railroad* (Springfield, Mass., 1863), 83.

25. WRR, CF, 1845, No. 25.

26. *Report of the Committees of the Boston and Worcester and Western Rail Road Corporations on the Subject of Uniting the Two Rail Roads. Also the Report of a Committee of the Stockholders of the Boston and Worcester Rail Road Instructed to Inquire into the*

Pecuniary Condition and Property of the Boston and Worcester and Western Rail Roads with Several Statements Appended Thereto (Boston, 1846), 7.

27. *Ibid.*, 9.

28. Bliss, *Memoir*, 86.

29. *Ibid.*, 91.

30. *"Our First Men": A Calendar of Wealth, Fashion and Gentility* . . . (Boston, 1846), 24.

31. A. Forbes and J. W. Greene, *The Rich Men of Massachusetts* . . . (Boston, 1851), 119.

32. *Ibid.*

33. *Sixteenth Annual Report of the Directors of the Western Rail-Road Corporation to the Stockholders* (Boston, 1851), 31-32.

34. WRR, Dir. Rec., III, 172–173.

35. WRR, CF, 1846, no. 104.

36. WRR, CF, 1846, no. 105.

37. WRR, Dir. Rec., III, 297.

38. WRR, CF, 1847, no. 29; WRR, CF, 1848, nos. 2, 36; WRR, Dir. Rec., III, 233-234, 266–269.

39. See the Dividend Records of the Western Railroad for the years 1846, 1847, 1848, and 1849.

40. Contract of 1846, B&W, Dir. Rec., V, 295–301.

41. Bliss, *Memoir*, 91.

42. Statistics drawn from various Western Railroad Directors' Reports to the Stockholders, 1846 through 1850.

43. WRR, CF, 1846, no. 63.

44. WRR, Dir. Rec., III, 183–186; WRR, CF, 1846, nos. 67, 79.

45. Bliss, *Memoir*, 93.

46. Rolling stock statistics.

ROLLING STOCK	1846	1850
Box cars, eight wheels	448	618
Box cars, four wheels	100	86
Flat cars, eight wheels	65	152
Passenger cars, eight wheels	23	34
Passenger cars, four wheels	4	7
Baggage cars, eight wheels	4	7
Baggage cars, four wheels	2	2

Source: Directors' Reports of the Western Railroad, 1847 and 1851.

47. Bliss, *Memoir*, 88.

48. *Sixteenth Annual Report of the Directors of the Western Rail-Road Corporation to the Stockholders* (Boston, 1851), 31.

49. *Ibid.*, 30.

50. *Ibid.*, 22–23.

51. Statistics from the Western Railroad Directors' Annual Reports to the Stockholders for the years 1850 through 1855.

52. WRR, CF, 1854, no. 25.

53. *Eighteenth Annual Report of the Directors of the Western Rail-Road Corporation to the Stockholders* (Boston, 1853), 10.

54. *The Railroad Jubilee, An Account of the Celebration Commemorative of the Opening of Railroad Communication between Boston and Canada* (Boston, 1852), 236–237.

55. Bliss, *Memoir,* 183.

56. WRR, CF, 1853, no. 21.

57. WRR, CF, 1852, no. 34.

58. Frank Walker Stevens, *The Beginnings of the New York Central Railroad: A History* (New York, 1926), 267.

59. WRR, CF, 1852, no. 27.

60. WRR, CF, 1852, nos. 27, 31.

61. Charles E. Fisher, "Whistler's Railroad: The Western Railroad of Massachusetts," *Railway and Locomotive Historical Society Bulletin* 69 (May 1947), 63.

62. WRR, CF, 1853, no. 22.

63. Fisher, *Railway and Locomotive Historical Society Bulletin* 69 (May 1947), 84–85.

64. The Boston & Worcester, although on a lesser scale, constructed motive power in its shops. By 1861 four of its fleet of thirty engines were home-built. *Thirty-first Annual Report of the Directors of the Boston and Worcester Railroad Corporation* (Boston, 1861), 8.

65. WRR, CF, 1853, no. 31.

CHAPTER XIII. *Chester W. Chapin and the Formation of the Boston & Albany*

1. Mason Arnold Green, *Springfield, 1636–1886 . . .* (Springfield, Mass., 1888), 478; A. Forbes and J. W. Greene, *The Rich Men of Massachusetts . . .* (Boston, 1851), 148–149.

2. Charles E. Fisher, "Whistler's Railroad: The Western Railroad of Massachusetts," *Railway and Locomotive Historical Society Bulletin* 69 (May 1947), 89–90; Moses King, ed., *King's Handbook of Springfield, Massachusetts . . .* (Springfield, Mass., 1884), 83–84, 86, 89, 91; Forbes and Green, *Rich Men of Massachusetts,* 149; WRR, Dividend Records, 1850 through 1854.

3. Previous data and generalizations are based on the comparison, at six-month intervals, of lists of all holders of forty or more shares of Western stock from 1846 through 1867. List compiled from WRR, Div. Rec.

4. *Eighteenth Annual Report of the Directors of the Western Rail-Road Corporation to the Stockholders* (Boston, 1853), 10–11.

5. Frank Walker Stevens, *The Beginnings of the New York Central Railroad: A History* (New York, 1926), 266–267.

6. For the Boston & Worcester's relationship to the Grand Junction, see *Twenty-ninth Annual Report of the Directors of the Boston & Worcester Railroad Corporation* (Boston, 1859), 10–14; *Thirty-first Annual Report of the Directors of the Boston & Worcester Railroad Corporation* (Boston, 1861), 12; B&W, Dir. Rec. Min., VIII, 23, 70–71, 73–74, 77, 144, 212, 221–222; and George Pierce Baker, *The Formation of the New England Railroad Systems . . .* (Cambridge, Mass., 1937), 6–7. For a graphic description of the effect of the Worcester's terminal facilities on the grain trade, see Edward Crane, *Abstract of an Address by Edward Crane Esq., on the Subject of Transportation at the Green Room, State House, February 13th, 14th, and 18th, 1868* (Boston, 1868), 17–22.

7. WRR, CF, 1854, no. 17.

8. Edward Chase Kirkland, *Men, Cities, and Transportation . . .* (Cambridge, Mass., 1948), I, 391–398.

9. WRR, CF, 1851, no. 20.

10. *Boston and the West* (Boston, 1851), 7.

11. *Ibid.*, 6.

12. *Ibid.*, 7.

13. See tabular statement of the arrivals and exports of flour at Boston from 1848 to 1862 published in *Report of the Commissioners upon the Troy and Greenfield Railroad and Hoosac Tunnel to His Excellency the Governor and the Honorable the Executive Council of the State of Massachusetts* (Boston, 1863), 86.

14. Elias H. Derby, *A Brief Review of the Speech of Hon. Thomas G. Cary . . .* (Boston, 1853), 5.

15. Elias Hasket Derby, *The Troy and Greenfield Railroad . . .* (Boston, 1856), 7.

16. *Ibid.*

17. Kirkland, *Men, Cities, and Transportation*, I, 431.

18. *Ibid.*, I, 398.

19. *Ibid.*, I, 431.

20. Justin Winsor, ed., *The Memorial History of Boston . . .* (Boston, 1881), IV, 142.

21. *Ibid.*, IV, 143.

22. Jackson to Chapin, October 25, 1854, WRR, CF, 1855, no. 2.

23. President Chapin's Communication to the Board on Rails and Double Tracking, April 11, 1854, WRR, CF, 1854, no. 10.

24. WRR, Dir. Rec., IV, 115–116; George Bliss, *Historical Memoir of the Western Railroad* (Springfield, Mass., 1863), 157.

25. Bliss, *Memoir*, 140.

26. WRR, Stockholders' Minutes, I, 182–185; WRR, Dir. Rec., IV, 126, 138; *Twenty-first Annual Report of the Directors of the Western Rail-Road Corporation to the Stock Holders* (Springfield, Mass., 1856), 12.

27. Bliss, *Memoir*, 125.

28. Benjamin Thomas Hill, "The Beginnings of the Boston and Worcester Railroad," *Proceedings of the Worcester Society of Antiquity 1900–1901*, XVII (1901), 530–532.

29. The data for the above paragraphs are drawn from Bliss, *Memoir*, 124–128.

30. Quoted in *ibid.*, 185–186.

31. These figures do not include the final 20,000 shares of capital stock (par value $2,000,000) that the shareholders received without payment of any money.

32. WRR, Dir. Rec., V, 12–14, 40–42.

33. WRR, Dir. Rec., V, 8–9.

34. Josiah Quincy, Jr., *The Railway System of Massachusetts . . .* (Boston, 1866), 4–5.

35. *Ibid.*, 24.

36. Boston Board of Trade, *Report of the Select Committee of the Boston Board of Trade on the Controversy between the Boston and Worcester and Western Railroads* (Boston, 1862), 5.

37. WRR, Dir. Rec., IV, 332–334.

38. B&W, Stockholders' Minutes for February 4, 1863, unpaged.

39. Charles Beck, *On the Consolidation of the Worcester and the Western Railroads* (n.p., 1864?), 7–10.

40. B&W, Dir. Rec., IX, 88–91.

41. WRR, Dir. Rec., V, 102–106.

42. Josiah Quincy, Jr., *Cheap Food Dependent on Cheap Transportation . . .* (Boston, 1869), 13–17.

43. *Ibid.*, 12.

44. Quoted in Wheaton J. Lane, *Commodore Vanderbilt . . .* (New York, 1942), 228–229.

45. Quoted in Kirkland, *Men, Cities, and Transportation*, I, 156.

CHAPTER XIV. *Conclusion*

1. Evelyn H. Knowlton, *Pepperell's Progress* . . . (Cambridge, Mass., 1948), 132.

2. Alfred D. Chandler, Jr., and Stephen Salsbury, "The Railroads: Innovators in Modern Business Administration," in Bruce Mazlish, ed., *The Railroad and the Space Program: An Exploration in Historical Analogy* (Cambridge, Mass., 1965), 131–140.

3. *Nineteenth Annual Report of the Directors of the Western Rail-Road Corporation to the Stockholders, January, 1854* (Boston, 1854), 6–7.